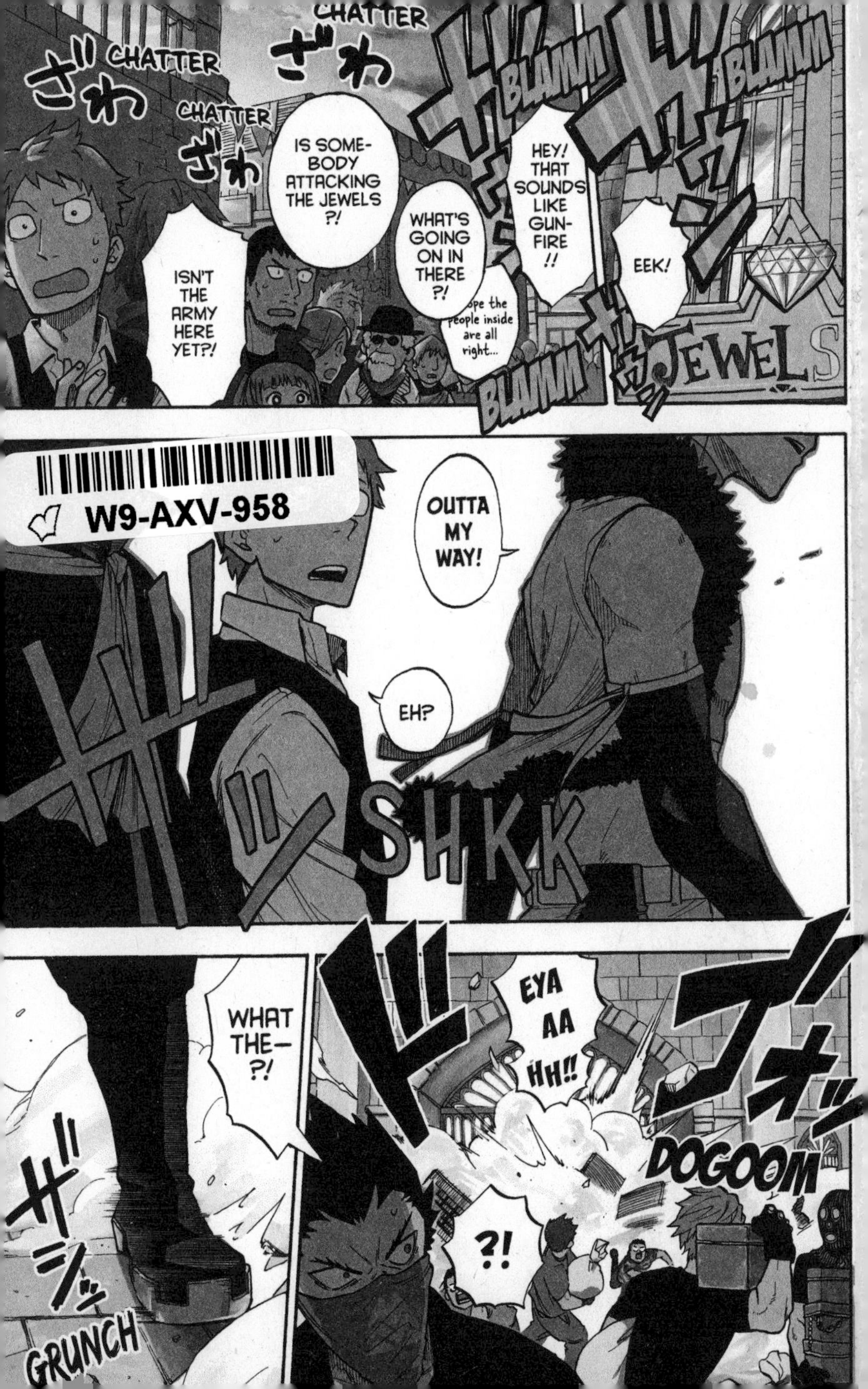
BLAMM
BLAMM
EEK!
HEY! THAT SOUNDS LIKE GUN-FIRE!!
JEWELS
BLAMM
ope the people inside are all right...
WHAT'S GOING ON IN THERE?!
IS SOME-BODY ATTACKING THE JEWELS?!
CHATTER
ISN'T THE ARMY HERE YET?!
CHATTER
CHATTER
OUTTA MY WAY!
EH?
SHKK
DOGOOM
EYA AA HH!!
?!
WHAT THE—?!
GRUNCH

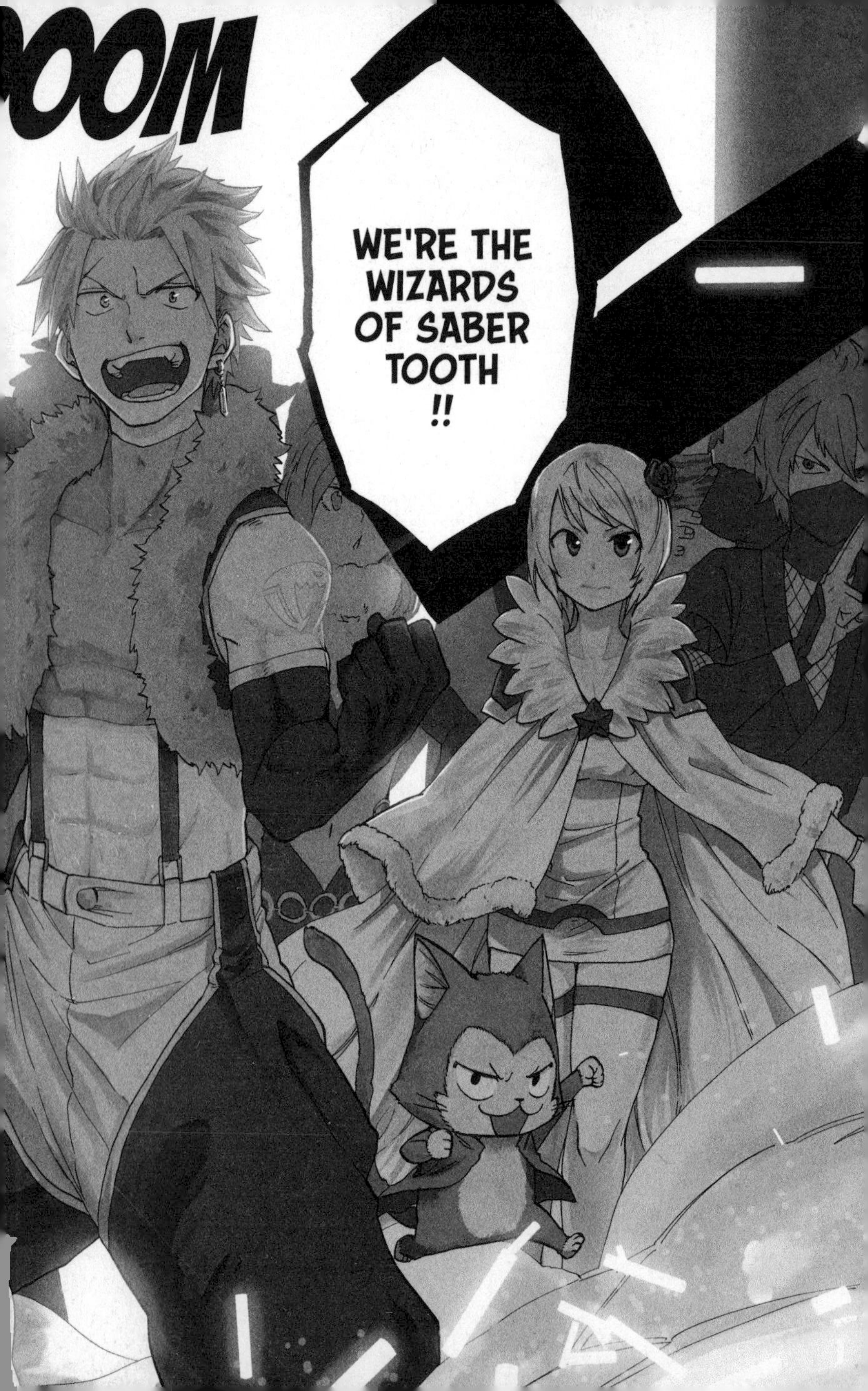
OOOM
WE'RE THE WIZARDS OF SABER TOOTH !!

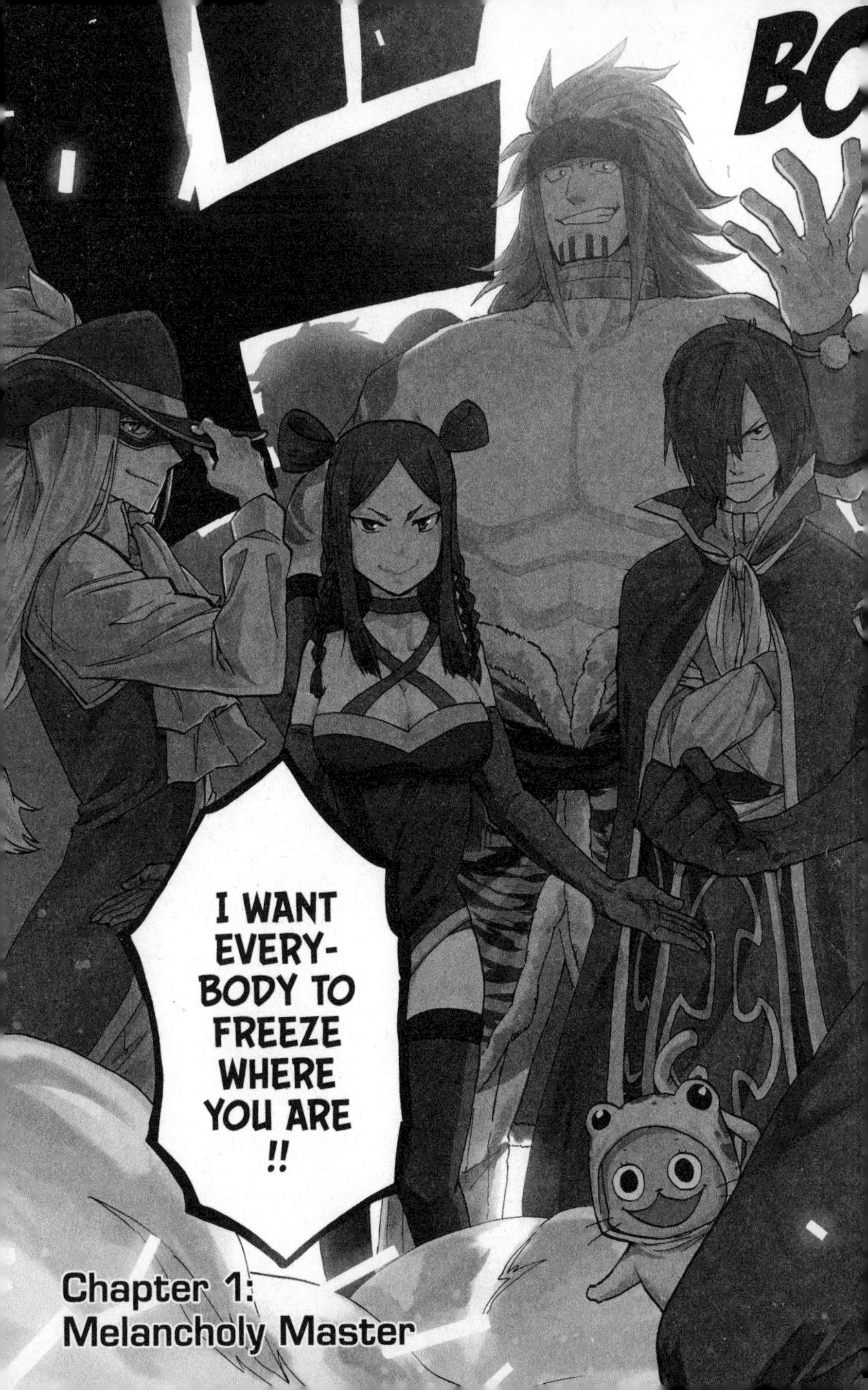
I WANT EVERY-BODY TO FREEZE WHERE YOU ARE !!

Chapter 1: Melancholy Master

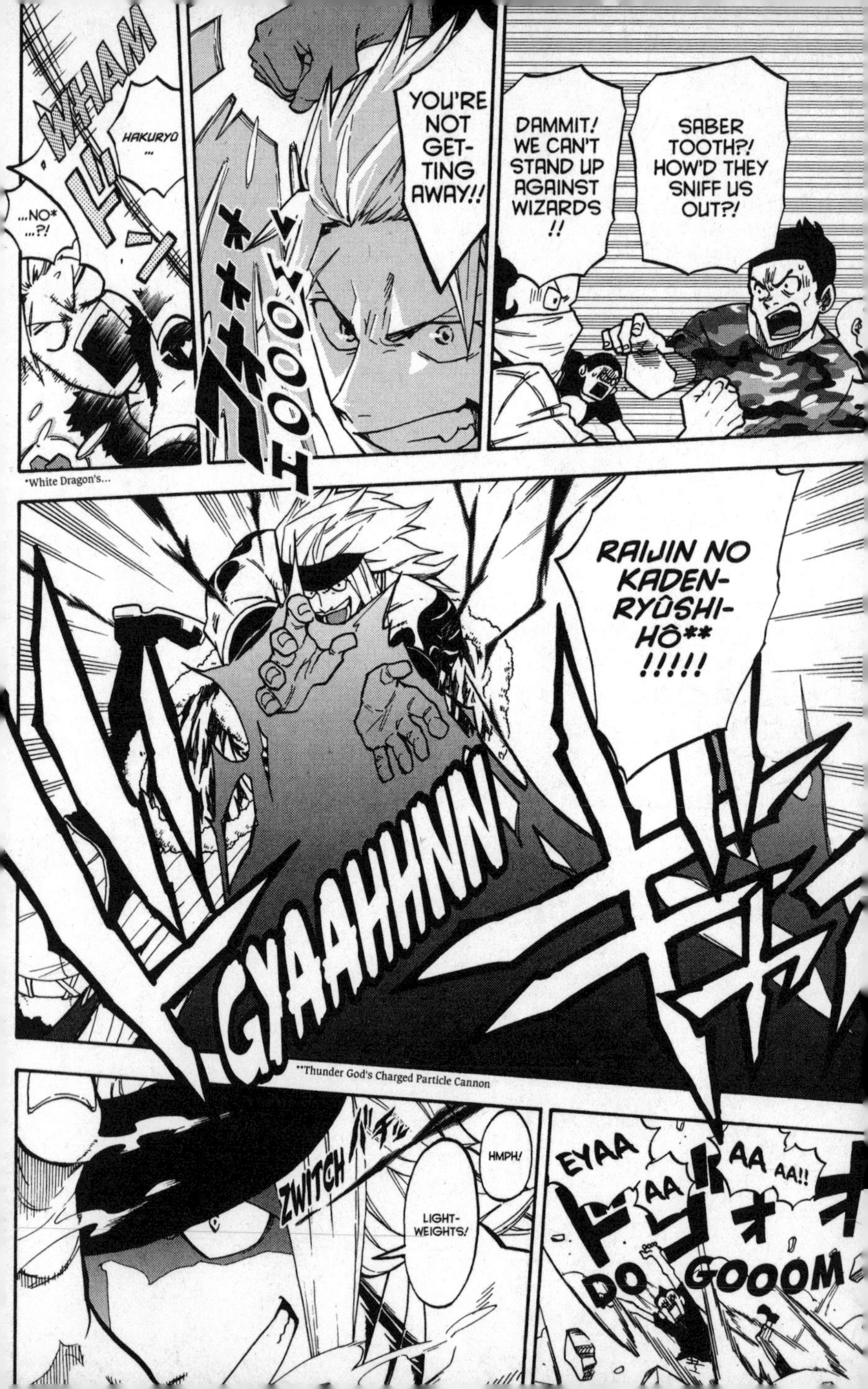
SABER TOOTH?! HOW'D THEY SNIFF US OUT?!
DAMMIT! WE CAN'T STAND UP AGAINST WIZARDS!!
YOU'RE NOT GETTING AWAY!!
WOOOOH
HAKURYO ...
...NO* ...?!
WHAM
RAIJIN NO KADEN-RYÛSHI-HÔ** !!!!!
GYAAHHNN
EYAA AA AA AA!!
DO GOOOM
HMPH!
LIGHT-WEIGHTS!
ZWITCH
*White Dragon's...
**Thunder God's Charged Particle Cannon

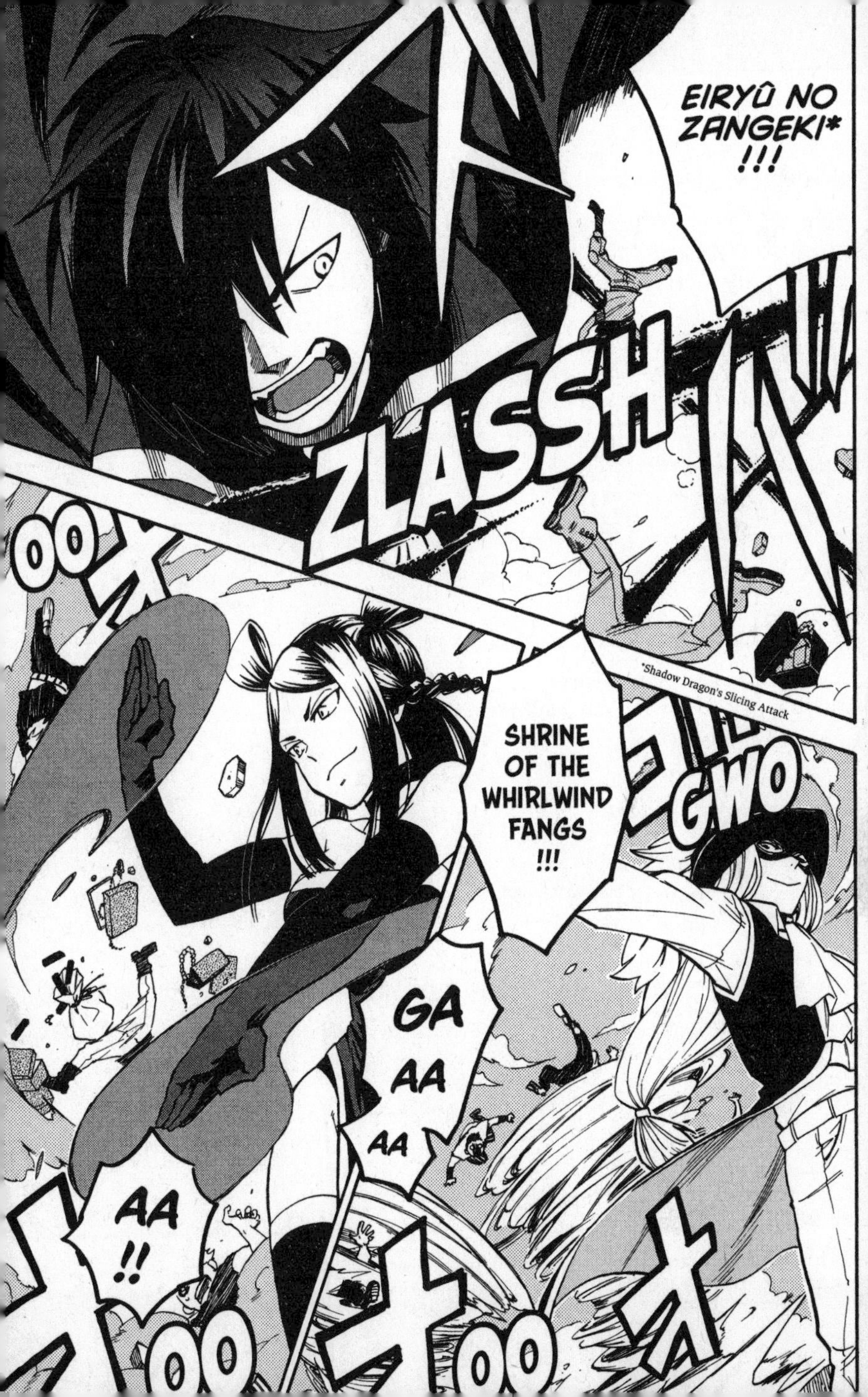
EIRYÛ NO ZANGEKI* !!!
ZLASSH
GWO
SHRINE OF THE WHIRLWIND FANGS !!!
OO
GA AA AA
AA !!
OO
OO
*Shadow Dragon's Slicing Attack

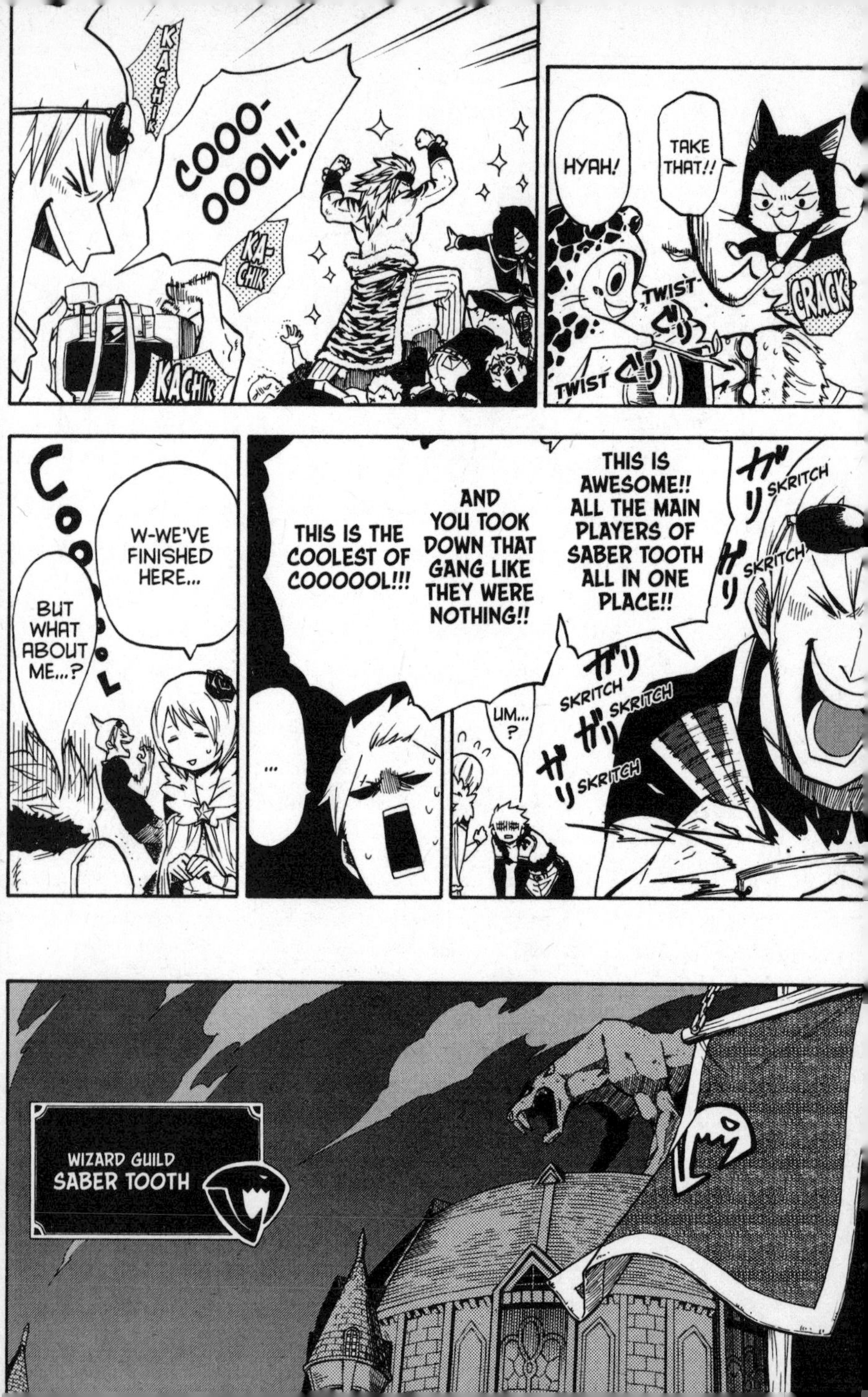
TAKE THAT!!
HYAH!
CRACK
TWIST
TWIST
KACHIK
COOO-OOOL!!
KA-CHIK
KACHIK
SKRITCH
SKRITCH
THIS IS AWESOME!! ALL THE MAIN PLAYERS OF SABER TOOTH ALL IN ONE PLACE!!
AND YOU TOOK DOWN THAT GANG LIKE THEY WERE NOTHING!!
THIS IS THE COOLEST OF COOOOOL!!!
SKRITCH
SKRITCH
SKRITCH
UM...?
...
COOOOOL
W-WE'VE FINISHED HERE...
BUT WHAT ABOUT ME...?
WIZARD GUILD
SABER TOOTH

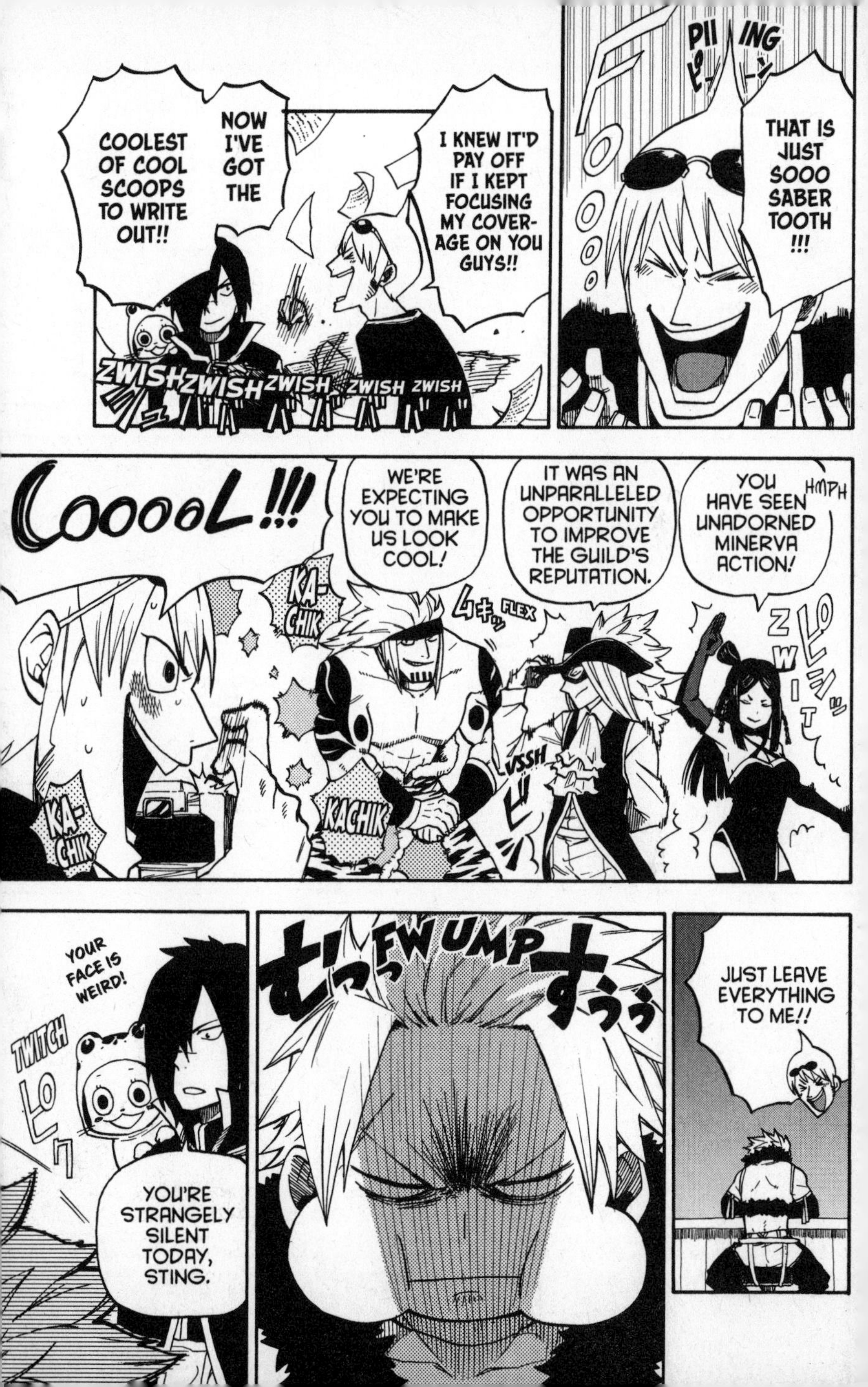
PII ING
THAT IS JUST SOOO SABER TOOTH!!!
I KNEW IT'D PAY OFF IF I KEPT FOCUSING MY COVERAGE ON YOU GUYS!!
NOW I'VE GOT THE
COOLEST OF COOL SCOOPS TO WRITE OUT!!
ZWISH ZWISH ZWISH ZWISH ZWISH
YOU HAVE SEEN UNADORNED MINERVA ACTION!
HMPH
ZWIT
IT WAS AN UNPARALLELED OPPORTUNITY TO IMPROVE THE GUILD'S REPUTATION.
FLEX
VSSH
WE'RE EXPECTING YOU TO MAKE US LOOK COOL!
KA-CHIK
KACHIK
KA-CHIK
COOOOL!!!
JUST LEAVE EVERYTHING TO ME!!
FWUMP
YOUR FACE IS WEIRD!
TWITCH
YOU'RE STRANGELY SILENT TODAY, STING.

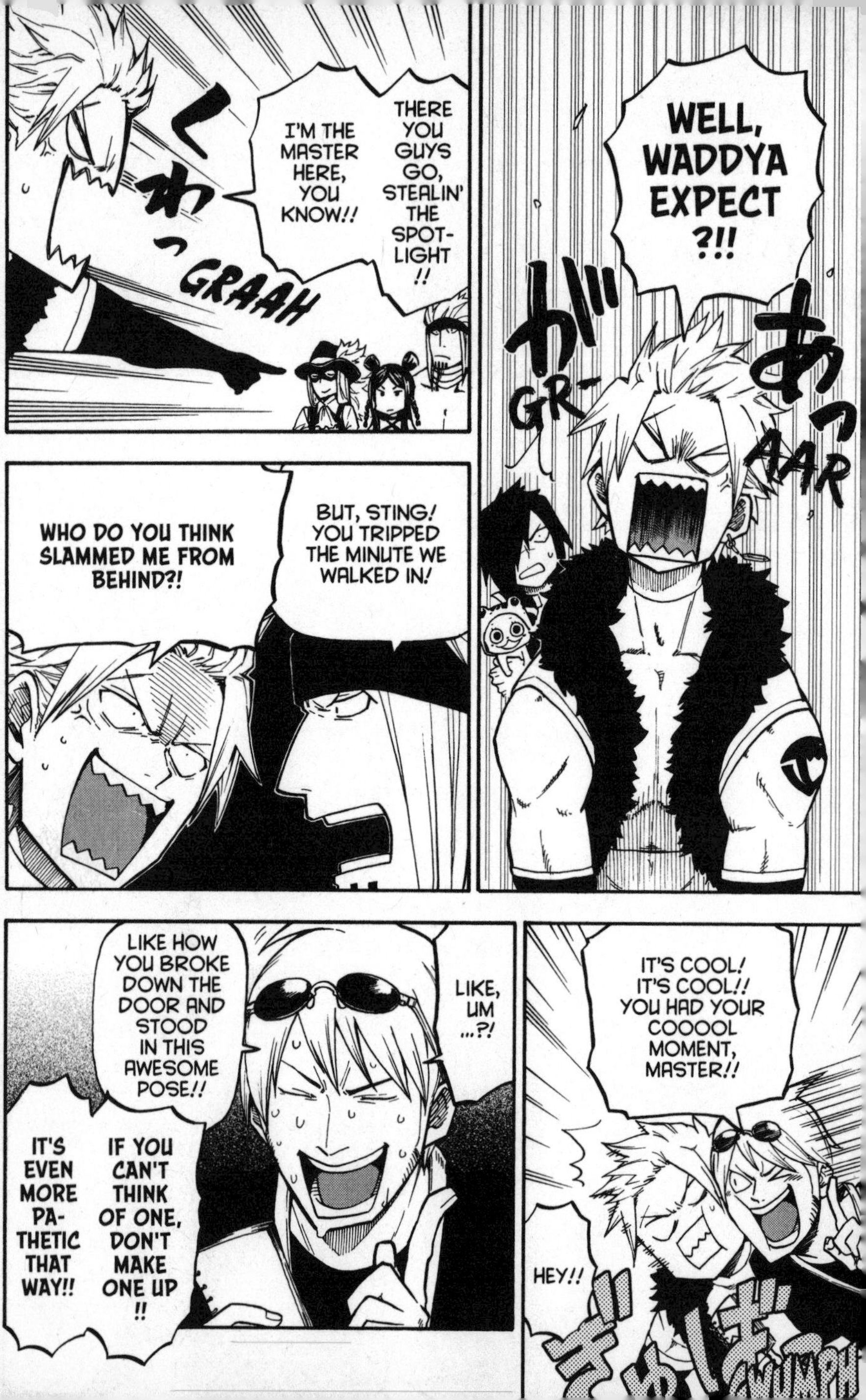

WELL, WADDYA EXPECT ?!!
わ゛
GR-
あっ
AAR
THERE YOU GUYS GO, STEALIN' THE SPOT-LIGHT !!
I'M THE MASTER HERE, YOU KNOW!!
くわっ
GRAAAH
BUT, STING! YOU TRIPPED THE MINUTE WE WALKED IN!
WHO DO YOU THINK SLAMMED ME FROM BEHIND?!
IT'S COOL! IT'S COOL!! YOU HAD YOUR COOOOL MOMENT, MASTER!!
HEY!!
LIKE, UM ...?!
LIKE HOW YOU BROKE DOWN THE DOOR AND STOOD IN THIS AWESOME POSE!!
IF YOU CAN'T THINK OF ONE, DON'T MAKE ONE UP !!
IT'S EVEN MORE PA-THETIC THAT WAY!!

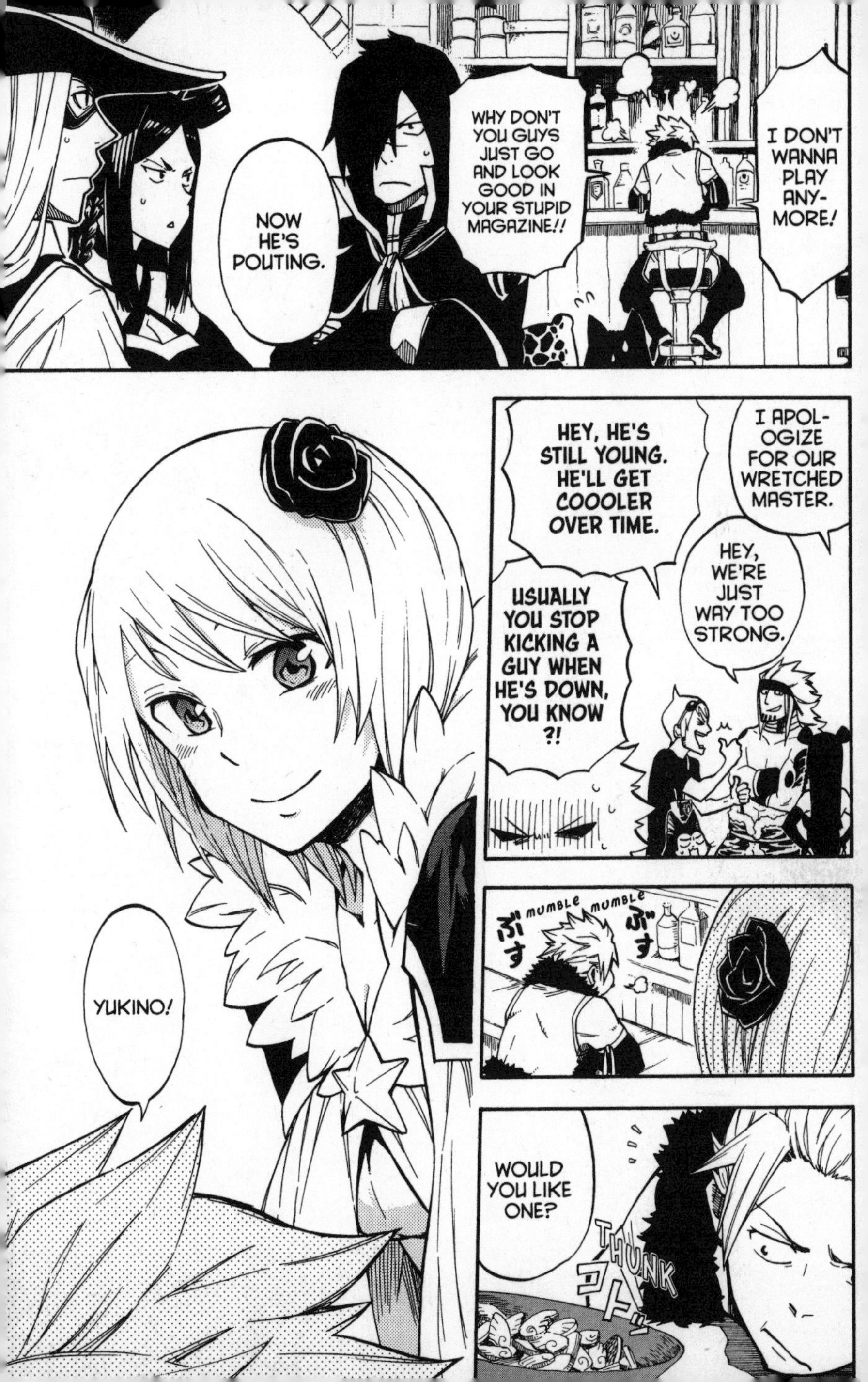

I DON'T WANNA PLAY ANY-MORE!
WHY DON'T YOU GUYS JUST GO AND LOOK GOOD IN YOUR STUPID MAGAZINE!!
NOW HE'S POUTING.
I APOL-OGIZE FOR OUR WRETCHED MASTER.
HEY, HE'S STILL YOUNG. HE'LL GET COOOLER OVER TIME.
HEY, WE'RE JUST WAY TOO STRONG.
USUALLY YOU STOP KICKING A GUY WHEN HE'S DOWN, YOU KNOW ?!
ぶす MUMBLE
ぶす MUMBLE
WOULD YOU LIKE ONE?
THUNK
コトッ
YUKINO!

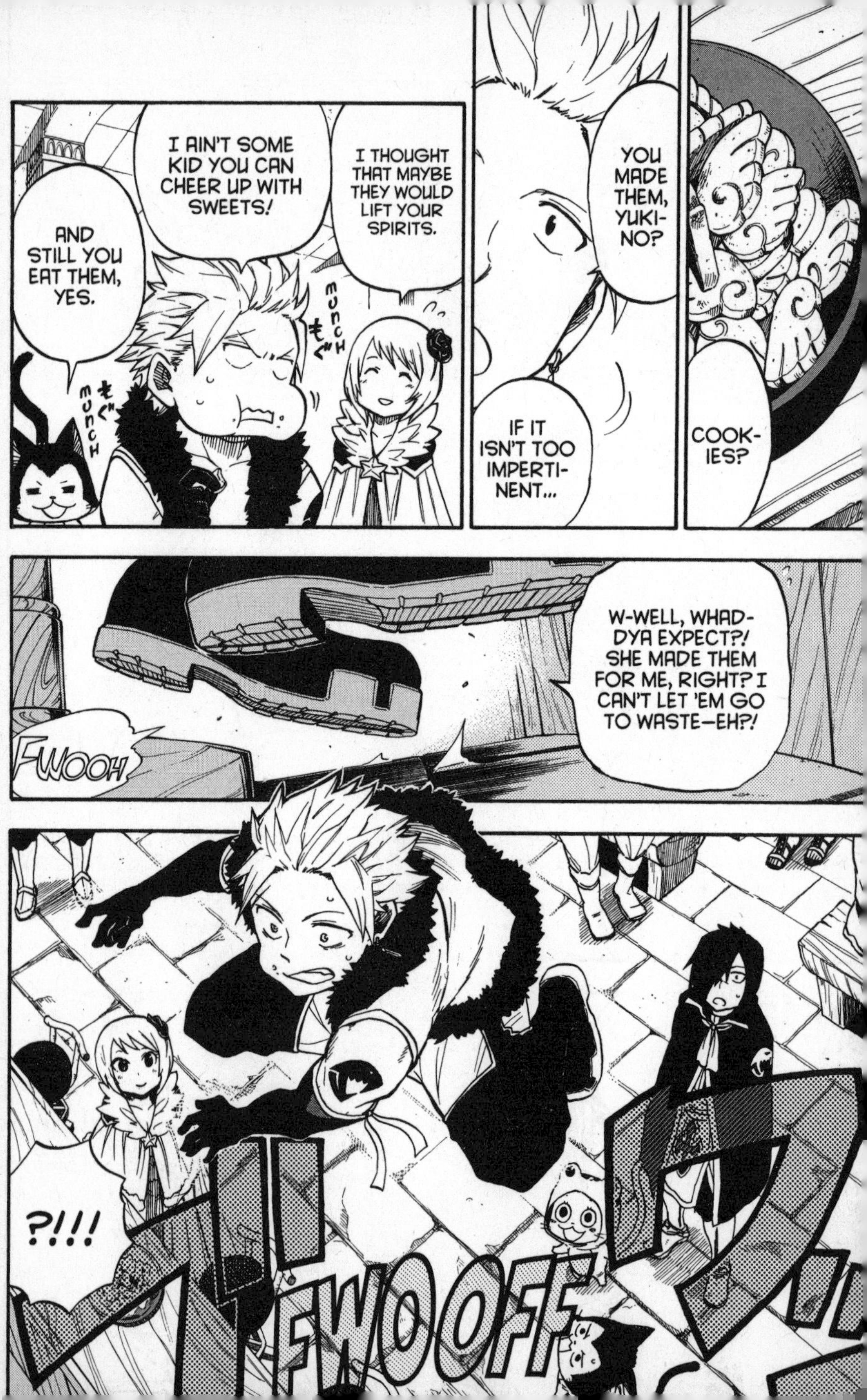
COOK-IES?
YOU MADE THEM, YUKI-NO?
IF IT ISN'T TOO IMPERTI-NENT...
I THOUGHT THAT MAYBE THEY WOULD LIFT YOUR SPIRITS.
I AIN'T SOME KID YOU CAN CHEER UP WITH SWEETS!
MUNCH もぐ
AND STILL YOU EAT THEM, YES.
もぐ MUNCH
W-WELL, WHAD-DYA EXPECT?! SHE MADE THEM FOR ME, RIGHT? I CAN'T LET 'EM GO TO WASTE—EH?!
FWOOH
?!!!
FWOOFF

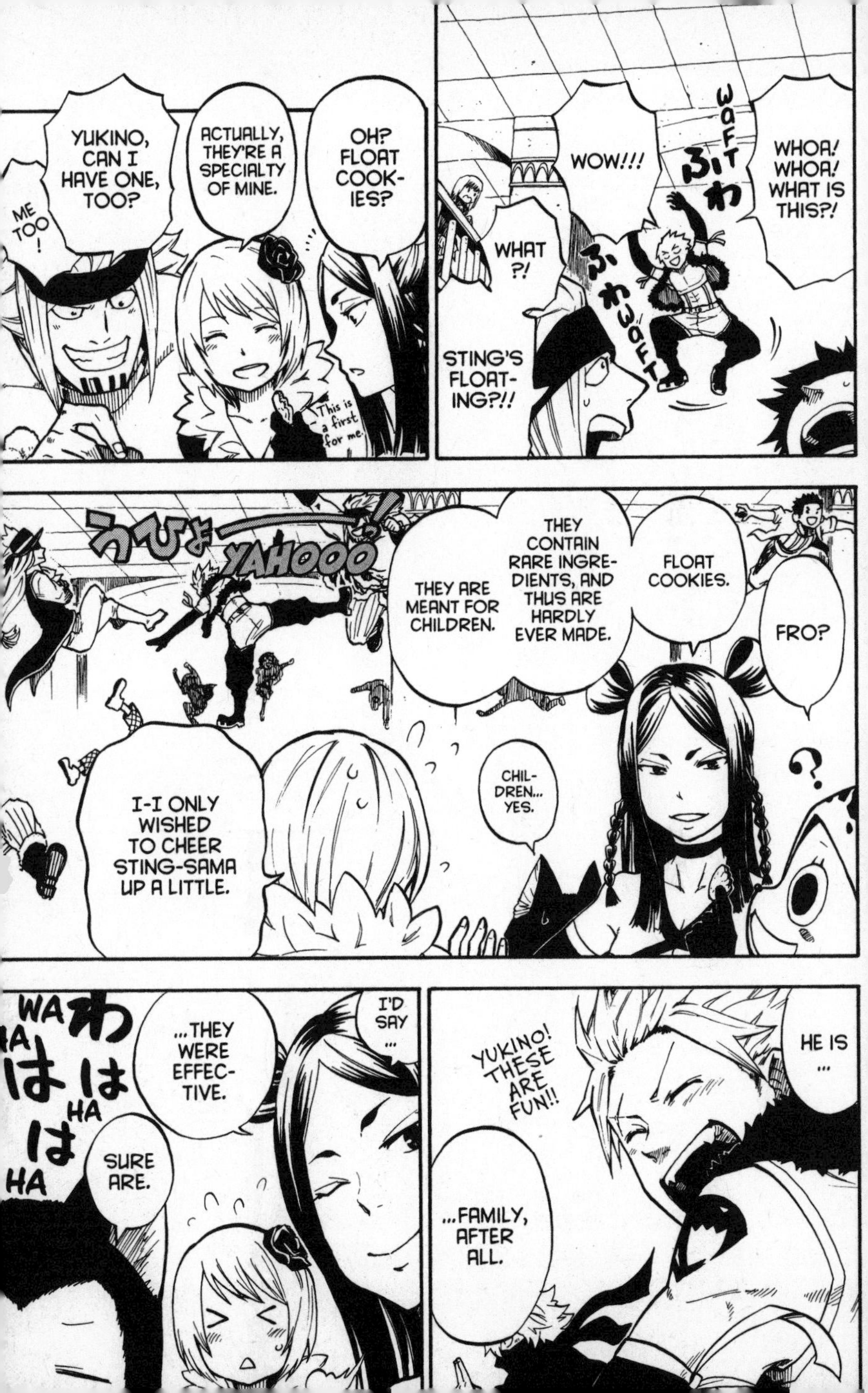
WHOA! WHOA! WHAT IS THIS?!
ふわ WAFT
WOW!!!
ふわ WAFT
WHAT?!
STING'S FLOAT-ING?!!
OH? FLOAT COOK-IES?
ACTUALLY, THEY'RE A SPECIALTY OF MINE.
YUKINO, CAN I HAVE ONE, TOO?
ME TOO!
This is a first for me.
FRO?
FLOAT COOKIES.
THEY CONTAIN RARE INGRE-DIENTS, AND THUS ARE HARDLY EVER MADE.
THEY ARE MEANT FOR CHILDREN.
うひょー YAHOOO
CHIL-DREN... YES.
I-I ONLY WISHED TO CHEER STING-SAMA UP A LITTLE.
HE IS ...
YUKINO! THESE ARE FUN!!
...FAMILY, AFTER ALL.
I'D SAY ...
...THEY WERE EFFEC-TIVE.
わははは WAHAHA
SURE ARE.

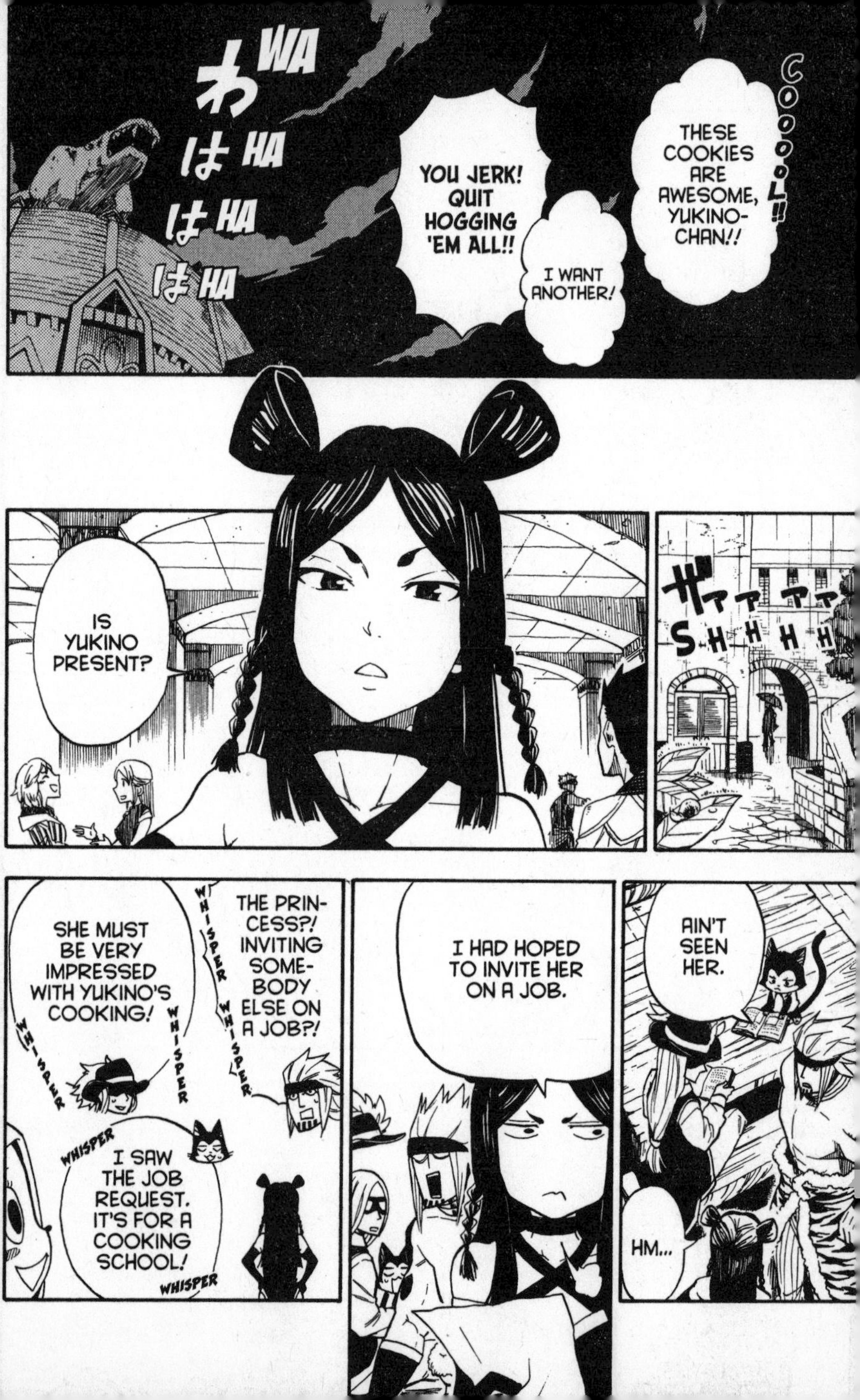
COOOOOL!!
THESE COOKIES ARE AWESOME, YUKINO-CHAN!!
I WANT ANOTHER!
YOU JERK! QUIT HOGGING 'EM ALL!!
わははは WA HA HA HA
ザァァァァ SHHHHH
IS YUKINO PRESENT?
AIN'T SEEN HER.
HM...
I HAD HOPED TO INVITE HER ON A JOB.
THE PRINCESS?! INVITING SOMEBODY ELSE ON A JOB?!
WHISPER
WHISPER
SHE MUST BE VERY IMPRESSED WITH YUKINO'S COOKING!
WHISPER
WHISPER
WHISPER
I SAW THE JOB REQUEST. IT'S FOR A COOKING SCHOOL!
WHISPER

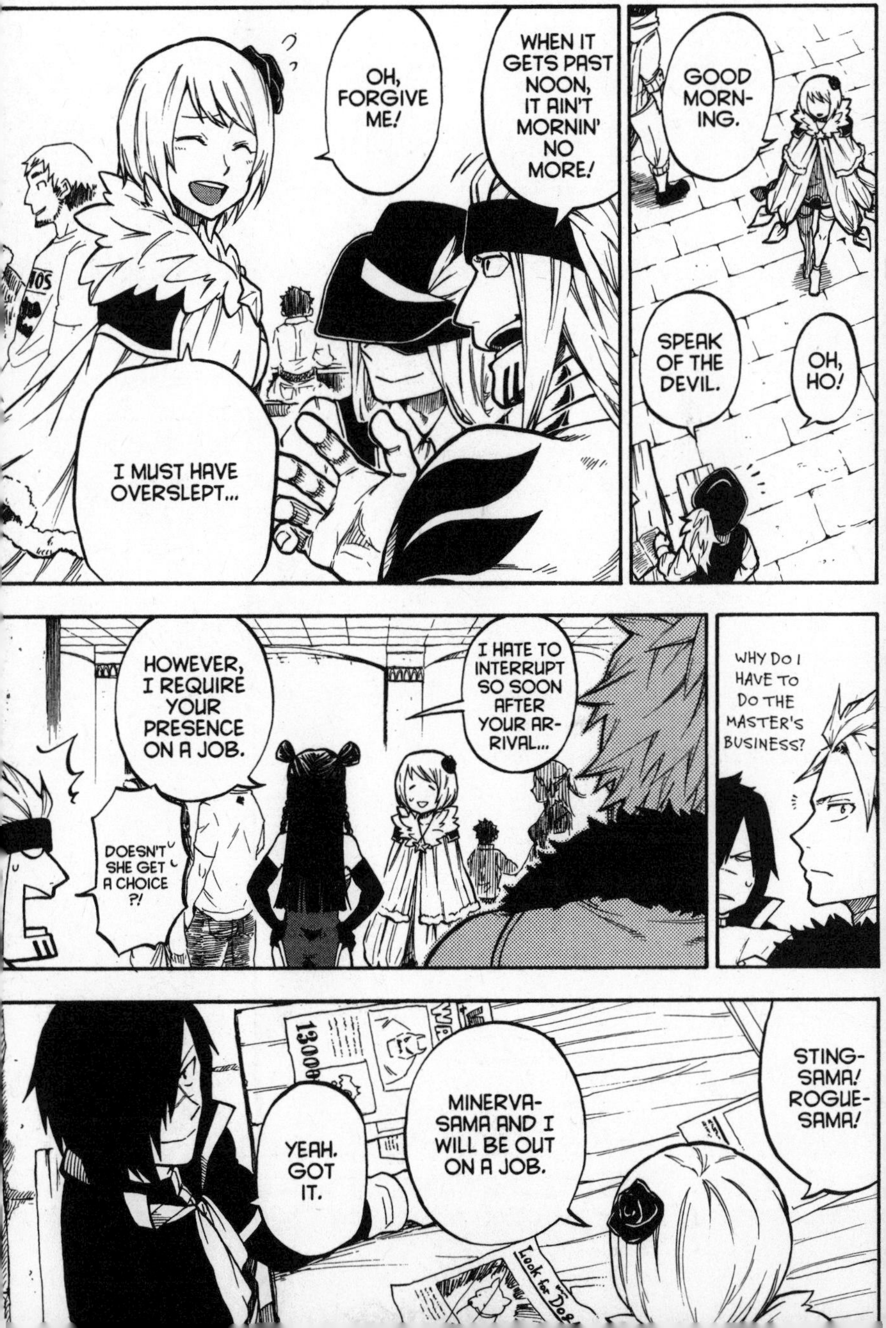
GOOD MORNING.
OH, HO!
SPEAK OF THE DEVIL.
WHEN IT GETS PAST NOON, IT AIN'T MORNIN' NO MORE!
OH, FORGIVE ME!
I MUST HAVE OVERSLEPT...
WHY DO I HAVE TO DO THE MASTER'S BUSINESS?
I HATE TO INTERRUPT SO SOON AFTER YOUR ARRIVAL...
HOWEVER, I REQUIRE YOUR PRESENCE ON A JOB.
DOESN'T SHE GET A CHOICE?!
STING-SAMA! ROGUE-SAMA!
MINERVA-SAMA AND I WILL BE OUT ON A JOB.
YEAH. GOT IT.

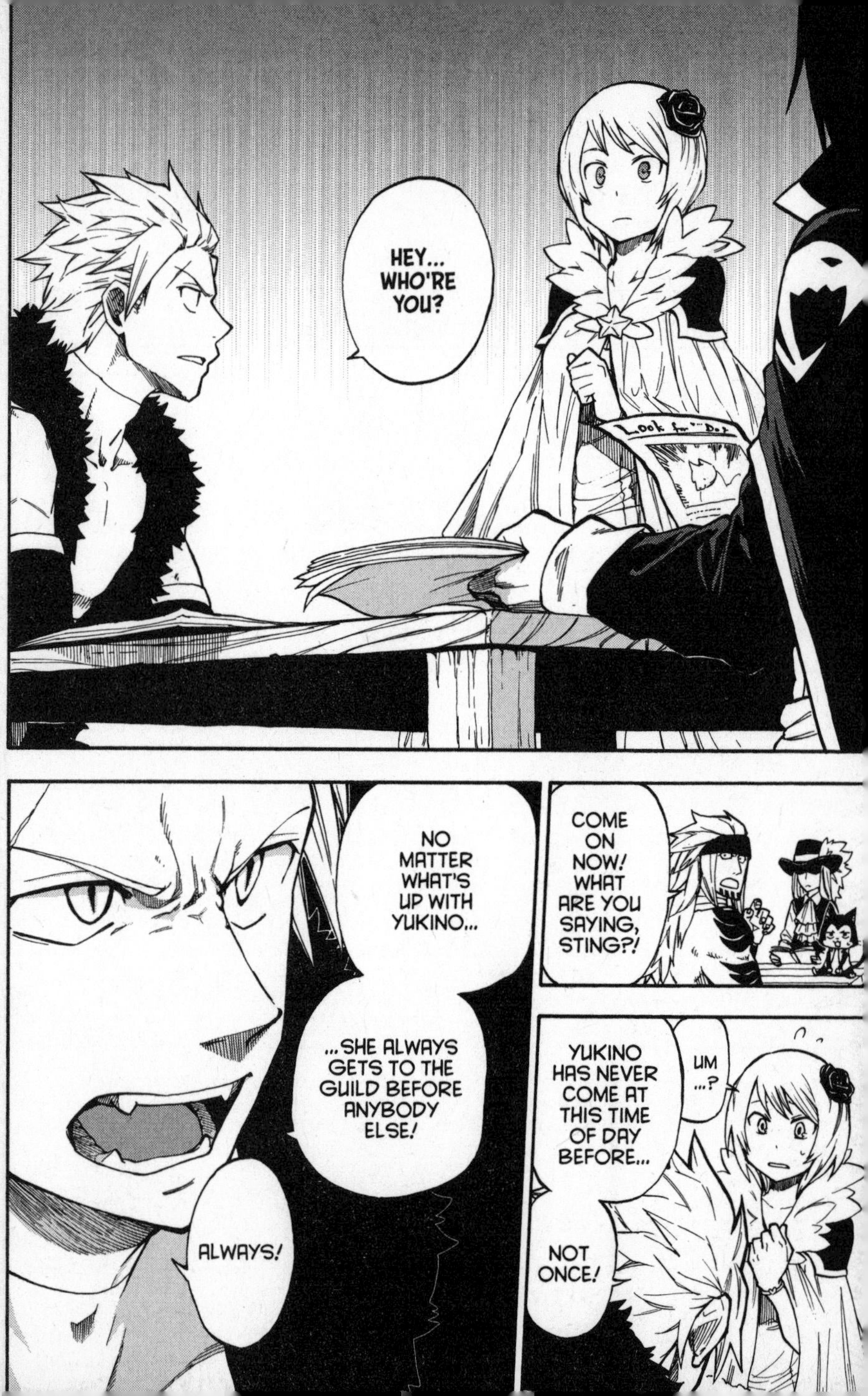
HEY... WHO'RE YOU?
COME ON NOW! WHAT ARE YOU SAYING, STING?!
UM ...?
YUKINO HAS NEVER COME AT THIS TIME OF DAY BEFORE...
NOT ONCE!
NO MATTER WHAT'S UP WITH YUKINO...
...SHE ALWAYS GETS TO THE GUILD BEFORE ANYBODY ELSE!
ALWAYS!

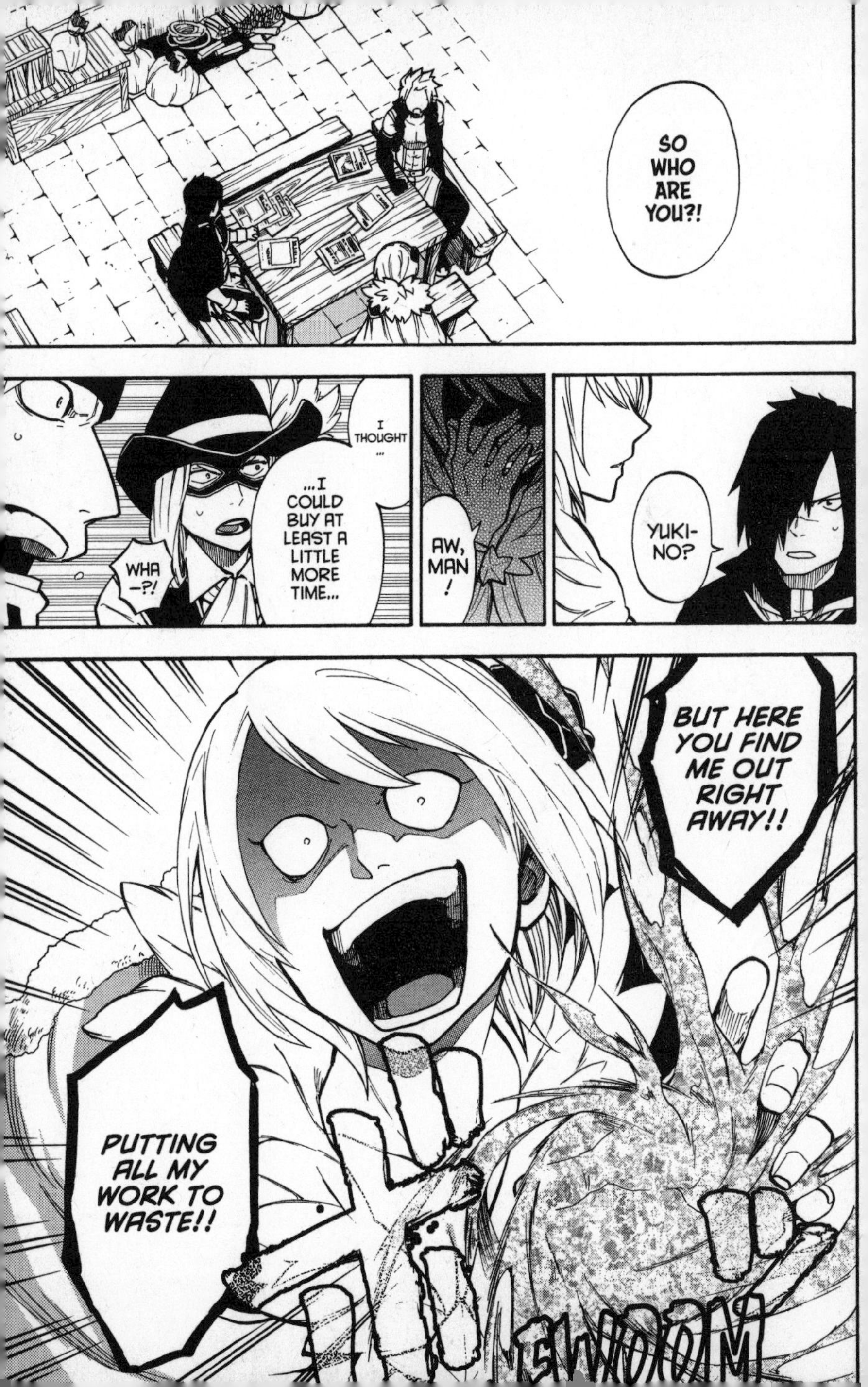
SO WHO ARE YOU?!
YUKI-NO?
AW, MAN!
I THOUGHT...
...I COULD BUY AT LEAST A LITTLE MORE TIME...
WHA—?!
BUT HERE YOU FIND ME OUT RIGHT AWAY!!
PUTTING ALL MY WORK TO WASTE!!
SWOOM

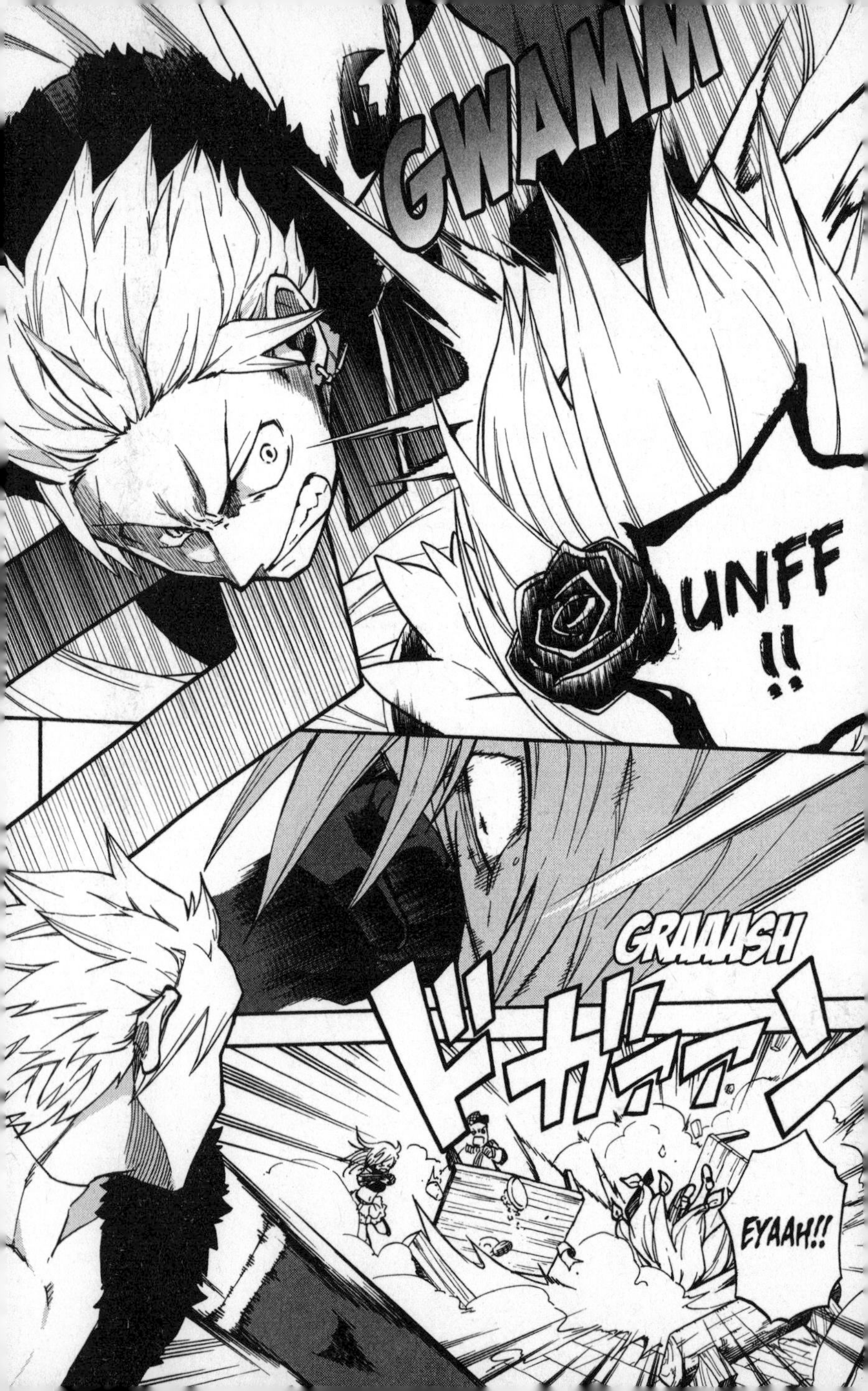
GWAMM
UNFF!!
GRAAASH
EYAAH!!

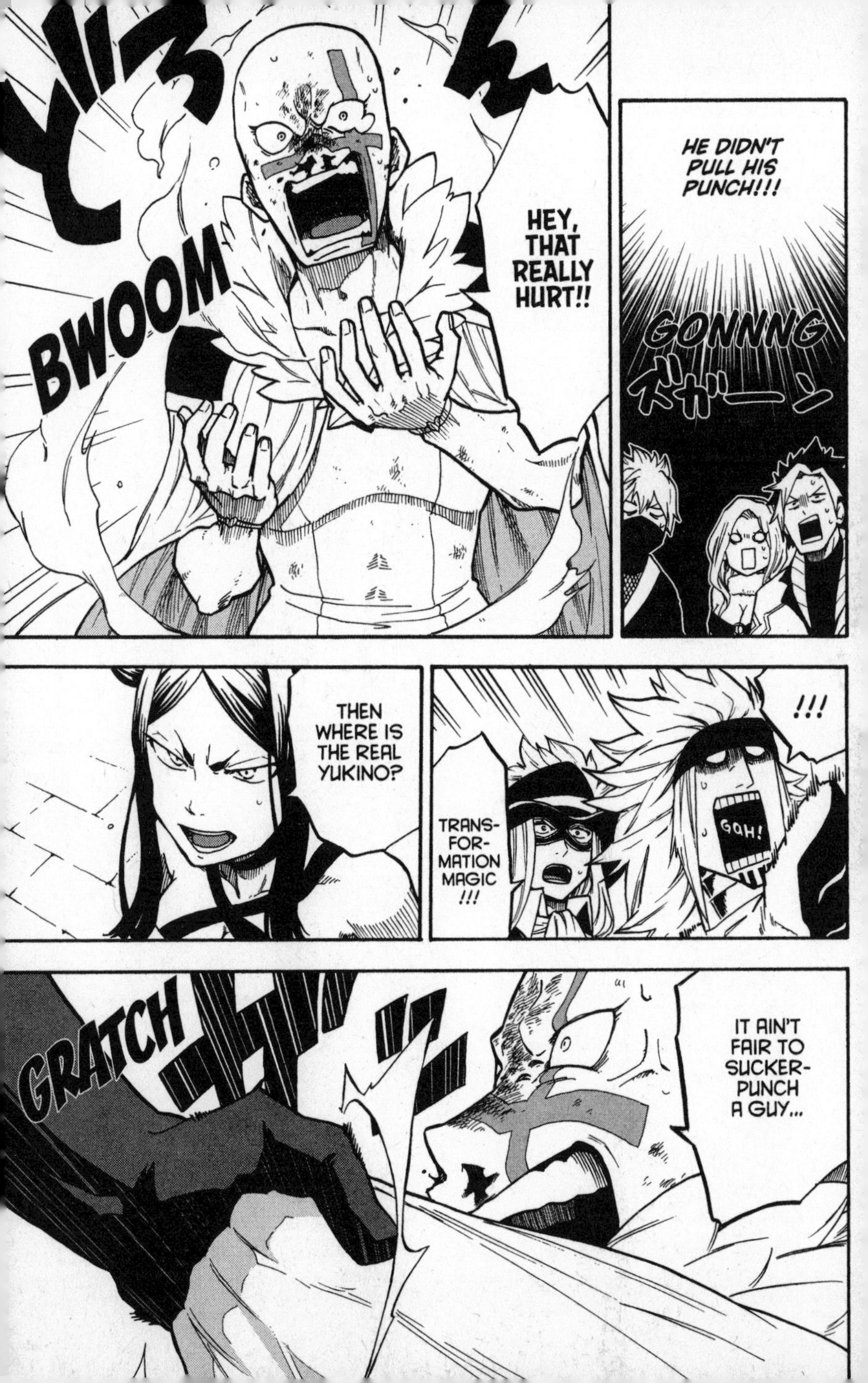
HE DIDN'T PULL HIS PUNCH!!!
GONNNG
ズガーーン
BWOOM
HEY, THAT REALLY HURT!!
!!!
GAH!
TRANS-FORMATION MAGIC !!!
THEN WHERE IS THE REAL YUKINO?
GRATCH
IT AIN'T FAIR TO SUCKER-PUNCH A GUY...

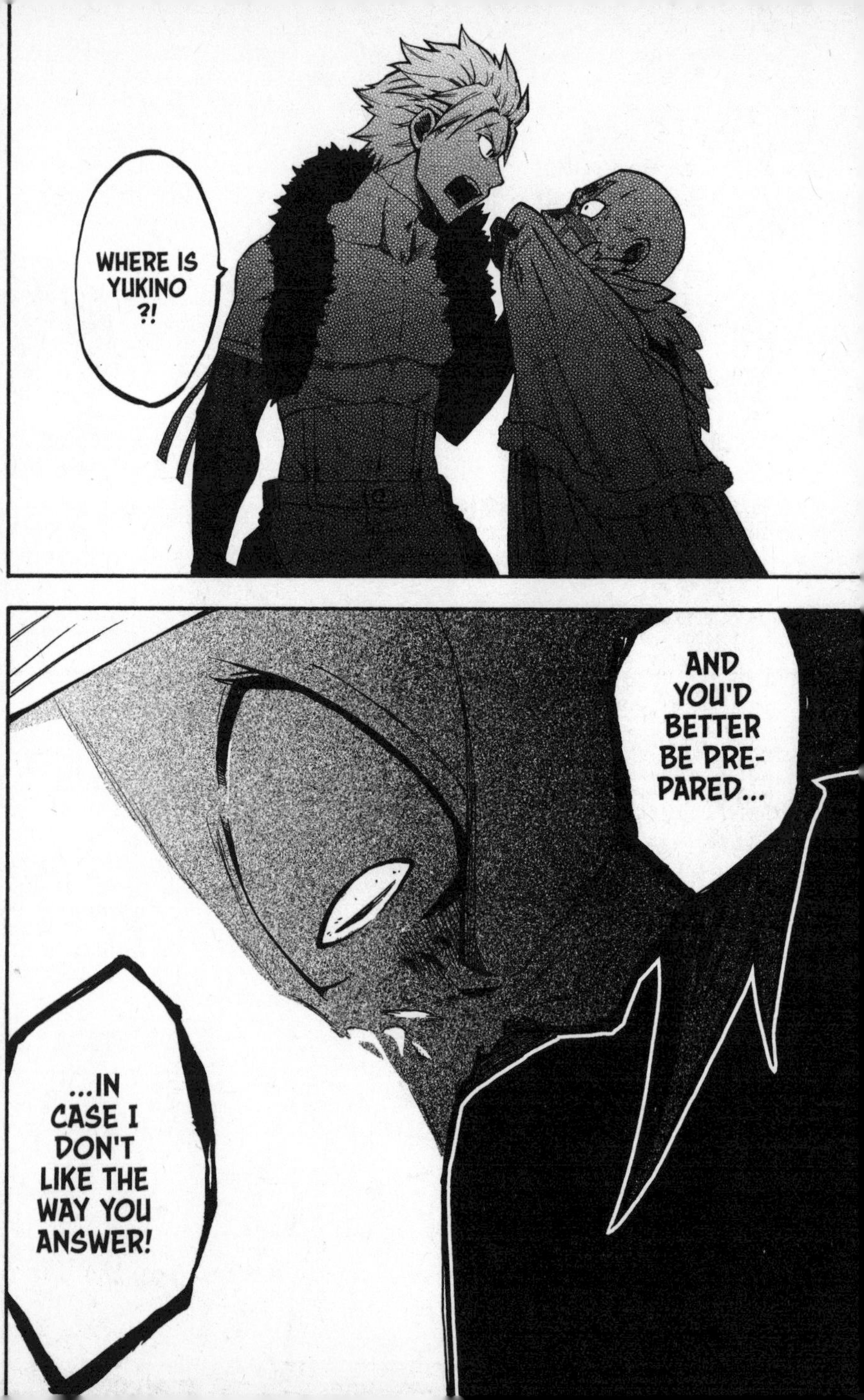
WHERE IS YUKINO ?!
AND YOU'D BETTER BE PRE-PARED...
...IN CASE I DON'T LIKE THE WAY YOU ANSWER!

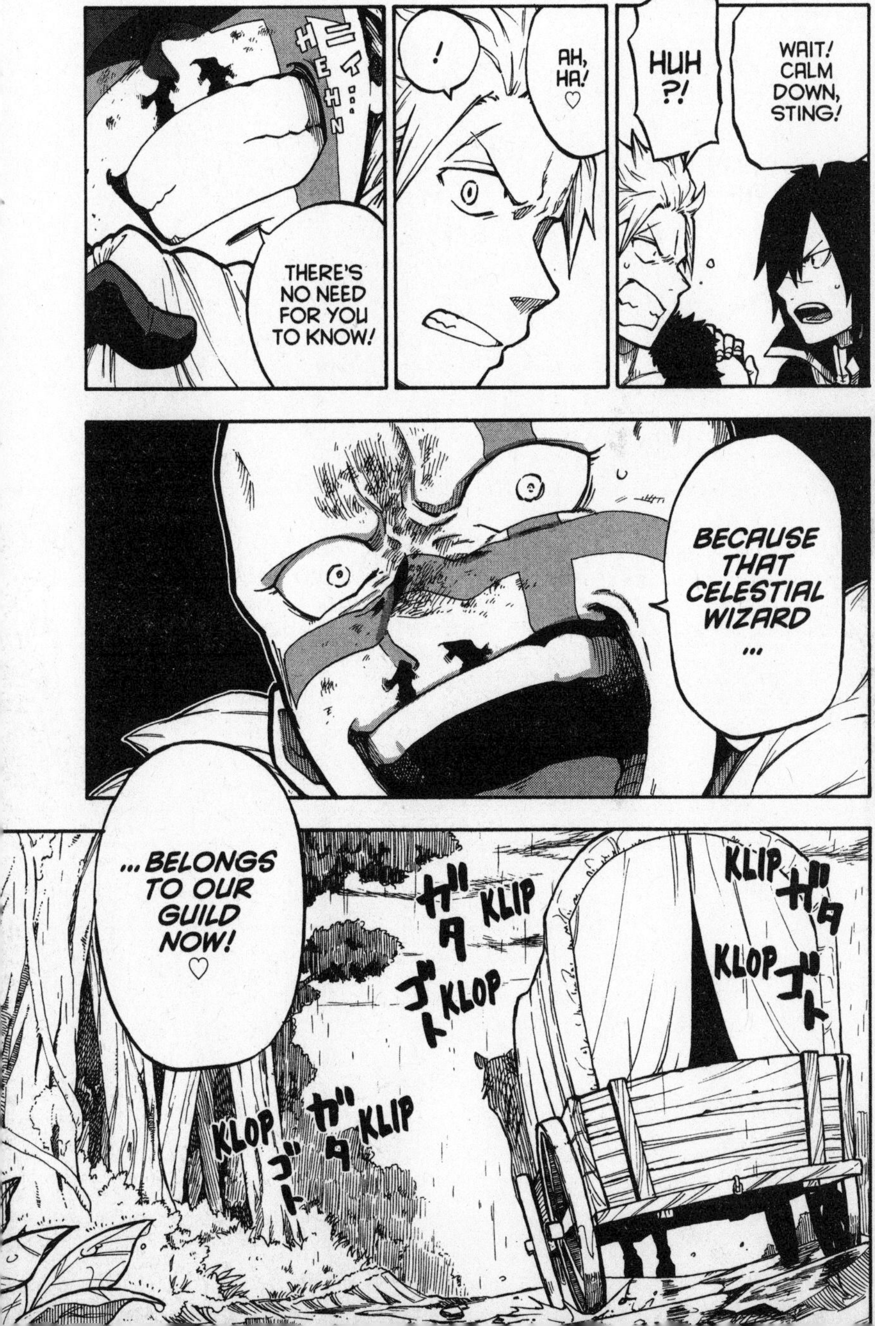
WAIT! CALM DOWN, STING!
HUH ?!
AH, HA! ♡
!
ニィ…
HEHN
THERE'S NO NEED FOR YOU TO KNOW!
BECAUSE THAT CELESTIAL WIZARD ...
...BELONGS TO OUR GUILD NOW! ♡
KLIP ガタ
KLOP ゴト
ガタ KLIP
ゴト KLOP
KLOP ゴト
ガタ KLIP

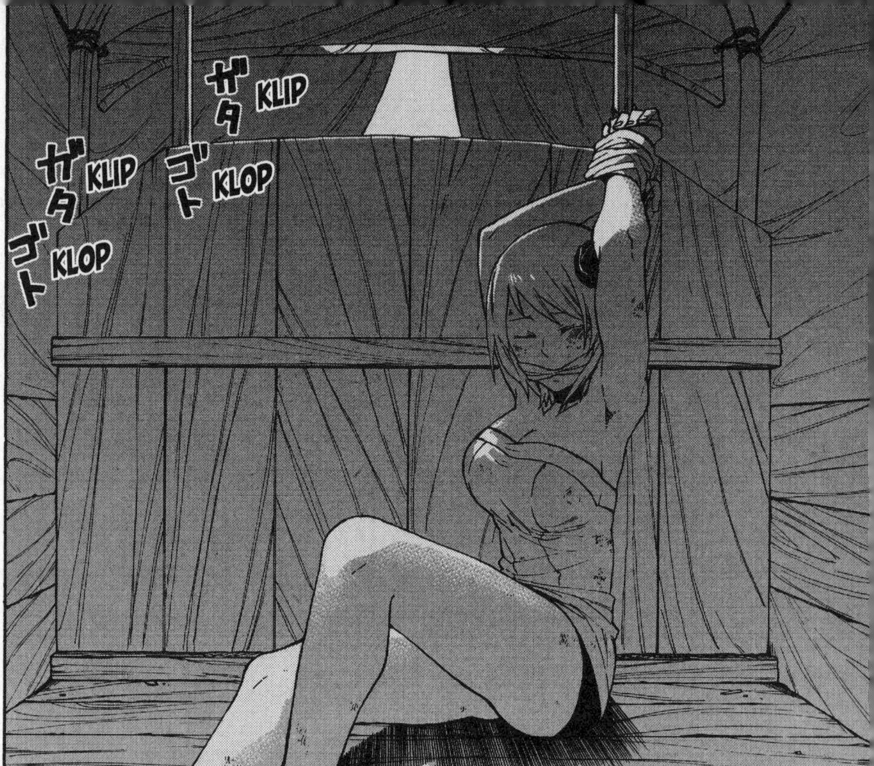
ガタ KLIP
ゴト KLOP
ガタ KLIP
ゴト KLOP

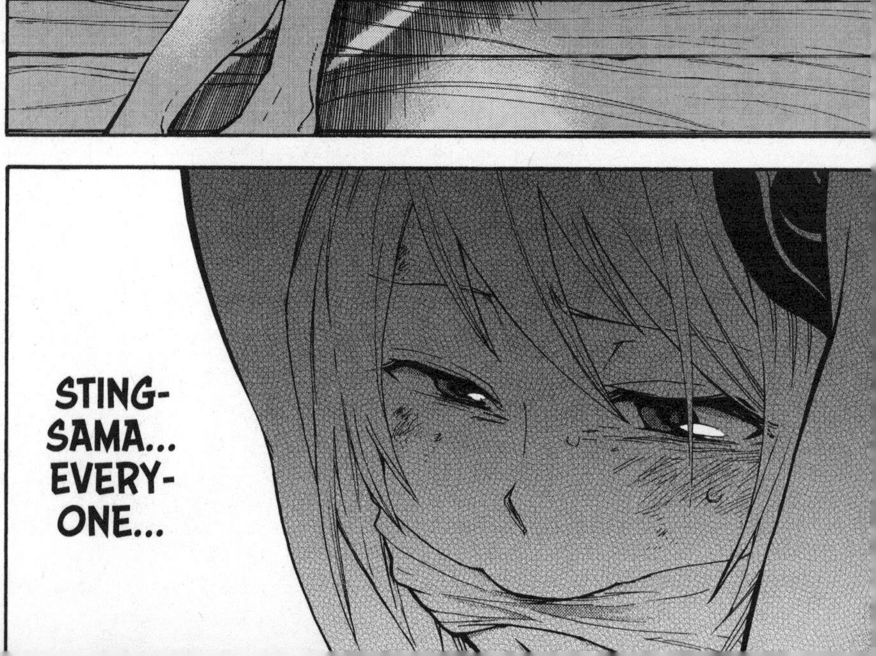
STING-SAMA... EVERY-ONE...

FAIRY TAIL: TWIN DRAGONS OF SABER TOOTH

Chapter 2: The Ancient Magic Weapon

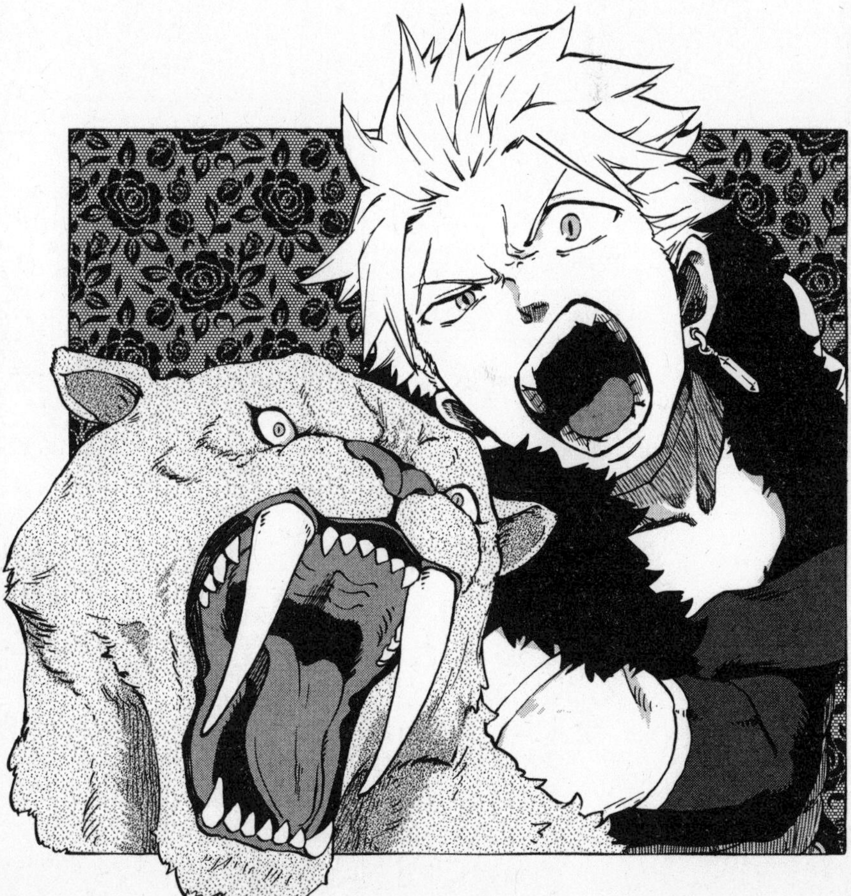

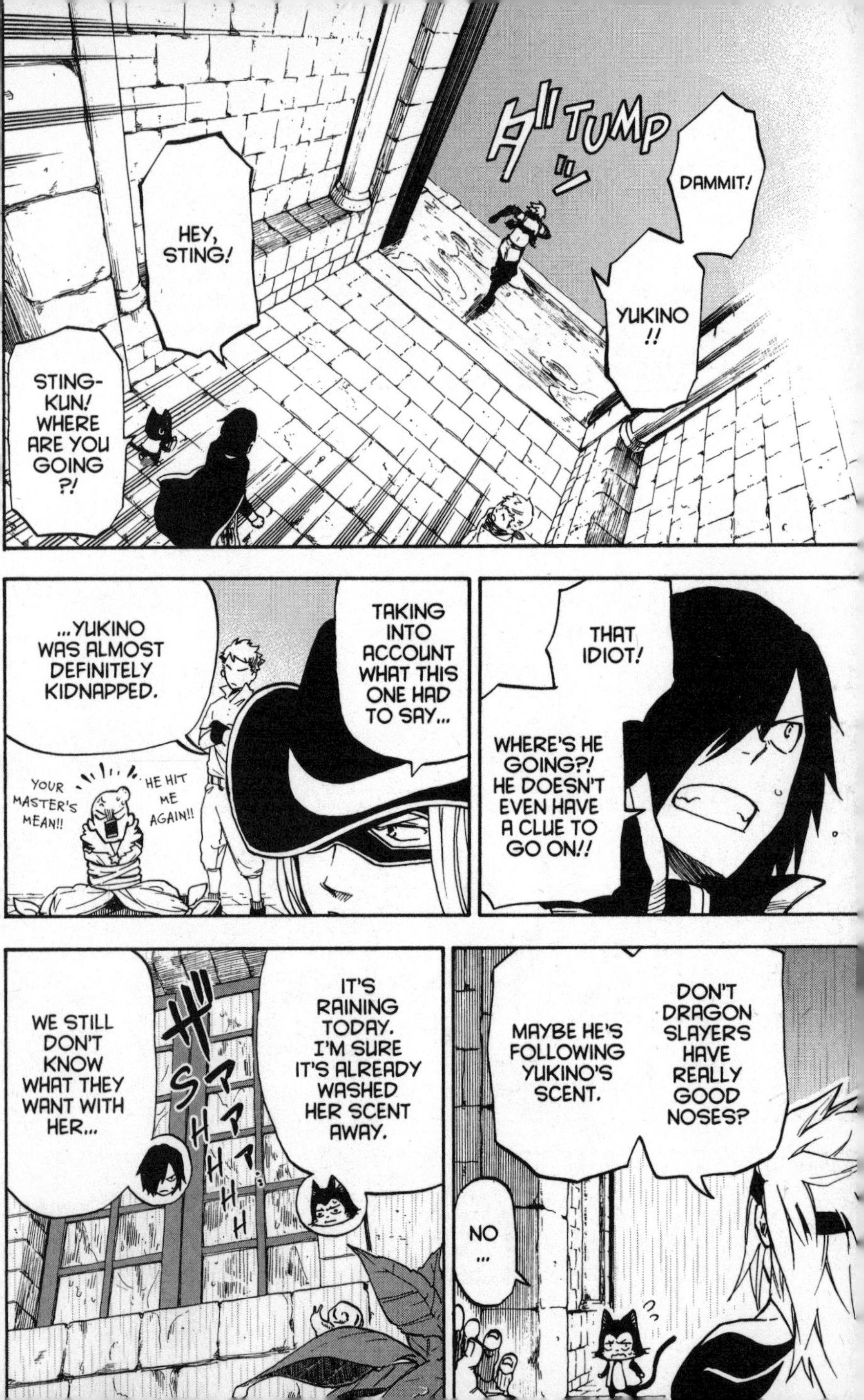
TUMP
DAMMIT!
YUKINO!!
HEY, STING!
STING-KUN! WHERE ARE YOU GOING?!
THAT IDIOT!
WHERE'S HE GOING?! HE DOESN'T EVEN HAVE A CLUE TO GO ON!!
TAKING INTO ACCOUNT WHAT THIS ONE HAD TO SAY...
...YUKINO WAS ALMOST DEFINITELY KIDNAPPED.
HE HIT ME AGAIN!!
YOUR MASTER'S MEAN!!
DON'T DRAGON SLAYERS HAVE REALLY GOOD NOSES?
MAYBE HE'S FOLLOWING YUKINO'S SCENT.
NO ...
IT'S RAINING TODAY. I'M SURE IT'S ALREADY WASHED HER SCENT AWAY.
SHHHHH
WE STILL DON'T KNOW WHAT THEY WANT WITH HER...

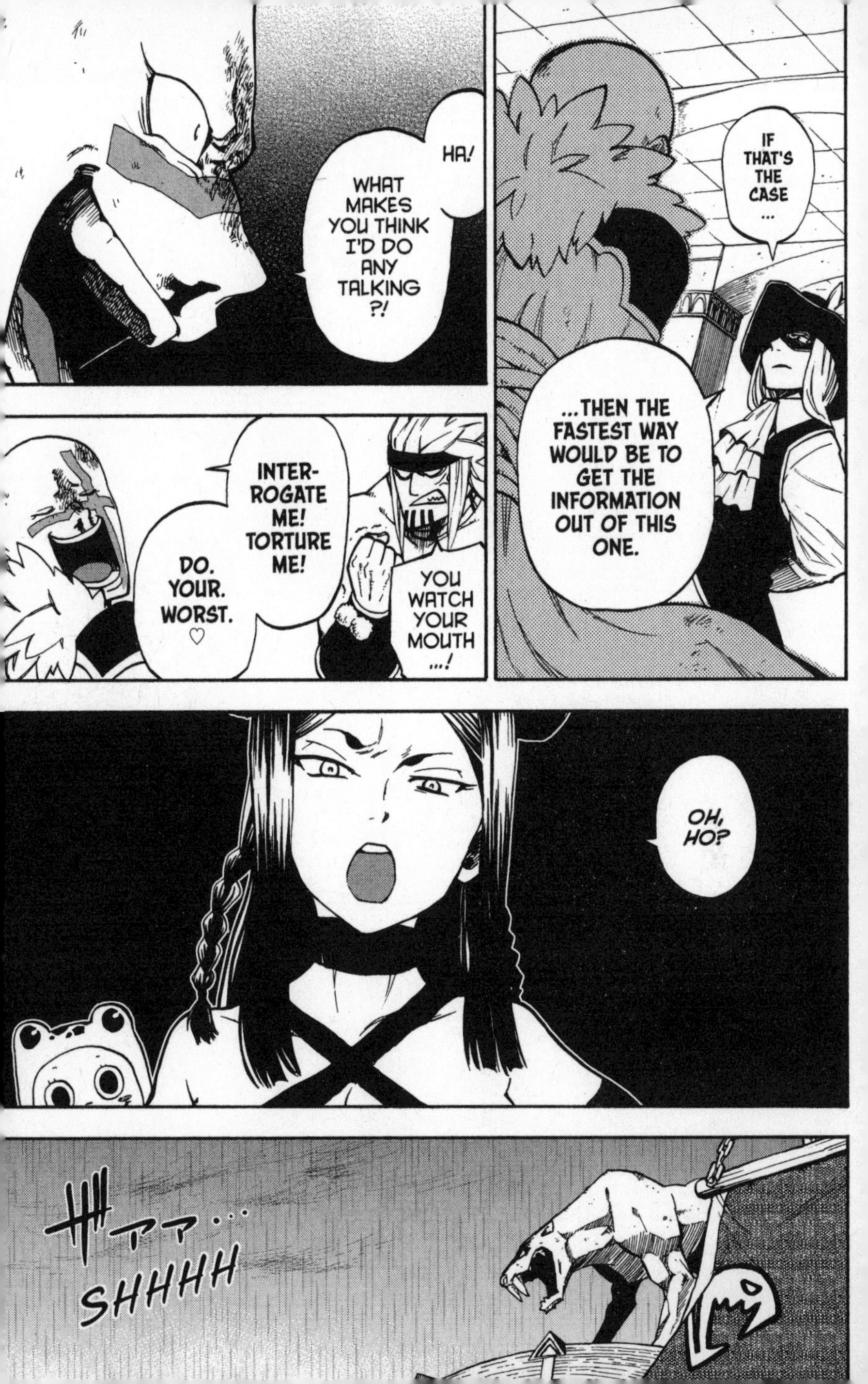
IF THAT'S THE CASE ...
...THEN THE FASTEST WAY WOULD BE TO GET THE INFORMATION OUT OF THIS ONE.
HA!
WHAT MAKES YOU THINK I'D DO ANY TALKING ?!
INTER-ROGATE ME! TORTURE ME!
DO. YOUR. WORST. ♡
YOU WATCH YOUR MOUTH ...!
OH, HO?
アア…
SHHHH

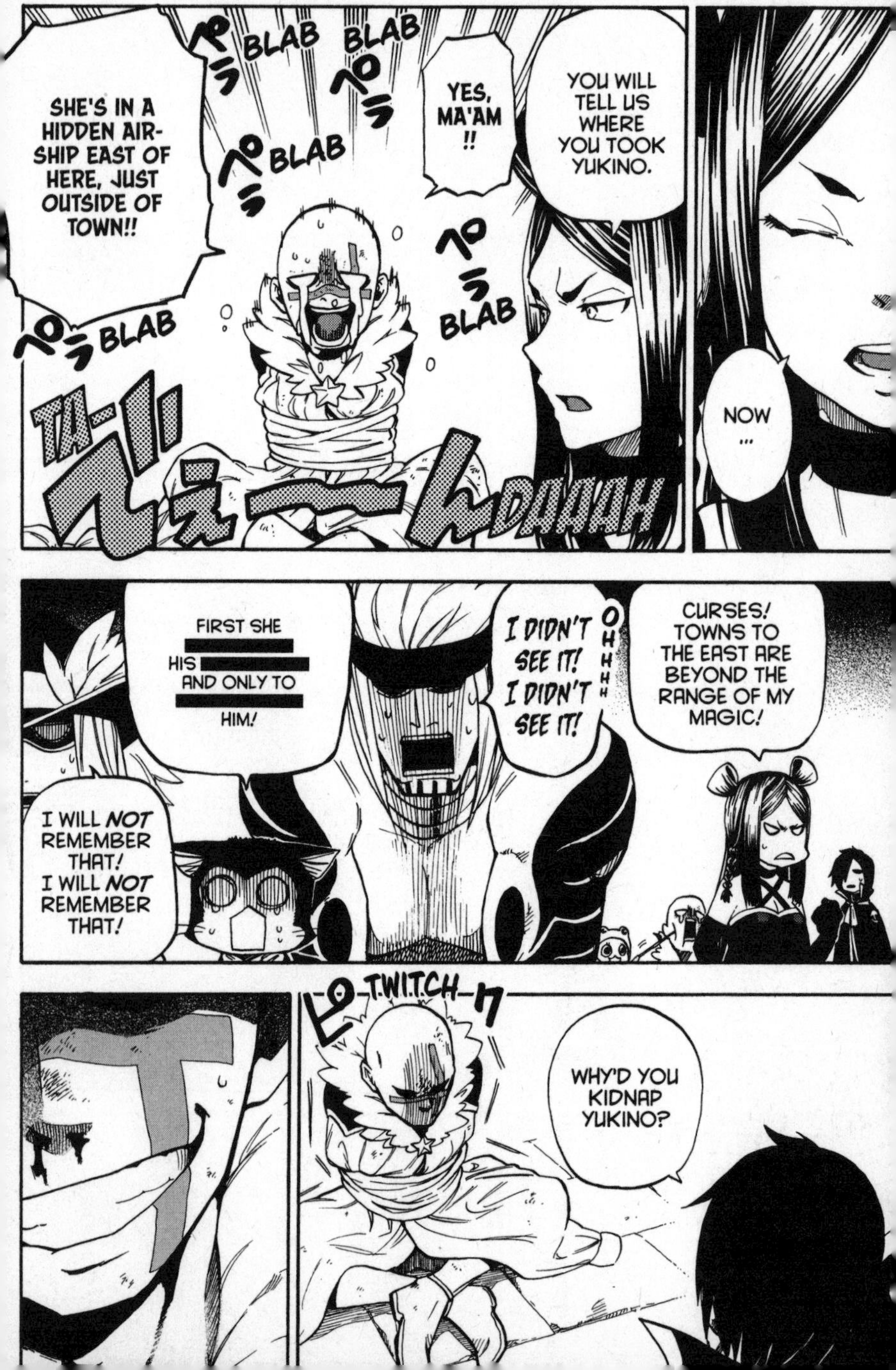
NOW ...
YOU WILL TELL US WHERE YOU TOOK YUKINO.
YES, MA'AM !!
BLAB BLAB BLAB BLAB BLAB
SHE'S IN A HIDDEN AIR-SHIP EAST OF HERE, JUST OUTSIDE OF TOWN!!
DAAAAH
CURSES! TOWNS TO THE EAST ARE BEYOND THE RANGE OF MY MAGIC!
OHHHHH
I DIDN'T SEE IT! I DIDN'T SEE IT!
FIRST SHE [redacted] HIS [redacted] AND ONLY TO [redacted] HIM!
I WILL NOT REMEMBER THAT! I WILL NOT REMEMBER THAT!
TWITCH
WHY'D YOU KIDNAP YUKINO?

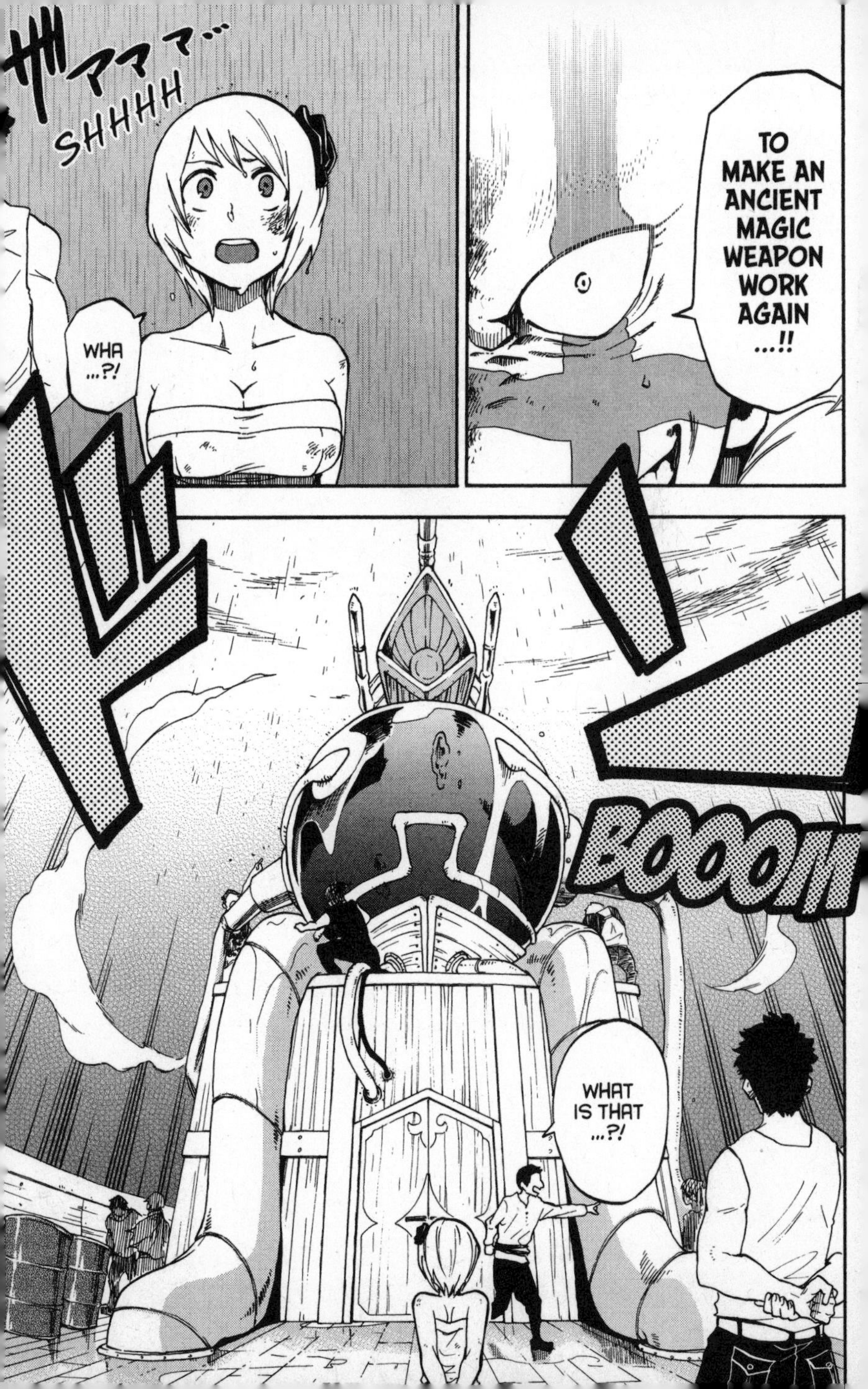
TO MAKE AN ANCIENT MAGIC WEAPON WORK AGAIN ...!!
SHHHH
WHA ...?!
BOOOM
WHAT IS THAT ...?!

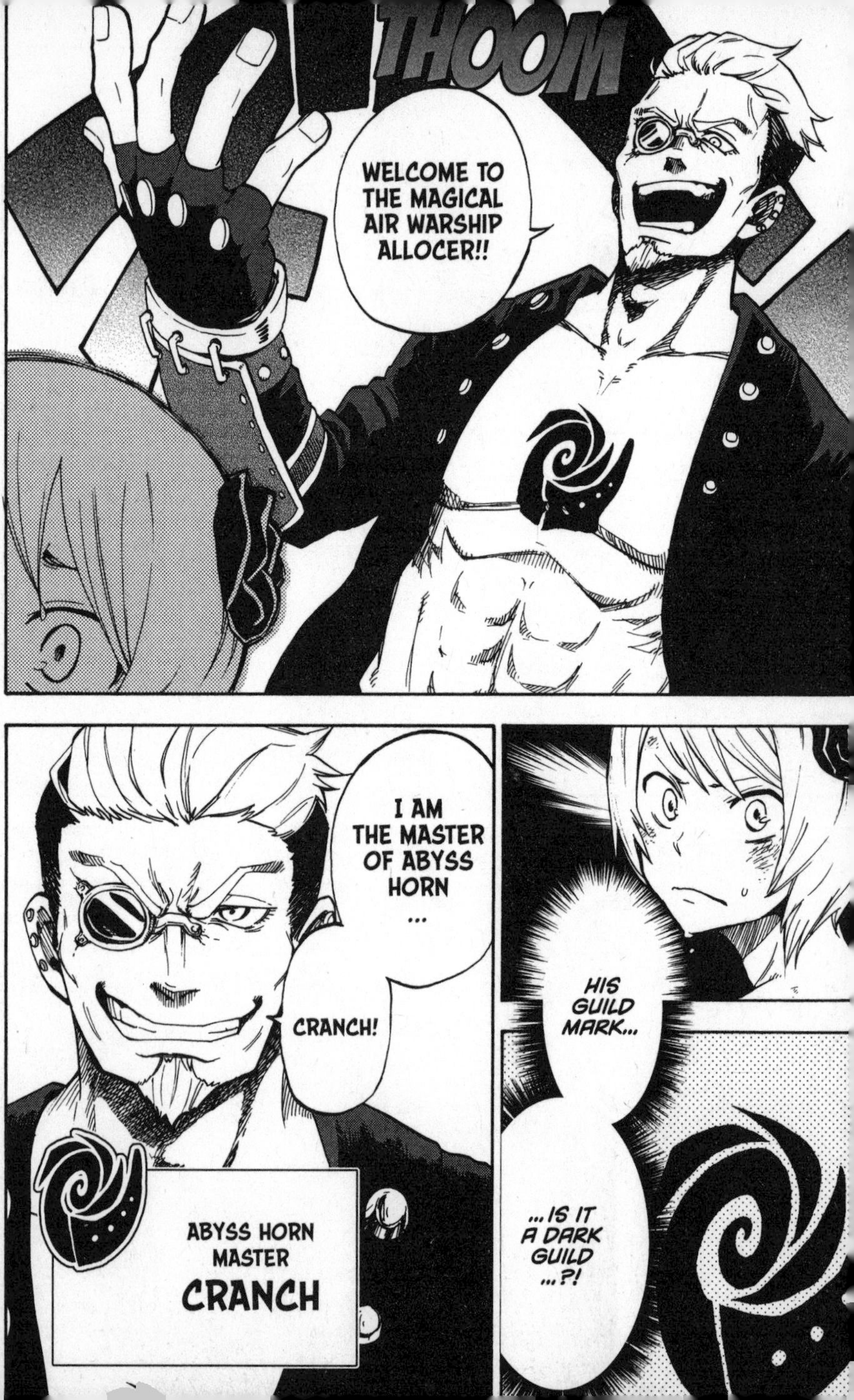
THOOM
WELCOME TO THE MAGICAL AIR WARSHIP ALLOCER!!
HIS GUILD MARK...
...IS IT A DARK GUILD ...?!
I AM THE MASTER OF ABYSS HORN ...
CRANCH!
ABYSS HORN MASTER CRANCH

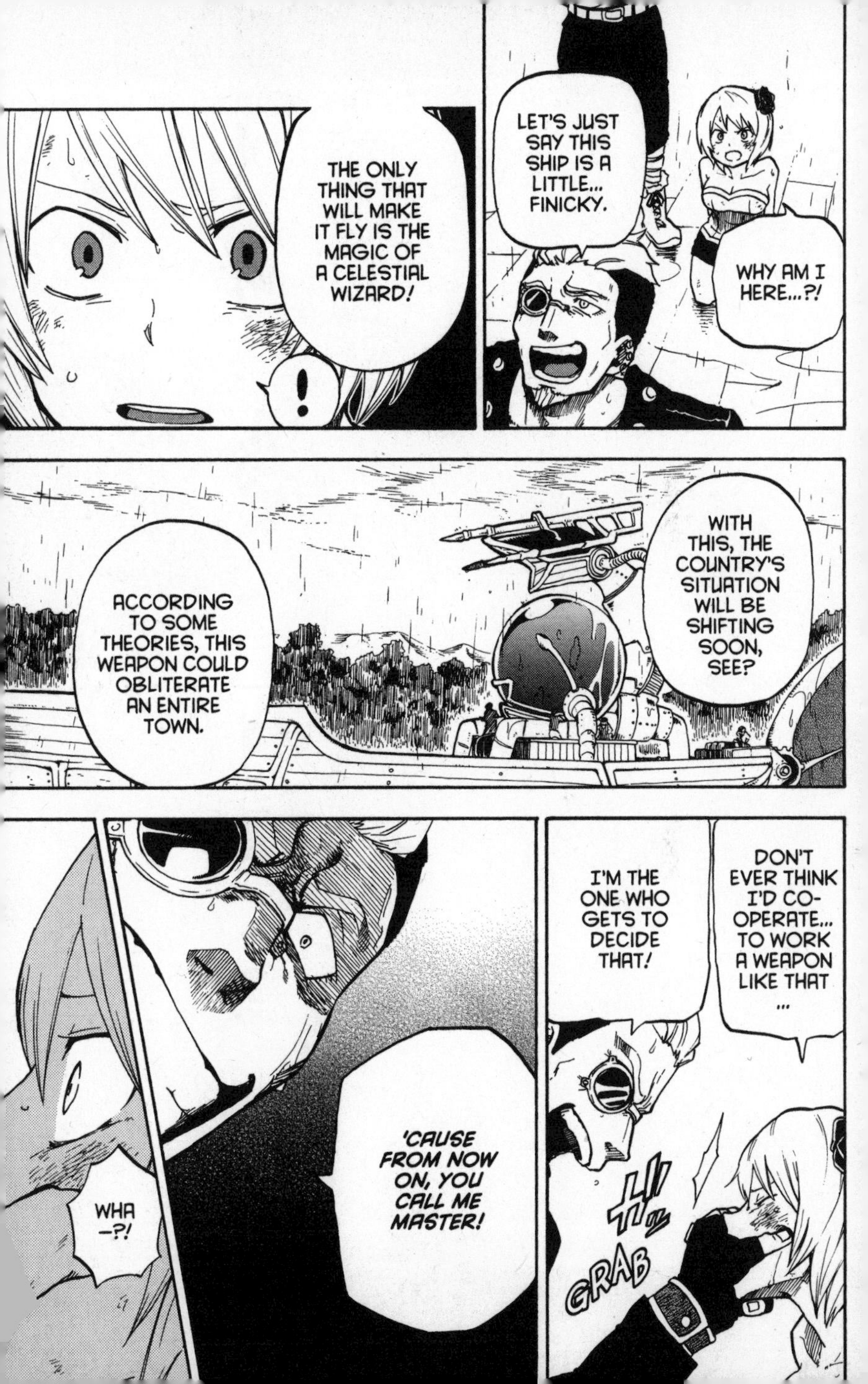
WHY AM I HERE...?!
LET'S JUST SAY THIS SHIP IS A LITTLE... FINICKY.
THE ONLY THING THAT WILL MAKE IT FLY IS THE MAGIC OF A CELESTIAL WIZARD!
!
WITH THIS, THE COUNTRY'S SITUATION WILL BE SHIFTING SOON, SEE?
ACCORDING TO SOME THEORIES, THIS WEAPON COULD OBLITERATE AN ENTIRE TOWN.
DON'T EVER THINK I'D CO-OPERATE... TO WORK A WEAPON LIKE THAT ...
I'M THE ONE WHO GETS TO DECIDE THAT!
GRAB
'CAUSE FROM NOW ON, YOU CALL ME MASTER!
WHA -?!

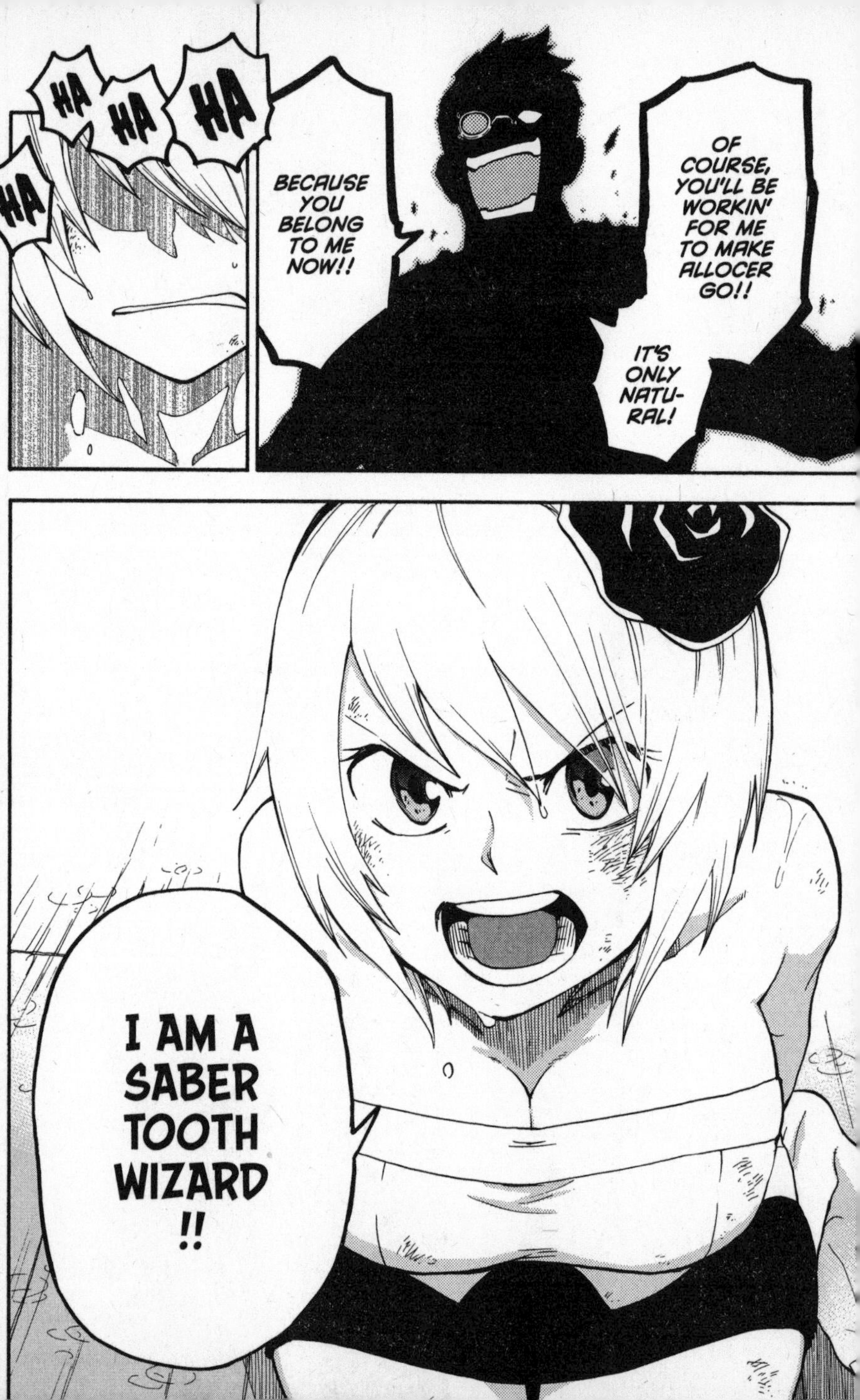
OF COURSE, YOU'LL BE WORKIN' FOR ME TO MAKE ALLOCER GO!!
IT'S ONLY NATU-RAL!
BECAUSE YOU BELONG TO ME NOW!!
HA
HA
HA
HA
I AM A SABER TOOTH WIZARD !!

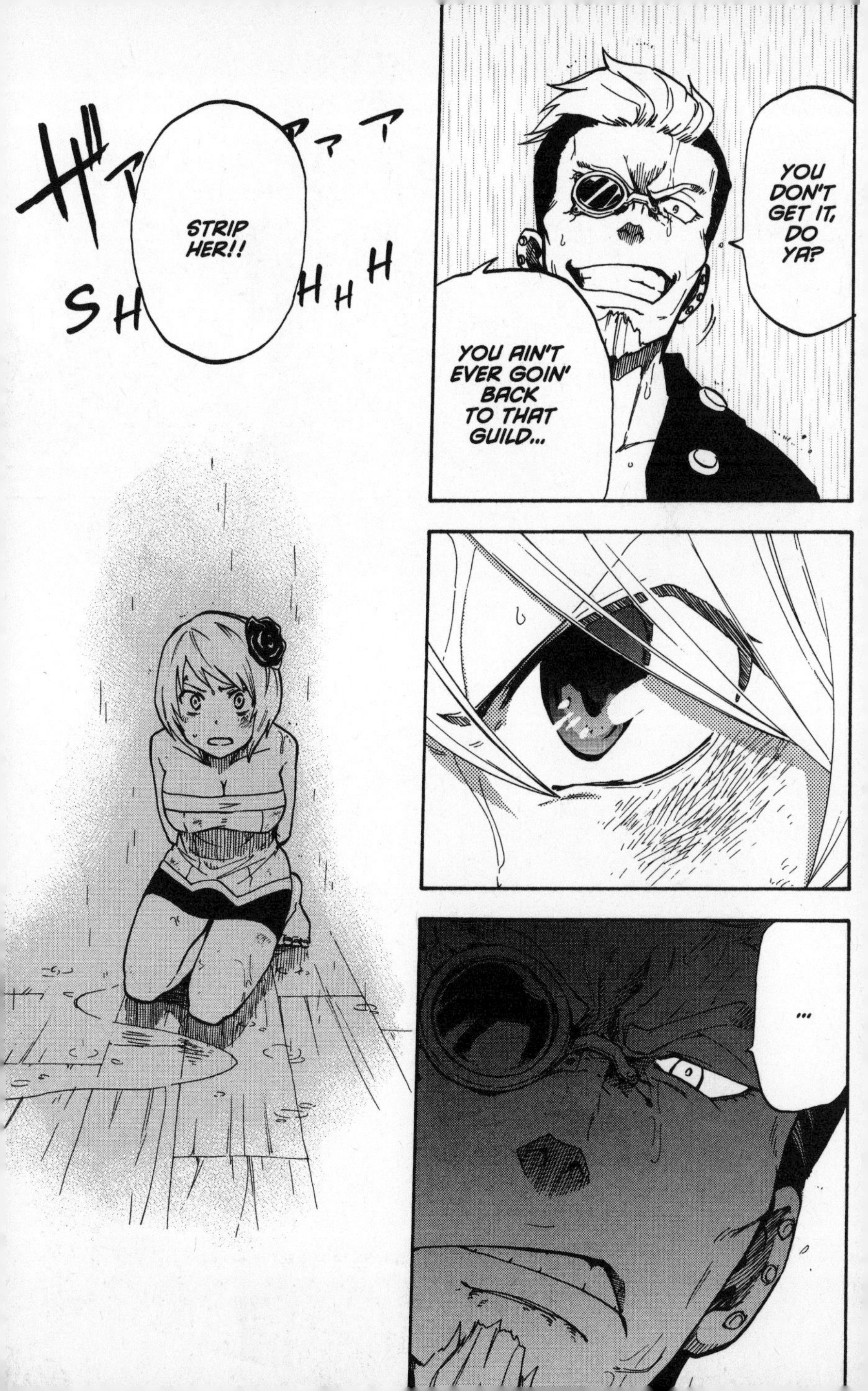
YOU DON'T GET IT, DO YA?
YOU AIN'T EVER GOIN' BACK TO THAT GUILD...
...
SH
HHH
STRIP HER!!

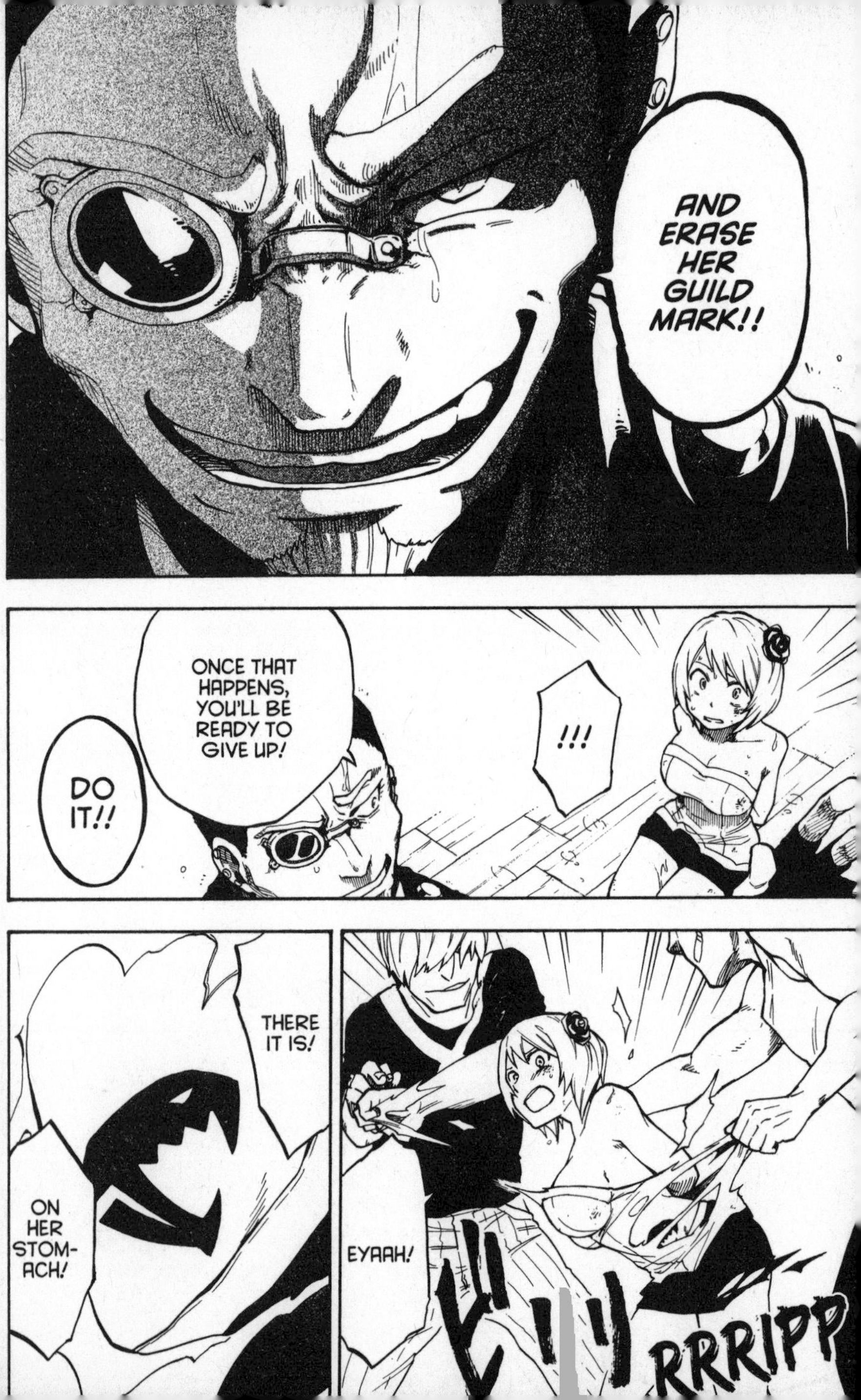
AND ERASE HER GUILD MARK!!
!!!
ONCE THAT HAPPENS, YOU'LL BE READY TO GIVE UP!
DO IT!!
RRRIPP
EYAAH!
THERE IT IS!
ON HER STOMACH!

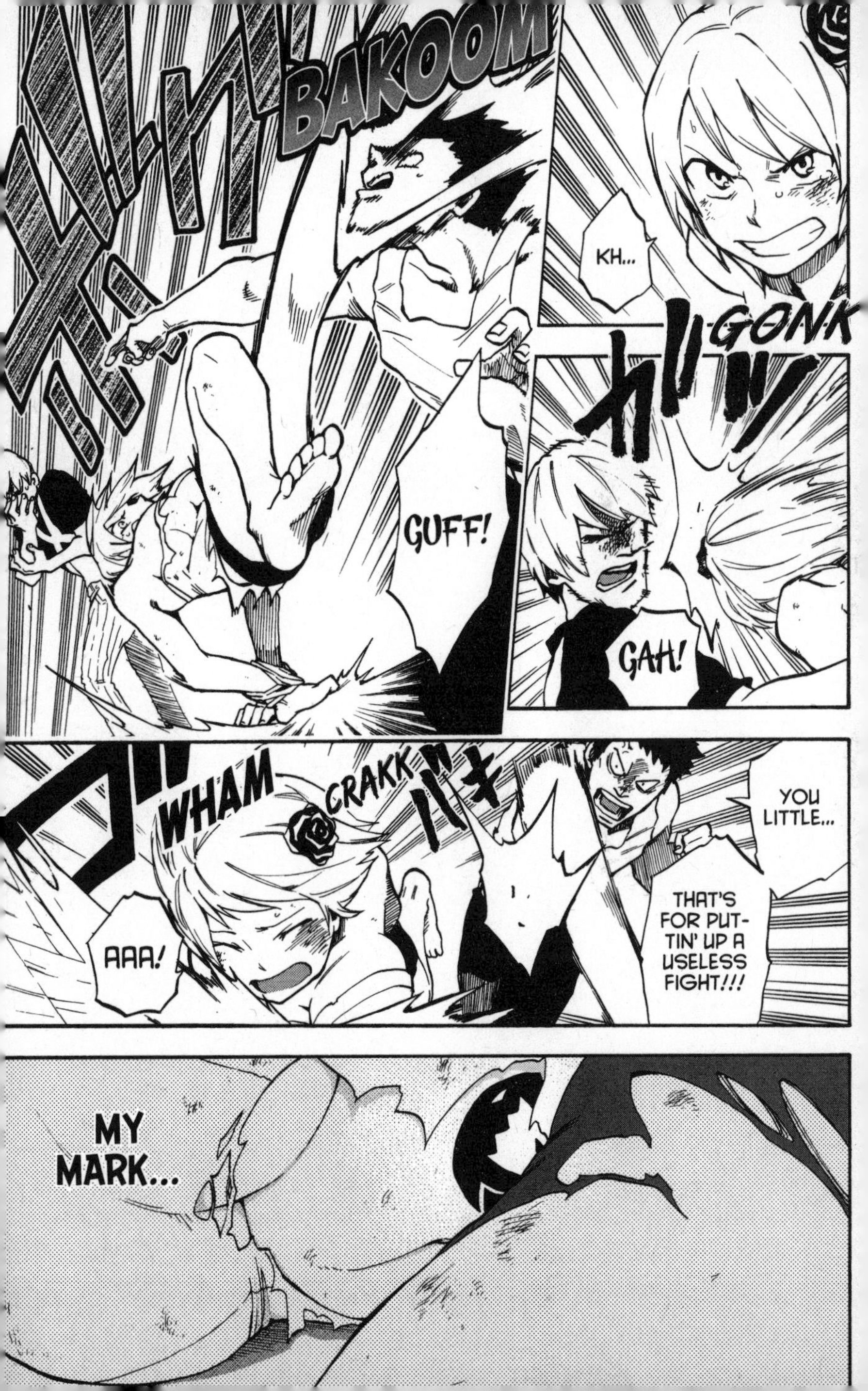
KH...
GONK
GAH!
BAKOOM
GUFF!
YOU LITTLE...
THAT'S FOR PUT-TIN' UP A USELESS FIGHT!!!
CRAKK
バキ
WHAM
AAA!
MY MARK...

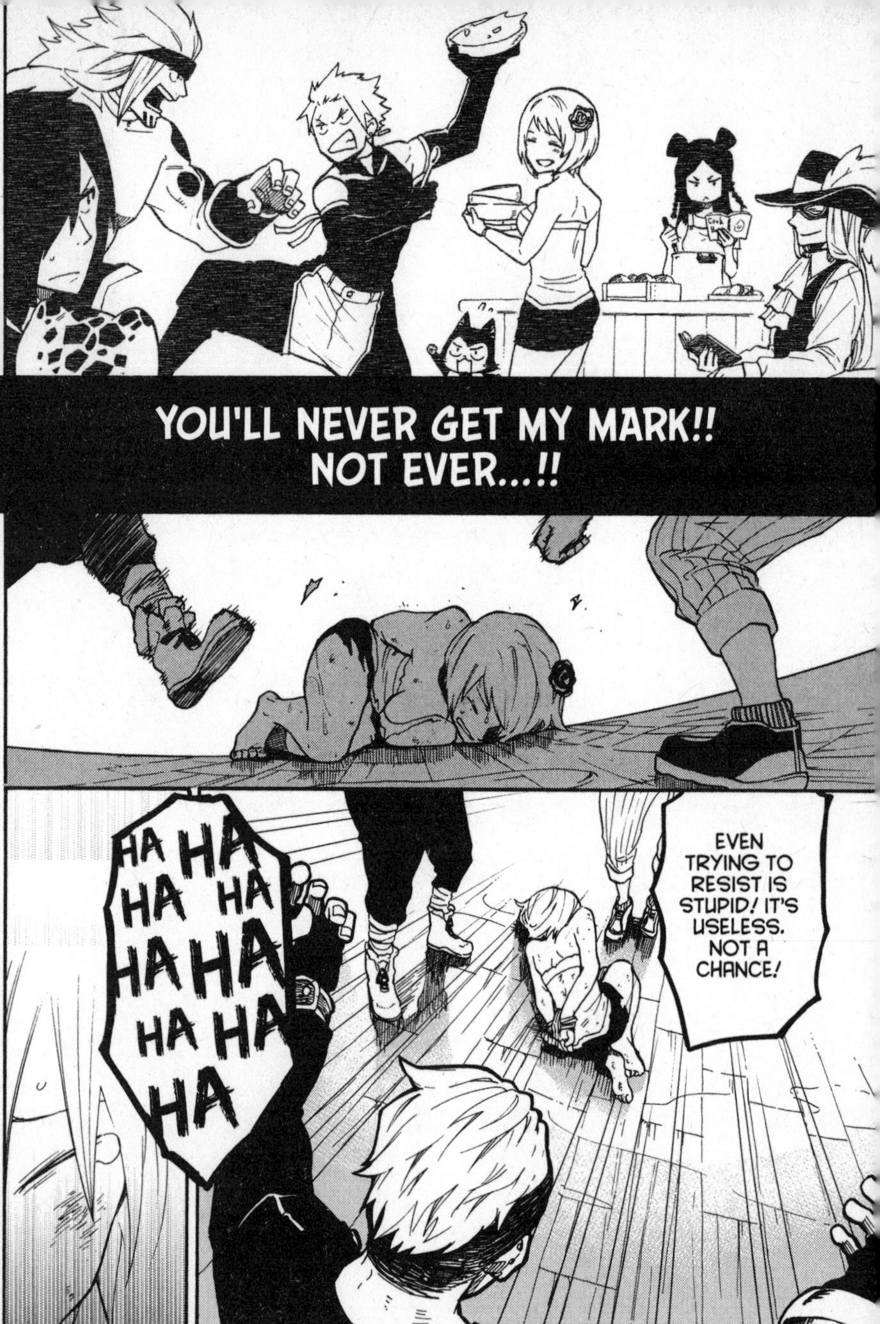
YOU'LL NEVER GET MY MARK!! NOT EVER...!!
EVEN TRYING TO RESIST IS STUPID! IT'S USELESS. NOT A CHANCE!
HA HA HA HA HA HA HA HA HA HA

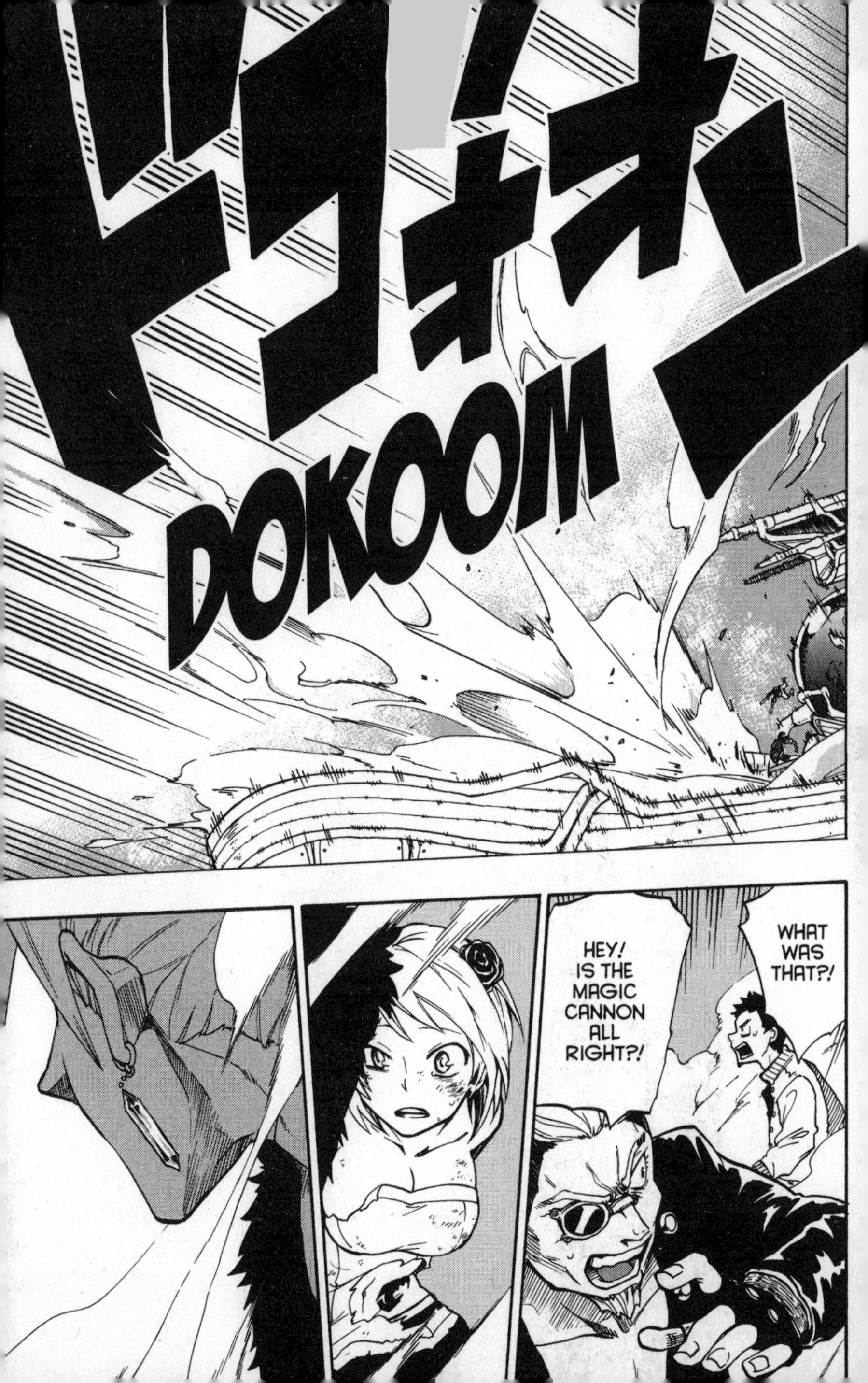
DOKOOM
WHAT WAS THAT?!
HEY! IS THE MAGIC CANNON ALL RIGHT?!

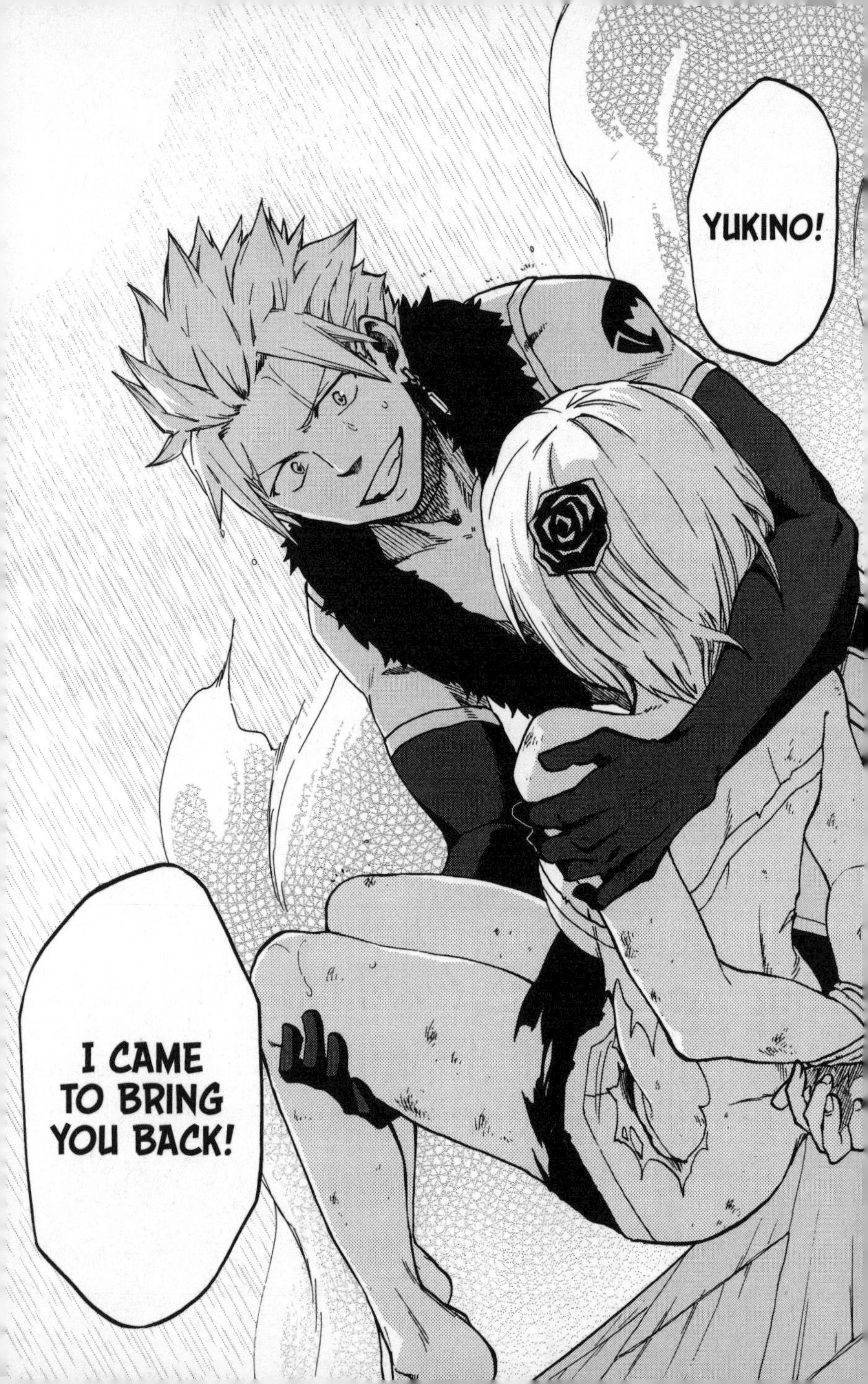
YUKINO!
I CAME TO BRING YOU BACK!

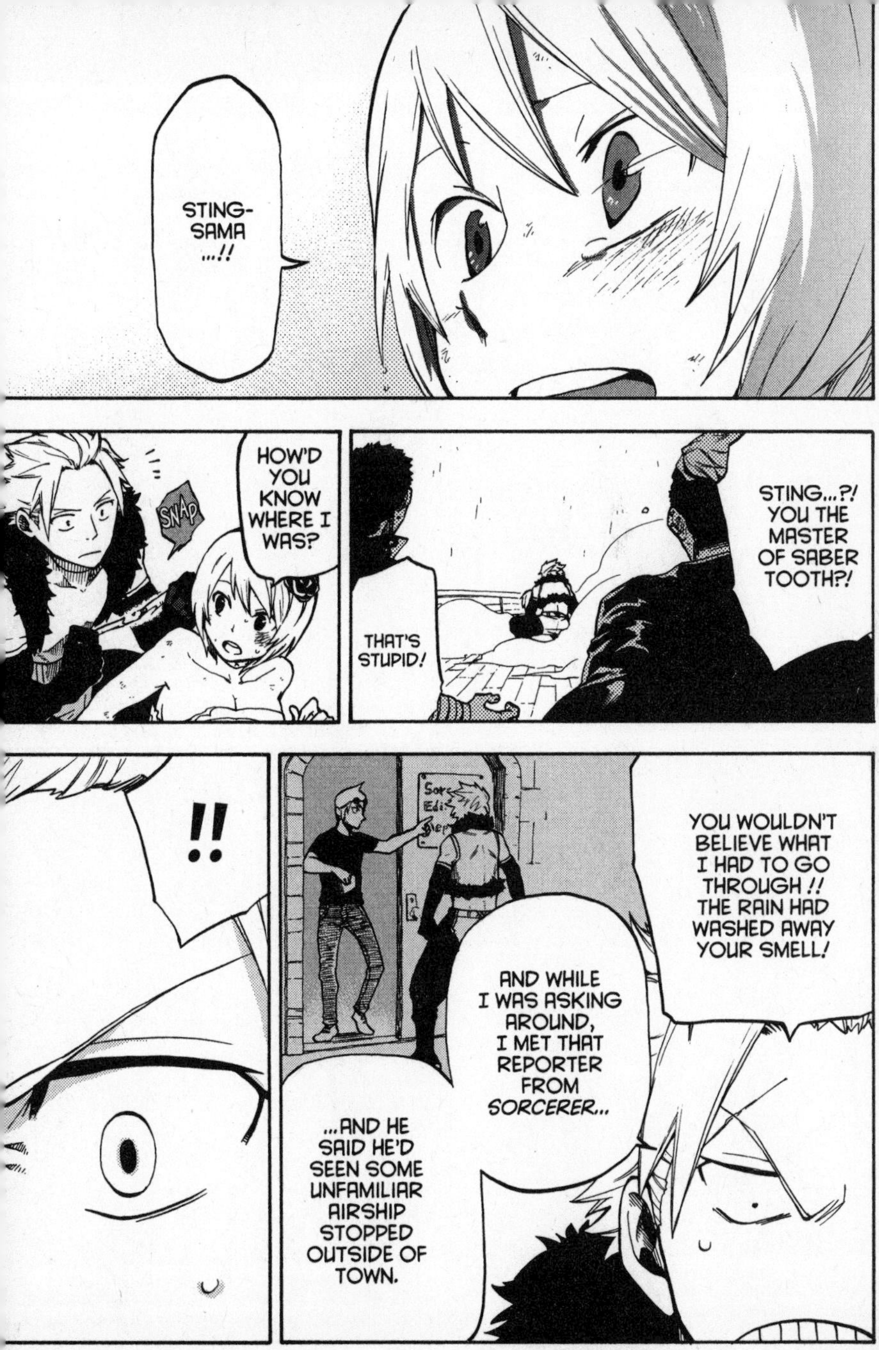
STING-SAMA ...!!
STING...?! YOU THE MASTER OF SABER TOOTH?!
THAT'S STUPID!
HOW'D YOU KNOW WHERE I WAS?
SNAP
YOU WOULDN'T BELIEVE WHAT I HAD TO GO THROUGH!! THE RAIN HAD WASHED AWAY YOUR SMELL!
AND WHILE I WAS ASKING AROUND, I MET THAT REPORTER FROM SORCERER...
...AND HE SAID HE'D SEEN SOME UNFAMILIAR AIRSHIP STOPPED OUTSIDE OF TOWN.
!!

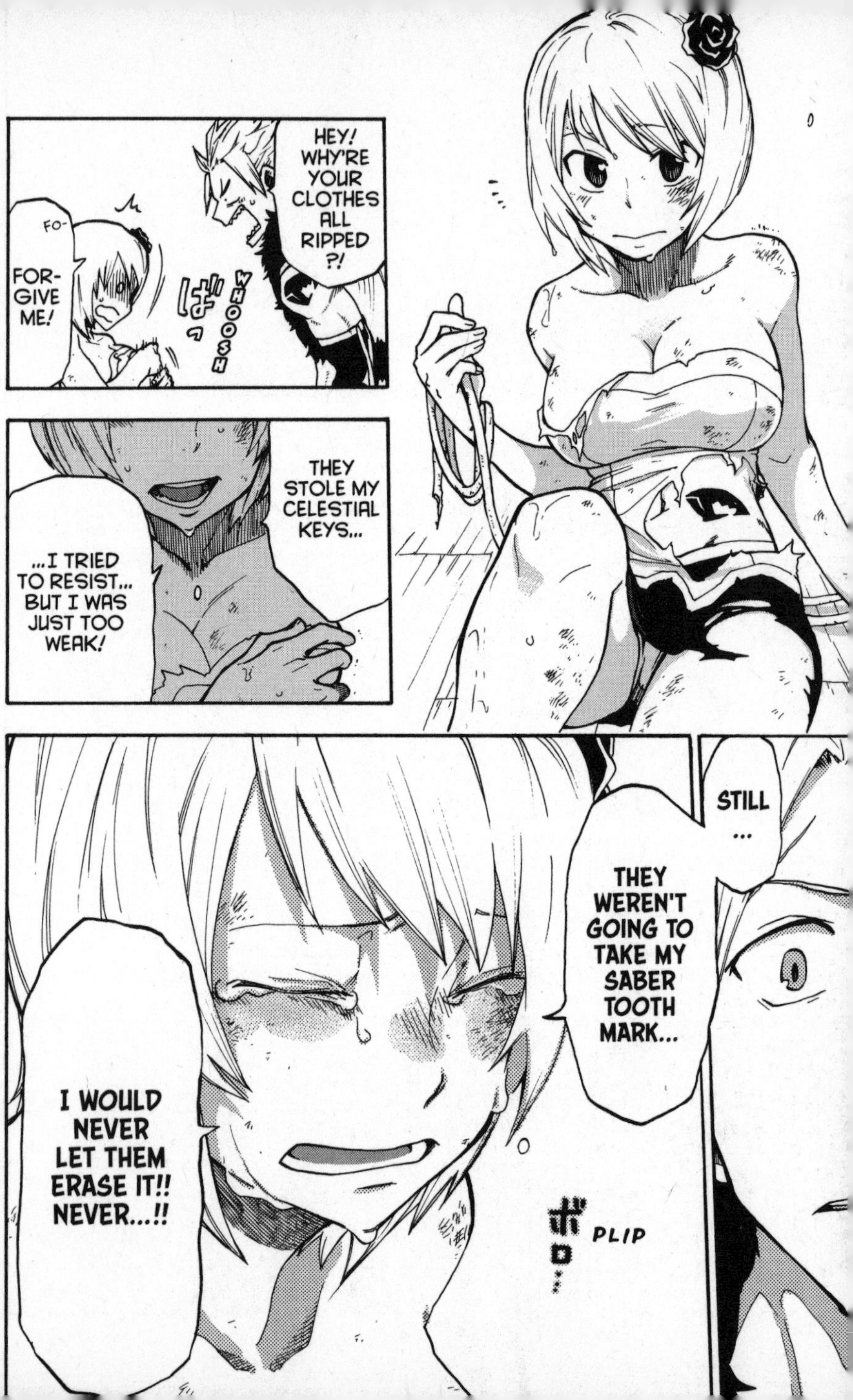
HEY! WHY'RE YOUR CLOTHES ALL RIPPED?!
ばっ
WHOOSH
FO-
FOR-GIVE ME!
THEY STOLE MY CELESTIAL KEYS...
...I TRIED TO RESIST... BUT I WAS JUST TOO WEAK!
STILL...
THEY WEREN'T GOING TO TAKE MY SABER TOOTH MARK...
I WOULD NEVER LET THEM ERASE IT!! NEVER...!!
ボロ…
PLIP

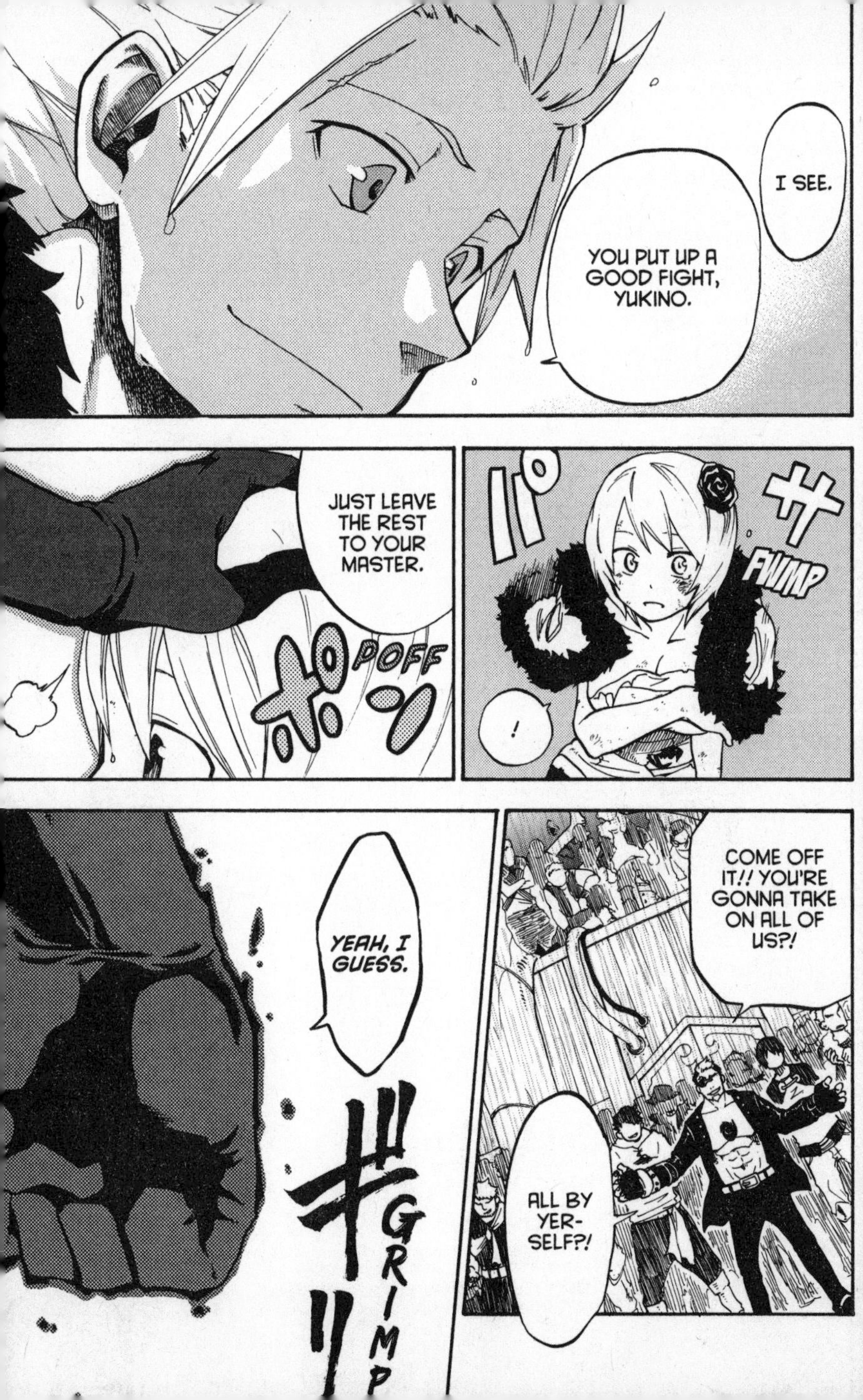
I SEE.
YOU PUT UP A GOOD FIGHT, YUKINO.
FWUMP
!
JUST LEAVE THE REST TO YOUR MASTER.
POFF
COME OFF IT!! YOU'RE GONNA TAKE ON ALL OF US?!
ALL BY YER-SELF?!
YEAH, I GUESS.
GRIMP

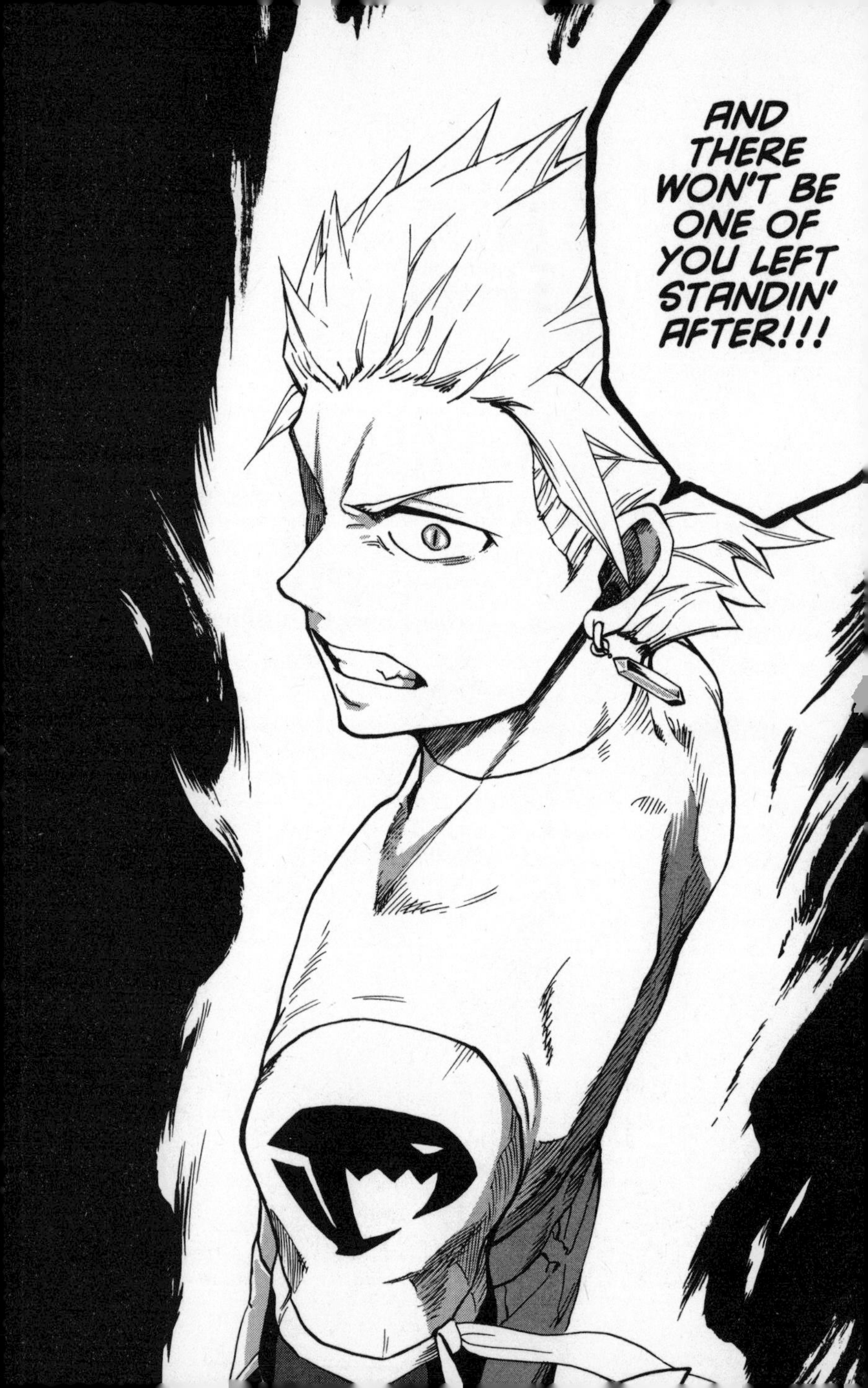
AND THERE WON'T BE ONE OF YOU LEFT STANDIN' AFTER!!!

FAIRY TAIL: TWIN DRAGONS OF SABER TOOTH

Chapter 3: Family

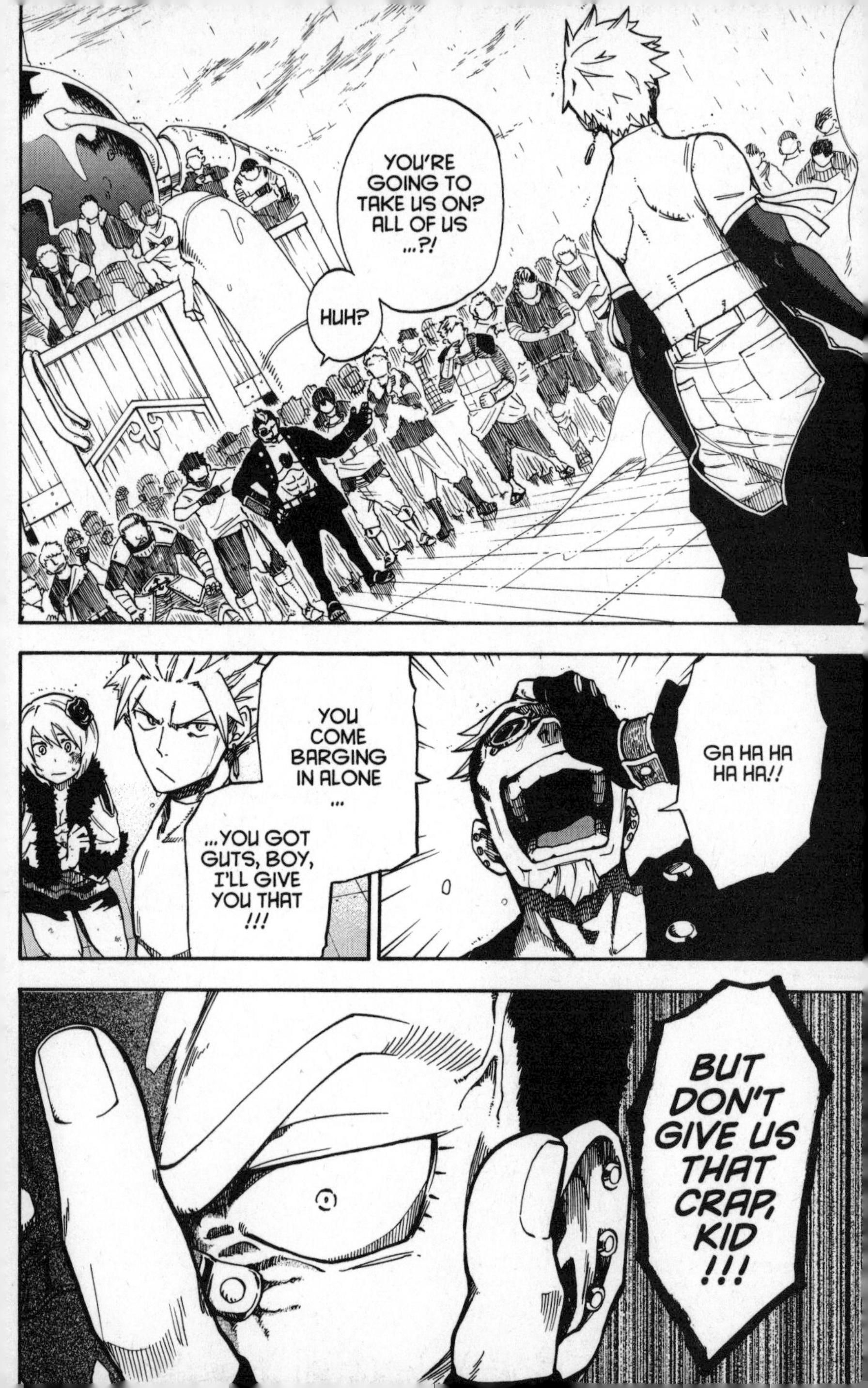
YOU'RE GOING TO TAKE US ON? ALL OF US ...?!
HUH?
GA HA HA HA HA!!
YOU COME BARGING IN ALONE ...
...YOU GOT GUTS, BOY, I'LL GIVE YOU THAT !!!
BUT DON'T GIVE US THAT CRAP, KID !!!

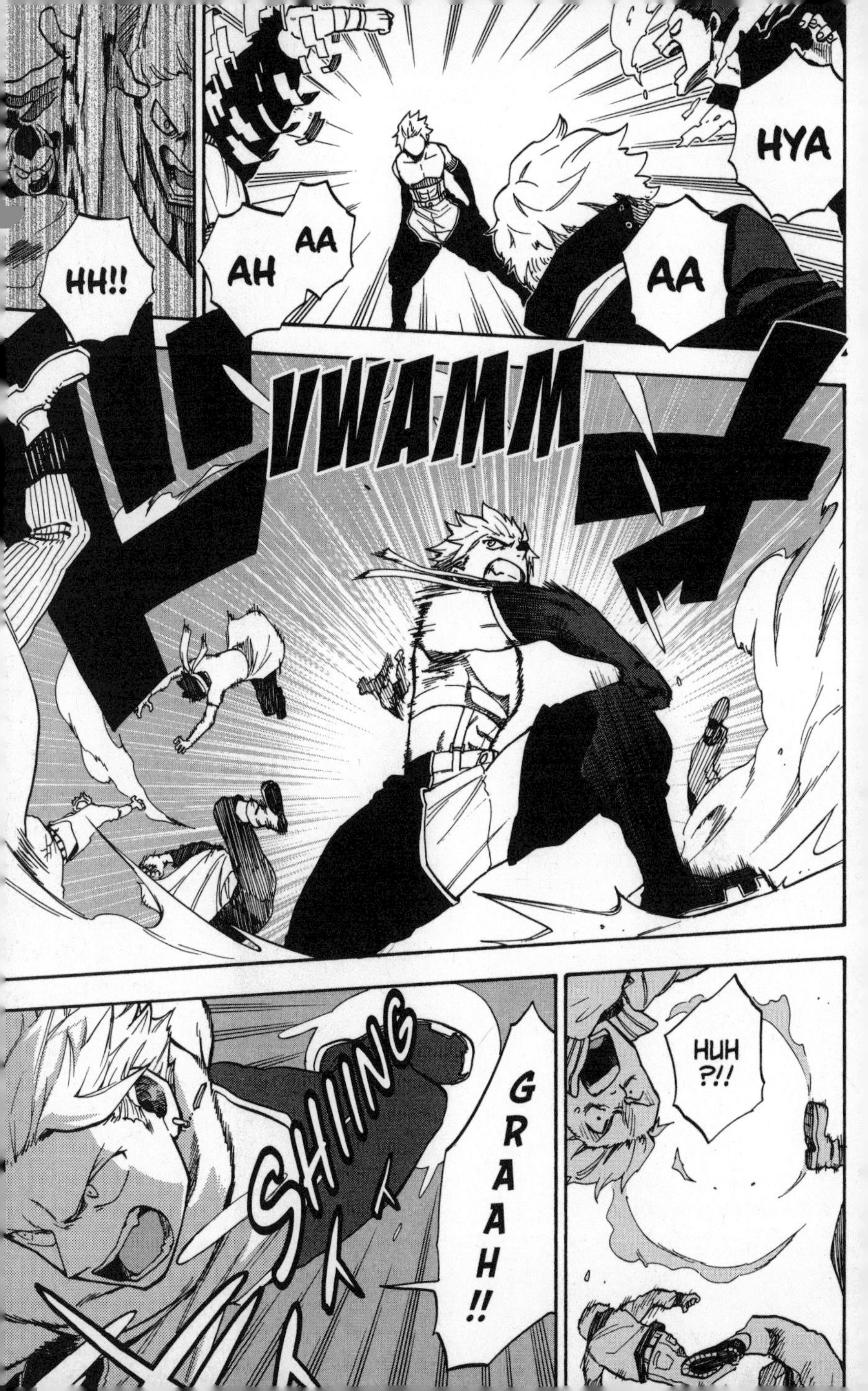
HYA
AA
AH AA
HH!!
VWAMM
HUH ?!!
GRAAAH!!
SHING

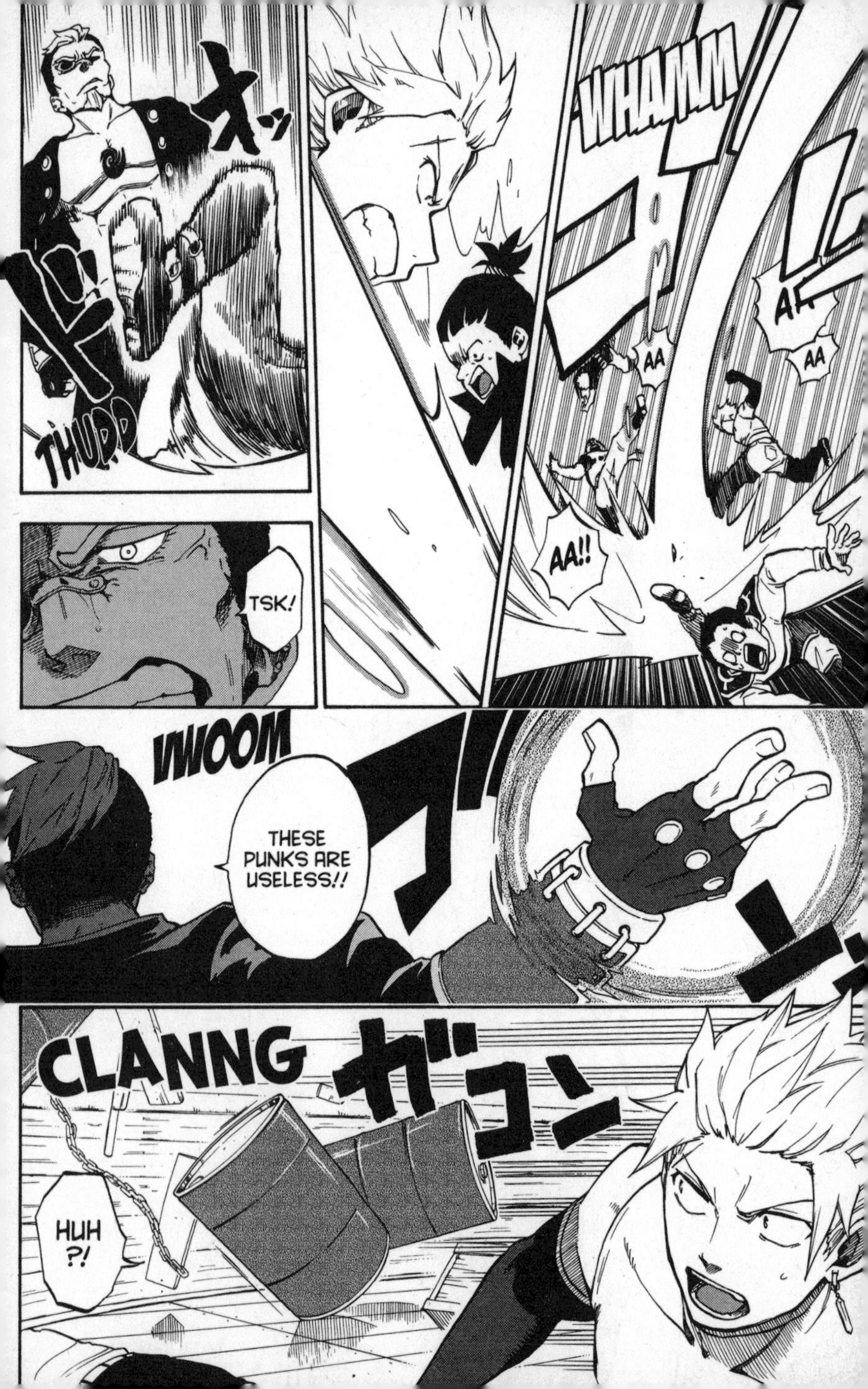
WHAMM
AA
AA
AA
AA!!
THUDD
TSK!
VWOOM
THESE PUNKS ARE USELESS!!
CLANNG
ガコン
HUH ?!

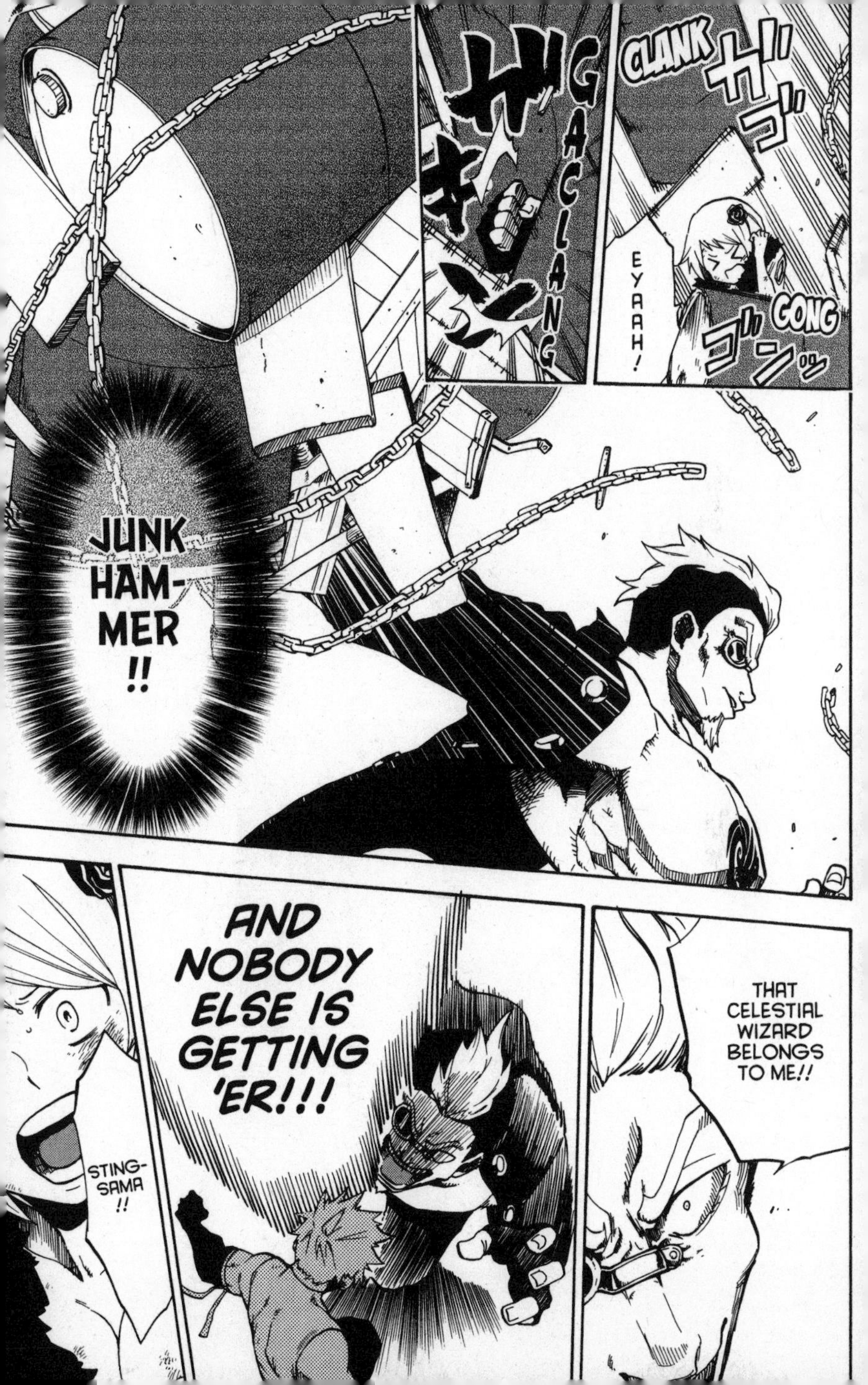
CLANK
EYAAH!
GONG
GACLANG
JUNK HAM-MER!!
THAT CELESTIAL WIZARD BELONGS TO ME!!
AND NOBODY ELSE IS GETTING 'ER!!!
STING-SAMA!!

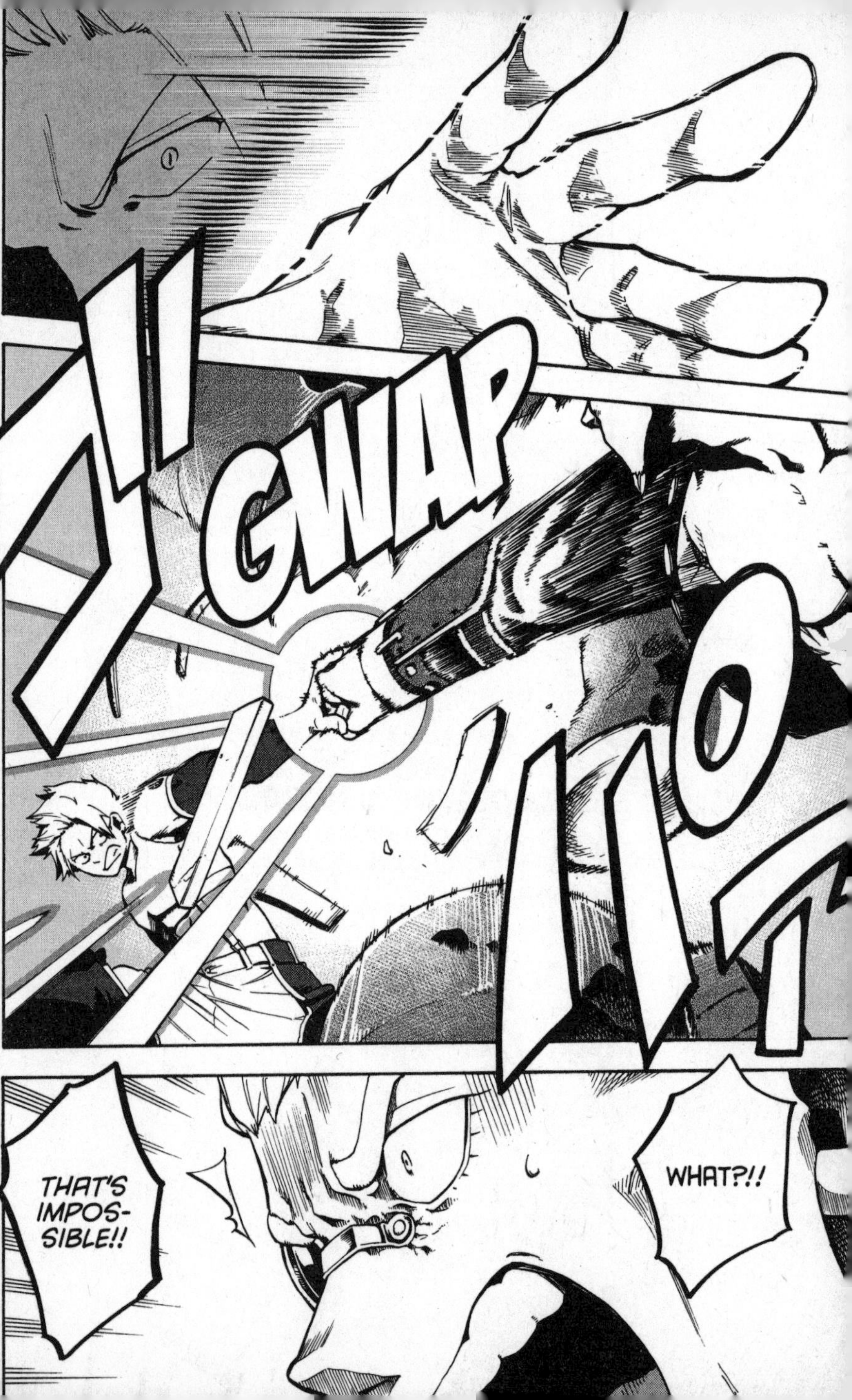
GWAP
WHAT?!!
THAT'S IMPOSSIBLE!!

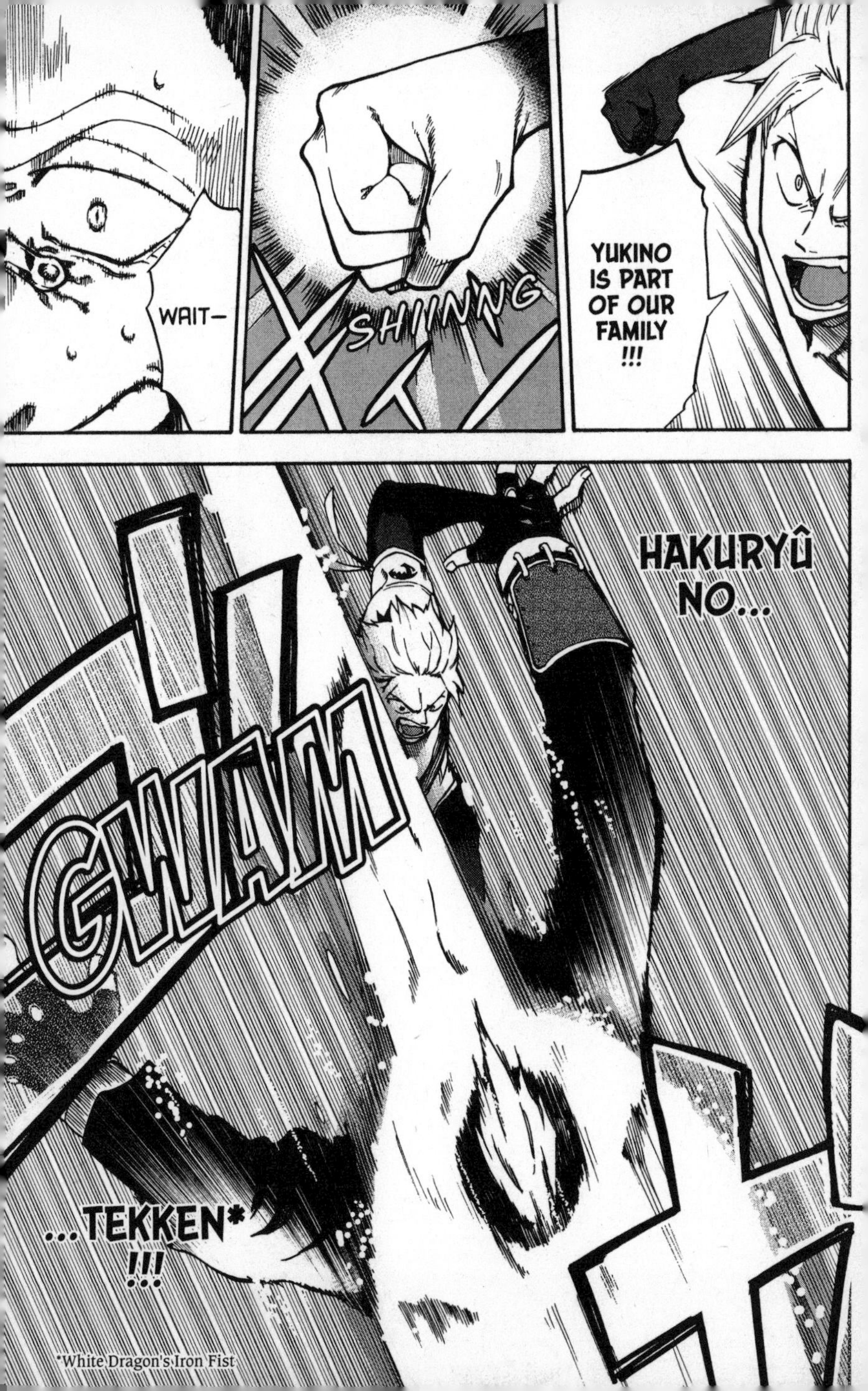
YUKINO IS PART OF OUR FAMILY !!!
SHIINNG
WAIT—
HAKURYÛ NO...
GWAM
...TEKKEN* !!!

*White Dragon's Iron Fist

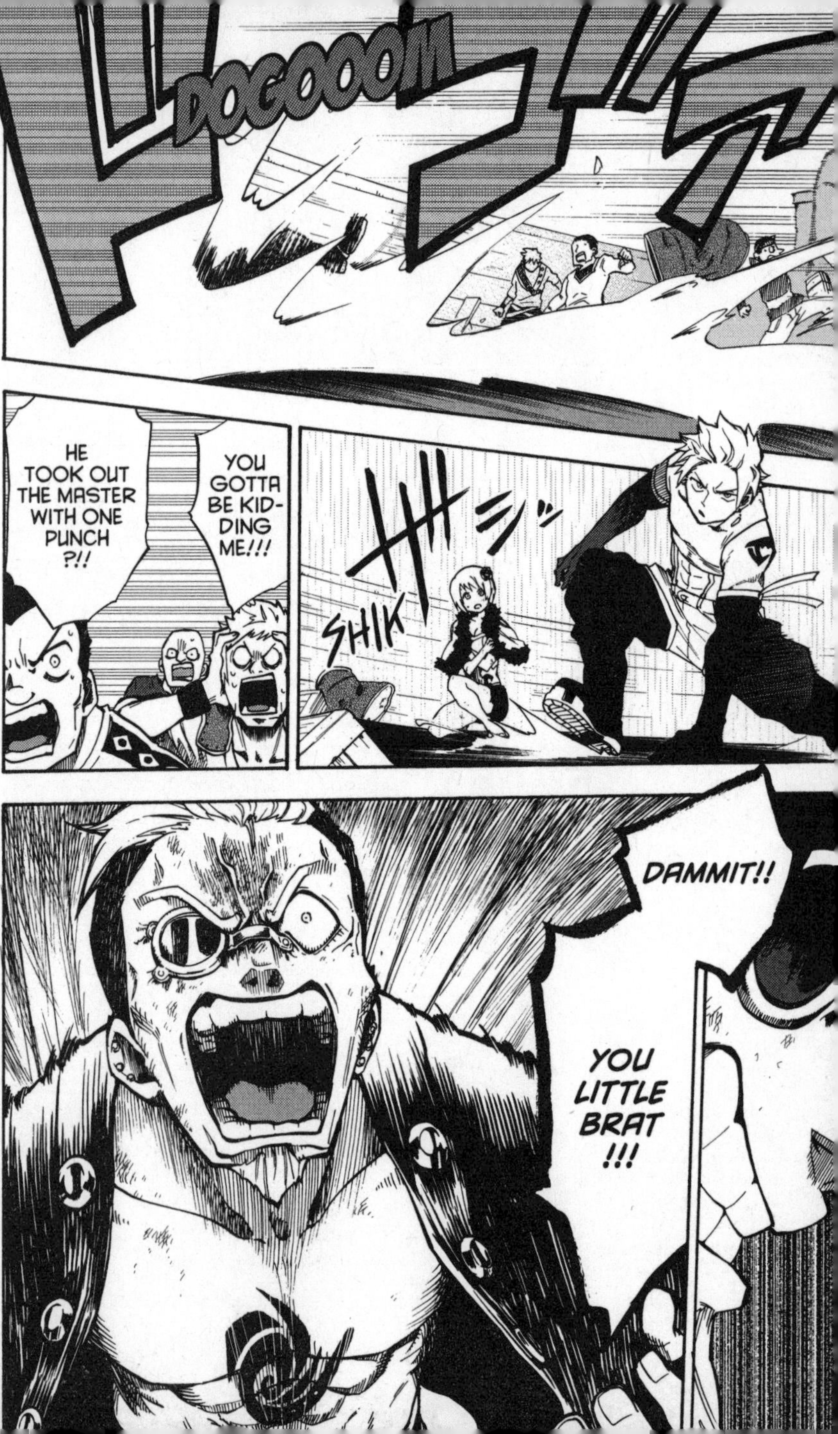
DOGOOOM
SHIK
YOU GOTTA BE KID-DING ME!!!
HE TOOK OUT THE MASTER WITH ONE PUNCH ?!!
DAMMIT!!
YOU LITTLE BRAT !!!

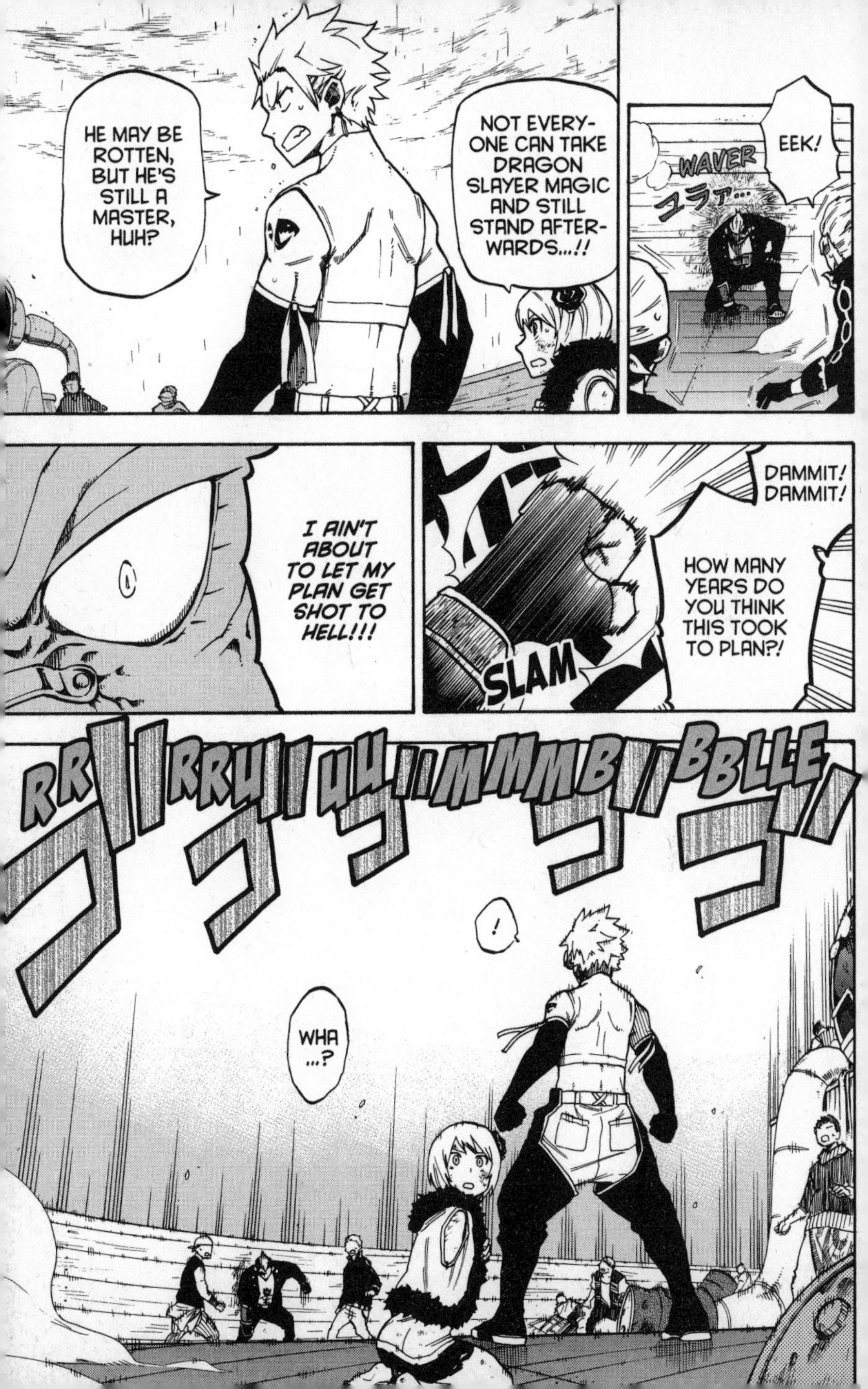
EEK!
WAVER
ユラア…
NOT EVERY-ONE CAN TAKE DRAGON SLAYER MAGIC AND STILL STAND AFTER-WARDS...!!
HE MAY BE ROTTEN, BUT HE'S STILL A MASTER, HUH?
DAMMIT! DAMMIT!
HOW MANY YEARS DO YOU THINK THIS TOOK TO PLAN?!
SLAM
I AIN'T ABOUT TO LET MY PLAN GET SHOT TO HELL!!!
RRRRUUUMMMMBBBLLE
!
WHA ...?

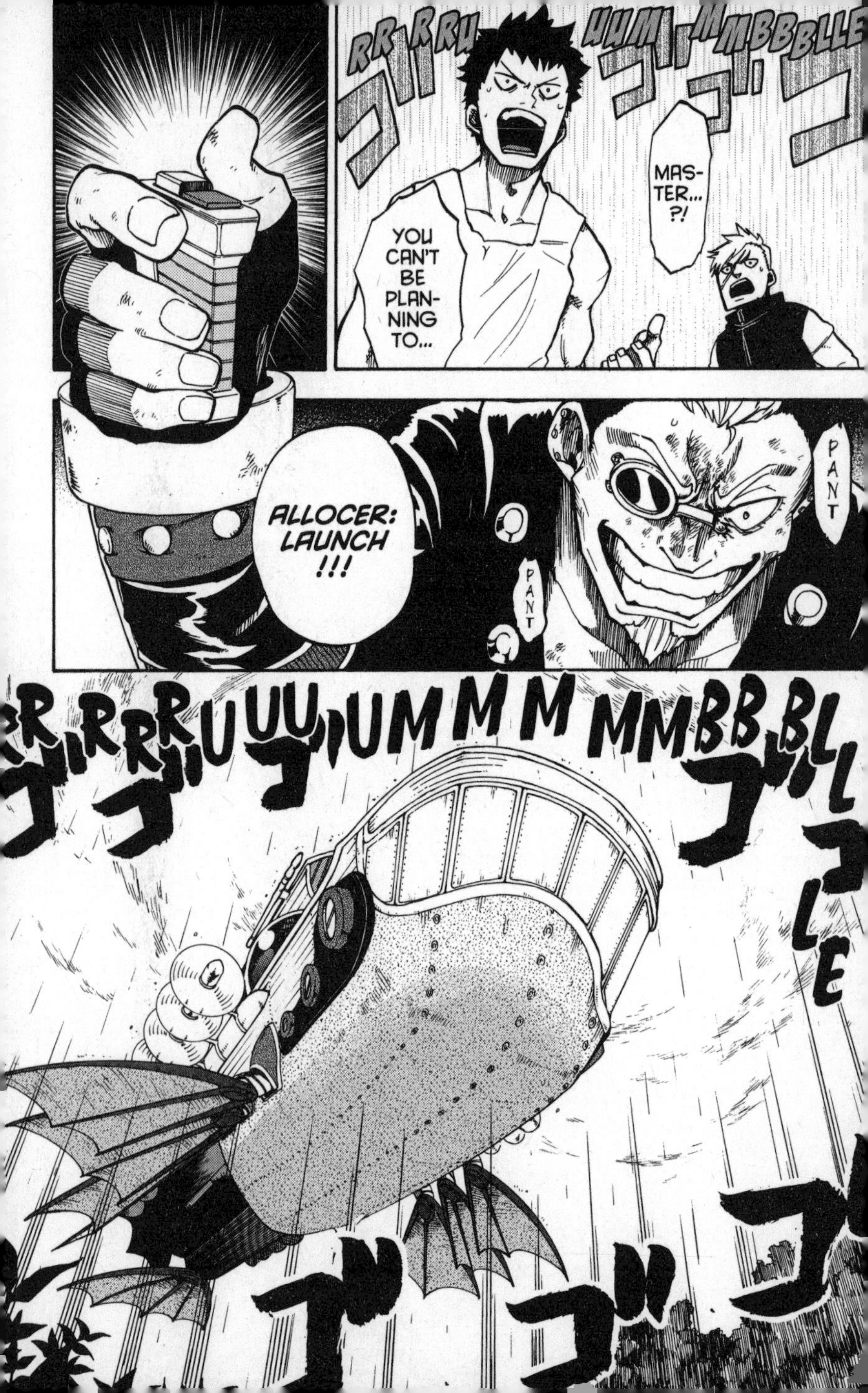
RRRRU UUMMMMBBBLLE
MASTER...?!
YOU CAN'T BE PLANNING TO...
PANT
ALLOCER: LAUNCH!!!
PANT
RRRRUUUUMMMMMMBBBLLLE

FAIRY TAIL: TWIN DRAGONS OF SABER TOOTH

Chapter 4: Nobody Can Stop It

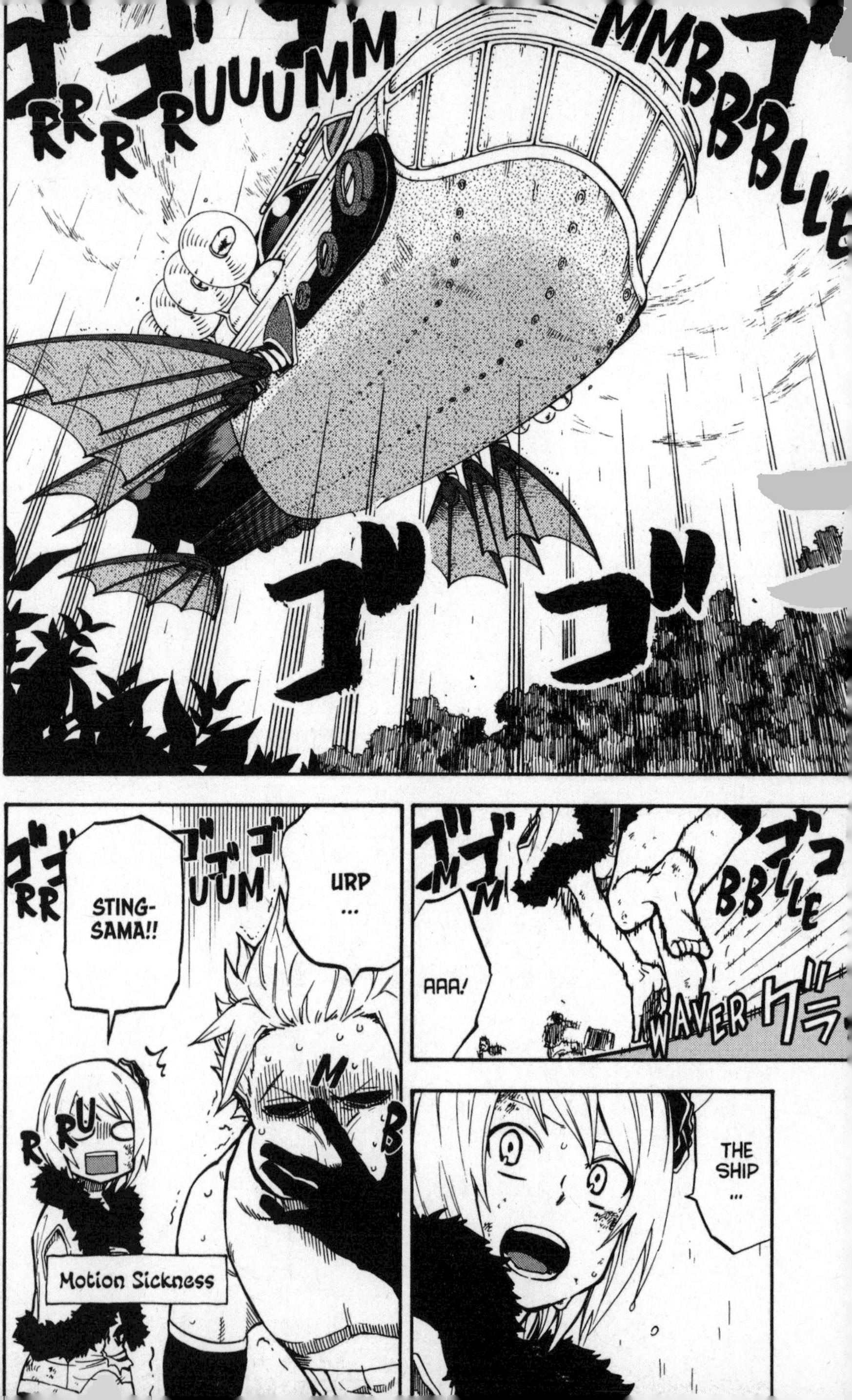
RRRRUUUUMMM
MMBBBLLE
ゴゴ
AAA!
WAVER グラ
THE SHIP ...
UUM
URP ...
STING-SAMA!!
RRUMB
Motion Sickness

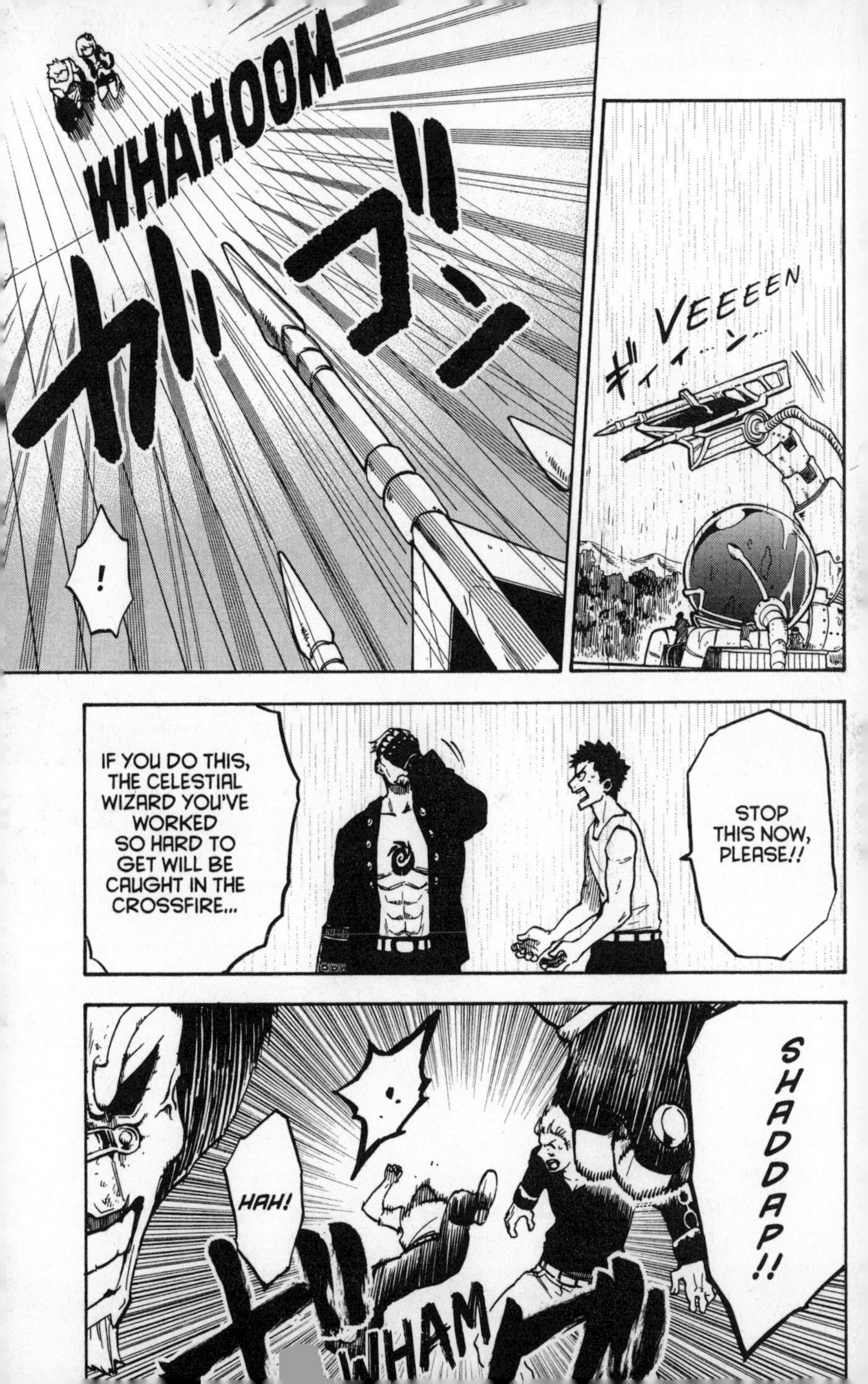
VEEEEN
ギィィ…ン…
WHAHOOM
ガゴン
!
STOP THIS NOW, PLEASE!!
IF YOU DO THIS, THE CELESTIAL WIZARD YOU'VE WORKED SO HARD TO GET WILL BE CAUGHT IN THE CROSSFIRE...
SHADDAP!!
HAH!
WHAM

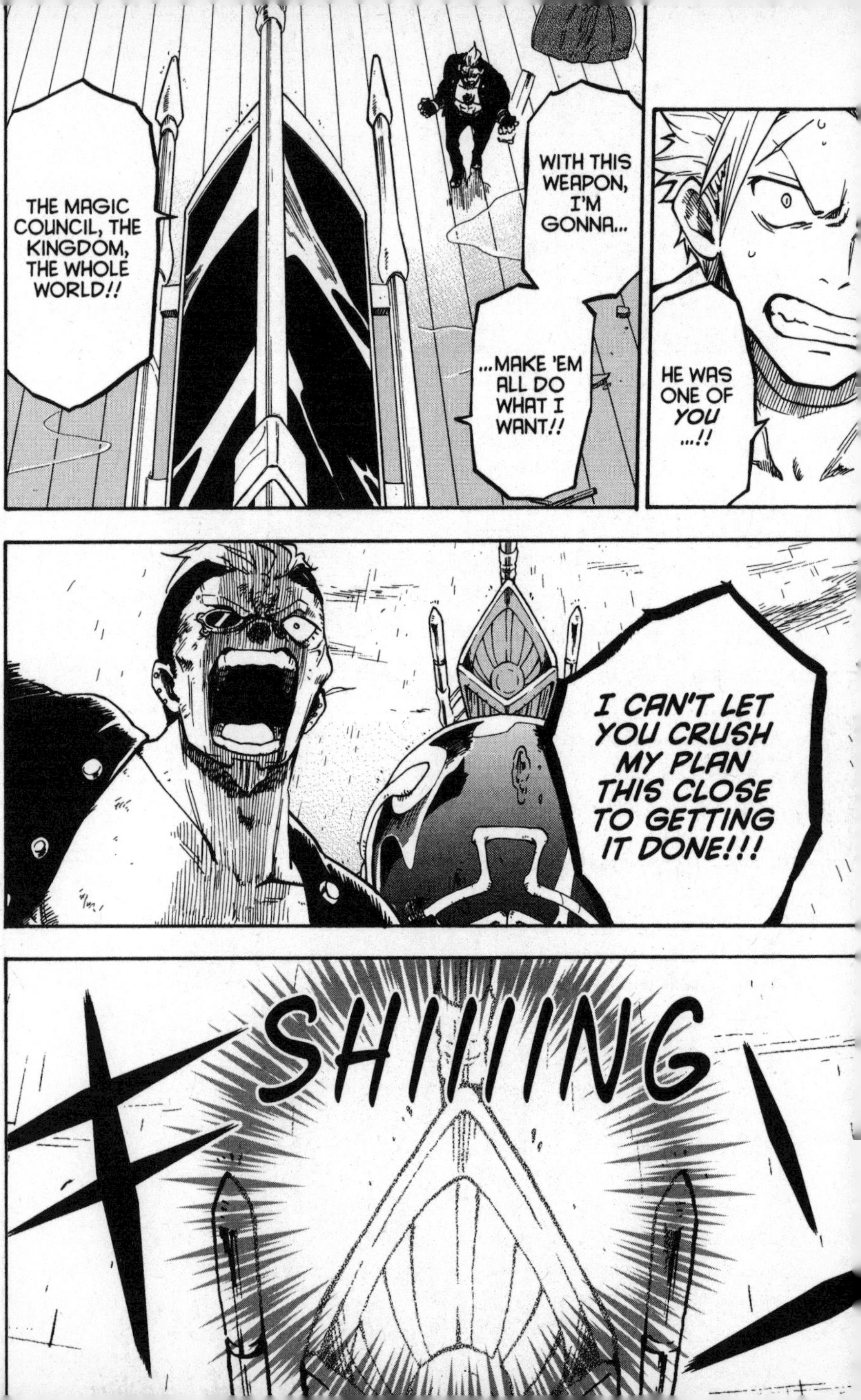
HE WAS ONE OF YOU ...!!
WITH THIS WEAPON, I'M GONNA...
...MAKE 'EM ALL DO WHAT I WANT!!
THE MAGIC COUNCIL, THE KINGDOM, THE WHOLE WORLD!!
I CAN'T LET YOU CRUSH MY PLAN THIS CLOSE TO GETTING IT DONE!!!
SHIIING

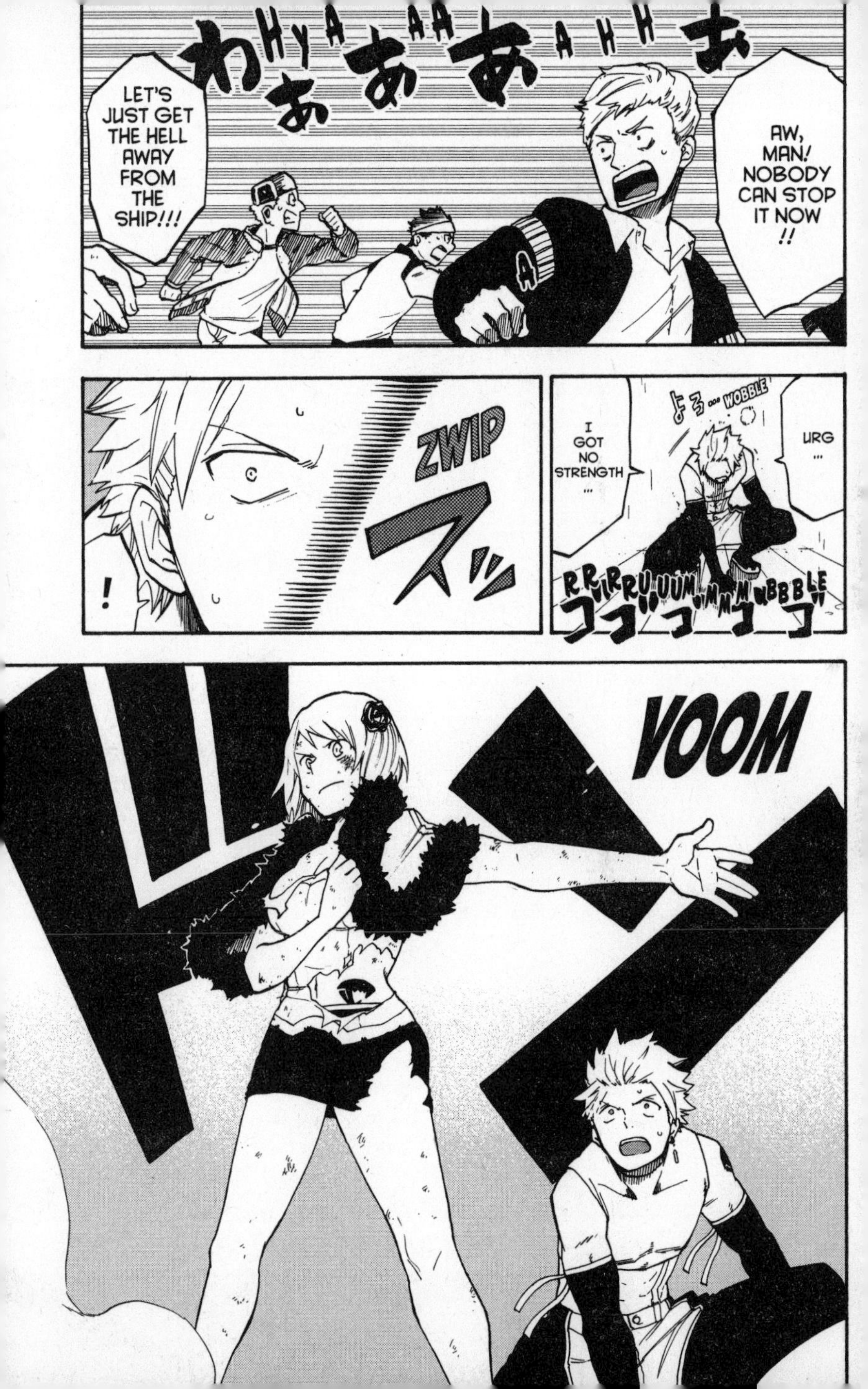

AW, MAN! NOBODY CAN STOP IT NOW!!
わあああ
HYAAAAHH
LET'S JUST GET THE HELL AWAY FROM THE SHIP!!!
URG ...
よろ… WOBBLE
I GOT NO STRENGTH ...
ゴゴゴゴゴ
RRRRRUUUMMMBBBLE
ZWIP
ス
!
VOOM

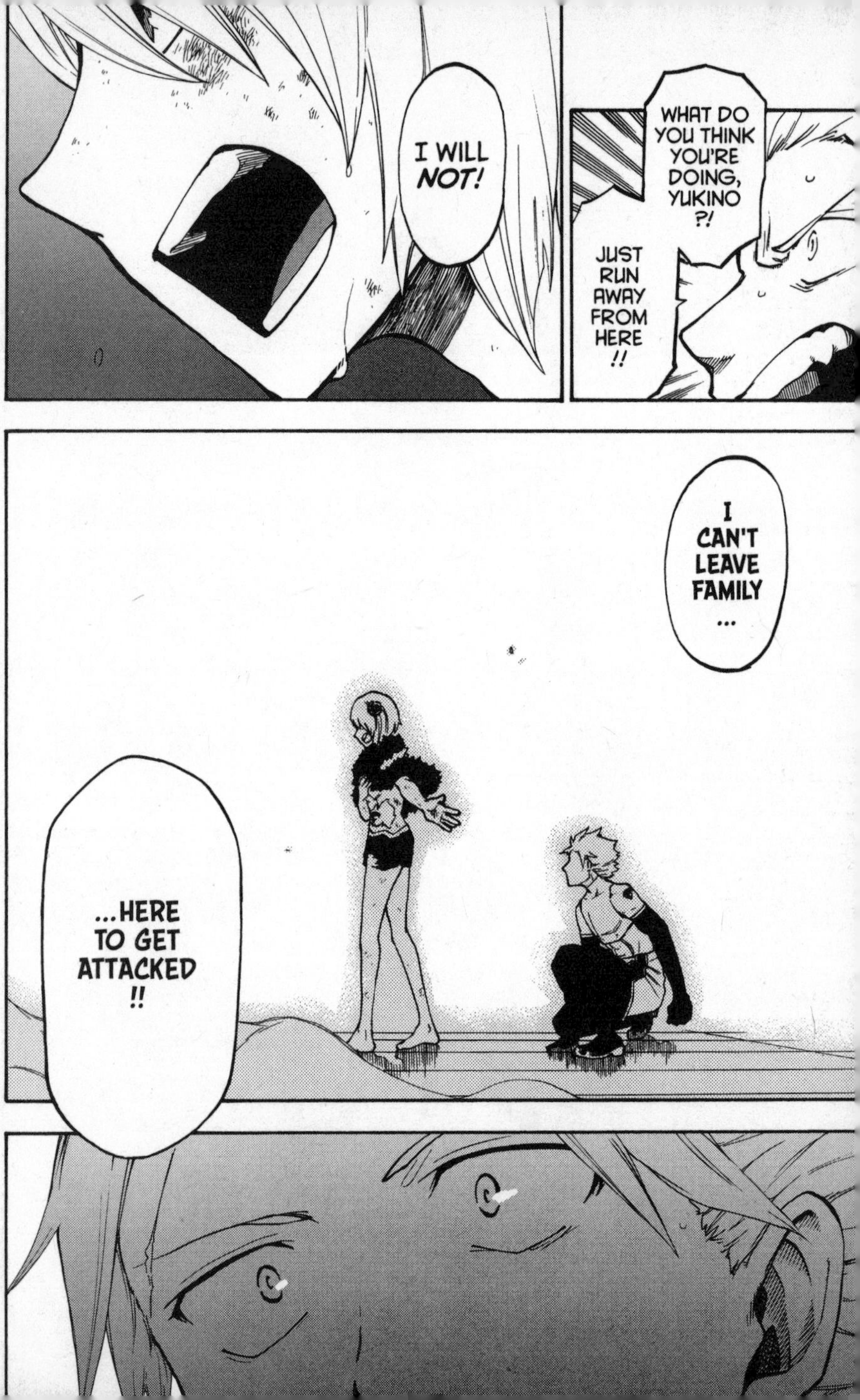
WHAT DO YOU THINK YOU'RE DOING, YUKINO?!
JUST RUN AWAY FROM HERE!!
I WILL *NOT*!
I CAN'T LEAVE FAMILY...
...HERE TO GET ATTACKED!!

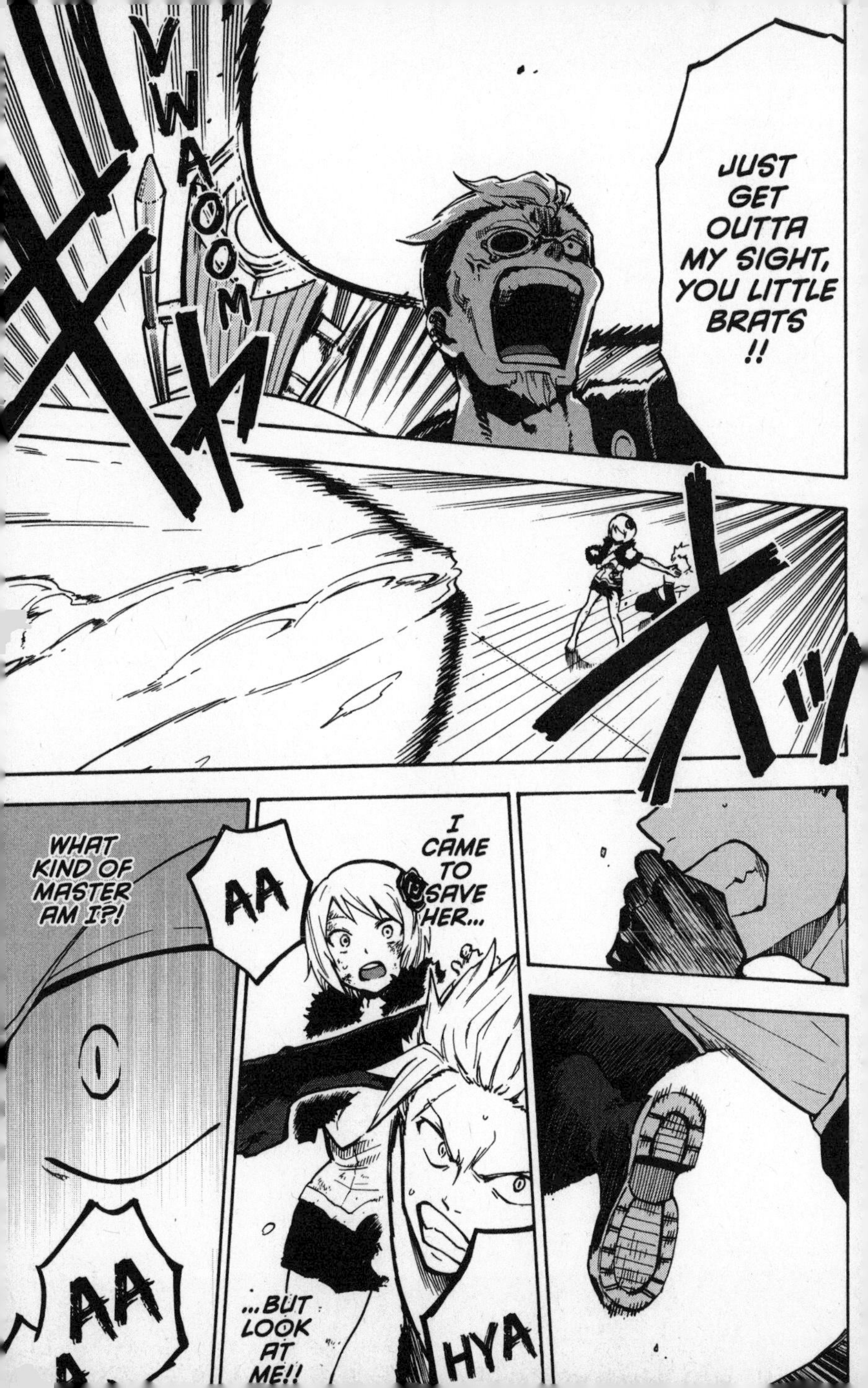
JUST GET OUTTA MY SIGHT, YOU LITTLE BRATS !!
VWAOOOM
HYA
I CAME TO SAVE HER...
AA
...BUT LOOK AT ME!!
WHAT KIND OF MASTER AM I?!
AA

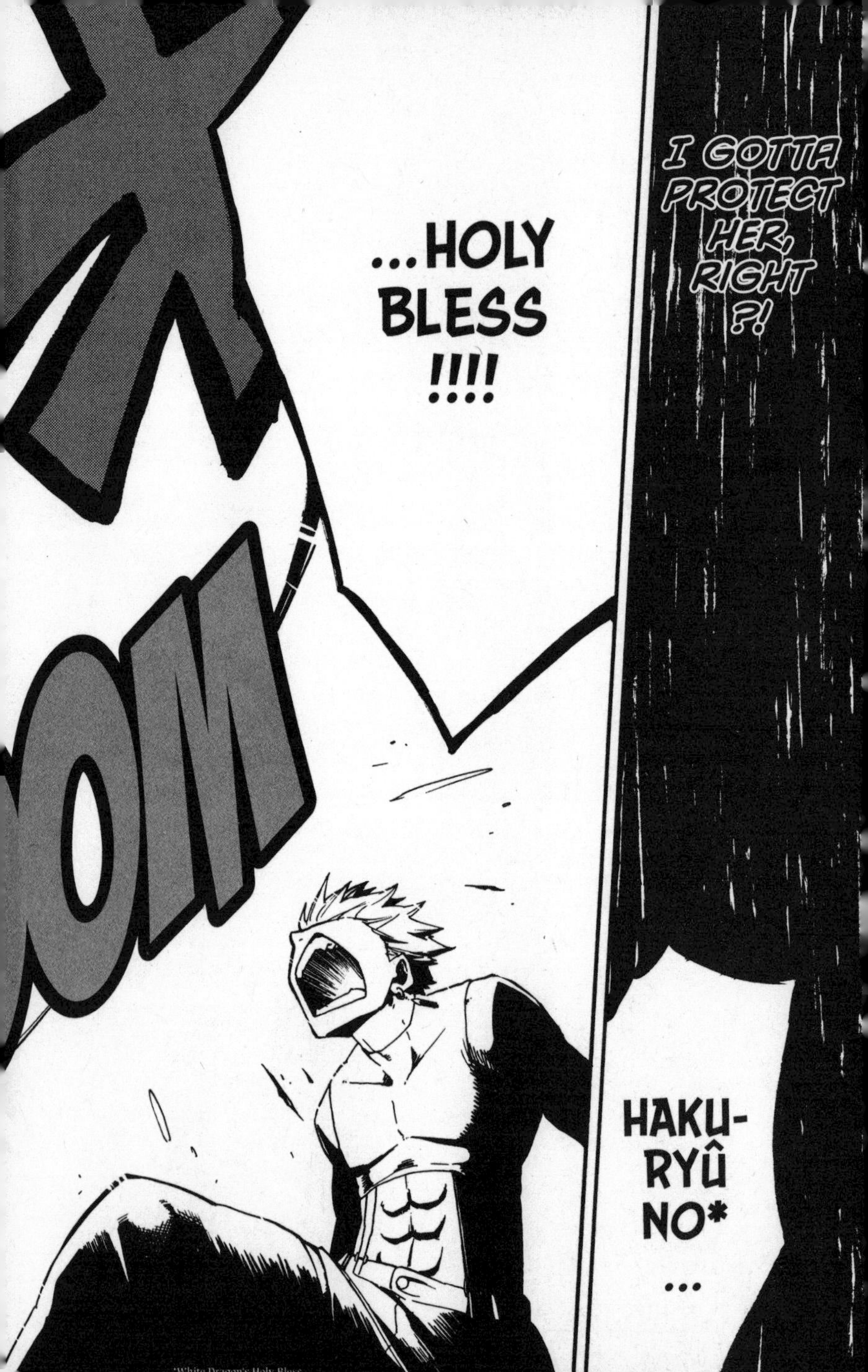
I GOTTA PROTECT HER, RIGHT?!
HAKU-RYÛ NO* ...
...HOLY BLESS!!!!

*White Dragon's Holy Bless

GWH

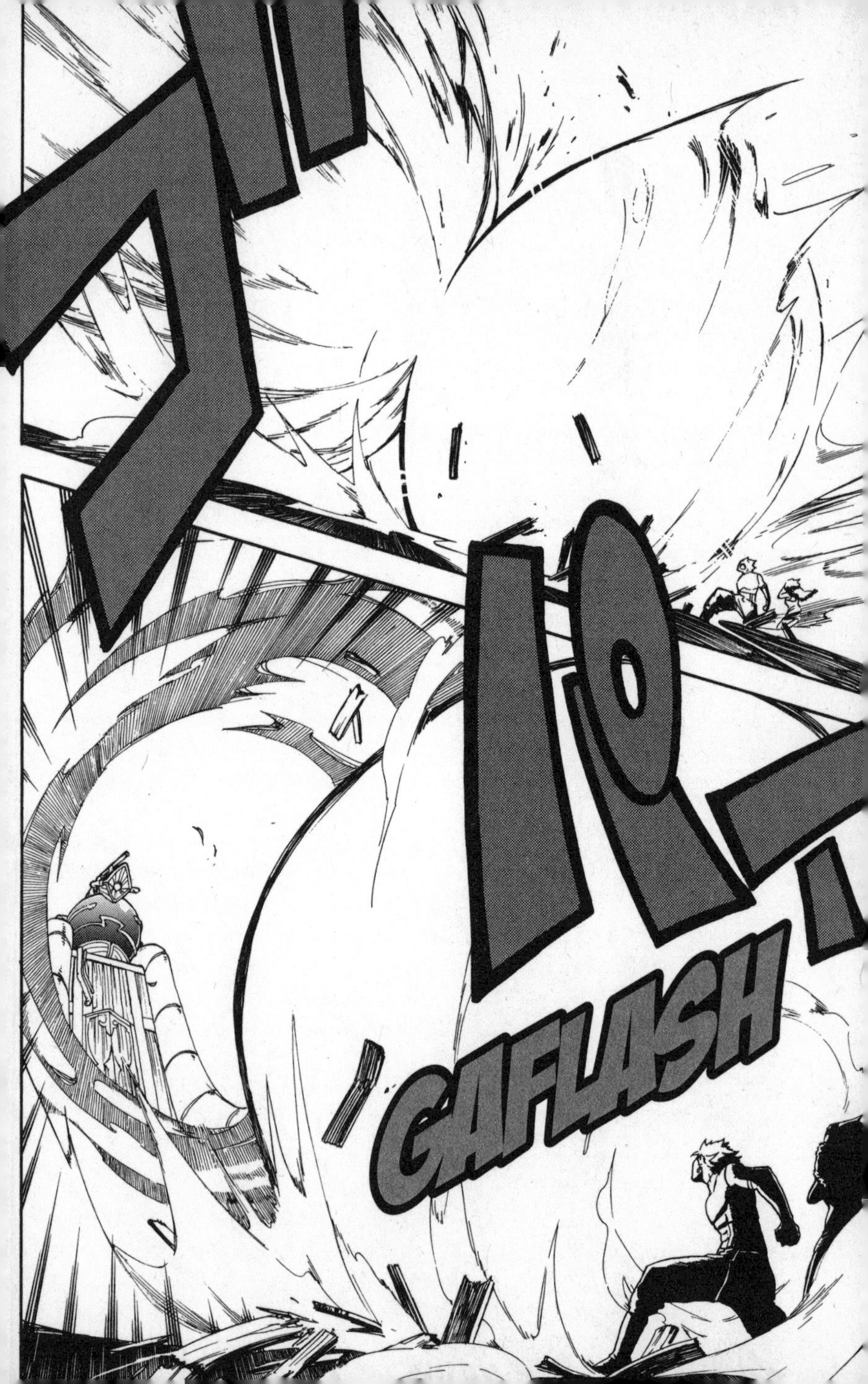
GAFLASH

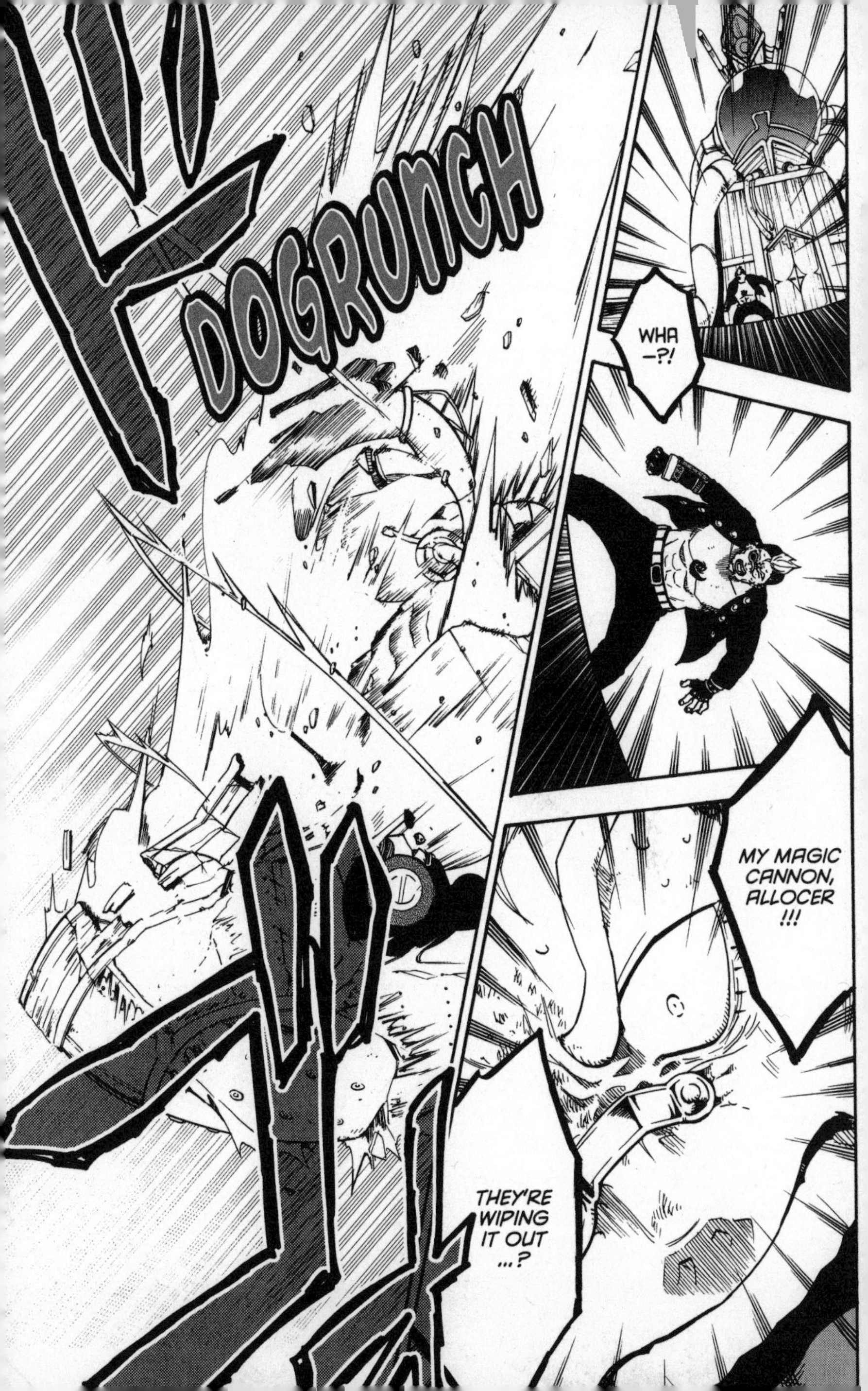
WHA—?!
MY MAGIC CANNON, ALLOCER!!!
THEY'RE WIPING IT OUT...?
DOGRUNCH

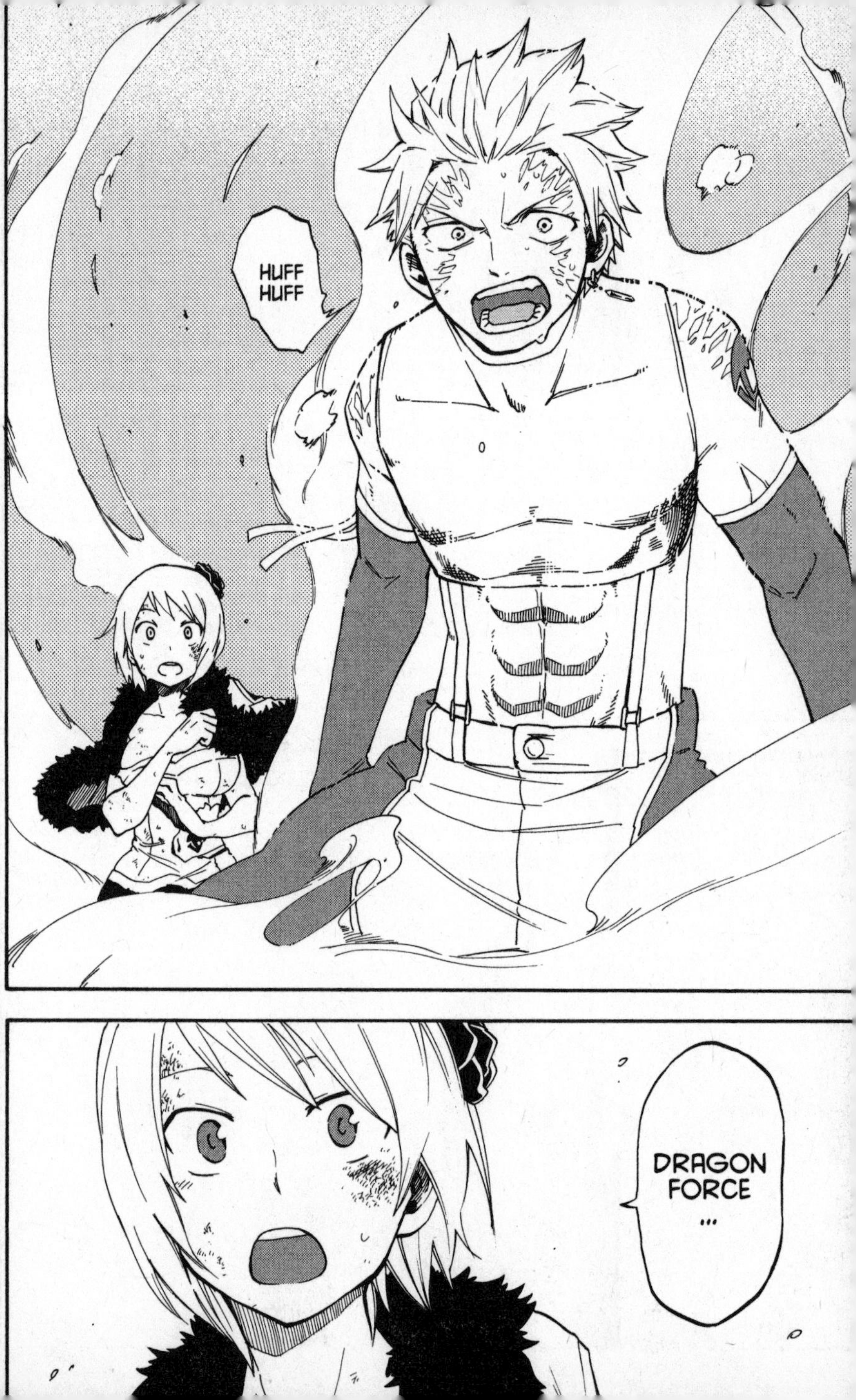
HUFF HUFF
DRAGON FORCE ...

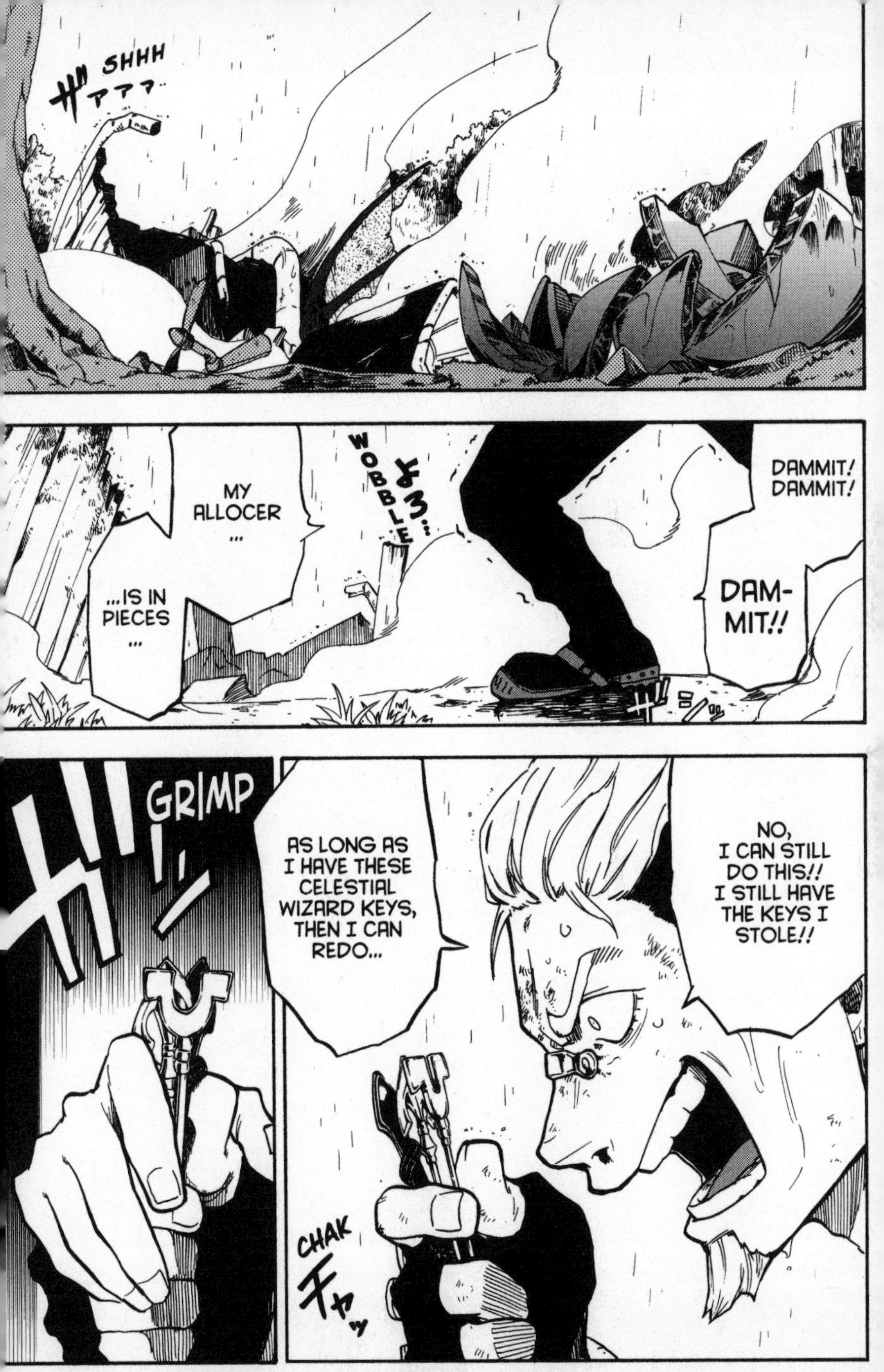
SHHH
ザァァァ…
DAMMIT! DAMMIT!
DAM-MIT!!
WOBBLE
よろ…
MY ALLOCER ...
...IS IN PIECES ...
NO, I CAN STILL DO THIS!! I STILL HAVE THE KEYS I STOLE!!
AS LONG AS I HAVE THESE CELESTIAL WIZARD KEYS, THEN I CAN REDO...
CHAK
チャッ
GRIMP
ガッ

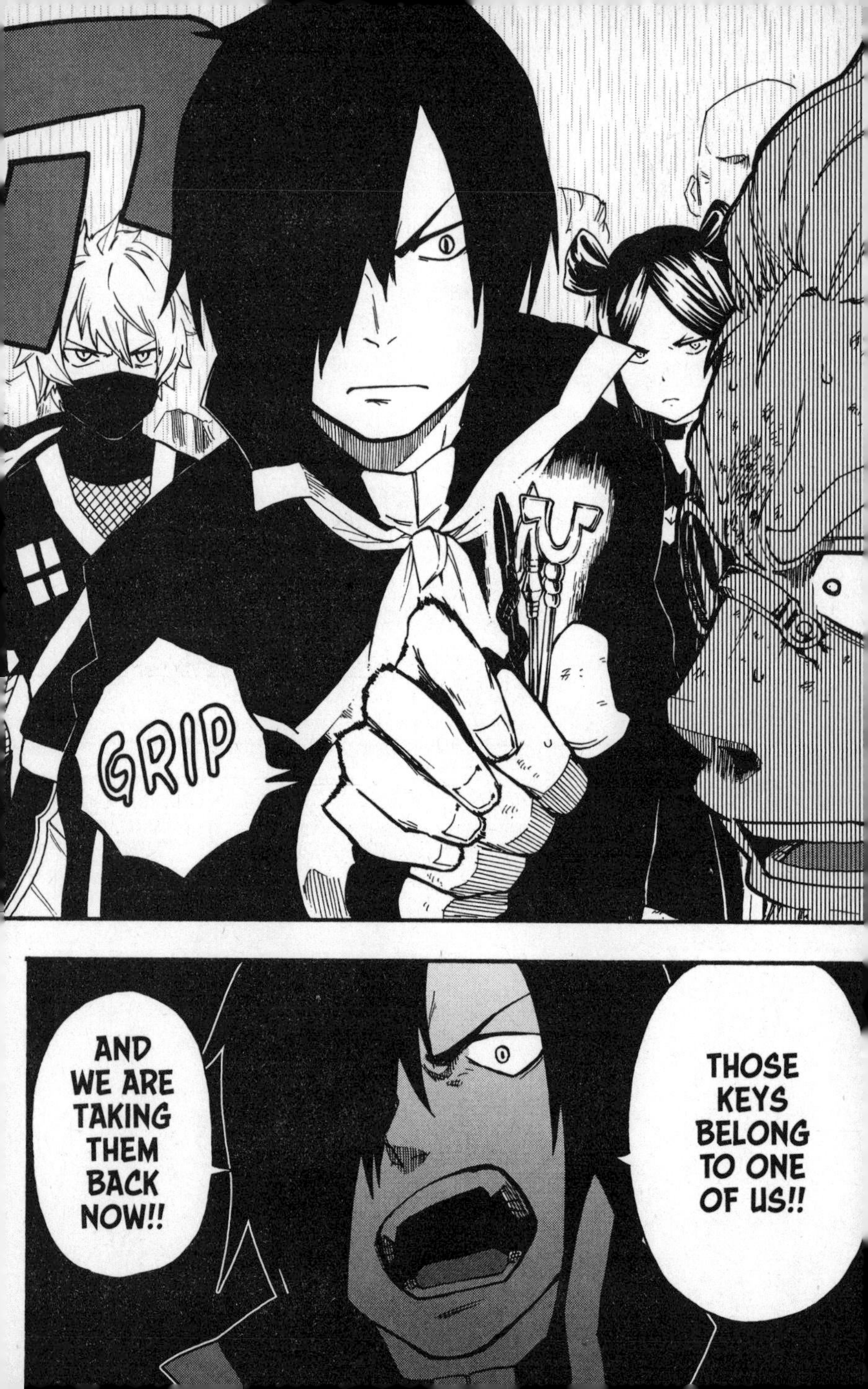
GRIP
THOSE KEYS BELONG TO ONE OF US!!
AND WE ARE TAKING THEM BACK NOW!!

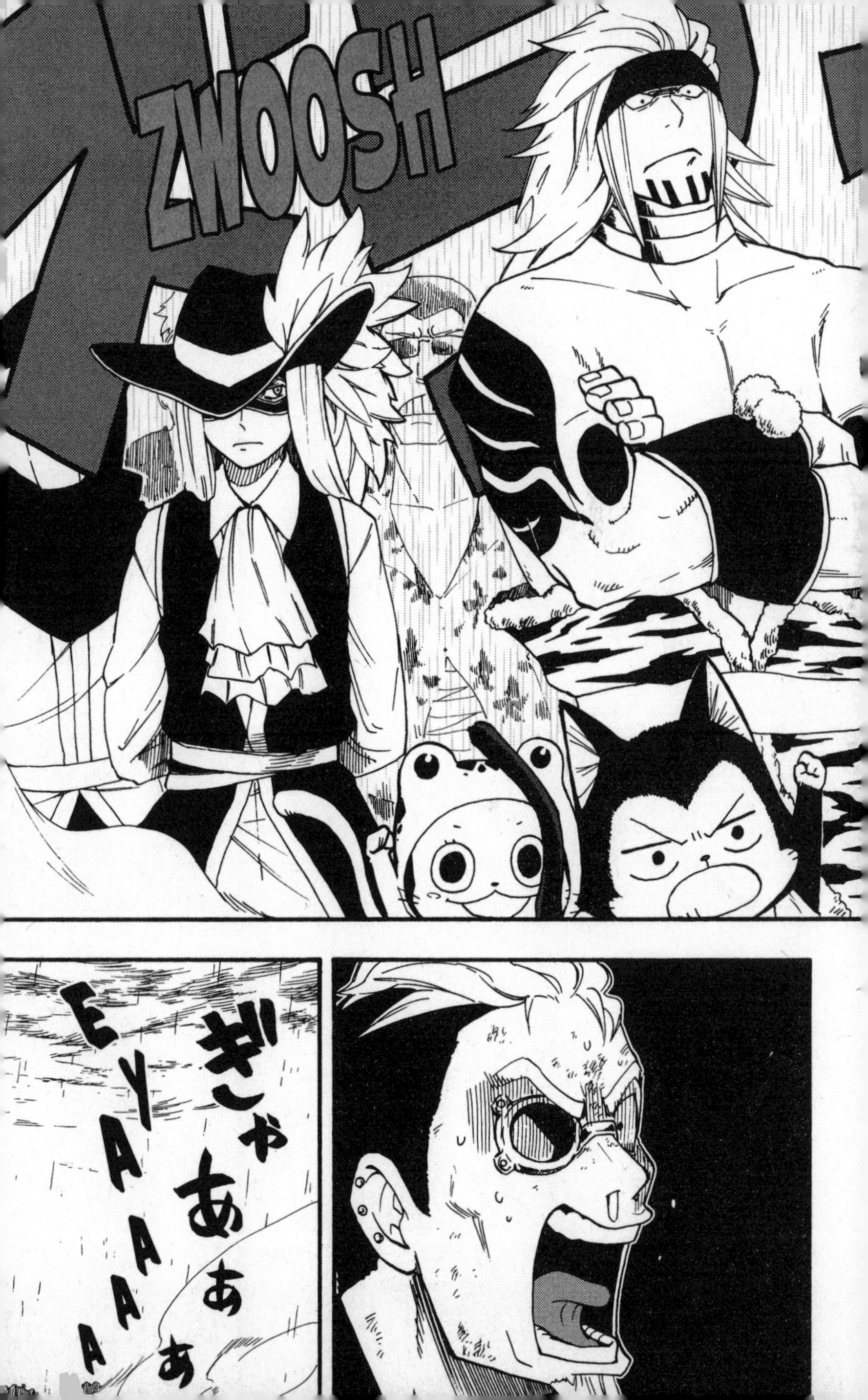
ZWOOSH
ぎゃあああ
EYAAAAA

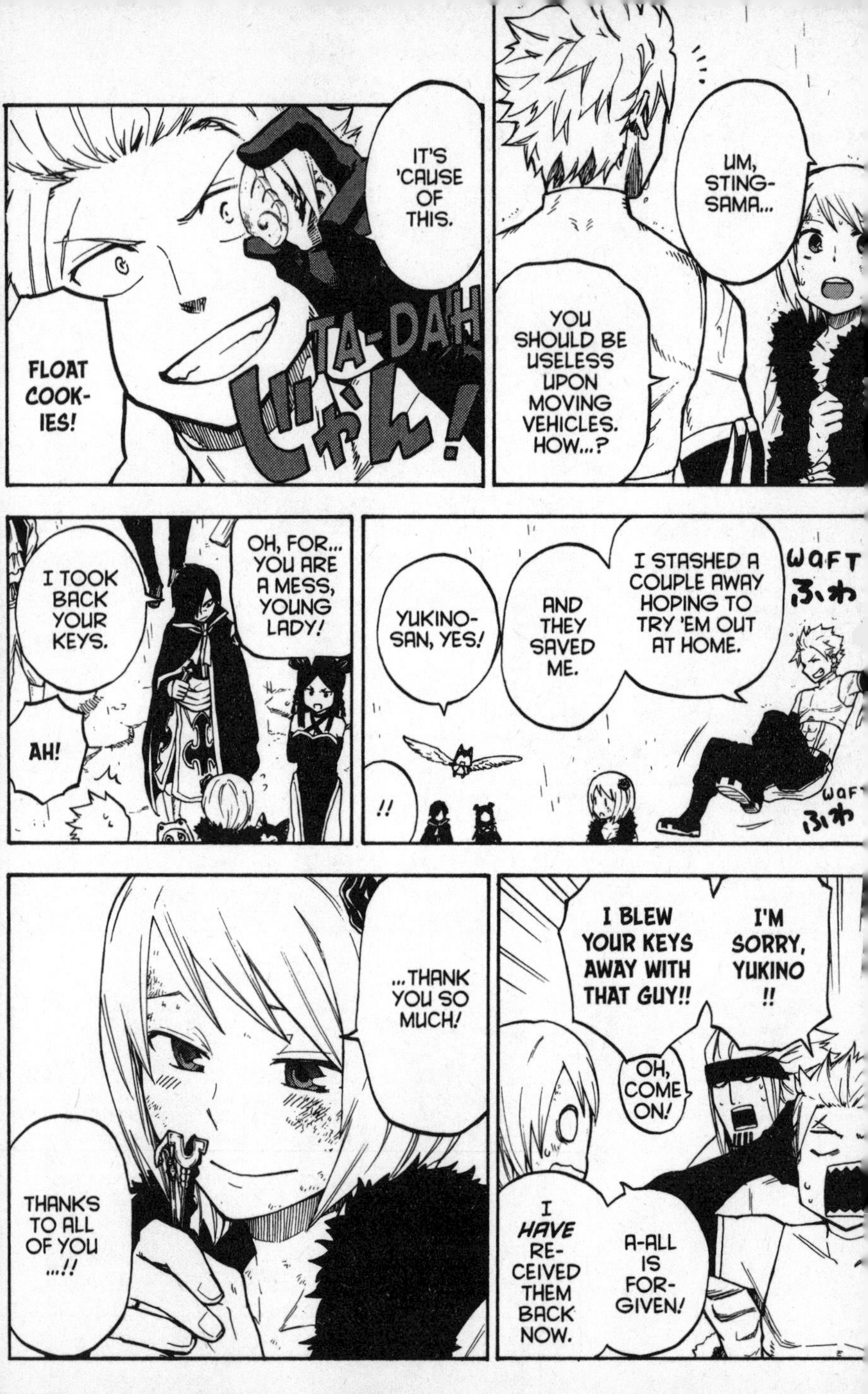
UM, STING-SAMA...
YOU SHOULD BE USELESS UPON MOVING VEHICLES. HOW...?
IT'S 'CAUSE OF THIS.
TA-DAH
じゃん!
FLOAT COOKIES!
WAFT
ふわ
I STASHED A COUPLE AWAY HOPING TO TRY 'EM OUT AT HOME.
AND THEY SAVED ME.
YUKINO-SAN, YES!
!!
WAFT
ふわ
OH, FOR... YOU ARE A MESS, YOUNG LADY!
I TOOK BACK YOUR KEYS.
AH!
I'M SORRY, YUKINO!!
I BLEW YOUR KEYS AWAY WITH THAT GUY!!
OH, COME ON!
A-ALL IS FORGIVEN!
I *HAVE* RECEIVED THEM BACK NOW.
...THANK YOU SO MUCH!
THANKS TO ALL OF YOU...!!

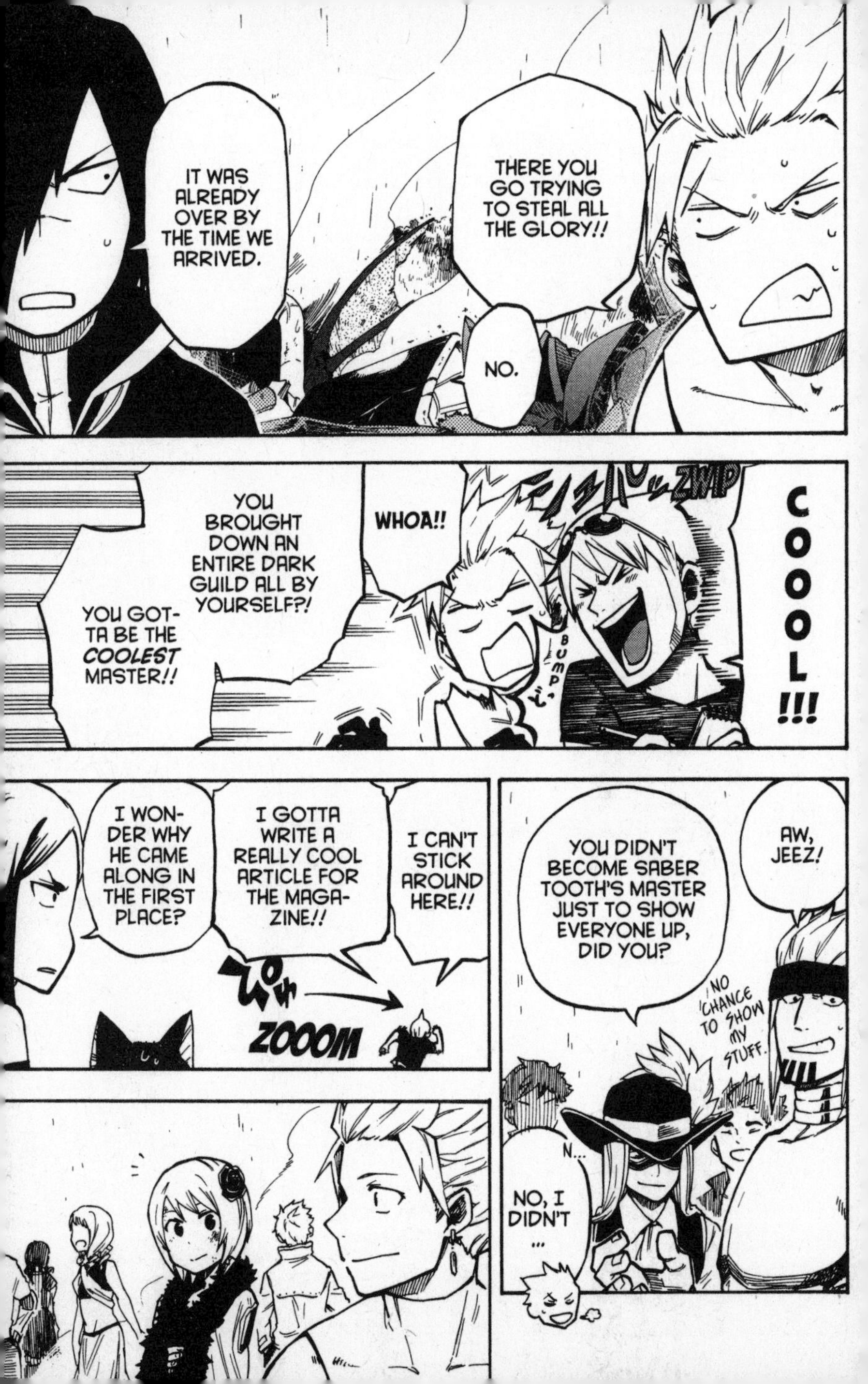
THERE YOU GO TRYING TO STEAL ALL THE GLORY!!
NO.
IT WAS ALREADY OVER BY THE TIME WE ARRIVED.
COOOL!!!
ZWIP
WHOA!!
BUMP
YOU BROUGHT DOWN AN ENTIRE DARK GUILD ALL BY YOURSELF?!
YOU GOT-TA BE THE *COOLEST* MASTER!!
AW, JEEZ!
YOU DIDN'T BECOME SABER TOOTH'S MASTER JUST TO SHOW EVERYONE UP, DID YOU?
NO CHANCE TO SHOW MY STUFF.
N...
NO, I DIDN'T ...
I CAN'T STICK AROUND HERE!!
I GOTTA WRITE A REALLY COOL ARTICLE FOR THE MAGA-ZINE!!
I WON-DER WHY HE CAME ALONG IN THE FIRST PLACE?
ZOOOM

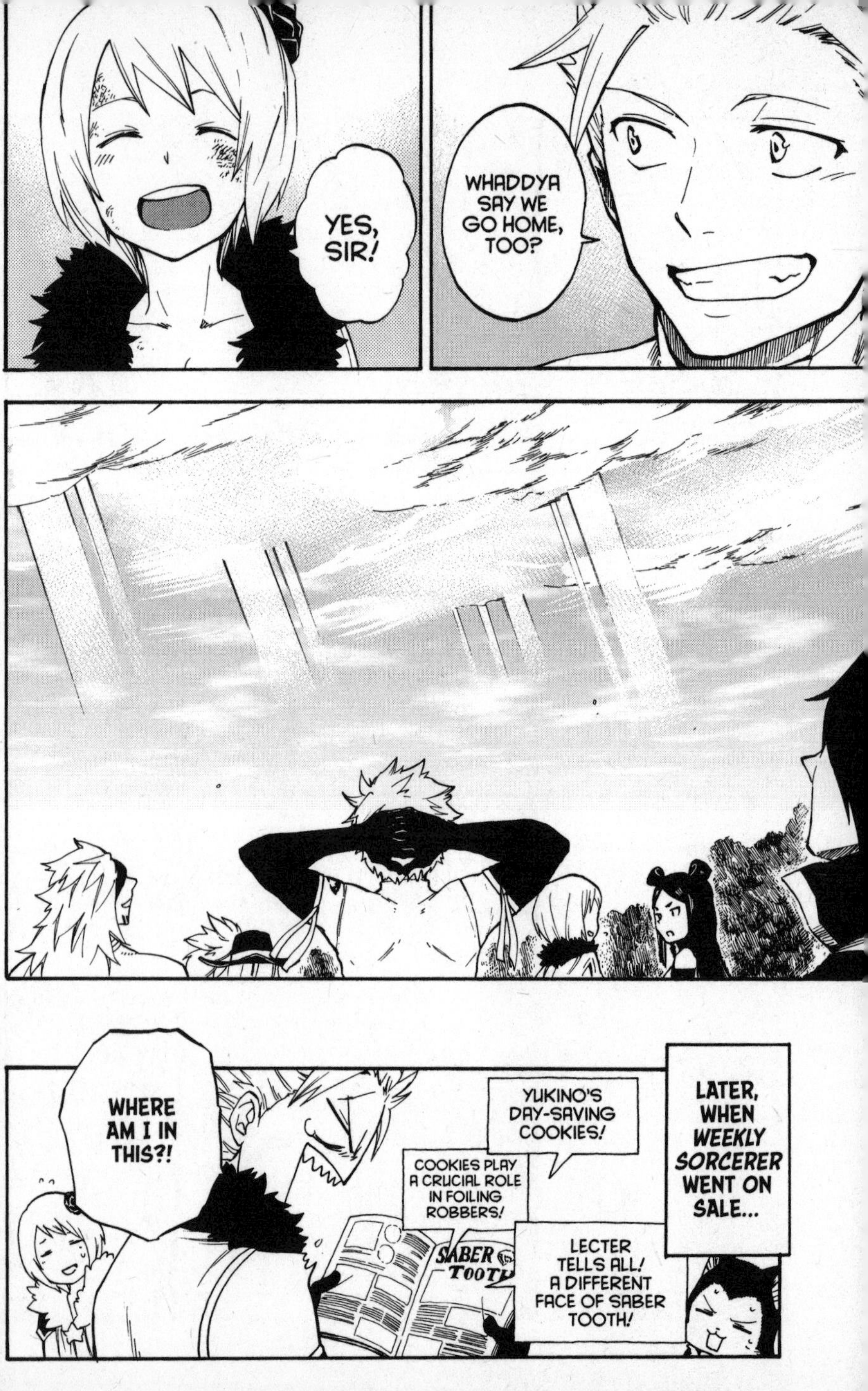
WHADDYA SAY WE GO HOME, TOO?
YES, SIR!
LATER, WHEN WEEKLY SORCERER WENT ON SALE...
YUKINO'S DAY-SAVING COOKIES!
LECTER TELLS ALL! A DIFFERENT FACE OF SABER TOOTH!
COOKIES PLAY A CRUCIAL ROLE IN FOILING ROBBERS!
WHERE AM I IN THIS?!

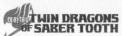

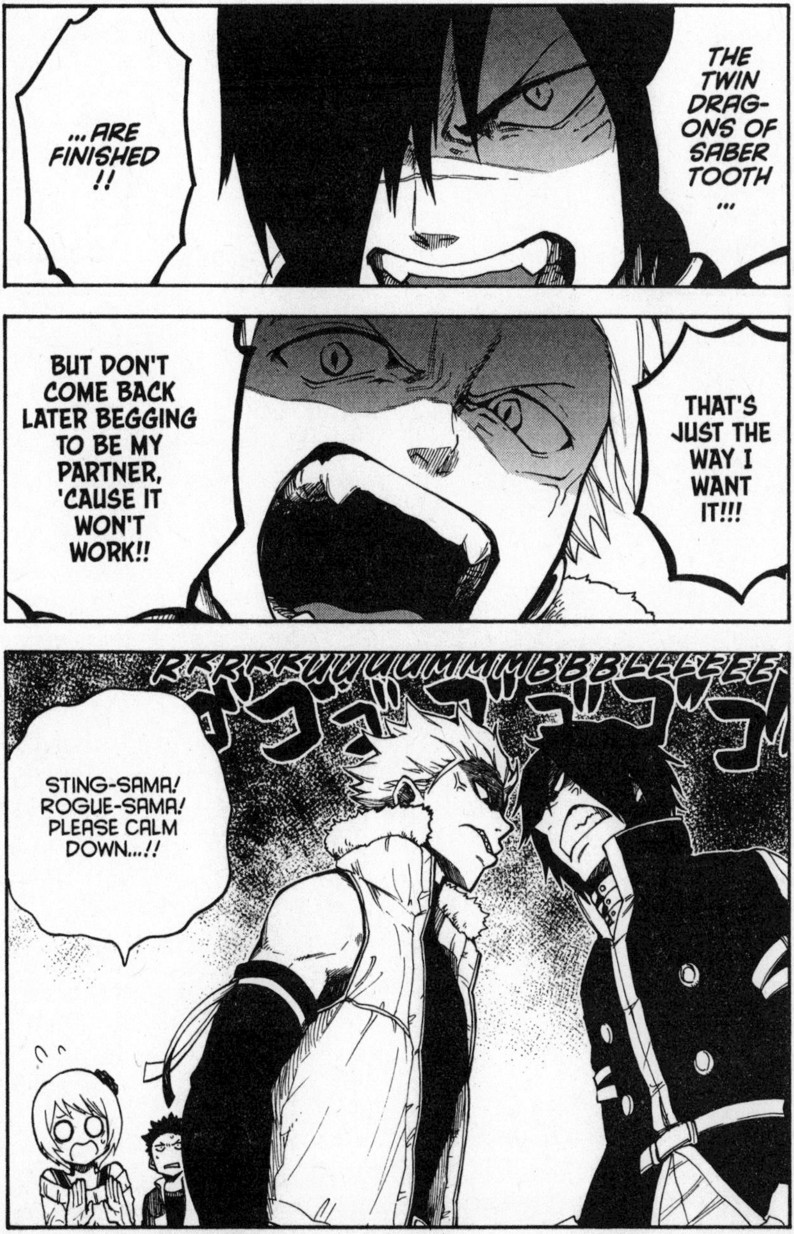
THE TWIN DRAGONS OF SABER TOOTH ...
...ARE FINISHED !!
THAT'S JUST THE WAY I WANT IT!!!
BUT DON'T COME BACK LATER BEGGING TO BE MY PARTNER, 'CAUSE IT WON'T WORK!!
RRRRRUUUUMMMMBBBLLLEEE
STING-SAMA! ROGUE-SAMA! PLEASE CALM DOWN...!!

FAIRY TAIL: TWIN DRAGONS OF SABER TOOTH

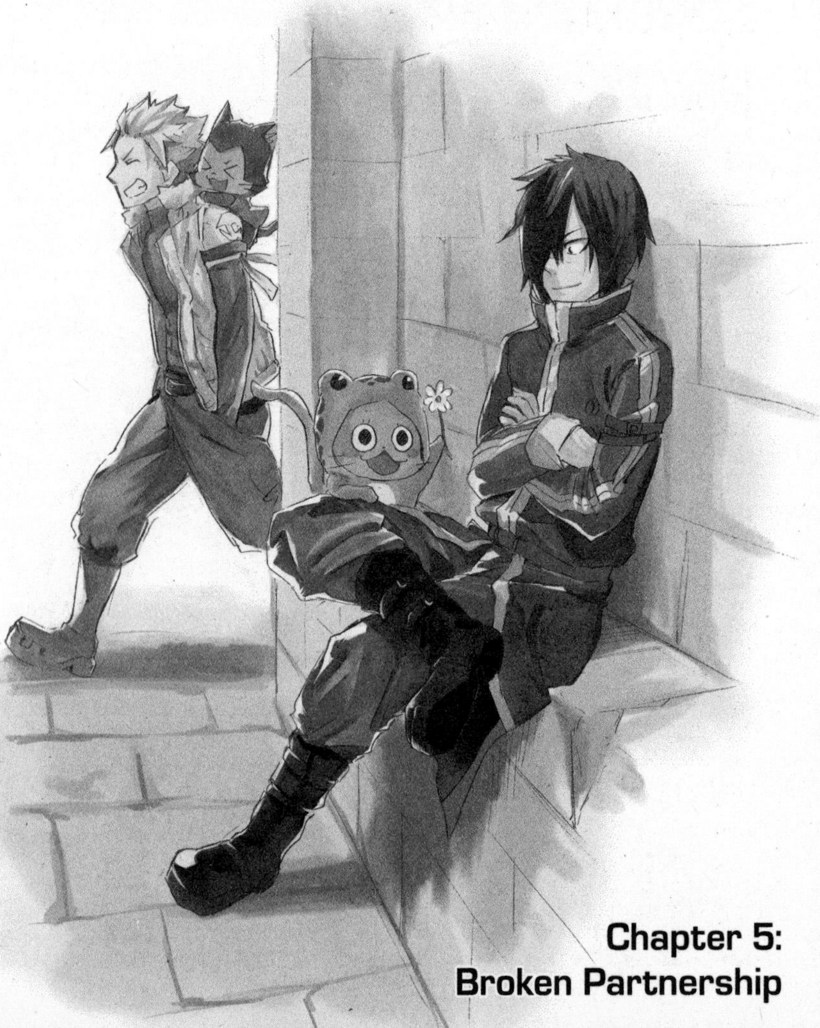

Chapter 5: Broken Partnership

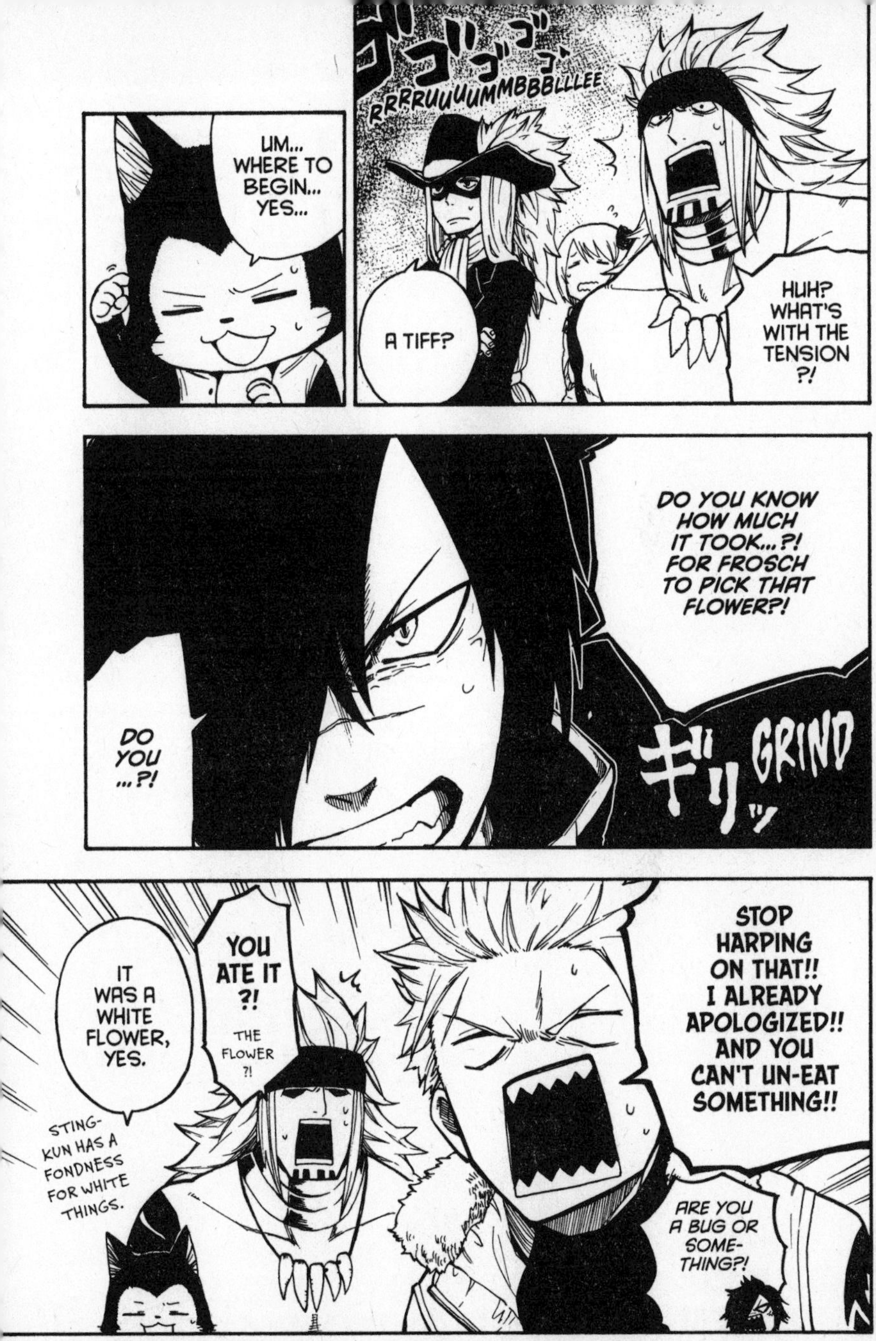
ゴゴゴゴ
RRRRUUUUMMBBBLLLEE
HUH? WHAT'S WITH THE TENSION ?!
A TIFF?
UM... WHERE TO BEGIN... YES...
DO YOU KNOW HOW MUCH IT TOOK...?! FOR FROSCH TO PICK THAT FLOWER?!
ギリッ
GRIND
DO YOU ...?!
STOP HARPING ON THAT!! I ALREADY APOLOGIZED!! AND YOU CAN'T UN-EAT SOMETHING!!
ARE YOU A BUG OR SOME-THING?!
YOU ATE IT ?!
THE FLOWER ?!
IT WAS A WHITE FLOWER, YES.
STING-KUN HAS A FONDNESS FOR WHITE THINGS.

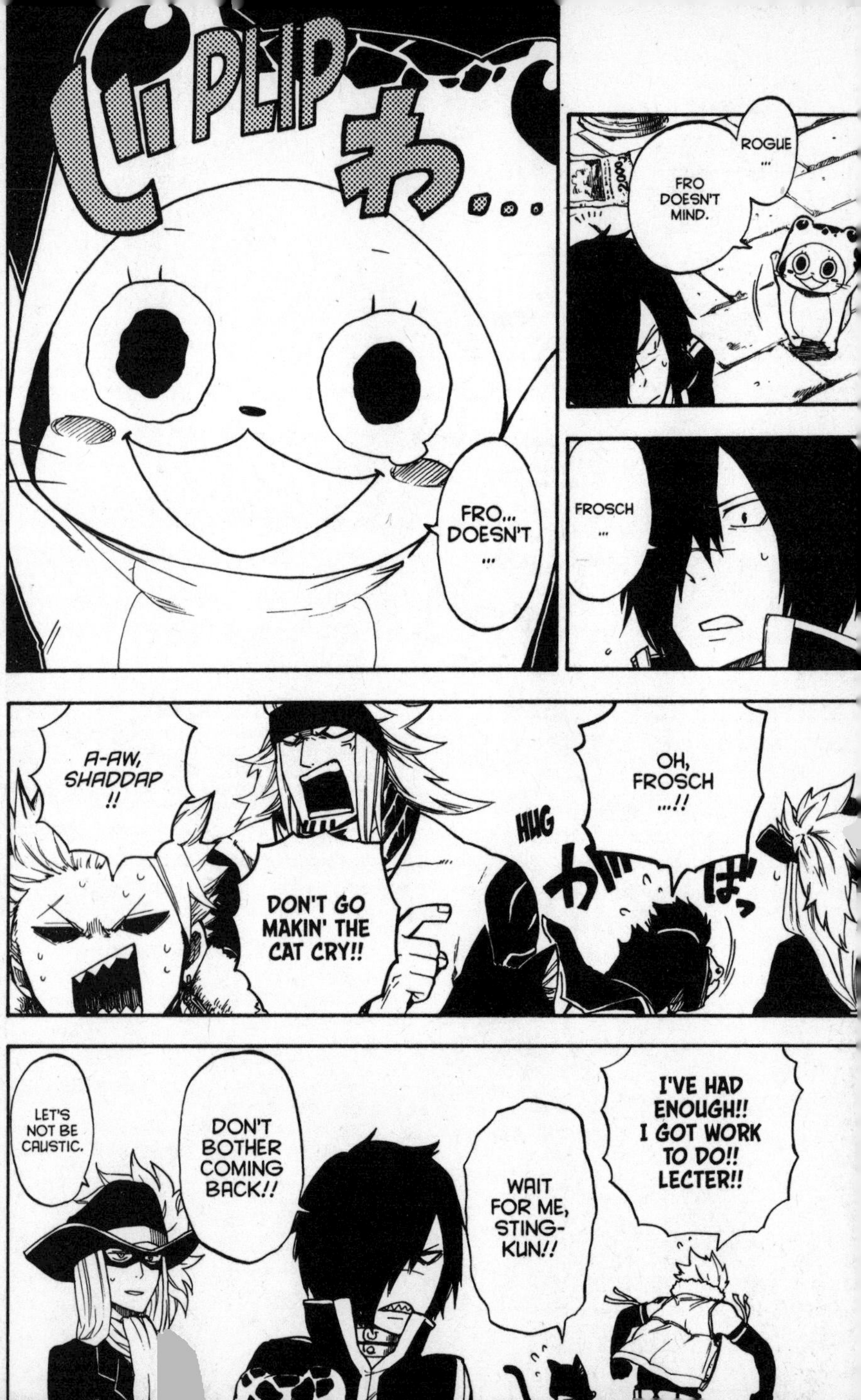
ROGUE ...
FRO DOESN'T MIND.
FROSCH ...
PLEIP
FRO... DOESN'T ...
OH, FROSCH ...!!
HUG
A-AW, SHADDAP!!
DON'T GO MAKIN' THE CAT CRY!!
I'VE HAD ENOUGH!! I GOT WORK TO DO!! LECTER!!
WAIT FOR ME, STING-KUN!!
DON'T BOTHER COMING BACK!!
LET'S NOT BE CAUSTIC.

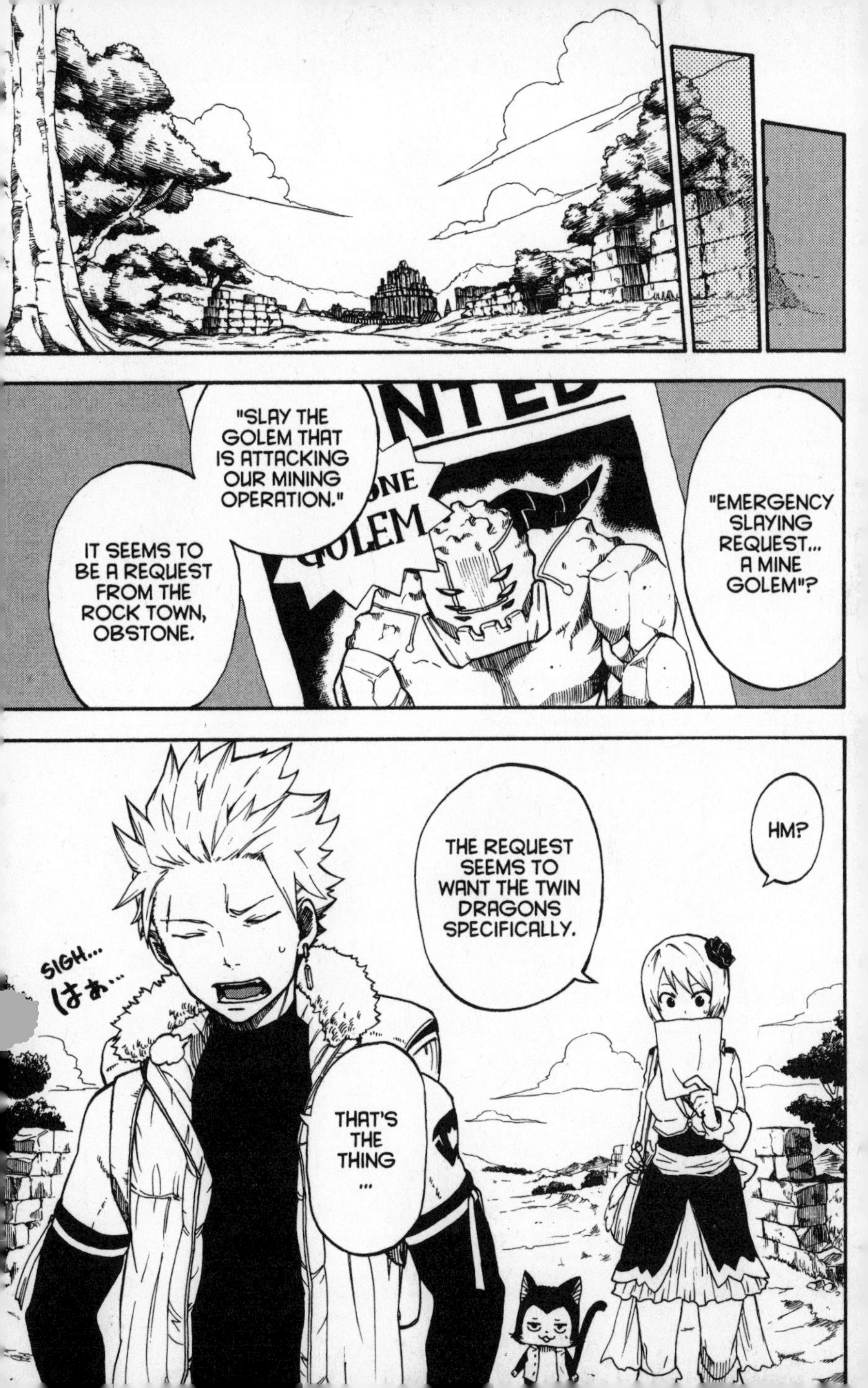
"EMERGENCY SLAYING REQUEST... A MINE GOLEM"?
"SLAY THE GOLEM THAT IS ATTACKING OUR MINING OPERATION."
IT SEEMS TO BE A REQUEST FROM THE ROCK TOWN, OBSTONE.
HM?
THE REQUEST SEEMS TO WANT THE TWIN DRAGONS SPECIFICALLY.
THAT'S THE THING ...
SIGH...
はぁ...

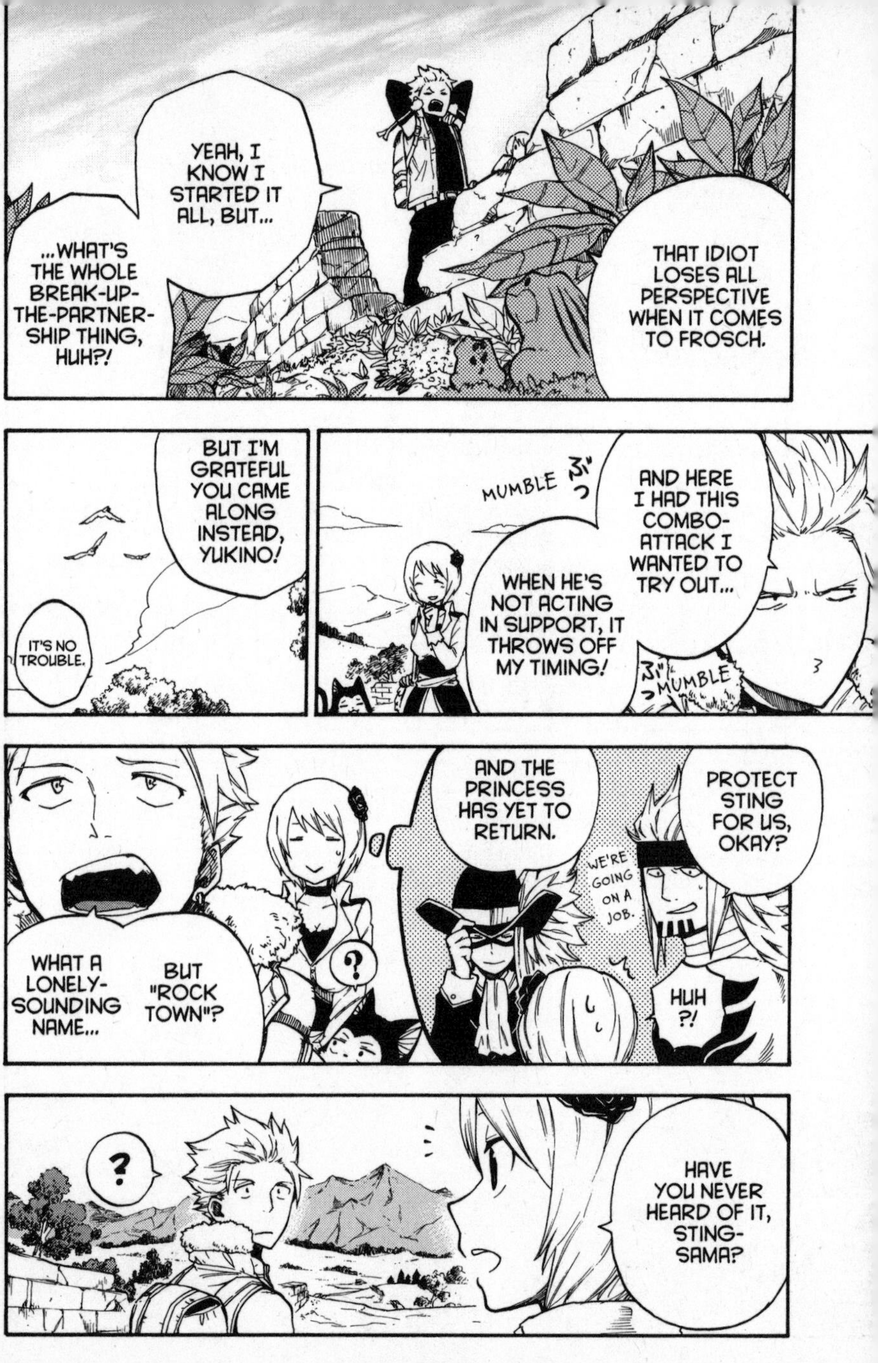
YEAH, I KNOW I STARTED IT ALL, BUT...
...WHAT'S THE WHOLE BREAK-UP-THE-PARTNERSHIP THING, HUH?!
THAT IDIOT LOSES ALL PERSPECTIVE WHEN IT COMES TO FROSCH.
AND HERE I HAD THIS COMBO-ATTACK I WANTED TO TRY OUT...
MUMBLE
WHEN HE'S NOT ACTING IN SUPPORT, IT THROWS OFF MY TIMING!
MUMBLE
BUT I'M GRATEFUL YOU CAME ALONG INSTEAD, YUKINO!
IT'S NO TROUBLE.
PROTECT STING FOR US, OKAY?
WE'RE GOING ON A JOB.
HUH ?!
AND THE PRINCESS HAS YET TO RETURN.
BUT "ROCK TOWN"?
WHAT A LONELY-SOUNDING NAME...
HAVE YOU NEVER HEARD OF IT, STING-SAMA?
?

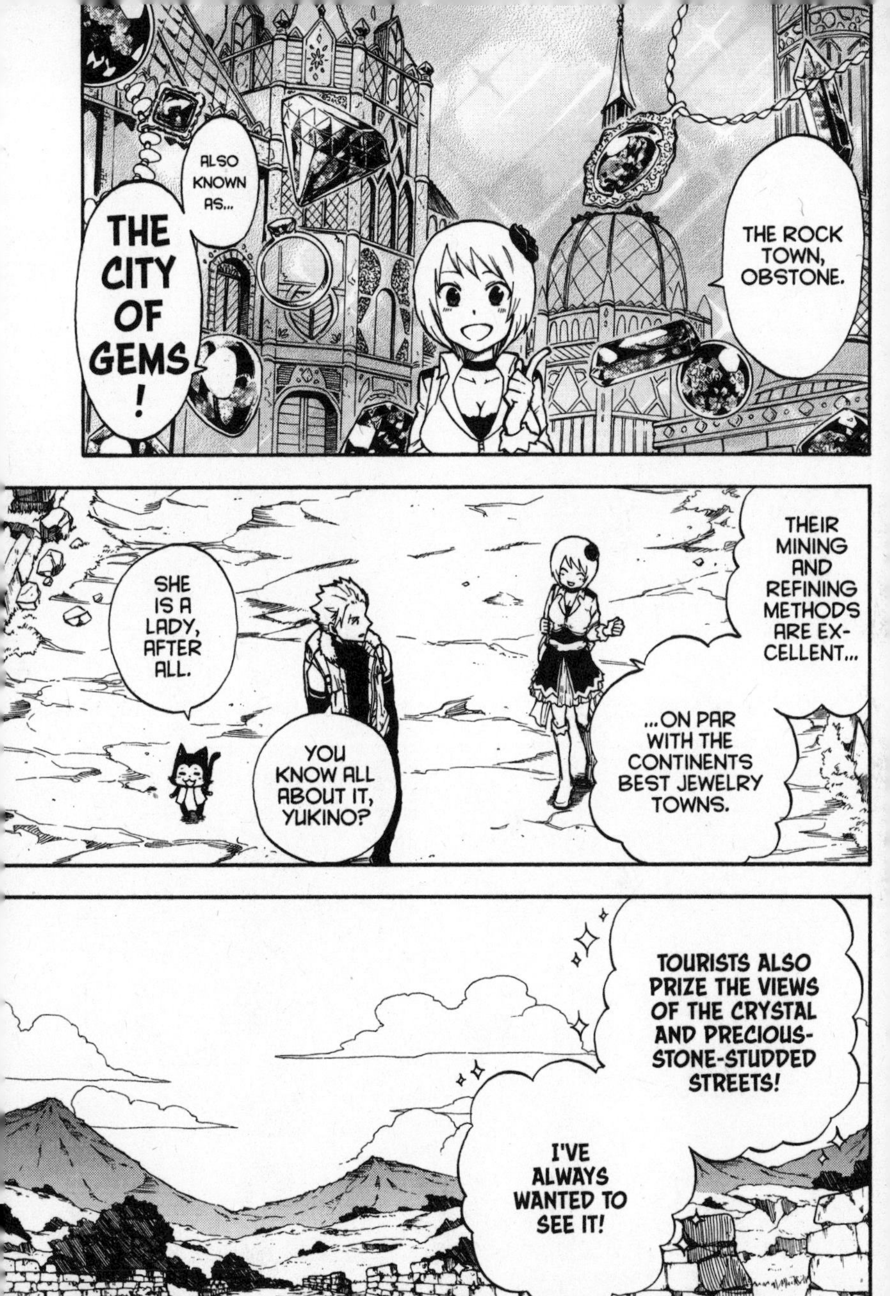
THE ROCK TOWN, OBSTONE.
ALSO KNOWN AS...
THE CITY OF GEMS!
THEIR MINING AND REFINING METHODS ARE EX-CELLENT...
...ON PAR WITH THE CONTINENTS BEST JEWELRY TOWNS.
YOU KNOW ALL ABOUT IT, YUKINO?
SHE IS A LADY, AFTER ALL.
TOURISTS ALSO PRIZE THE VIEWS OF THE CRYSTAL AND PRECIOUS-STONE-STUDDED STREETS!
I'VE ALWAYS WANTED TO SEE IT!

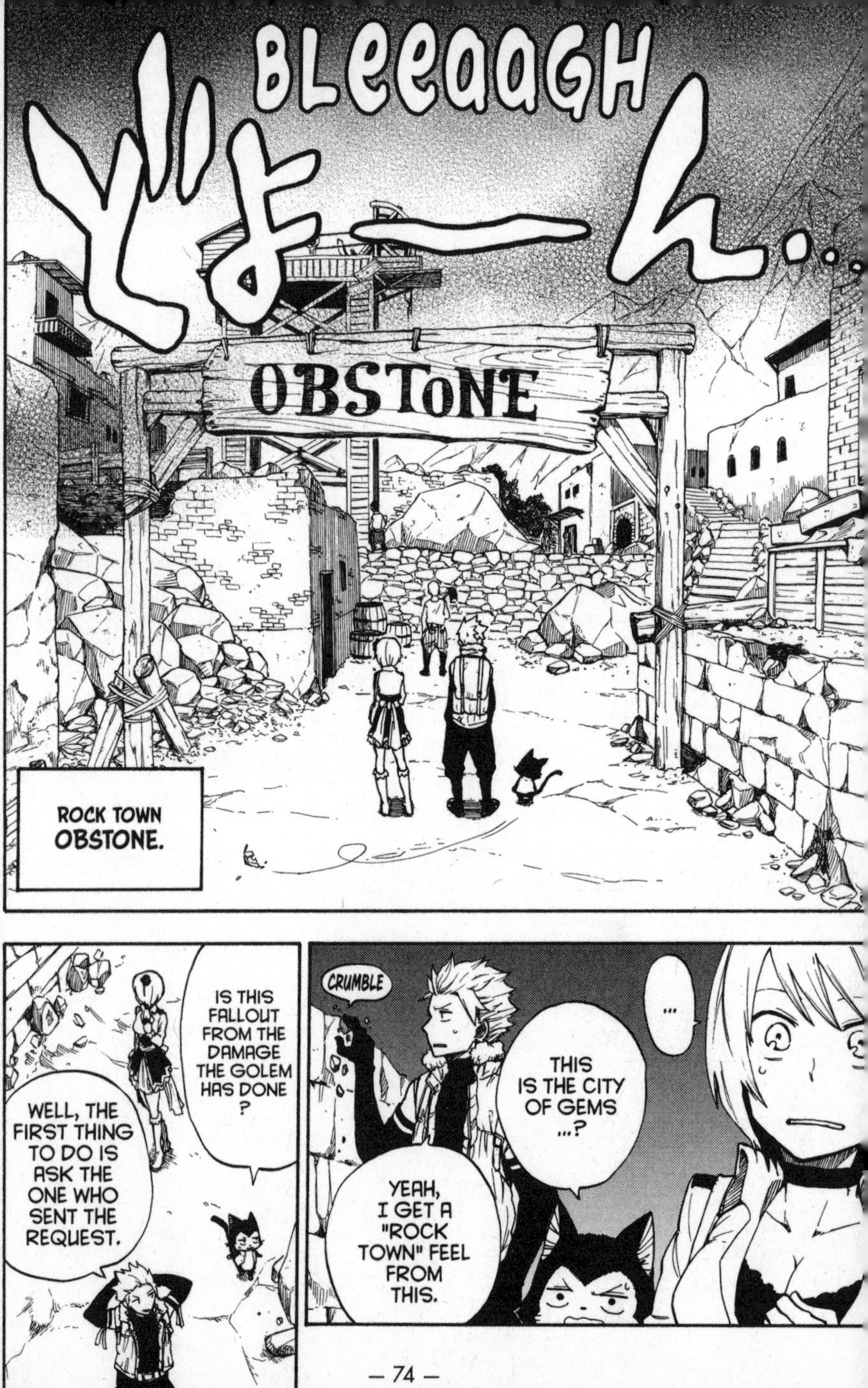
BLEEAAGH
どよーん...
OBSTONE
ROCK TOWN OBSTONE.
...
THIS IS THE CITY OF GEMS ...?
CRUMBLE
YEAH, I GET A "ROCK TOWN" FEEL FROM THIS.
IS THIS FALLOUT FROM THE DAMAGE THE GOLEM HAS DONE?
WELL, THE FIRST THING TO DO IS ASK THE ONE WHO SENT THE REQUEST.

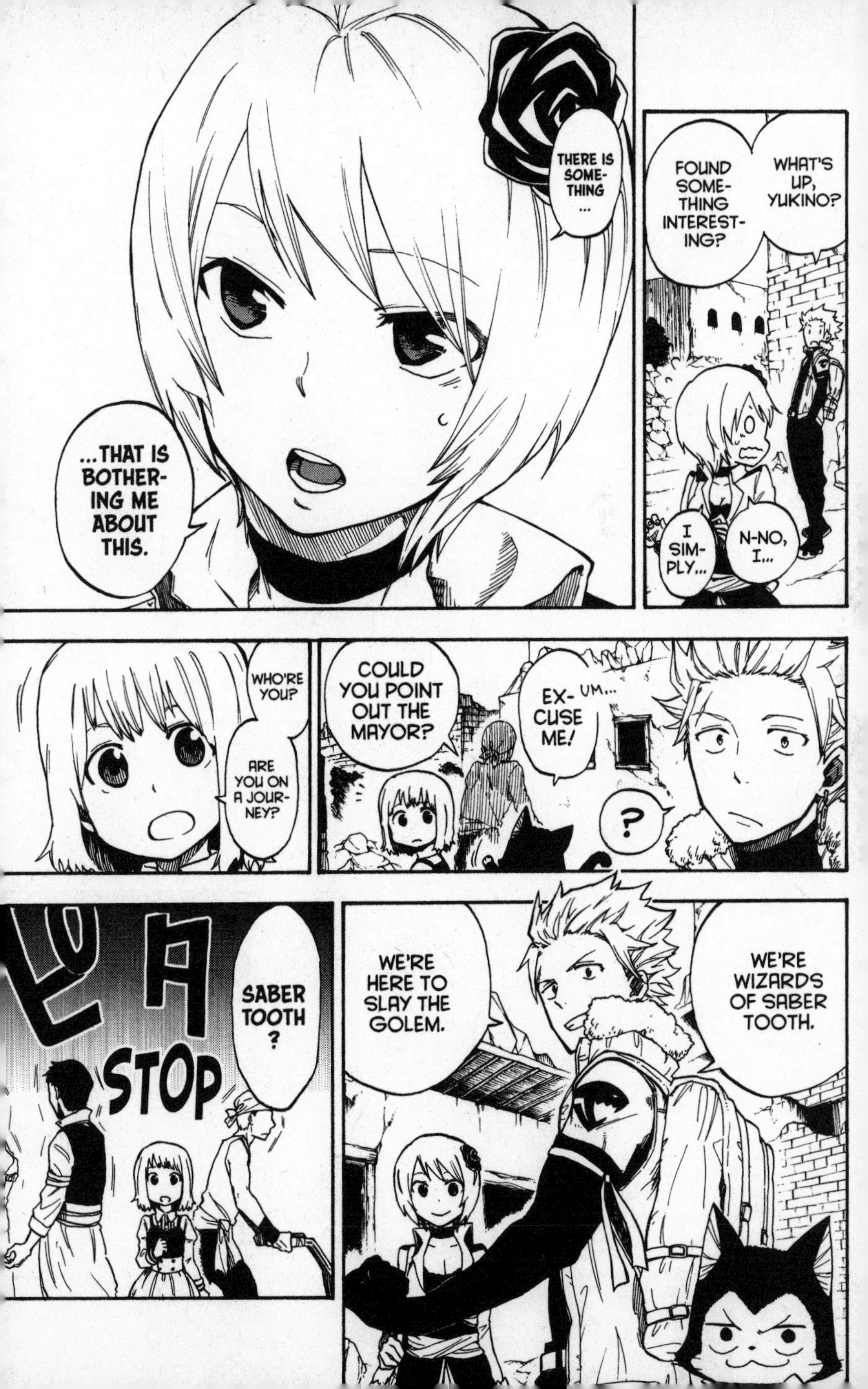
WHAT'S UP, YUKINO?
FOUND SOMETHING INTERESTING?
N-NO, I...
I SIMPLY...
THERE IS SOMETHING...
...THAT IS BOTHERING ME ABOUT THIS.
UM...
EXCUSE ME!
?
COULD YOU POINT OUT THE MAYOR?
WHO'RE YOU?
ARE YOU ON A JOURNEY?
WE'RE WIZARDS OF SABER TOOTH.
WE'RE HERE TO SLAY THE GOLEM.
SABER TOOTH?
STOP

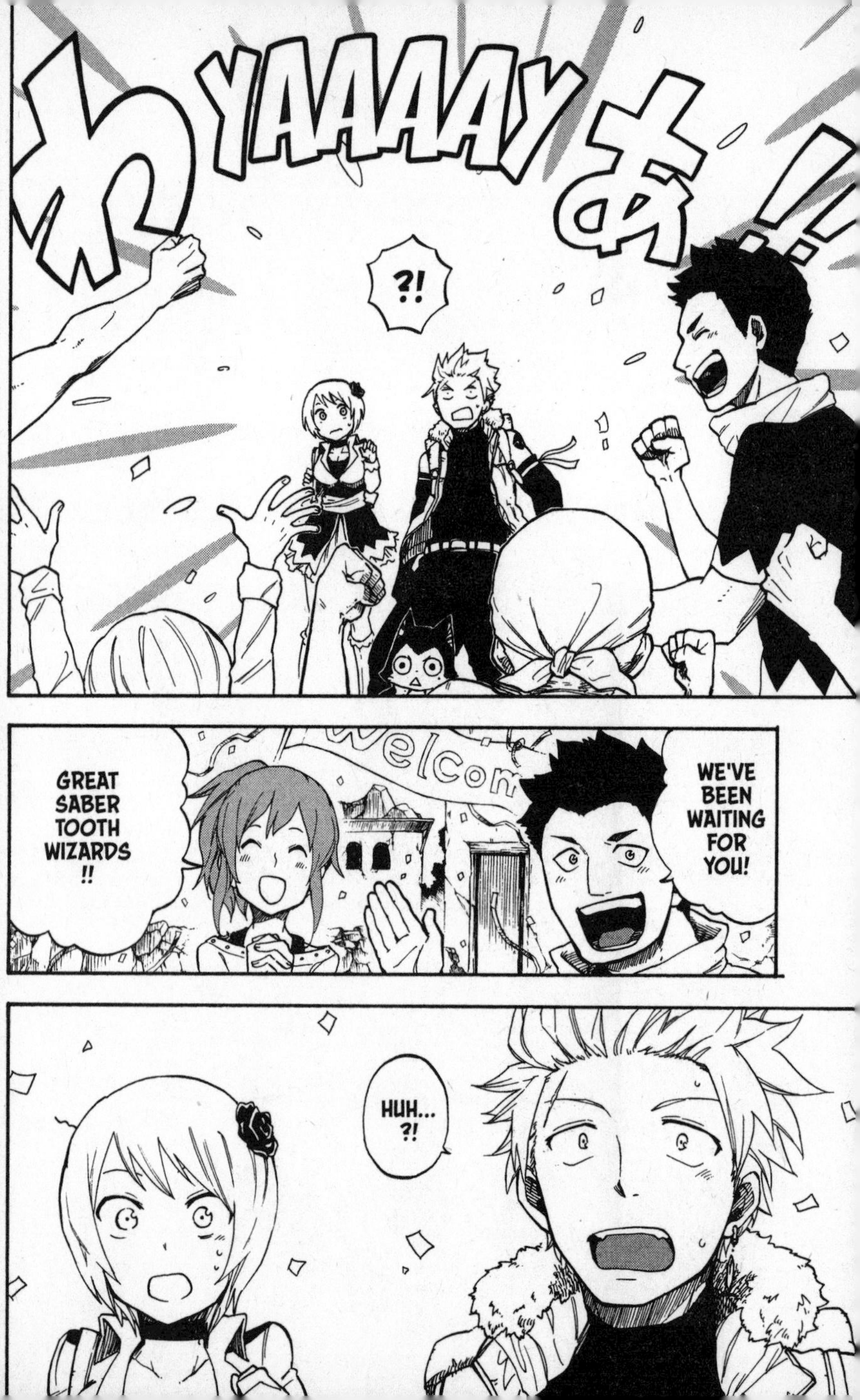
わYAAAAYあ!!
?!
WE'VE BEEN WAITING FOR YOU!
Welcom
GREAT SABER TOOTH WIZARDS !!
HUH... ?!

FAIRY TAIL: TWIN DRAGONS OF SABER TOOTH

Chapter 6: The Mystery of Rock Town

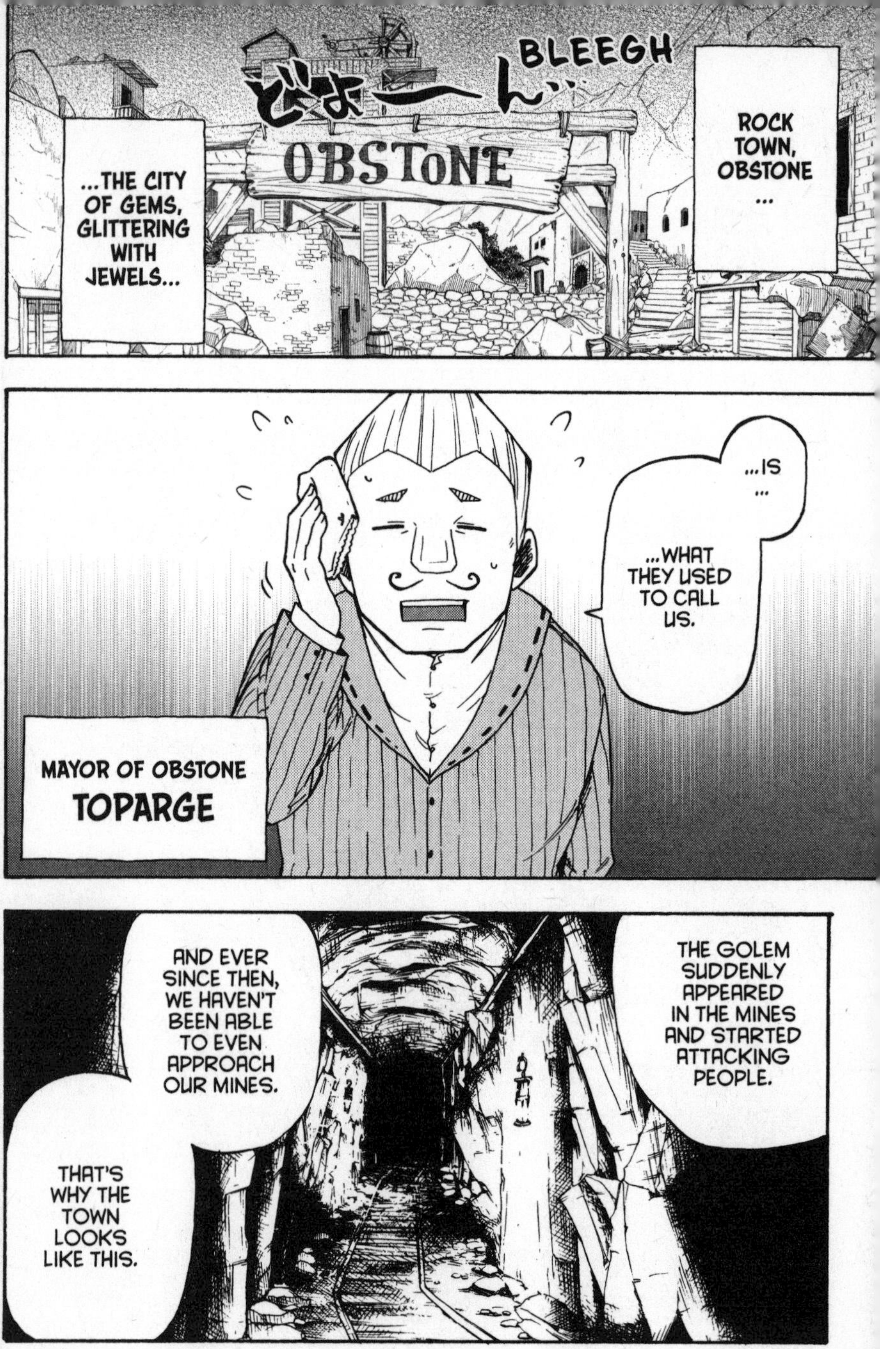
ROCK TOWN, OBSTONE ...
どよーん
BLEEGH
OBSTONE
...THE CITY OF GEMS, GLITTERING WITH JEWELS...
...IS ...
...WHAT THEY USED TO CALL US.
MAYOR OF OBSTONE
TOPARGE
THE GOLEM SUDDENLY APPEARED IN THE MINES AND STARTED ATTACKING PEOPLE.
AND EVER SINCE THEN, WE HAVEN'T BEEN ABLE TO EVEN APPROACH OUR MINES.
THAT'S WHY THE TOWN LOOKS LIKE THIS.

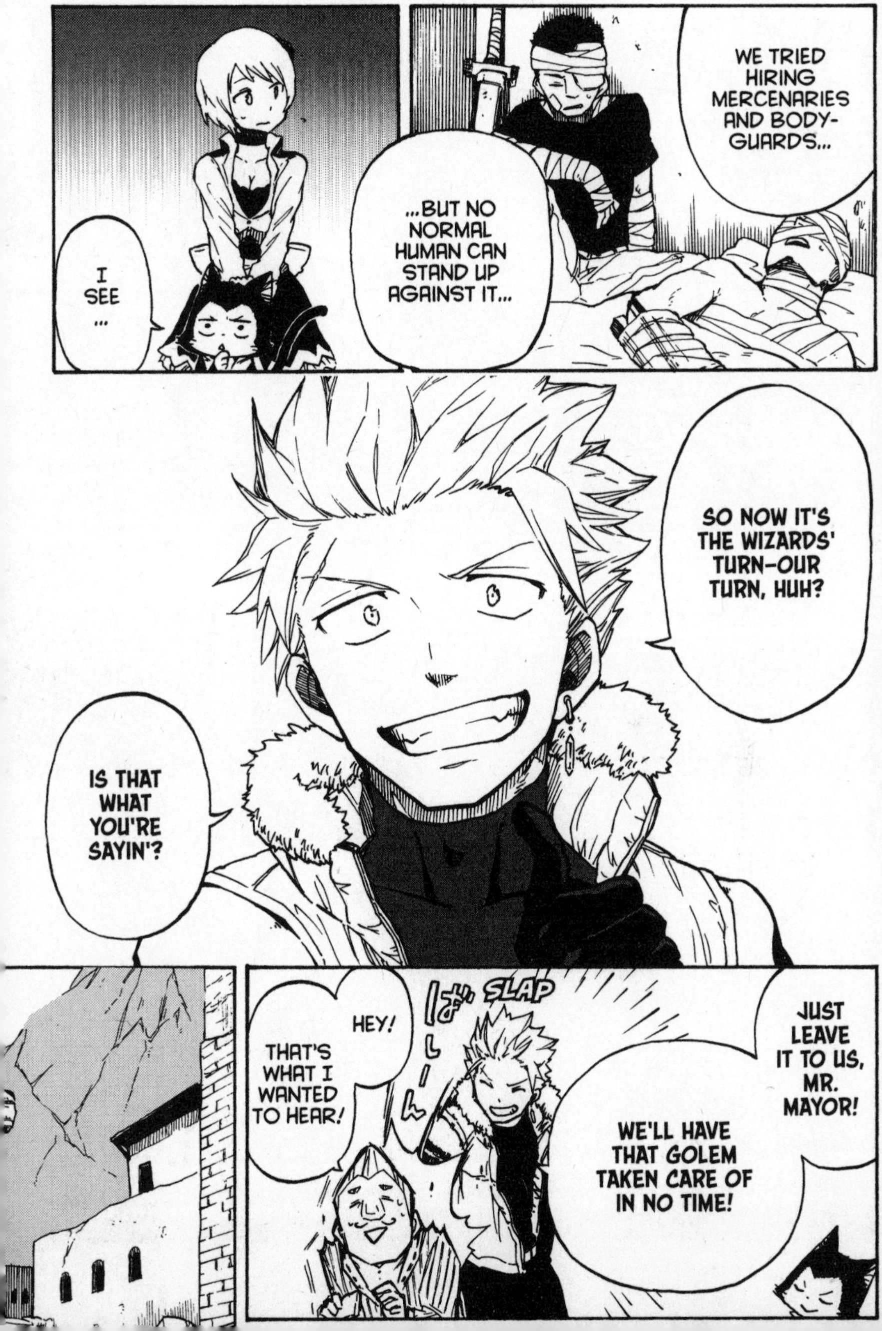
WE TRIED HIRING MERCENARIES AND BODY-GUARDS...
...BUT NO NORMAL HUMAN CAN STAND UP AGAINST IT...
I SEE ...
SO NOW IT'S THE WIZARDS' TURN—OUR TURN, HUH?
IS THAT WHAT YOU'RE SAYIN'?
JUST LEAVE IT TO US, MR. MAYOR!
WE'LL HAVE THAT GOLEM TAKEN CARE OF IN NO TIME!
SLAP
ばしーん
HEY!
THAT'S WHAT I WANTED TO HEAR!

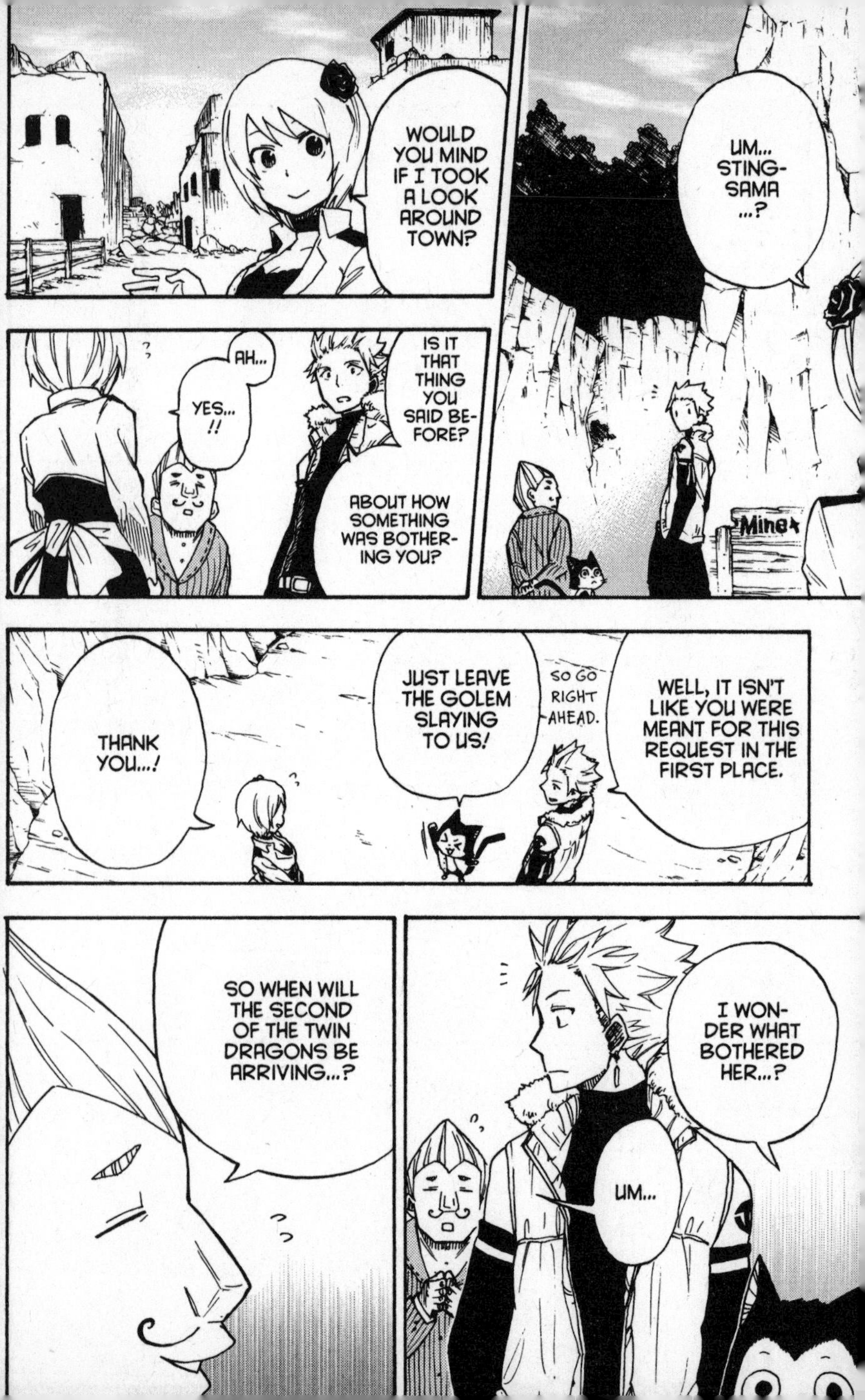
UM... STING-SAMA ...?
Mine
WOULD YOU MIND IF I TOOK A LOOK AROUND TOWN?
IS IT THAT THING YOU SAID BEFORE?
ABOUT HOW SOMETHING WAS BOTHERING YOU?
AH...
YES... !!
WELL, IT ISN'T LIKE YOU WERE MEANT FOR THIS REQUEST IN THE FIRST PLACE.
SO GO RIGHT AHEAD.
JUST LEAVE THE GOLEM SLAYING TO US!
THANK YOU...!
I WONDER WHAT BOTHERED HER...?
UM...
SO WHEN WILL THE SECOND OF THE TWIN DRAGONS BE ARRIVING...?

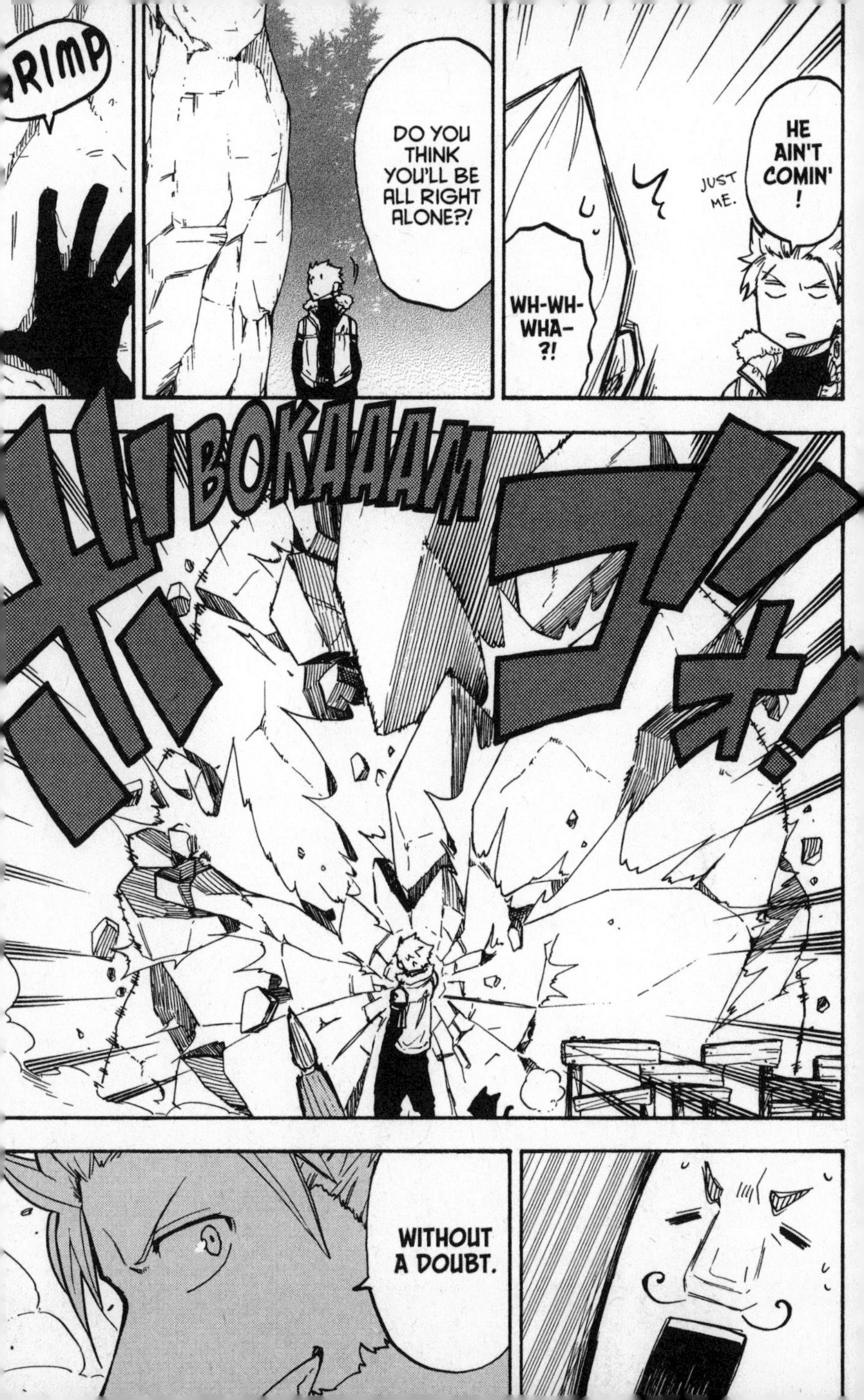
HE AIN'T COMIN'!
JUST ME.
WH-WH-WHA-?!
DO YOU THINK YOU'LL BE ALL RIGHT ALONE?!
RIMP
BOKAAAM
WITHOUT A DOUBT.

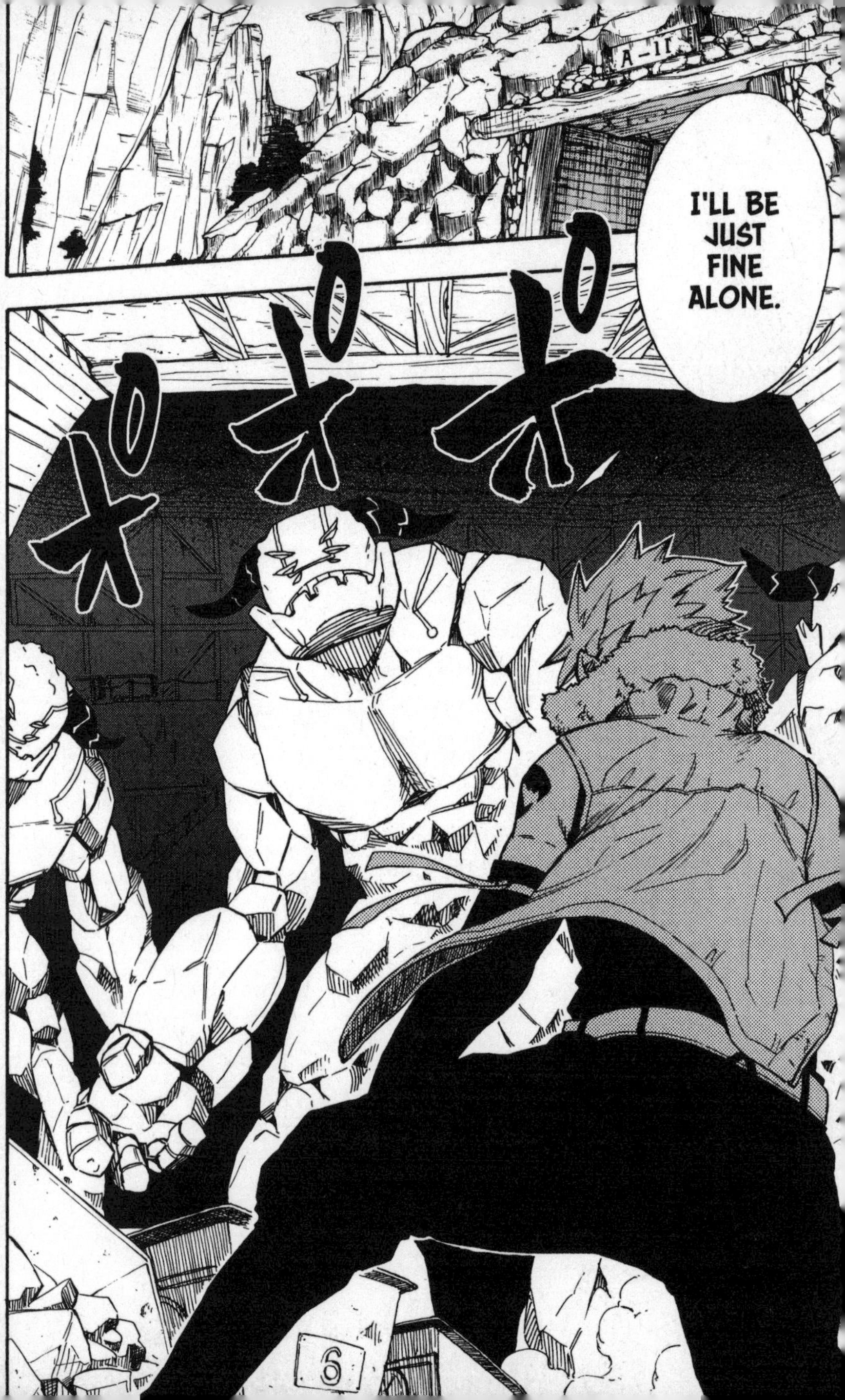
A-11
I'LL BE JUST FINE ALONE.
6

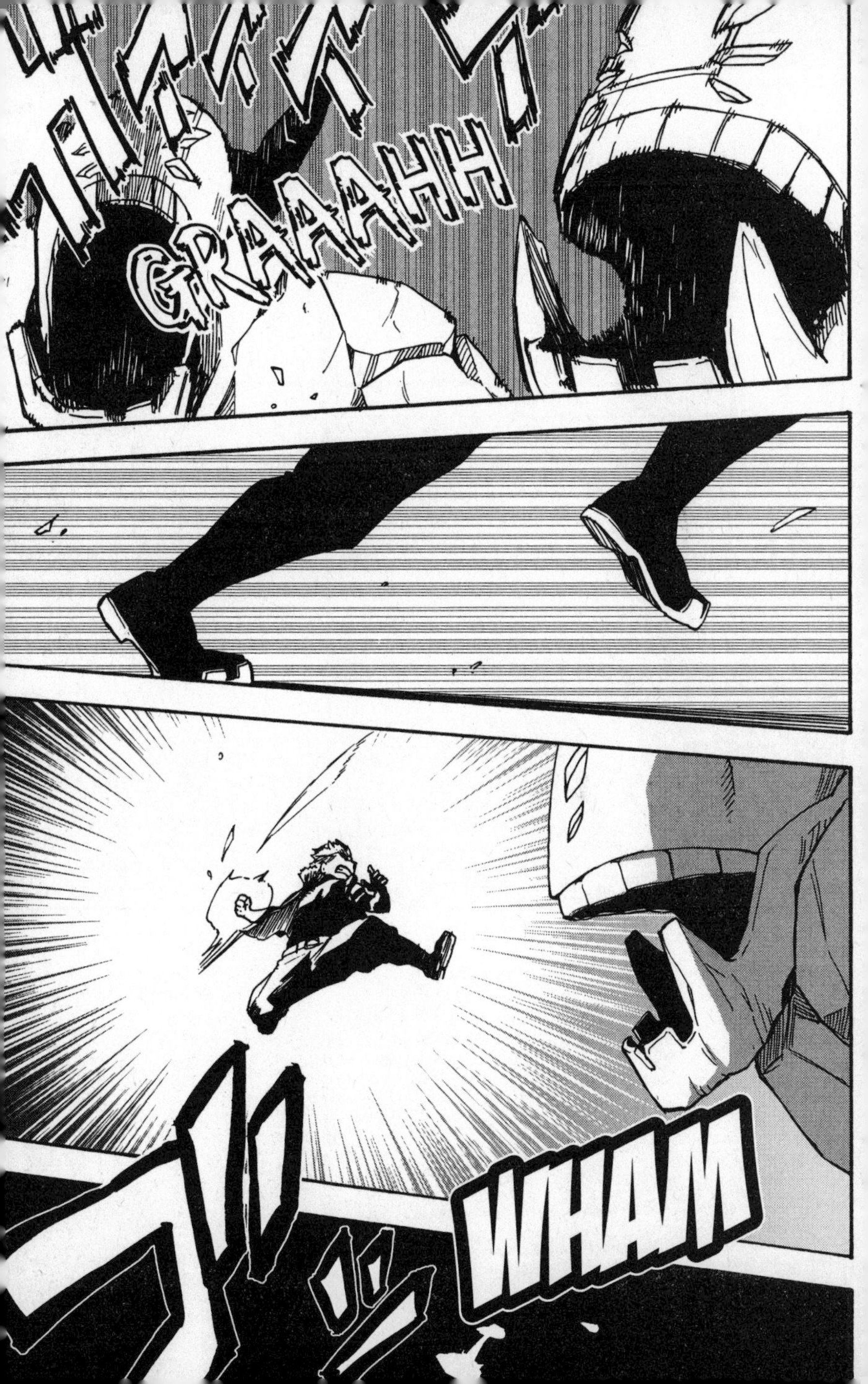
GRAAHH
WHAM

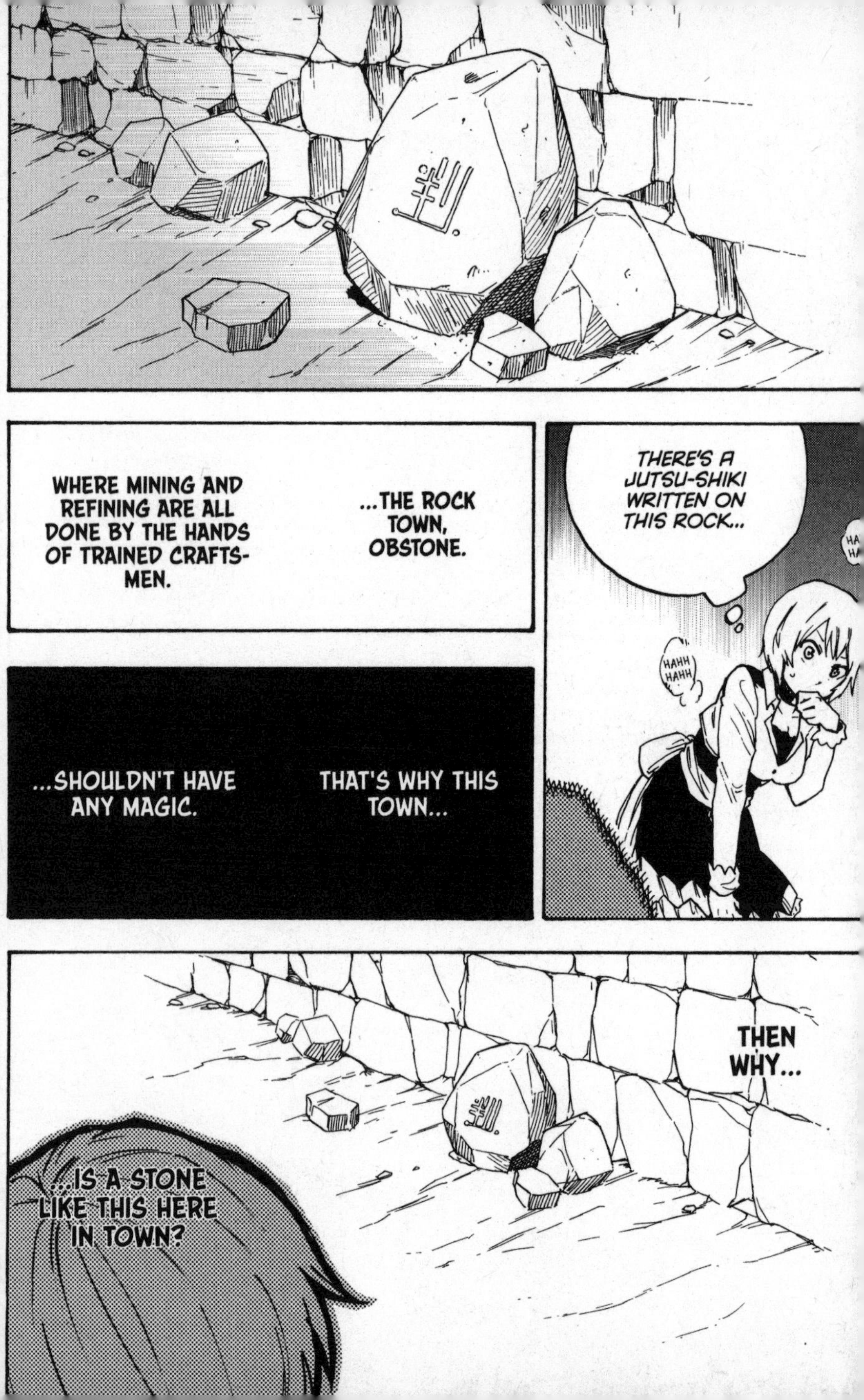
THERE'S A JUTSU-SHIKI WRITTEN ON THIS ROCK...
HAHH HAHH
...THE ROCK TOWN, OBSTONE.
WHERE MINING AND REFINING ARE ALL DONE BY THE HANDS OF TRAINED CRAFTSMEN.
THAT'S WHY THIS TOWN...
...SHOULDN'T HAVE ANY MAGIC.
THEN WHY...
...IS A STONE LIKE THIS HERE IN TOWN?

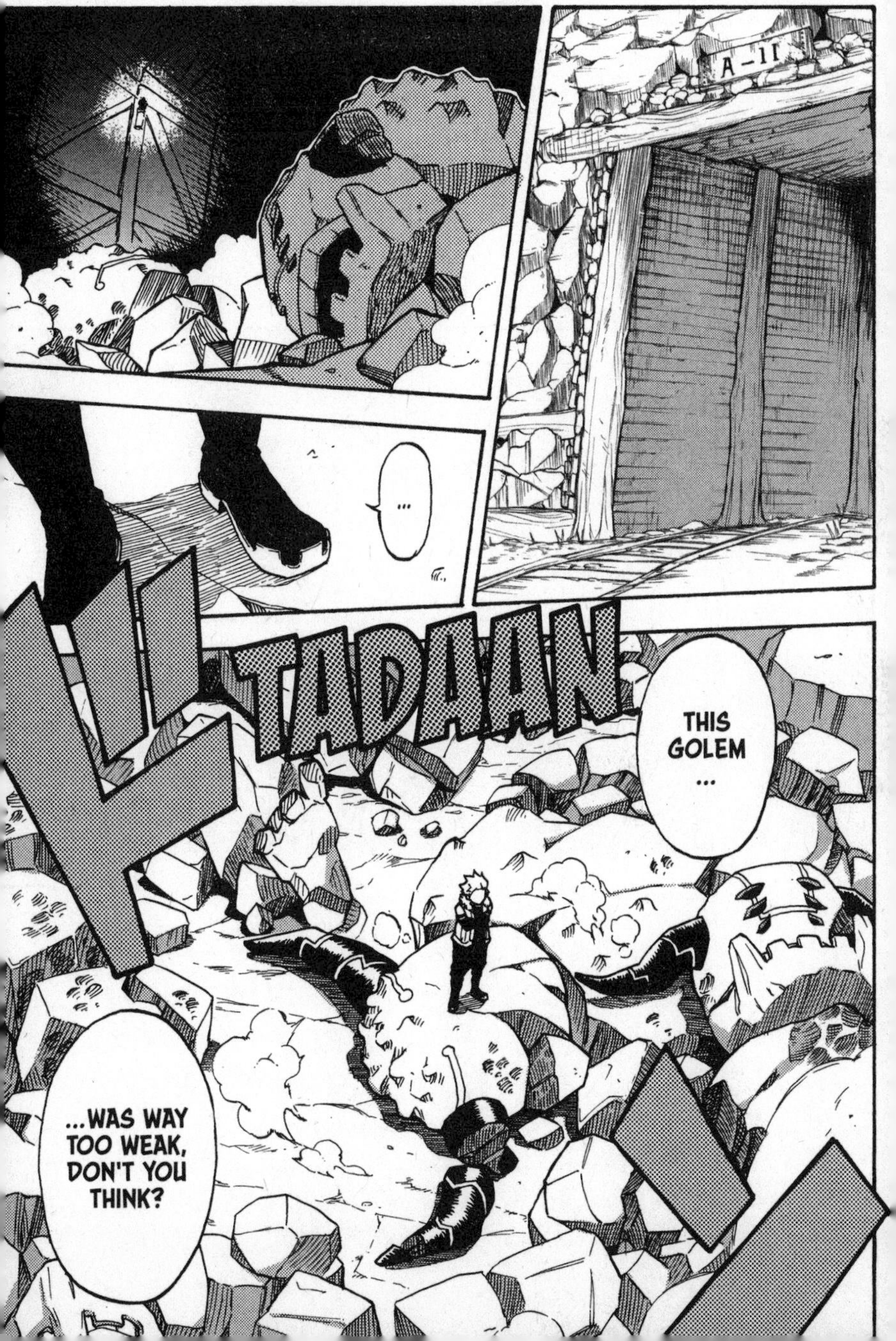
A-11
...
TADAAN
THIS GOLEM ...
...WAS WAY TOO WEAK, DON'T YOU THINK?

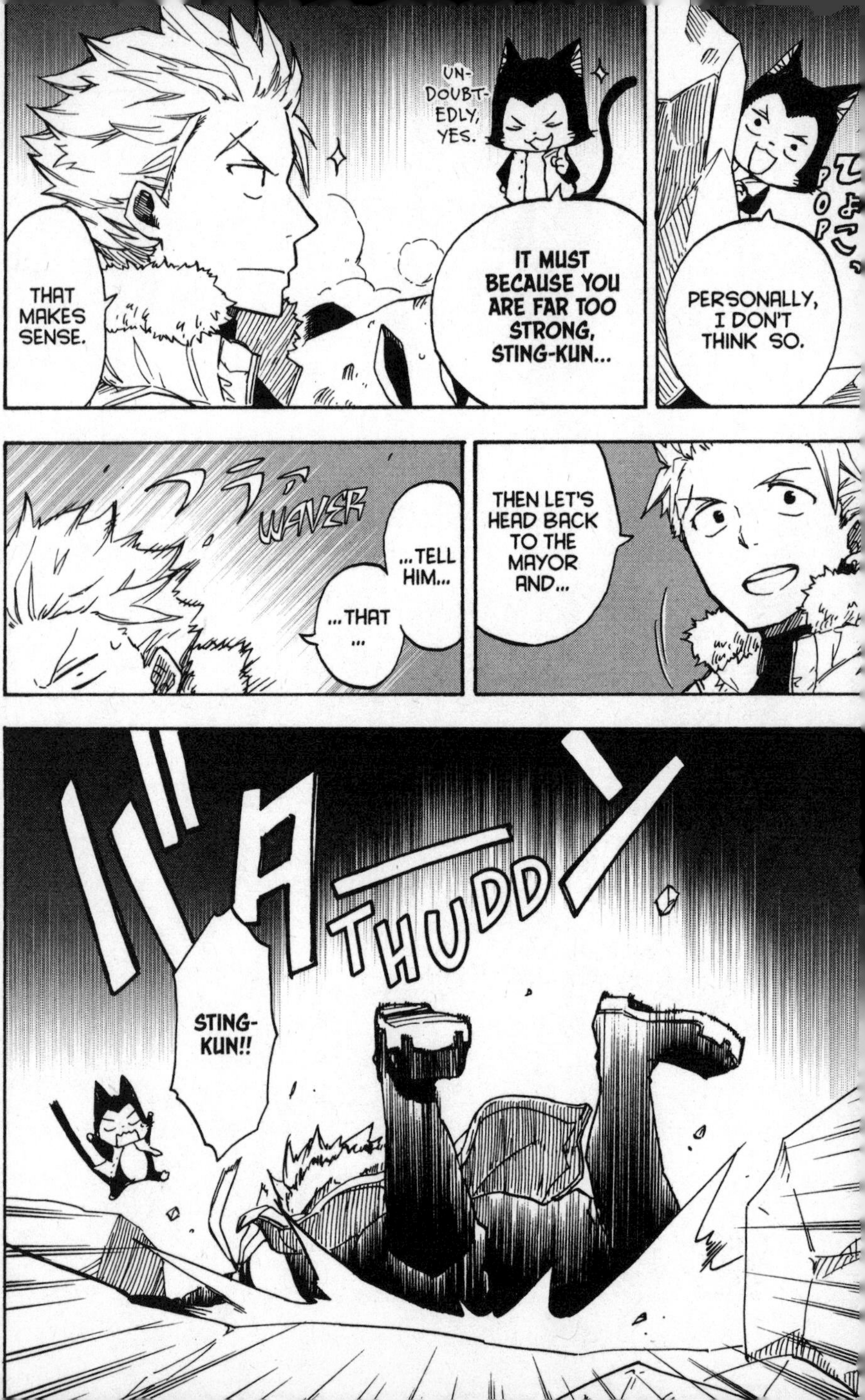
PERSONALLY, I DON'T THINK SO.
IT MUST BECAUSE YOU ARE FAR TOO STRONG, STING-KUN...
UN-DOUBT-EDLY, YES.
THAT MAKES SENSE.
THEN LET'S HEAD BACK TO THE MAYOR AND...
WAVER
...TELL HIM...
...THAT ...
THUDD
STING-KUN!!

FAIRY TAIL: TWIN DRAGONS OF SABER TOOTH

Chapter 7: A Tiger's Cage

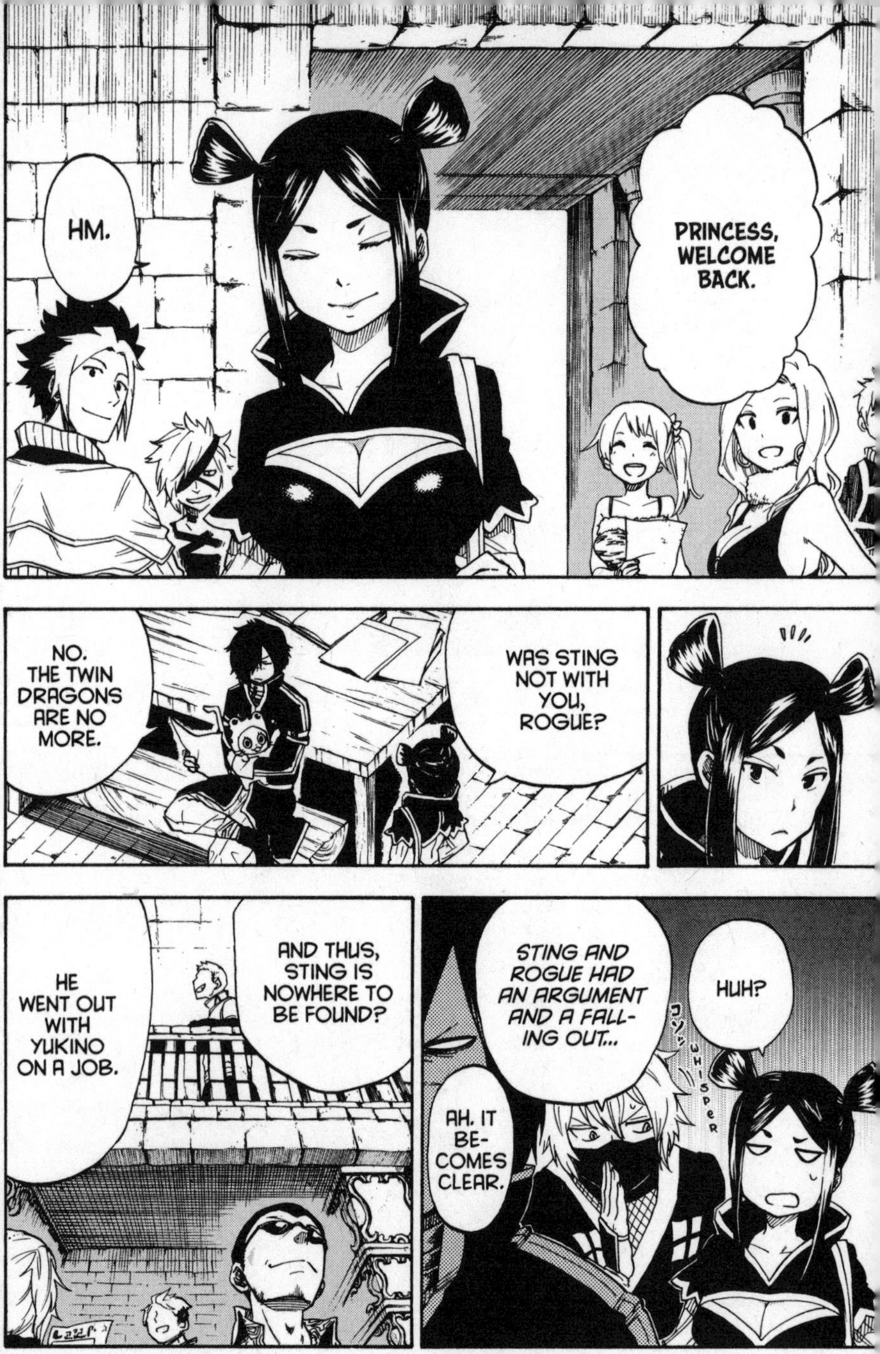
PRINCESS, WELCOME BACK.
HM.
WAS STING NOT WITH YOU, ROGUE?
NO. THE TWIN DRAGONS ARE NO MORE.
HUH?
STING AND ROGUE HAD AN ARGUMENT AND A FALL-ING OUT...
WHISPER
AH. IT BE-COMES CLEAR.
AND THUS, STING IS NOWHERE TO BE FOUND?
HE WENT OUT WITH YUKINO ON A JOB.

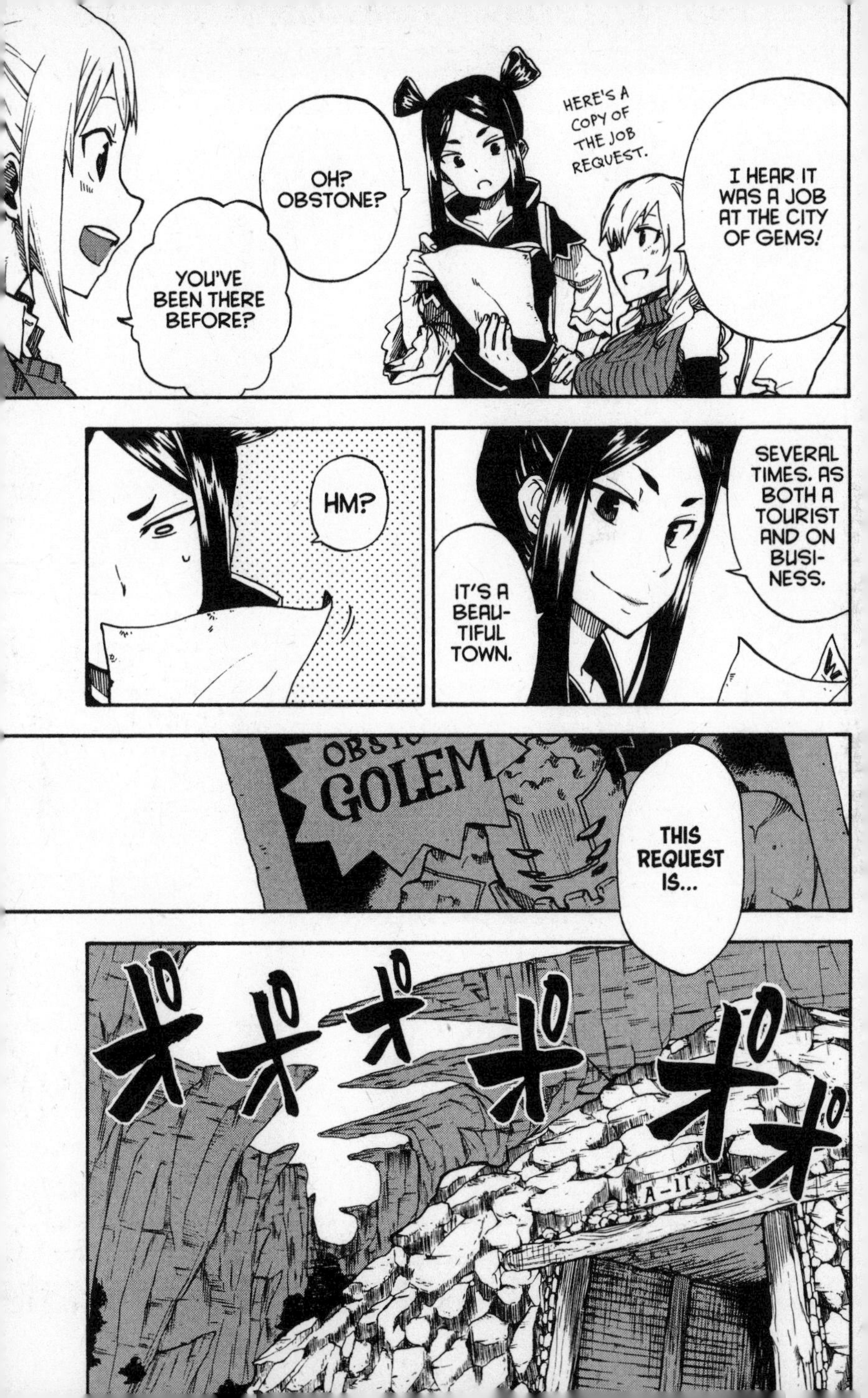
I HEAR IT WAS A JOB AT THE CITY OF GEMS!
HERE'S A COPY OF THE JOB REQUEST.
OH? OBSTONE?
YOU'VE BEEN THERE BEFORE?
SEVERAL TIMES. AS BOTH A TOURIST AND ON BUSINESS.
IT'S A BEAUTIFUL TOWN.
HM?
THIS REQUEST IS...
GOLEM
A-11

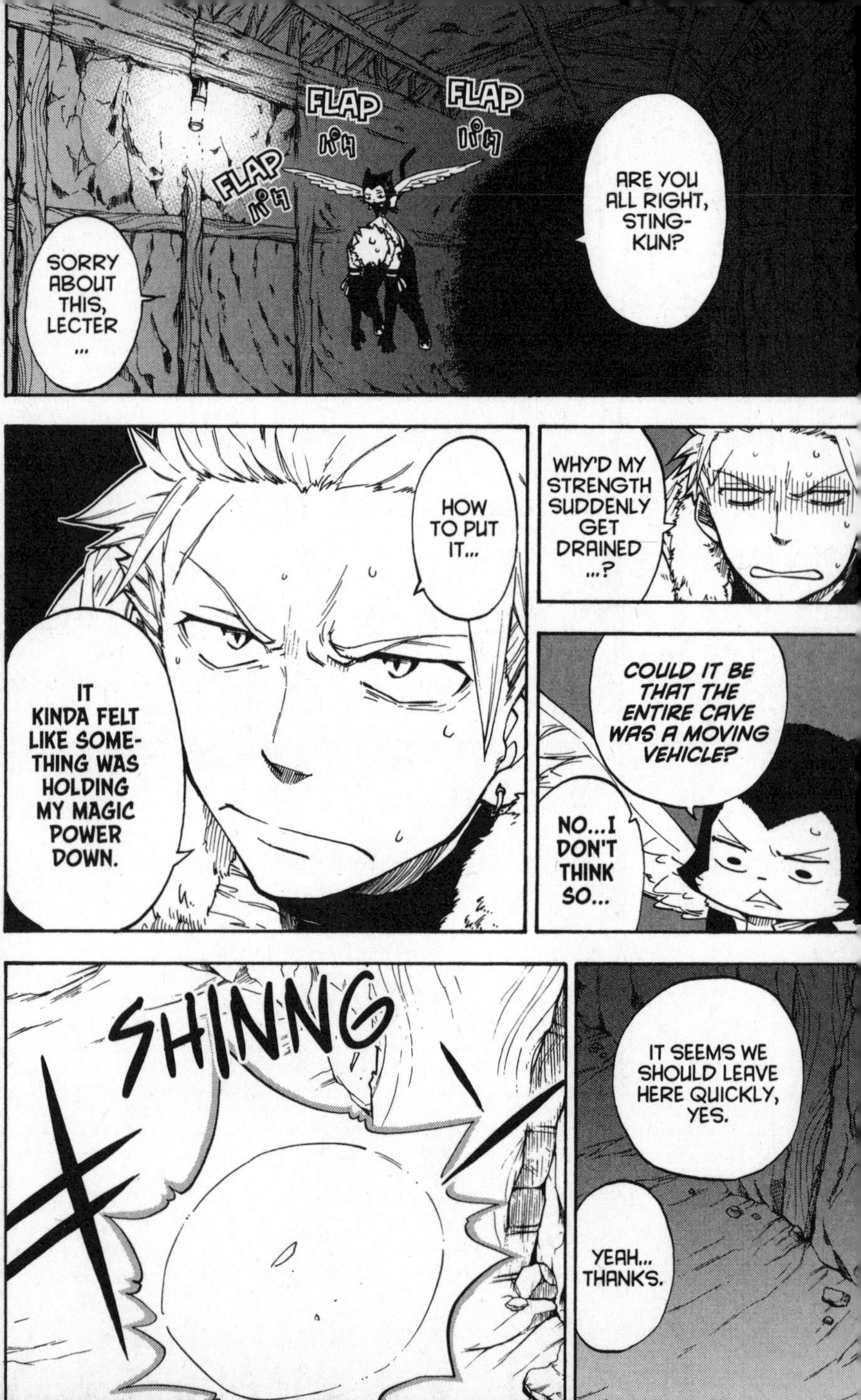
ARE YOU ALL RIGHT, STING-KUN?
FLAP
パタ
FLAP
パタ
FLAP
パタ
SORRY ABOUT THIS, LECTER ...
WHY'D MY STRENGTH SUDDENLY GET DRAINED ...?
COULD IT BE THAT THE ENTIRE CAVE WAS A MOVING VEHICLE?
NO...I DON'T THINK SO...
HOW TO PUT IT...
IT KINDA FELT LIKE SOME-THING WAS HOLDING MY MAGIC POWER DOWN.
IT SEEMS WE SHOULD LEAVE HERE QUICKLY, YES.
YEAH... THANKS.
SHINNG

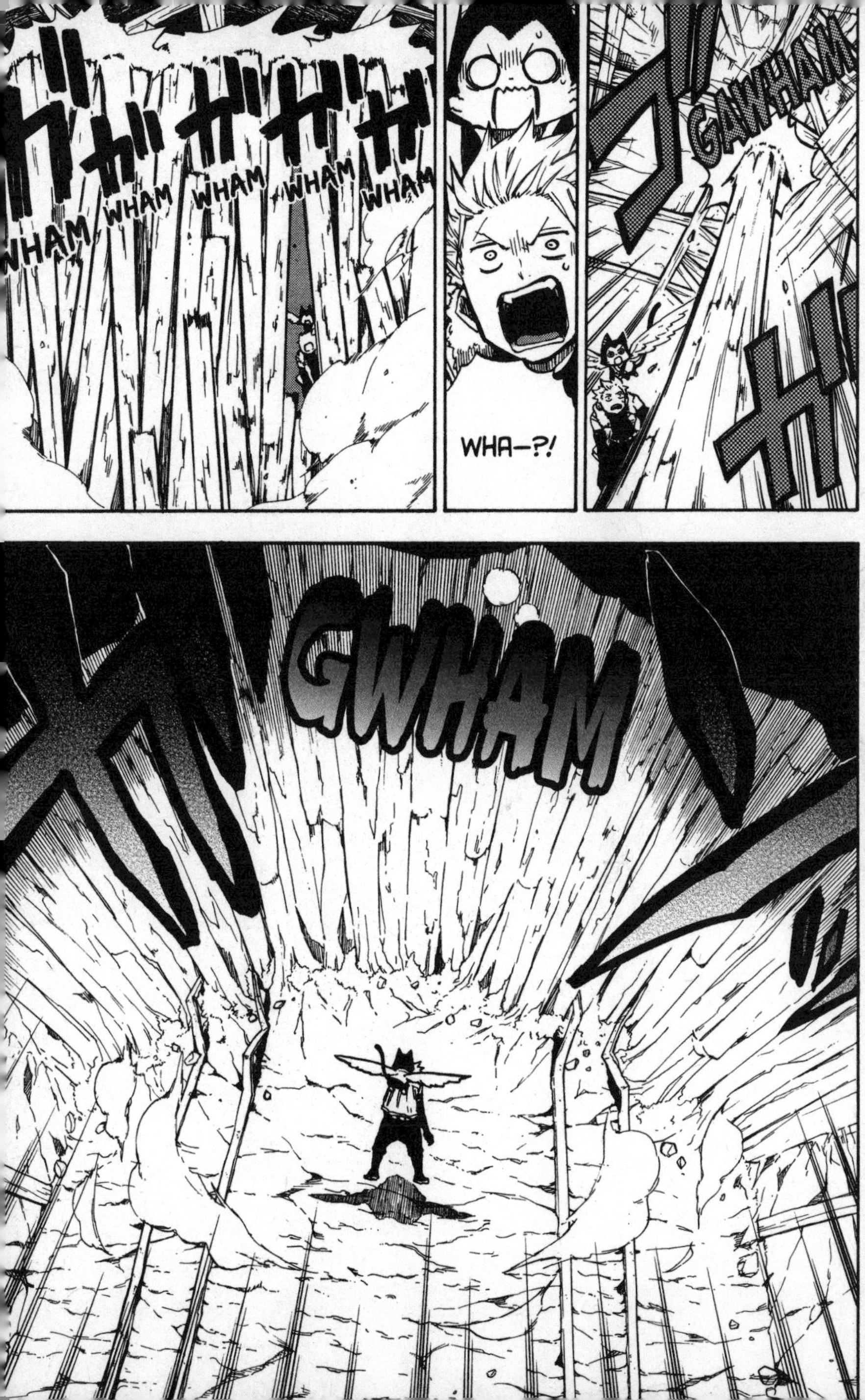

GAWHAM
WHA-?!
WHAM
WHAM
WHAM
WHAM
WHAM
GWHAM

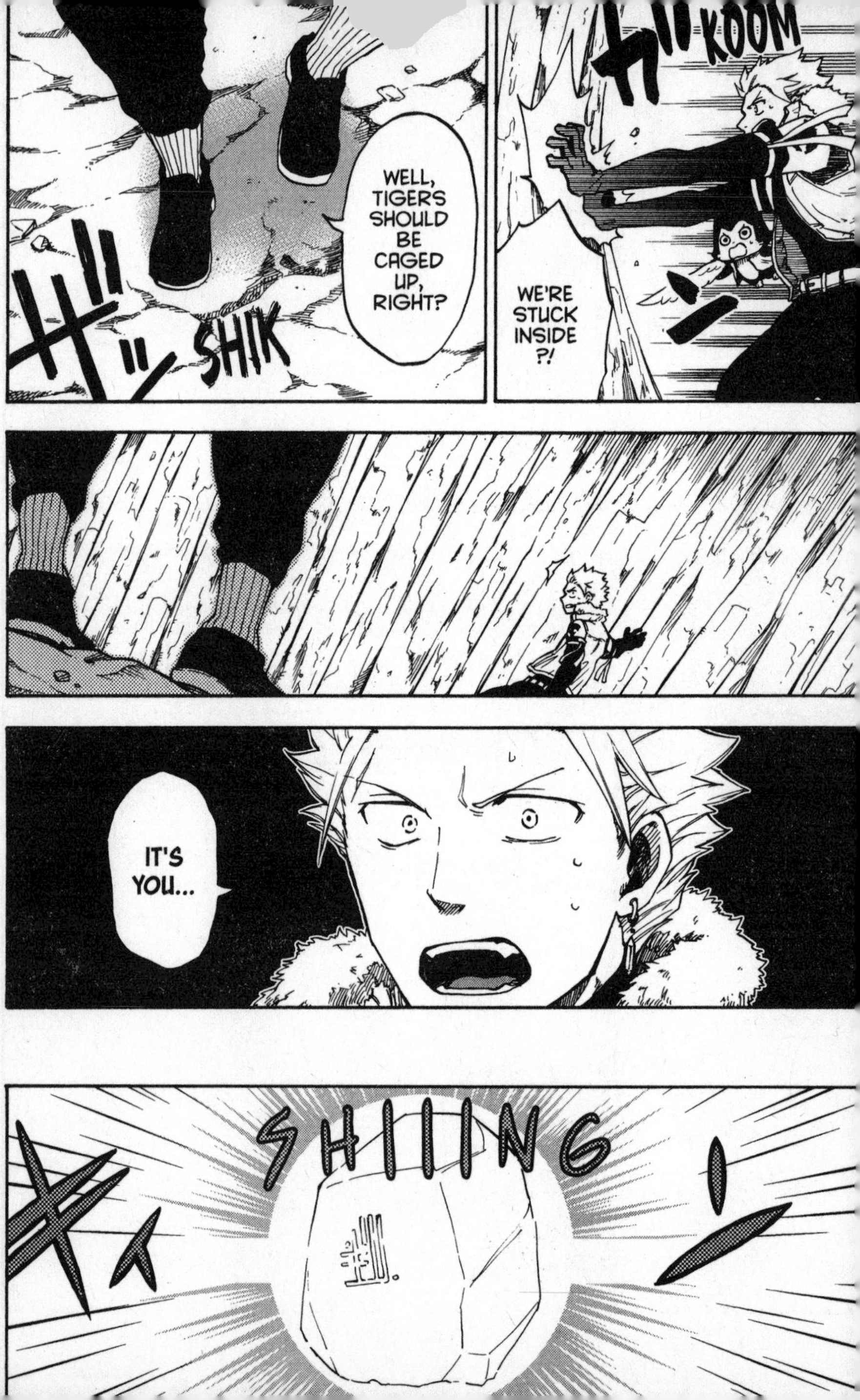
KOOM
WE'RE STUCK INSIDE?!
WELL, TIGERS SHOULD BE CAGED UP, RIGHT?
SHIK
IT'S YOU...
SHIIING

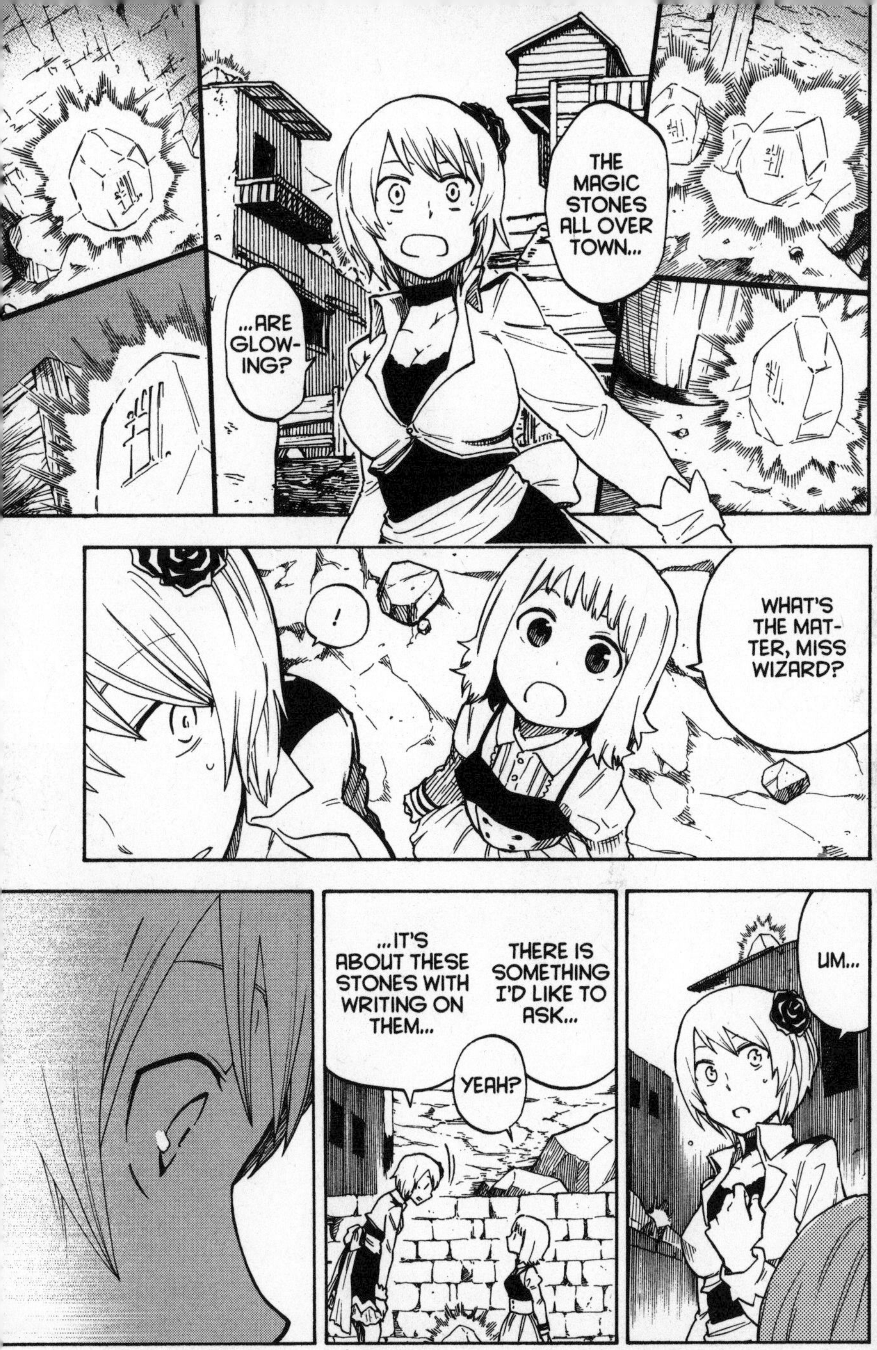
THE MAGIC STONES ALL OVER TOWN...
...ARE GLOWING?
WHAT'S THE MATTER, MISS WIZARD?
!
UM...
THERE IS SOMETHING I'D LIKE TO ASK...
...IT'S ABOUT THESE STONES WITH WRITING ON THEM...
YEAH?

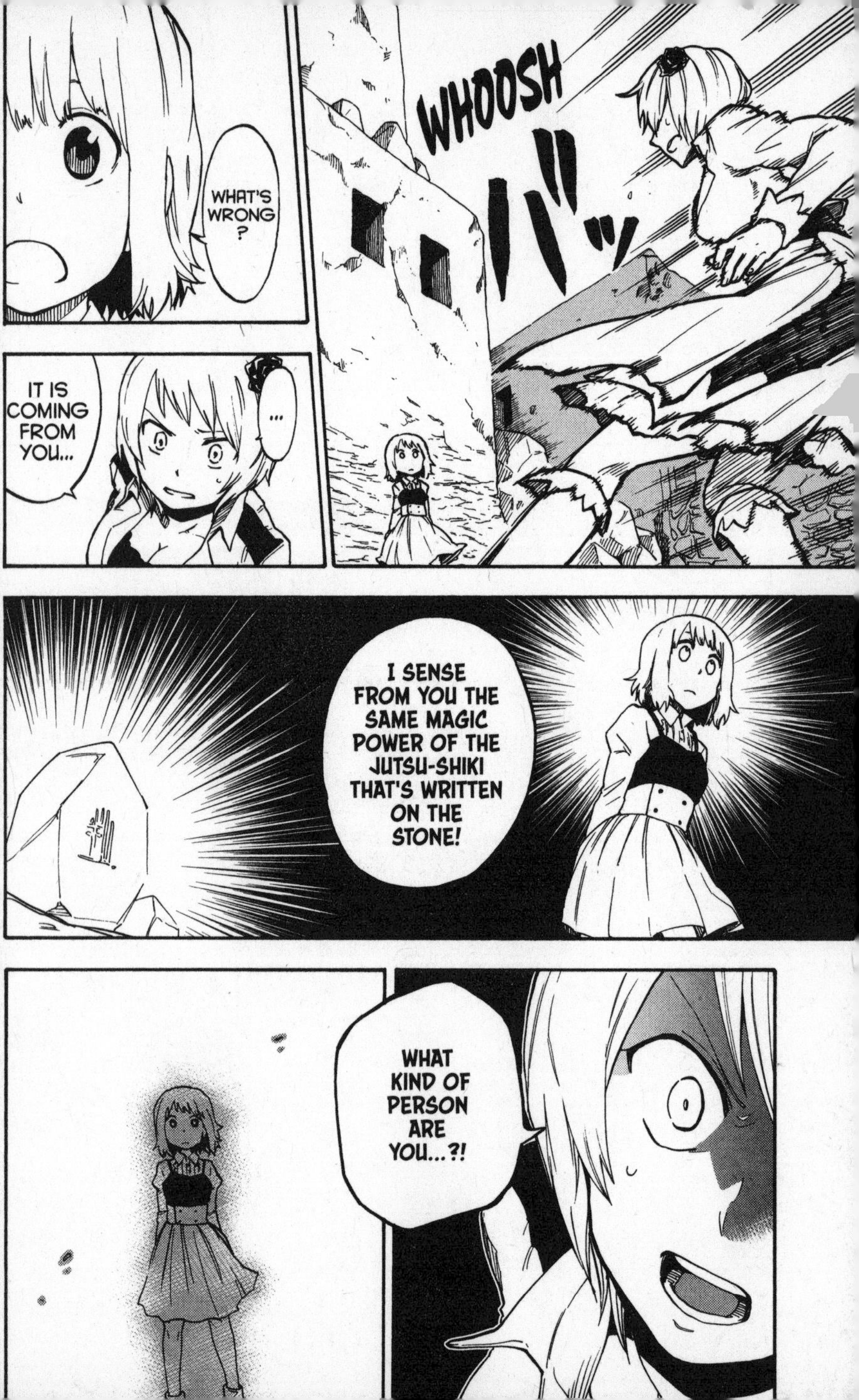
WHOOSH
バッ
WHAT'S WRONG?
...
IT IS COMING FROM YOU...
I SENSE FROM YOU THE SAME MAGIC POWER OF THE JUTSU-SHIKI THAT'S WRITTEN ON THE STONE!
WHAT KIND OF PERSON ARE YOU...?!

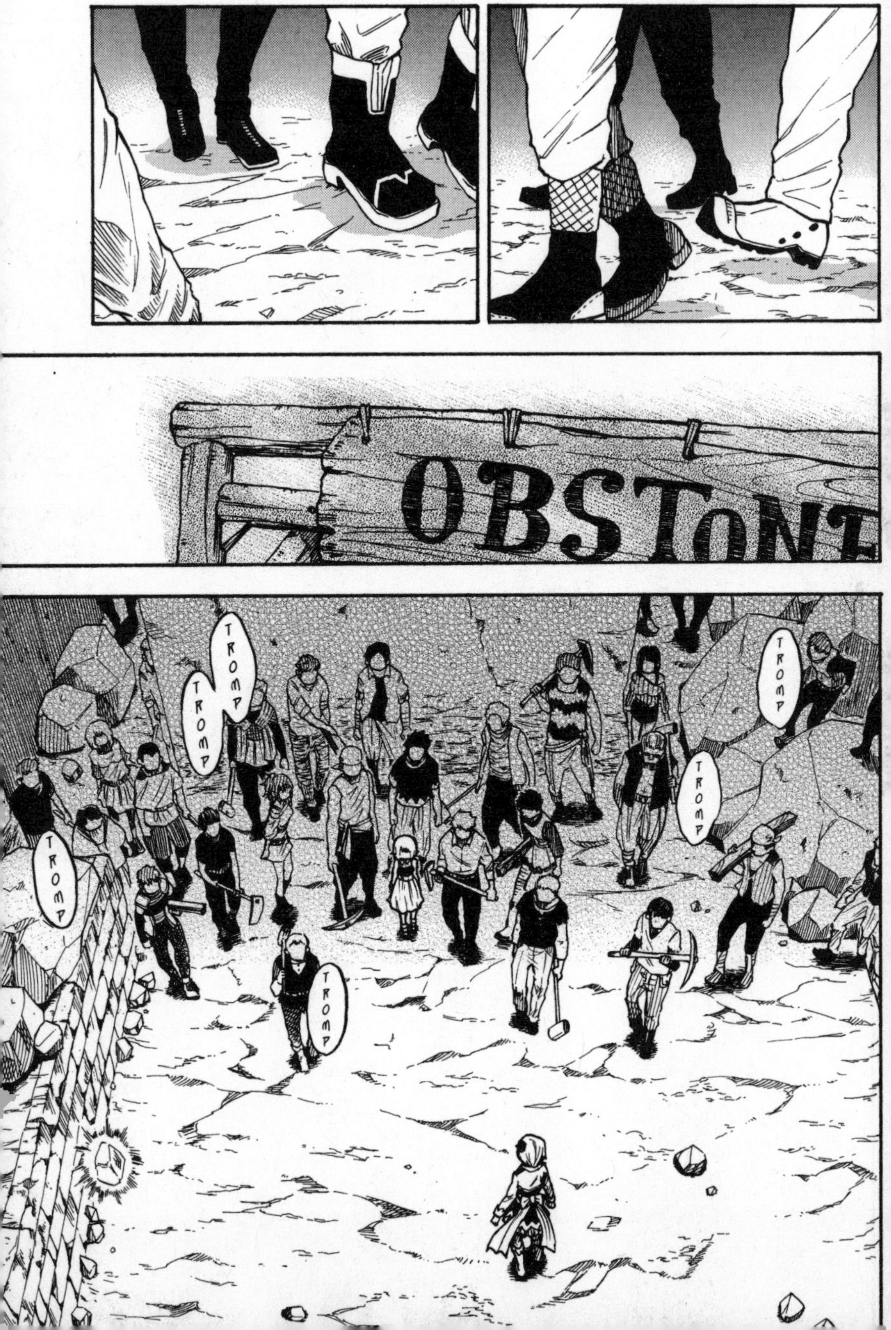
OBSTON
TROMP
TROMP
TROMP
TROMP
TROMP
TROMP

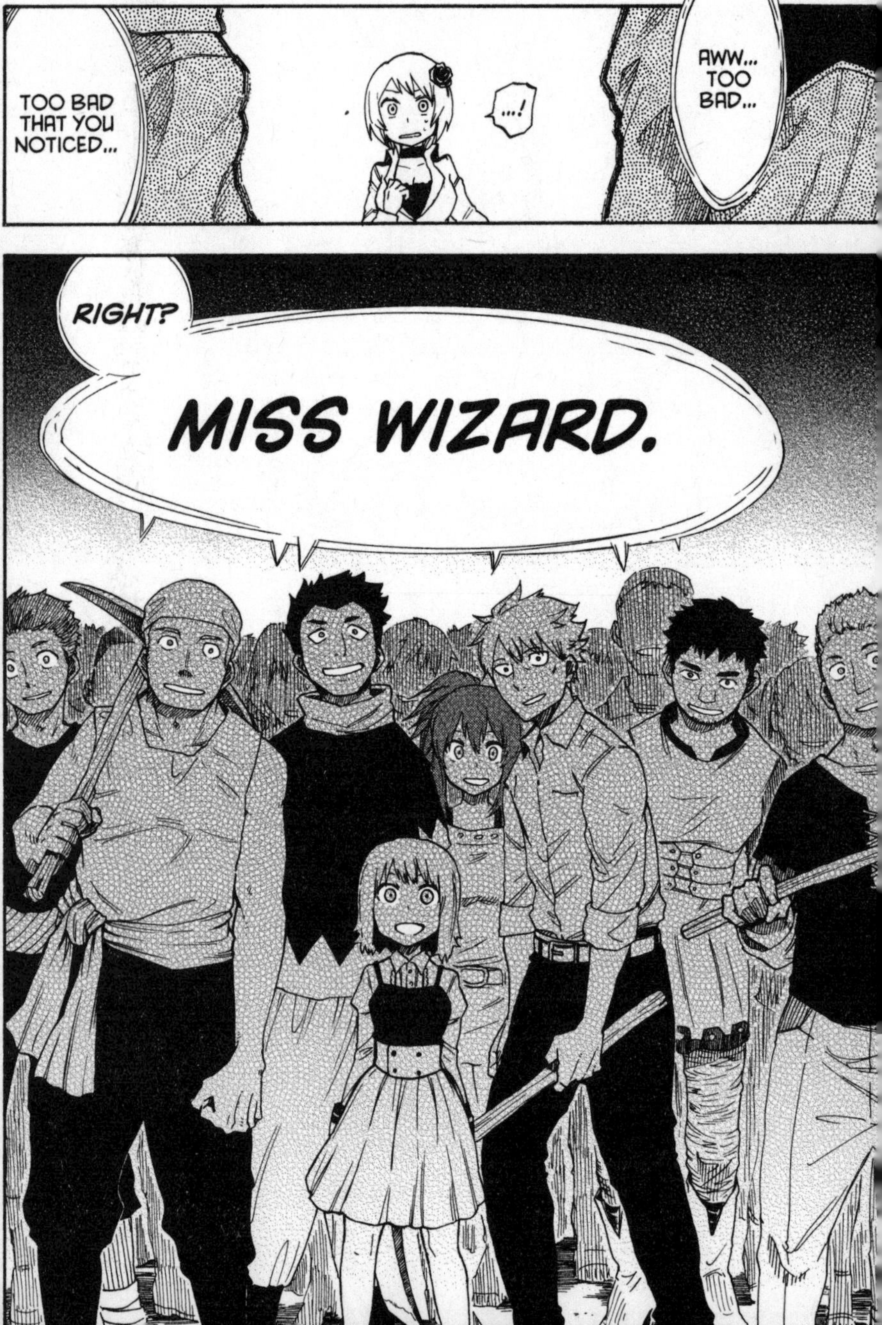
AWW... TOO BAD...
...!
TOO BAD THAT YOU NOTICED...
RIGHT?
MISS WIZARD.

FAIRYTAIL: TWIN DRAGONS OF SABER TOOTH

Chapter 8: The One Who Wants Dragon Power

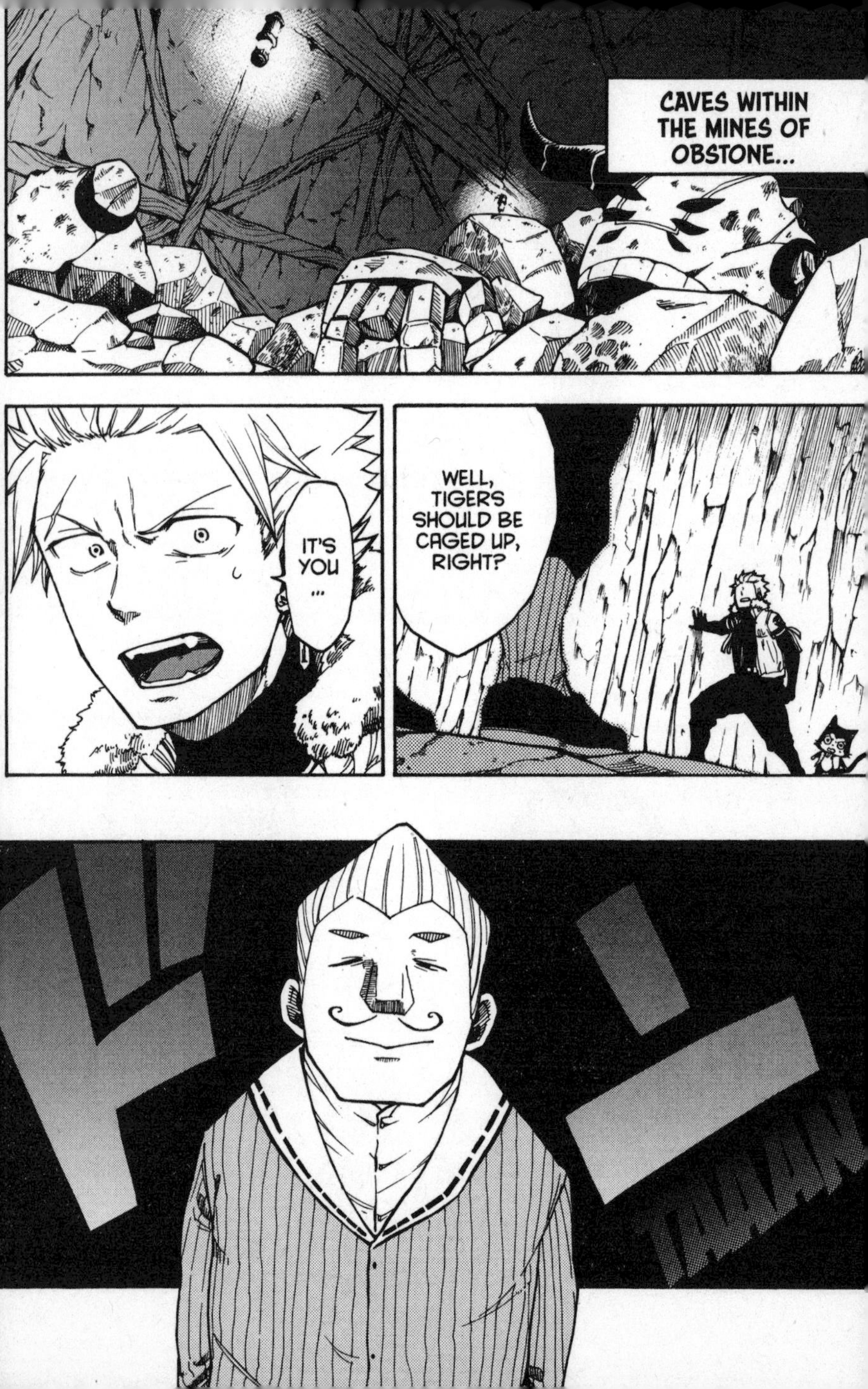
CAVES WITHIN THE MINES OF OBSTONE...
WELL, TIGERS SHOULD BE CAGED UP, RIGHT?
IT'S YOU ...

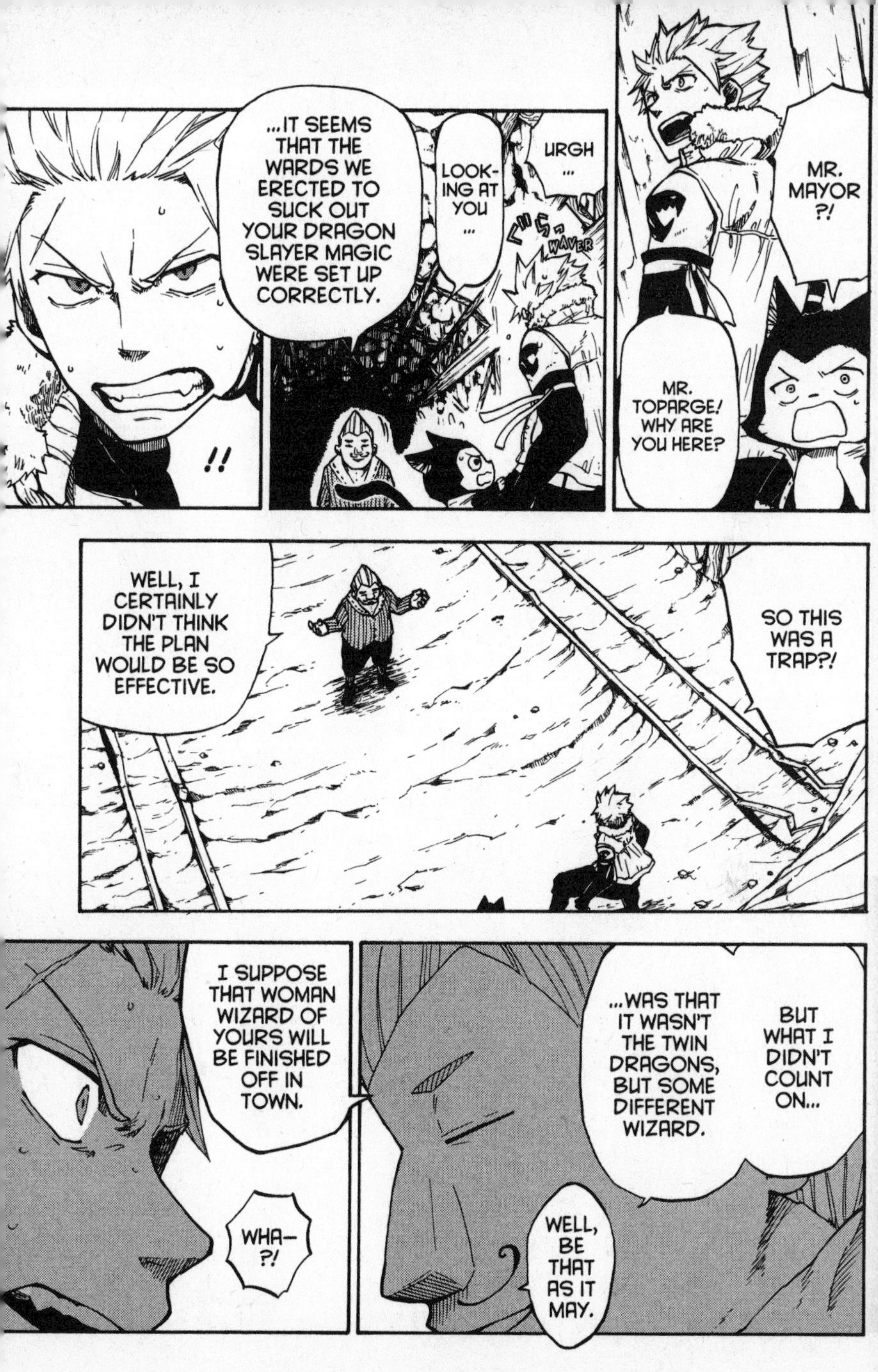
MR. MAYOR?!
MR. TOPARGE! WHY ARE YOU HERE?
URGH...
LOOKING AT YOU...
WAVER
...IT SEEMS THAT THE WARDS WE ERECTED TO SUCK OUT YOUR DRAGON SLAYER MAGIC WERE SET UP CORRECTLY.
!!
SO THIS WAS A TRAP?!
WELL, I CERTAINLY DIDN'T THINK THE PLAN WOULD BE SO EFFECTIVE.
BUT WHAT I DIDN'T COUNT ON...
...WAS THAT IT WASN'T THE TWIN DRAGONS, BUT SOME DIFFERENT WIZARD.
WELL, BE THAT AS IT MAY.
I SUPPOSE THAT WOMAN WIZARD OF YOURS WILL BE FINISHED OFF IN TOWN.
WHA—?!

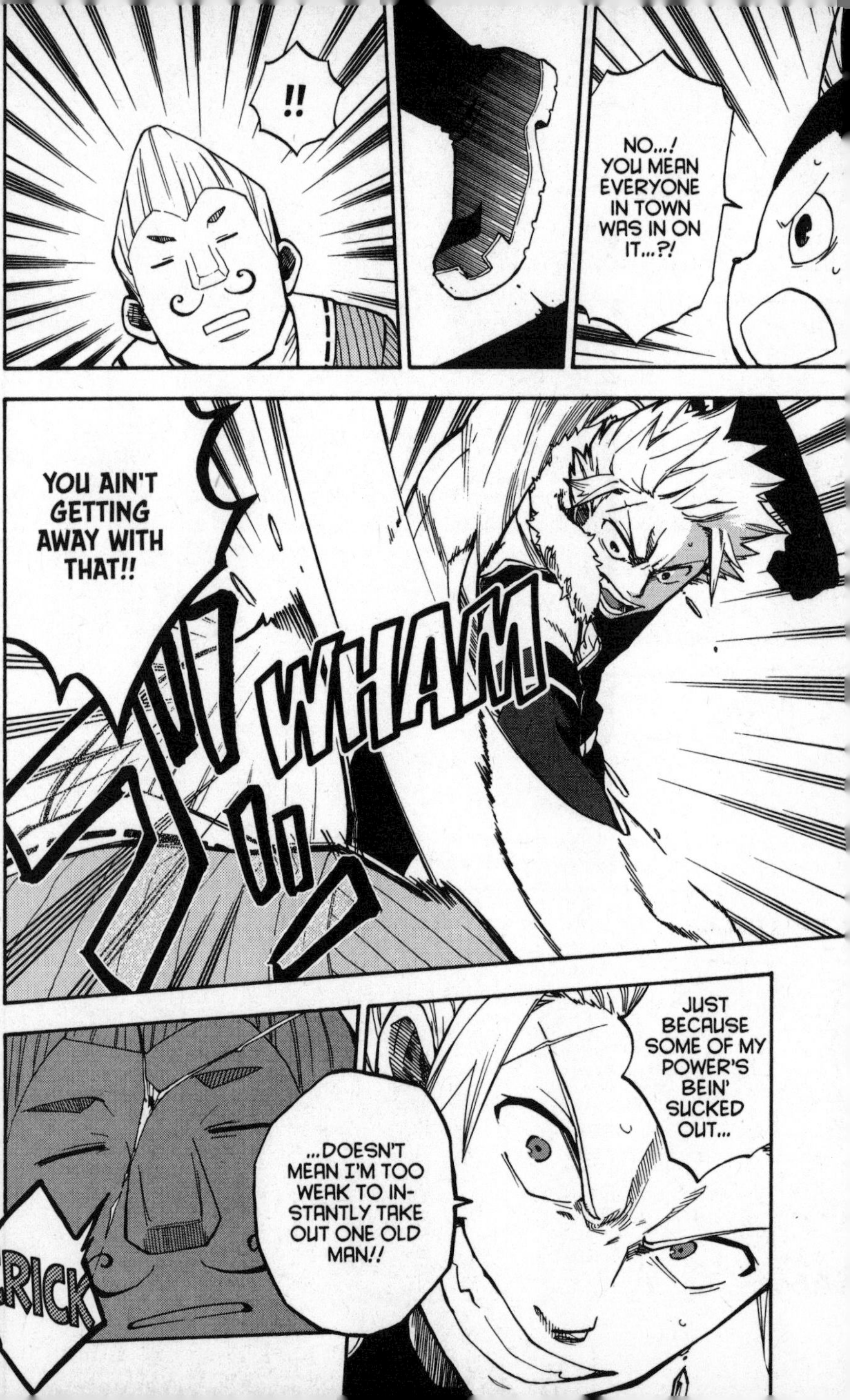
NO...! YOU MEAN EVERYONE IN TOWN WAS IN ON IT...?!
!!
YOU AIN'T GETTING AWAY WITH THAT!!
WHAM
JUST BECAUSE SOME OF MY POWER'S BEIN' SUCKED OUT...
...DOESN'T MEAN I'M TOO WEAK TO IN-STANTLY TAKE OUT ONE OLD MAN!!
CRICK

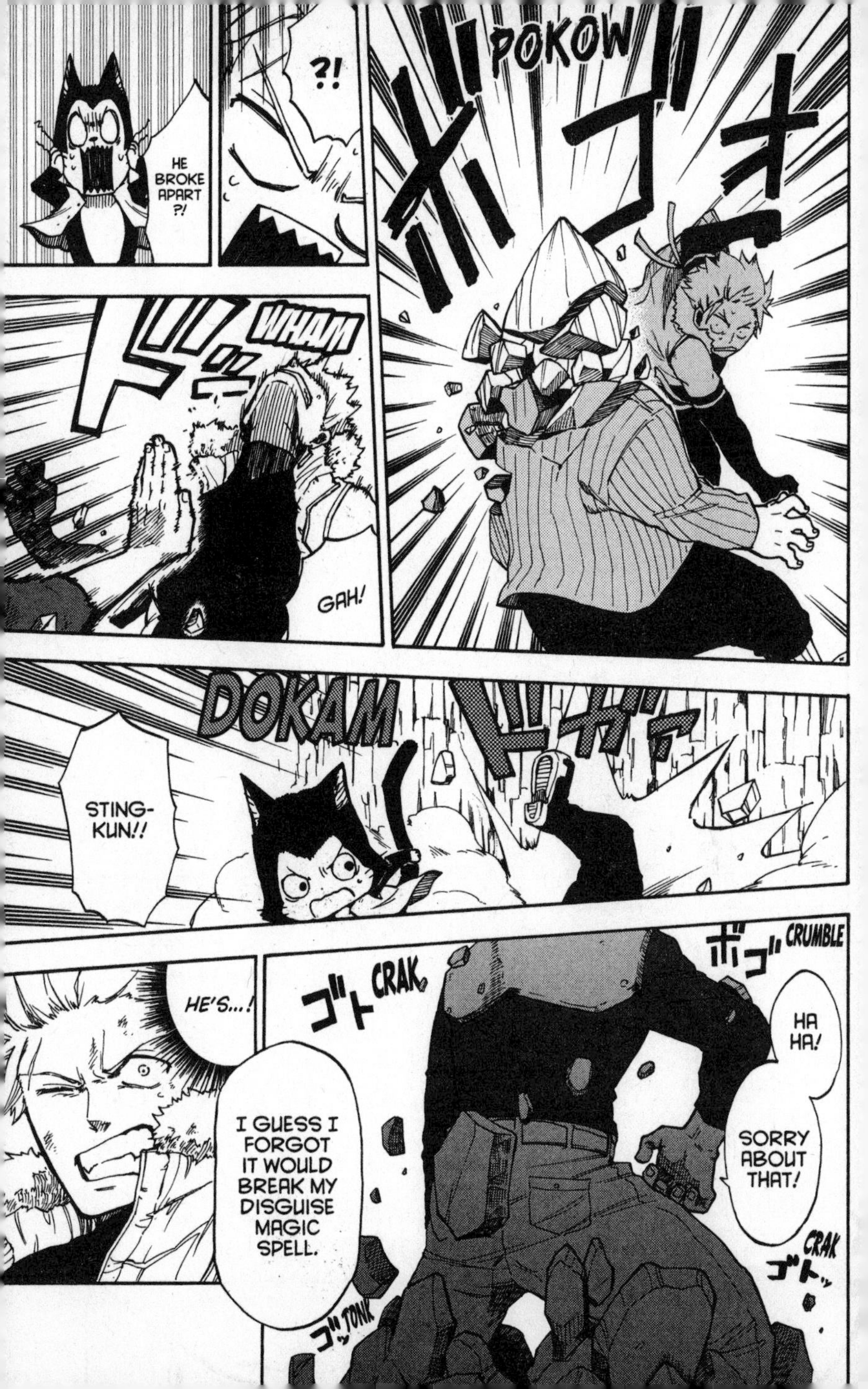
POKOW
?!
HE BROKE APART?!
WHAM
GAH!
DOKAM
STING-KUN!!
CRUMBLE
HA HA!
CRAK
SORRY ABOUT THAT!
I GUESS I FORGOT IT WOULD BREAK MY DISGUISE MAGIC SPELL.
CRAK
TONK
HE'S...!

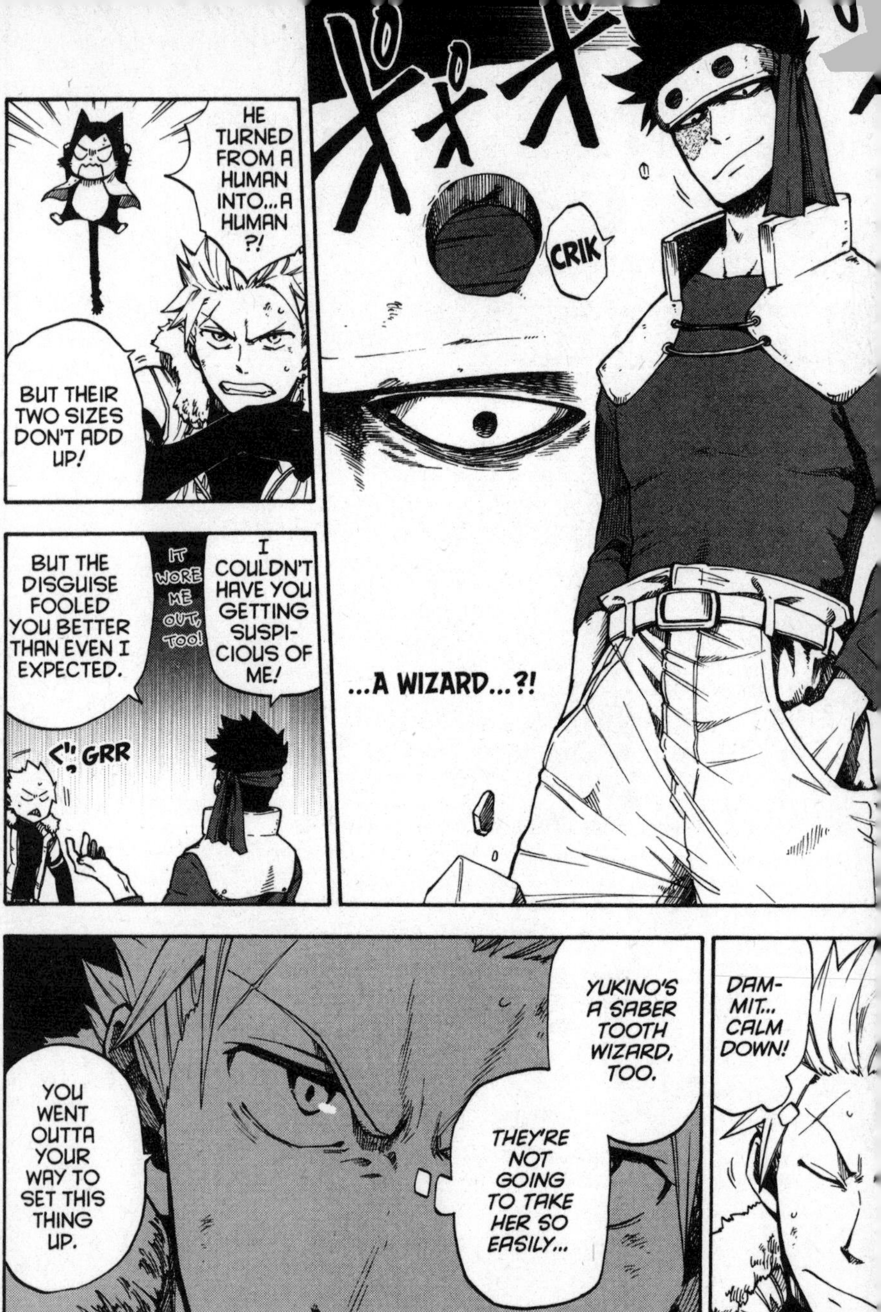
CRIK
...A WIZARD...?!
HE TURNED FROM A HUMAN INTO...A HUMAN?!
BUT THEIR TWO SIZES DON'T ADD UP!
I COULDN'T HAVE YOU GETTING SUSPICIOUS OF ME!
IT WORE ME OUT, TOO!
BUT THE DISGUISE FOOLED YOU BETTER THAN EVEN I EXPECTED.
GRR
DAMMIT... CALM DOWN!
YUKINO'S A SABER TOOTH WIZARD, TOO.
THEY'RE NOT GOING TO TAKE HER SO EASILY...
YOU WENT OUTTA YOUR WAY TO SET THIS THING UP.

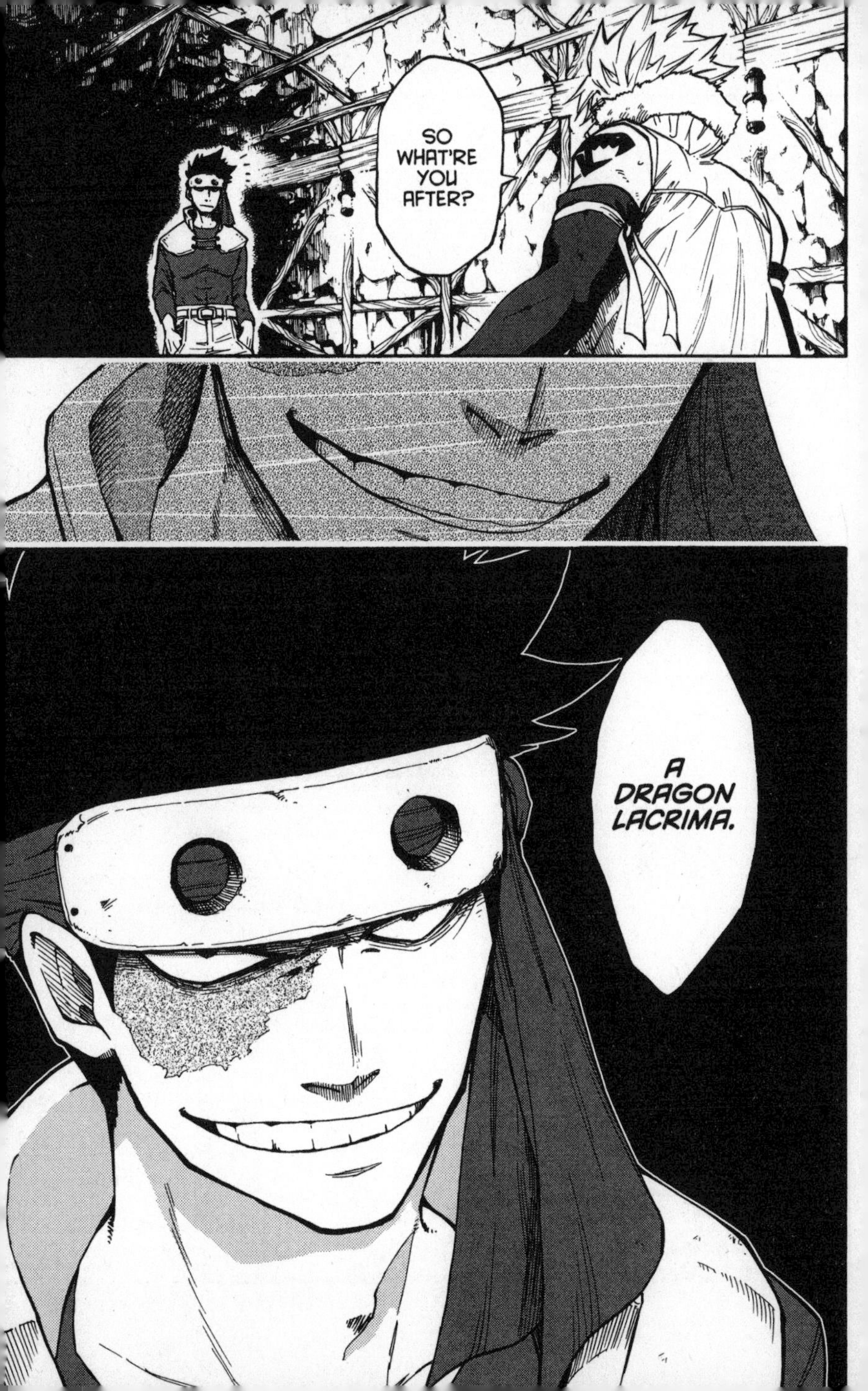
SO WHAT'RE YOU AFTER?
A DRAGON LACRIMA.

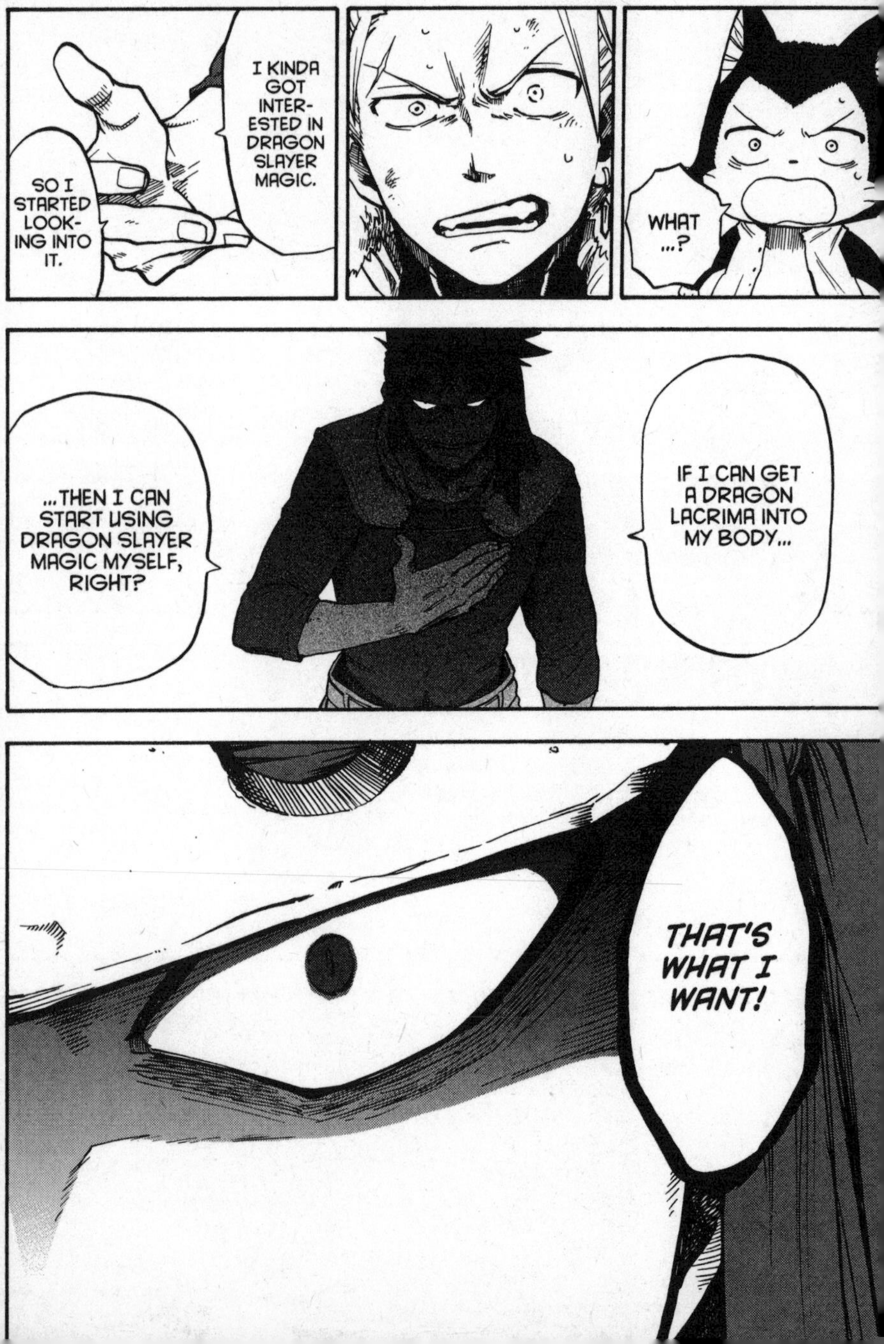
WHAT ...?
I KINDA GOT INTER-ESTED IN DRAGON SLAYER MAGIC.
SO I STARTED LOOK-ING INTO IT.
IF I CAN GET A DRAGON LACRIMA INTO MY BODY...
...THEN I CAN START USING DRAGON SLAYER MAGIC MYSELF, RIGHT?
THAT'S WHAT I WANT!

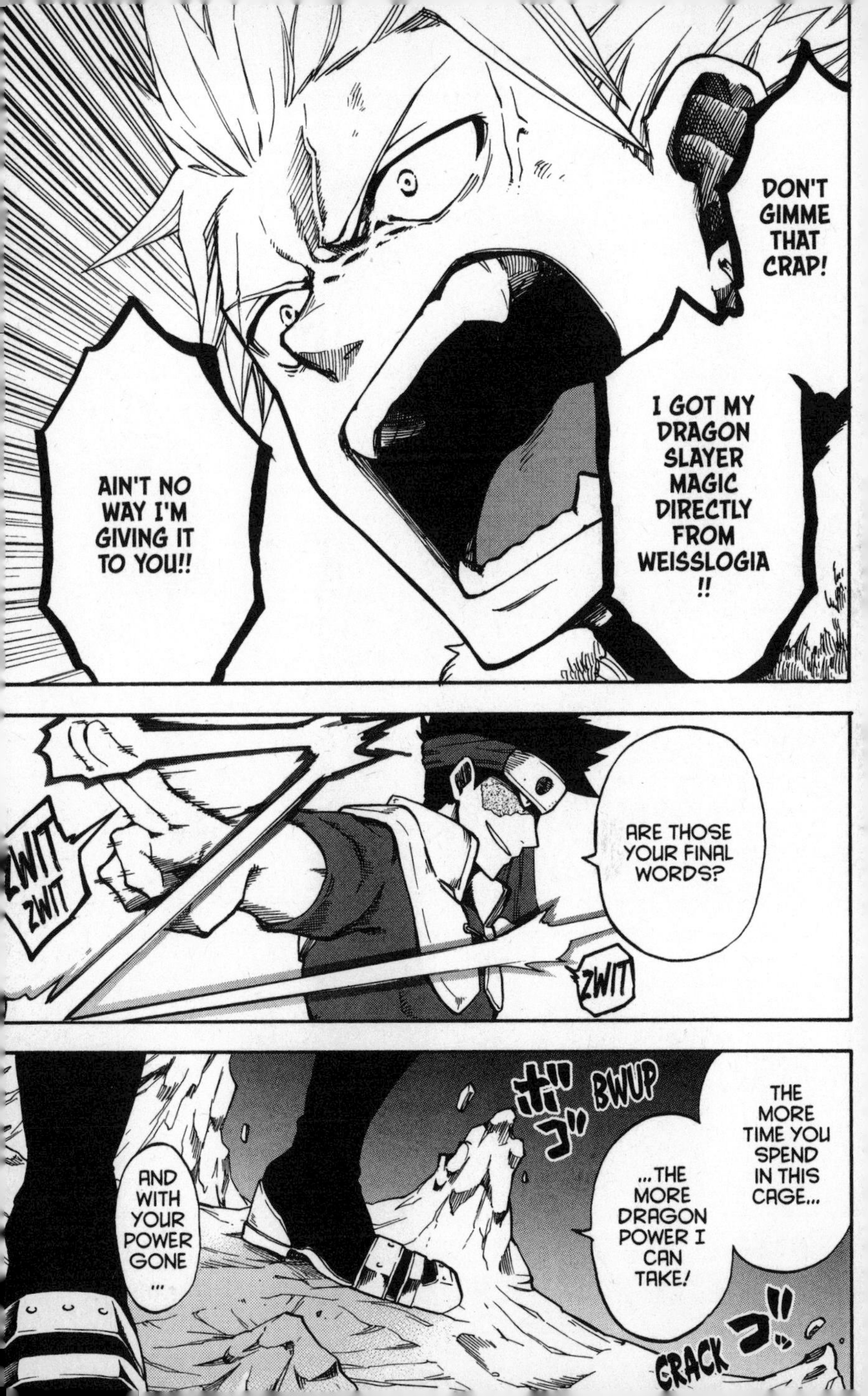
DON'T GIMME THAT CRAP!
I GOT MY DRAGON SLAYER MAGIC DIRECTLY FROM WEISSLOGIA !!
AIN'T NO WAY I'M GIVING IT TO YOU!!
ARE THOSE YOUR FINAL WORDS?
ZWIT
ZWIT ZWIT
BWUP
THE MORE TIME YOU SPEND IN THIS CAGE...
...THE MORE DRAGON POWER I CAN TAKE!
AND WITH YOUR POWER GONE ...
CRACK

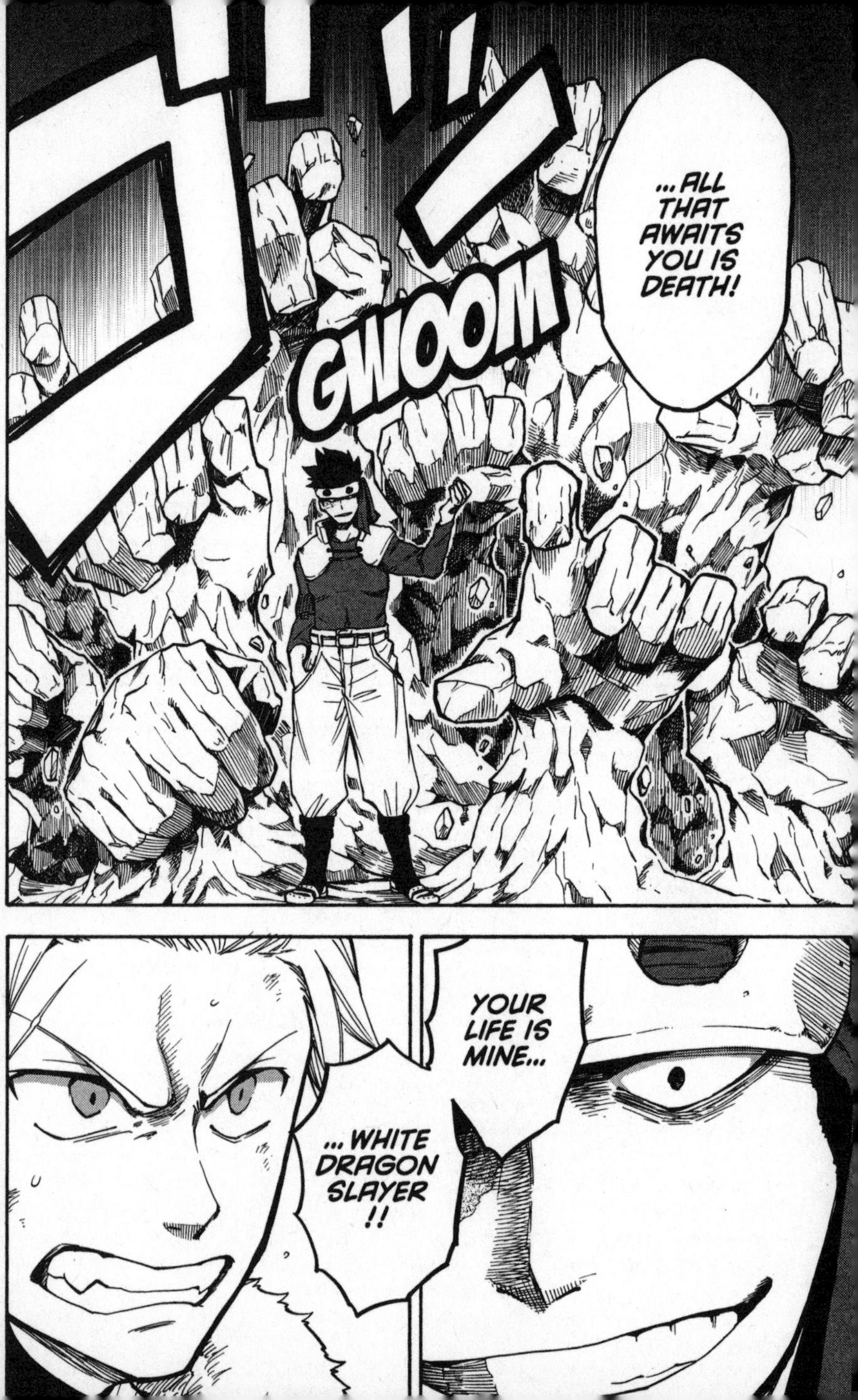
...ALL THAT AWAITS YOU IS DEATH!
GWOOM
YOUR LIFE IS MINE...
...WHITE DRAGON SLAYER !!

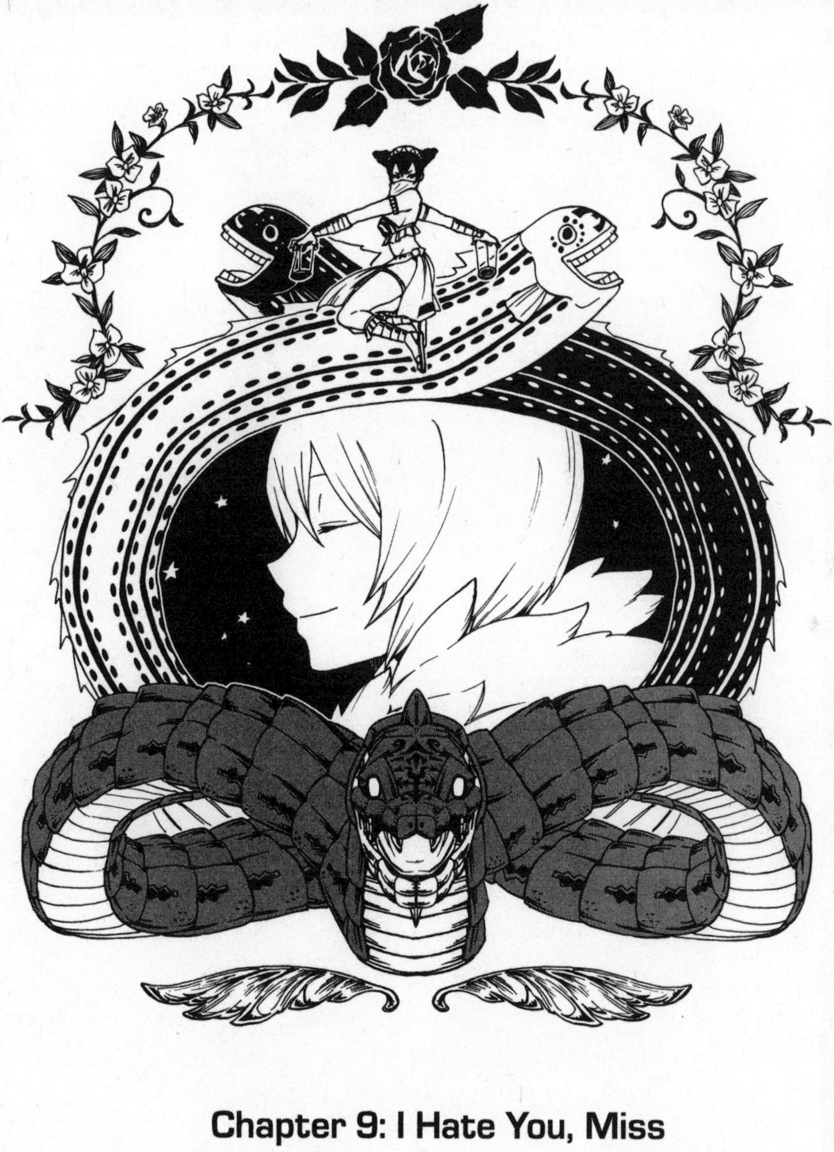

Chapter 9: I Hate You, Miss

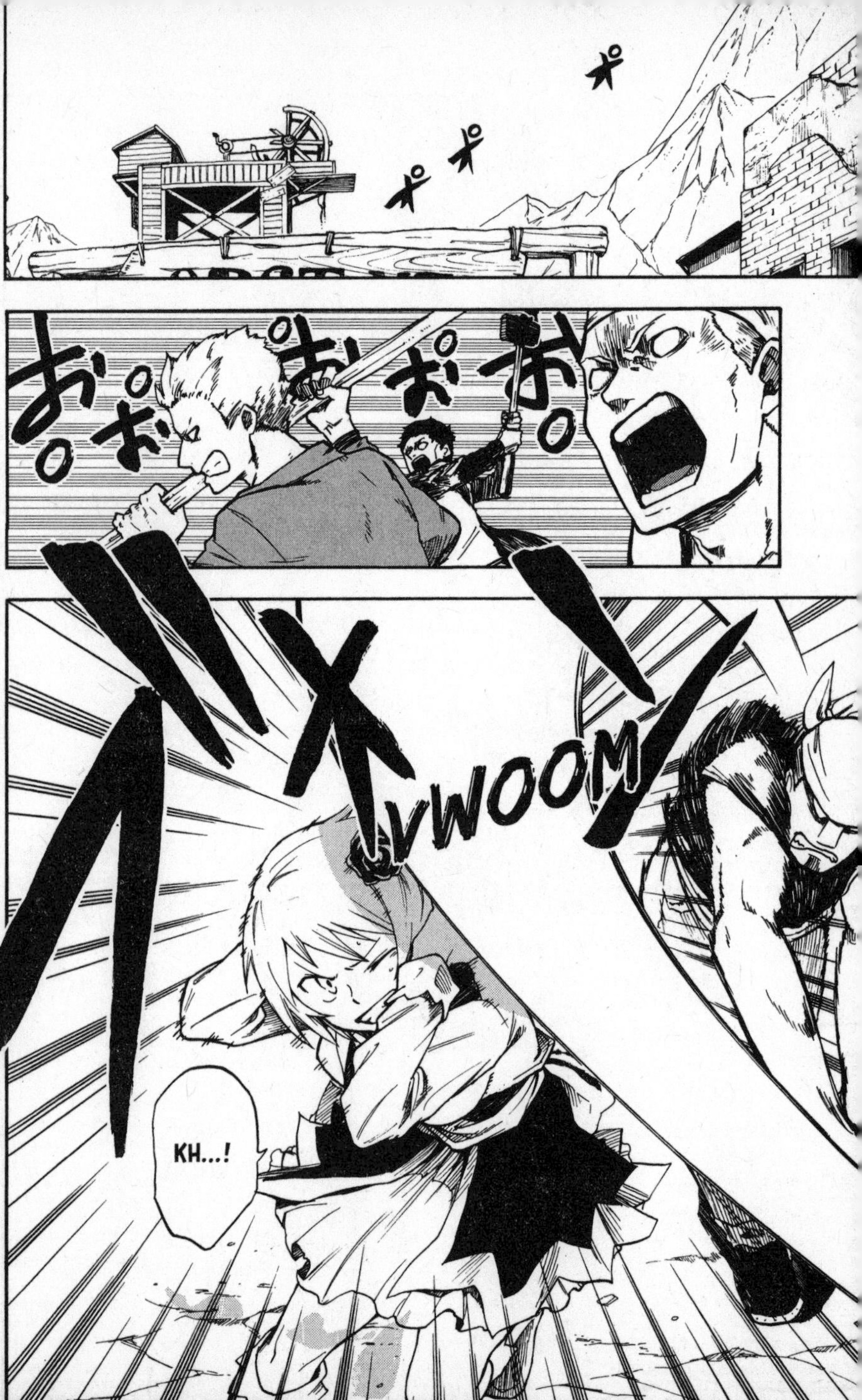
ポ
ポ
ポ
VWOOM
KH...!

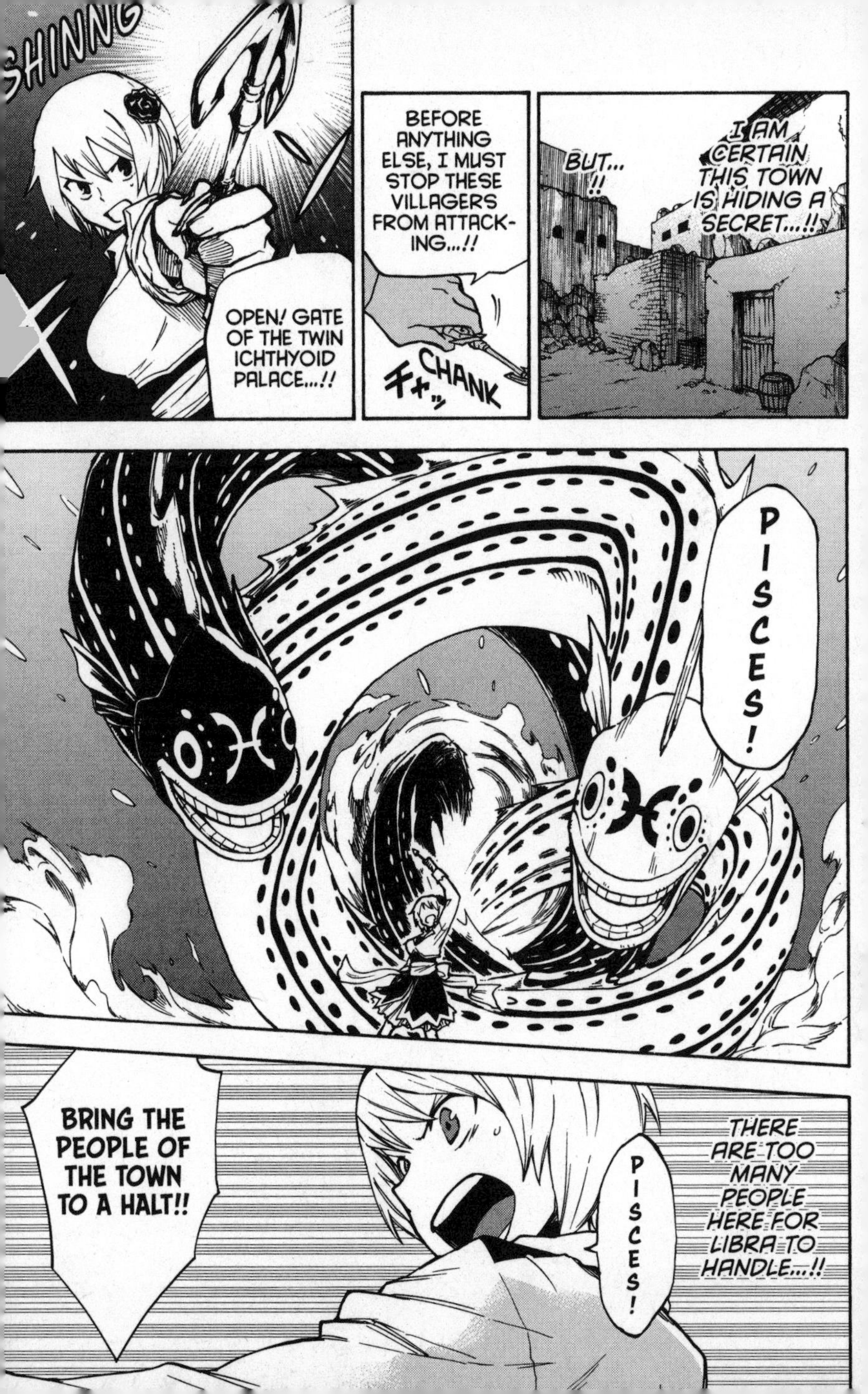
I AM CERTAIN THIS TOWN IS HIDING A SECRET...!!
BUT...!!
BEFORE ANYTHING ELSE, I MUST STOP THESE VILLAGERS FROM ATTACKING...!!
CHANK
チャッ
SHINNG
OPEN! GATE OF THE TWIN ICHTHYOID PALACE...!!
PISCES!
THERE ARE TOO MANY PEOPLE HERE FOR LIBRA TO HANDLE...!!
PISCES!
BRING THE PEOPLE OF THE TOWN TO A HALT!!

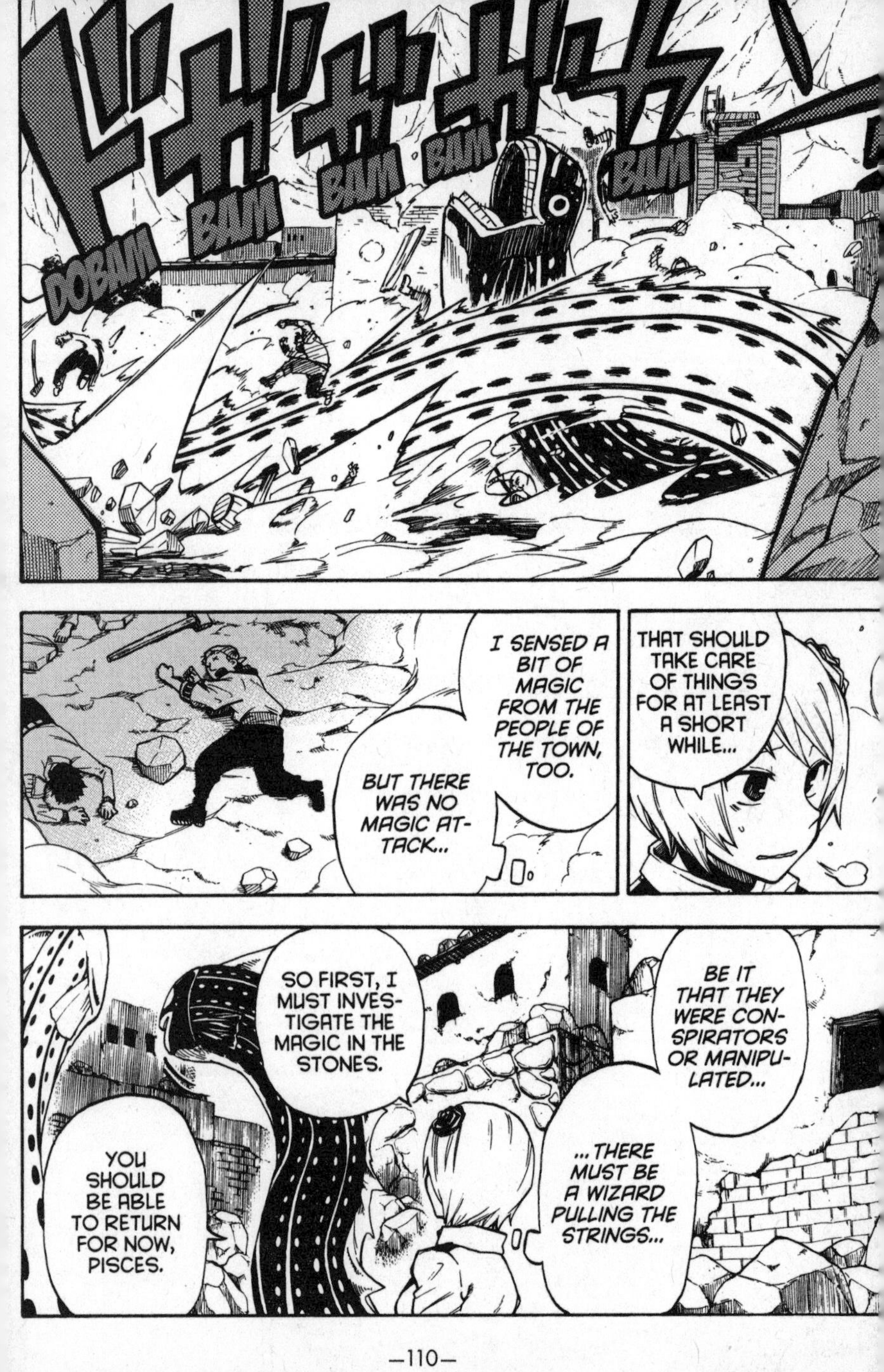
DOBAM BAM BAM BAM BAM
THAT SHOULD TAKE CARE OF THINGS FOR AT LEAST A SHORT WHILE...
I SENSED A BIT OF MAGIC FROM THE PEOPLE OF THE TOWN, TOO.
BUT THERE WAS NO MAGIC ATTACK...
BE IT THAT THEY WERE CONSPIRATORS OR MANIPULATED...
...THERE MUST BE A WIZARD PULLING THE STRINGS...
SO FIRST, I MUST INVESTIGATE THE MAGIC IN THE STONES.
YOU SHOULD BE ABLE TO RETURN FOR NOW, PISCES.

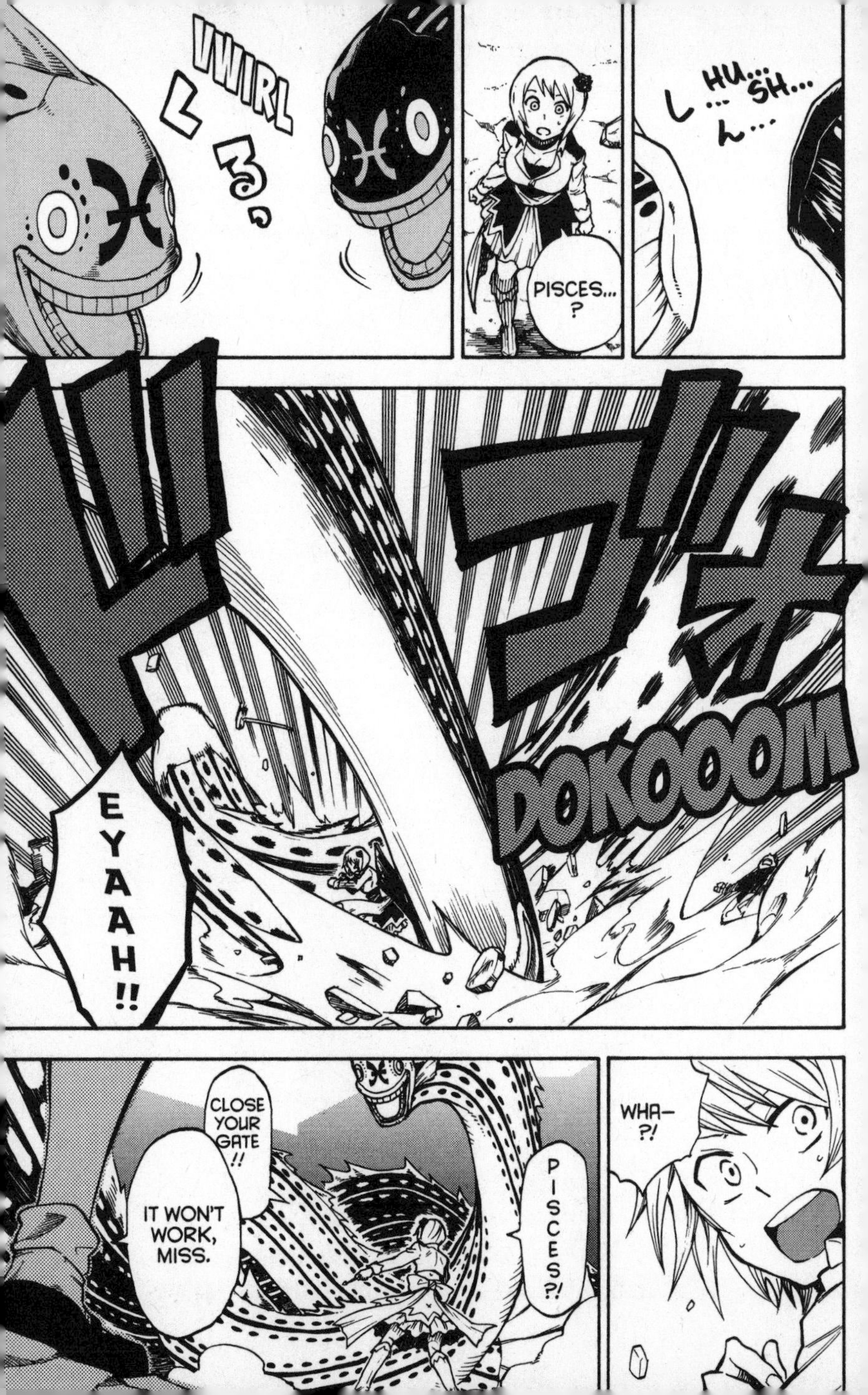

HU... SH...
し… ん…
PISCES... ?
VWIRL
くるっ
DOKOOOM
EYAAH!!
WHA— ?!
PISCES?!
CLOSE YOUR GATE!!
IT WON'T WORK, MISS.

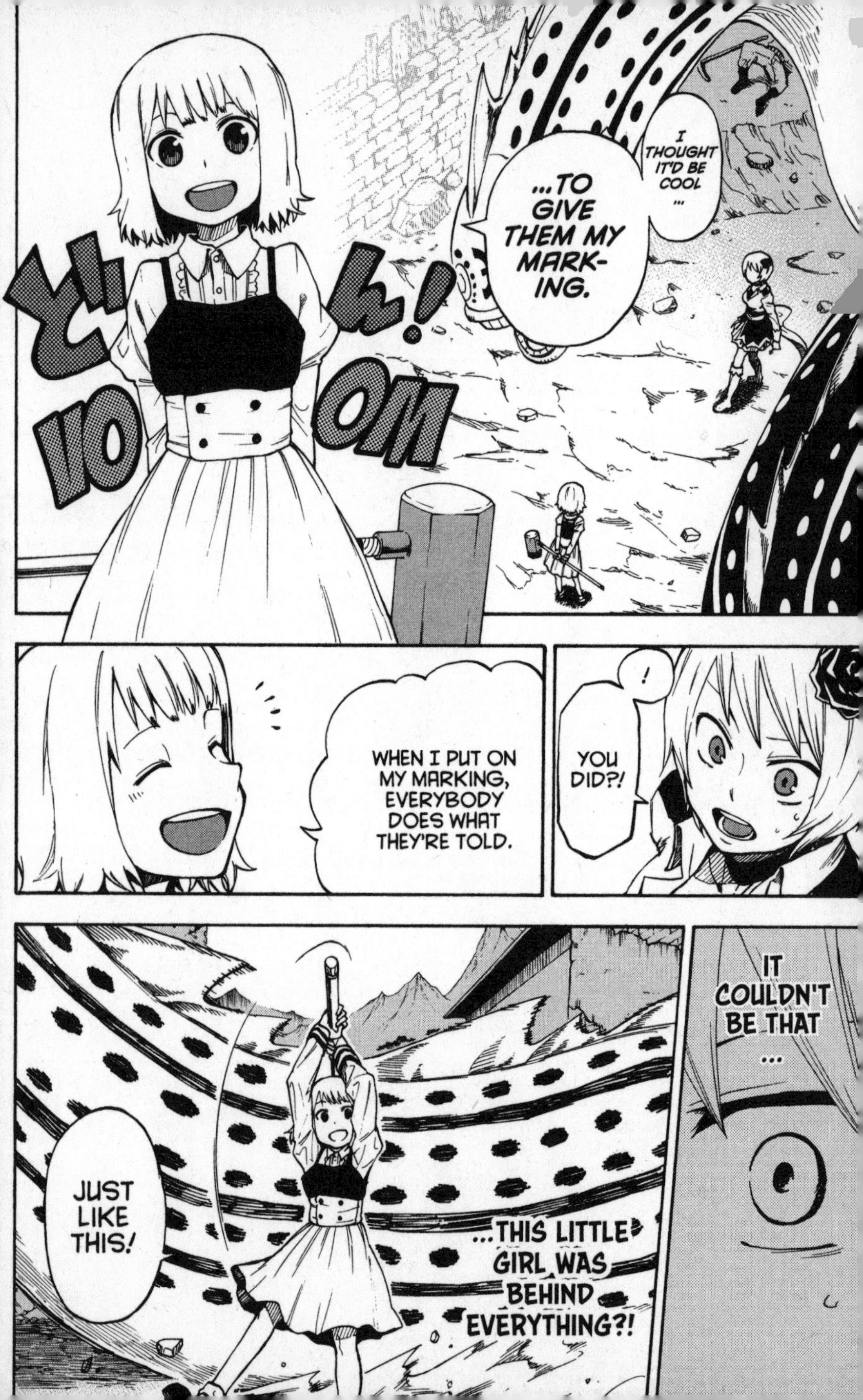
I THOUGHT IT'D BE COOL ...
...TO GIVE THEM MY MARKING.
どん!
!
YOU DID?!
WHEN I PUT ON MY MARKING, EVERYBODY DOES WHAT THEY'RE TOLD.
IT COULDN'T BE THAT ...
...THIS LITTLE GIRL WAS BEHIND EVERYTHING?!
JUST LIKE THIS!

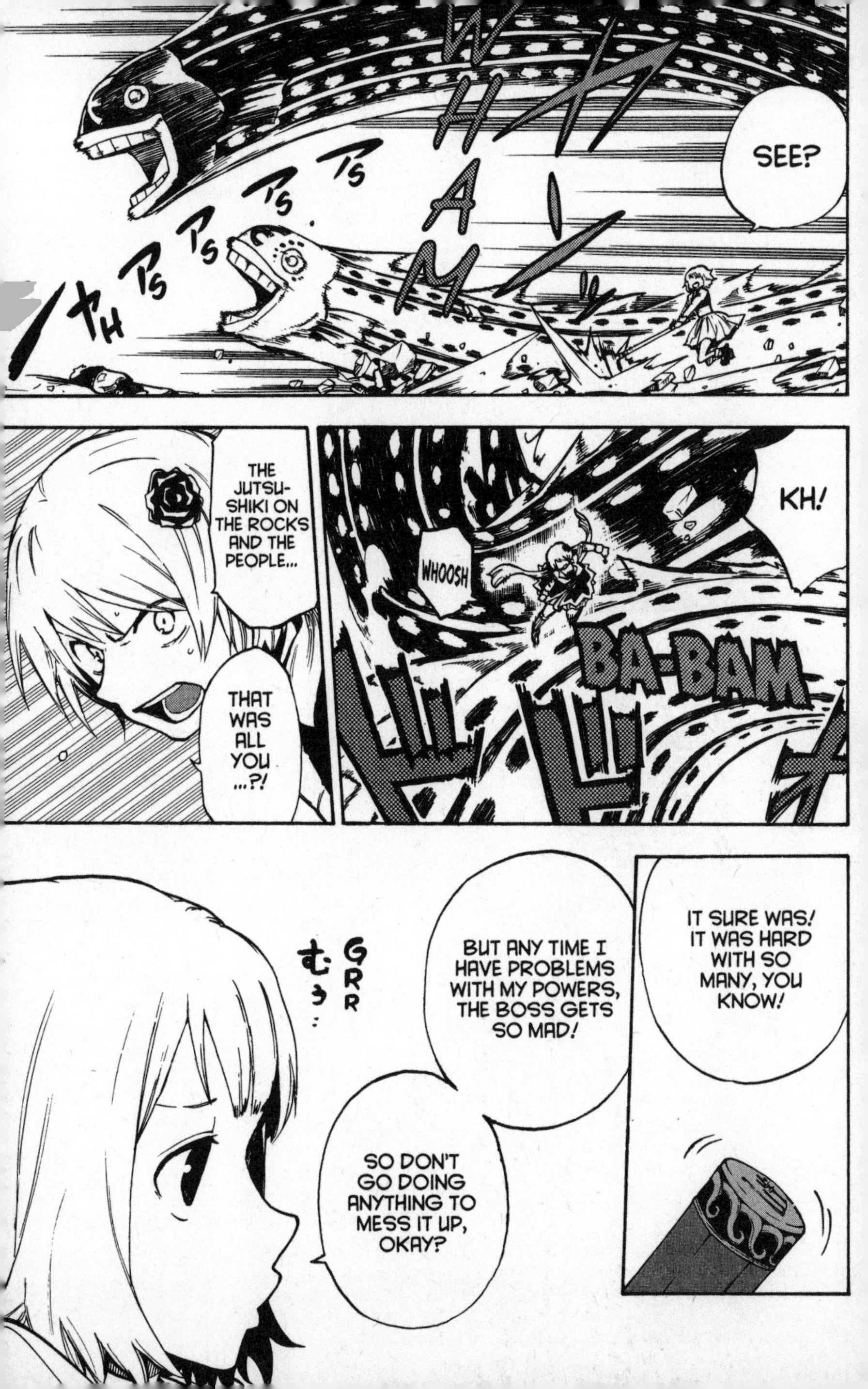
SEE?
WHAM
KH!
WHOOSH
BA-BAM
THE JUTSU-SHIKI ON THE ROCKS AND THE PEOPLE...
THAT WAS ALL YOU ...?!
IT SURE WAS! IT WAS HARD WITH SO MANY, YOU KNOW!
BUT ANY TIME I HAVE PROBLEMS WITH MY POWERS, THE BOSS GETS SO MAD!
GRR
むぅ
SO DON'T GO DOING ANYTHING TO MESS IT UP, OKAY?

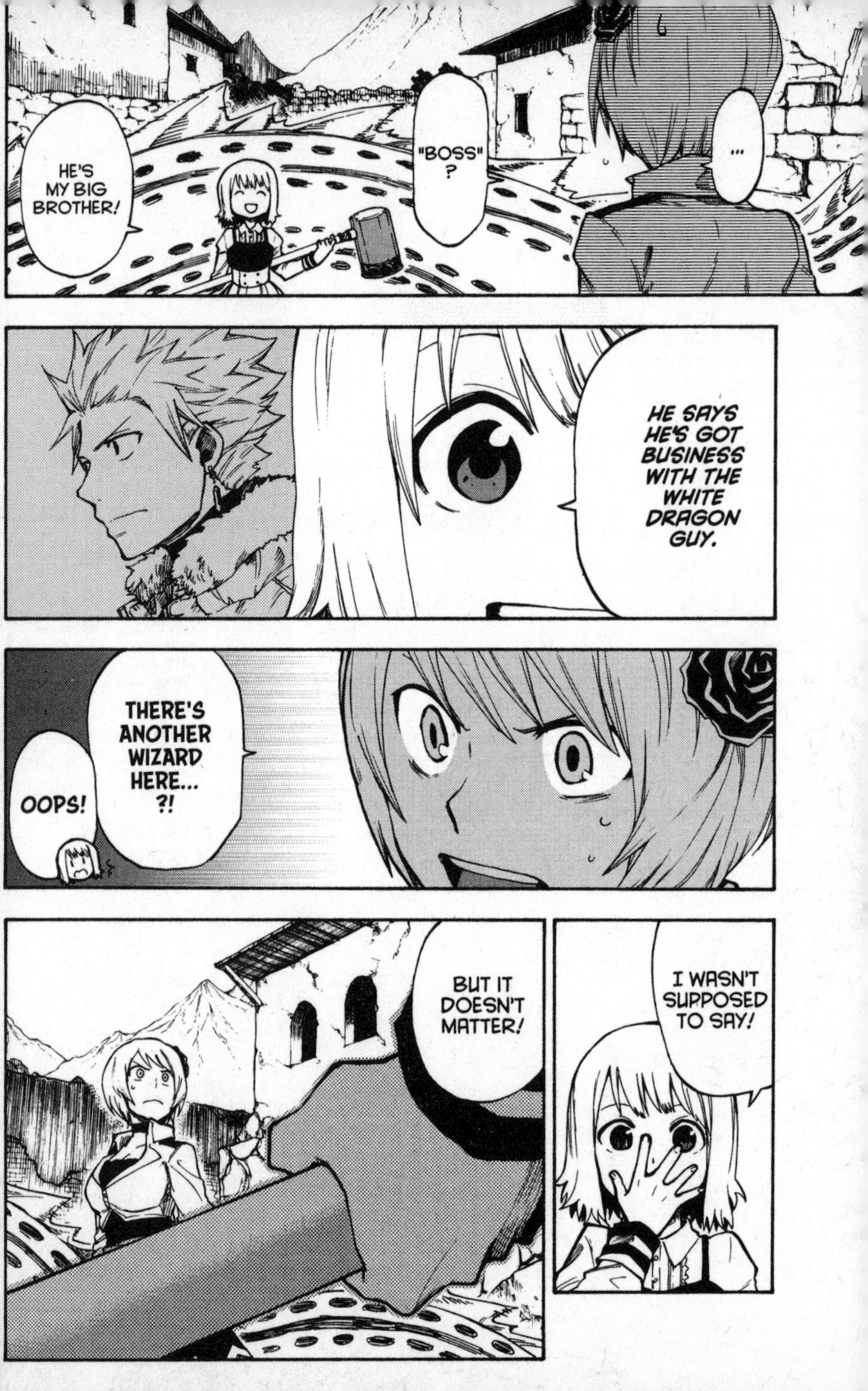
...
"BOSS"?
HE'S MY BIG BROTHER!
HE SAYS HE'S GOT BUSINESS WITH THE WHITE DRAGON GUY.
THERE'S ANOTHER WIZARD HERE...?!
OOPS!
I WASN'T SUPPOSED TO SAY!
BUT IT DOESN'T MATTER!

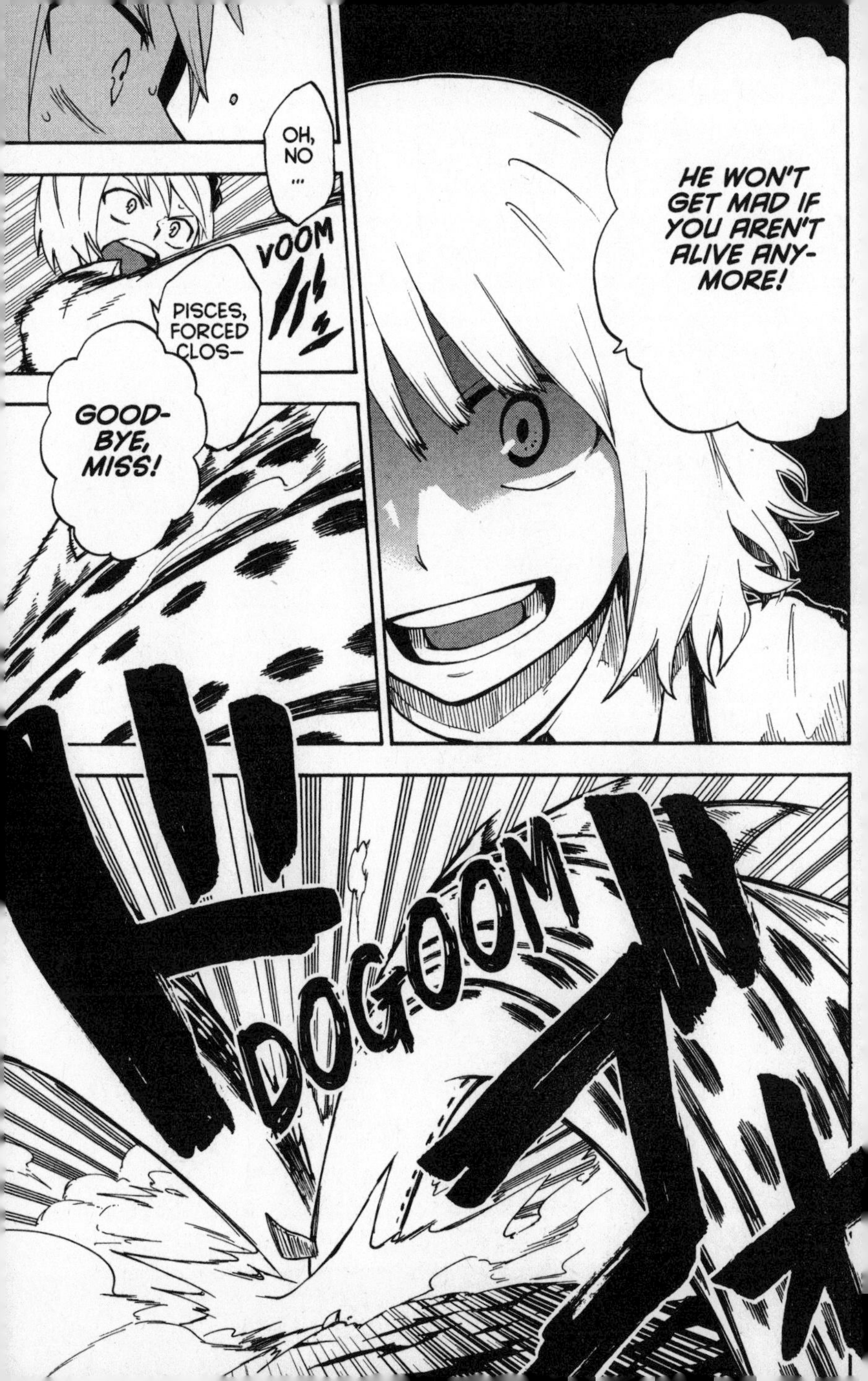
HE WON'T GET MAD IF YOU AREN'T ALIVE ANY-MORE!
OH, NO ...
VOOM
PISCES, FORCED CLOS—
GOOD-BYE, MISS!
DOGOOM

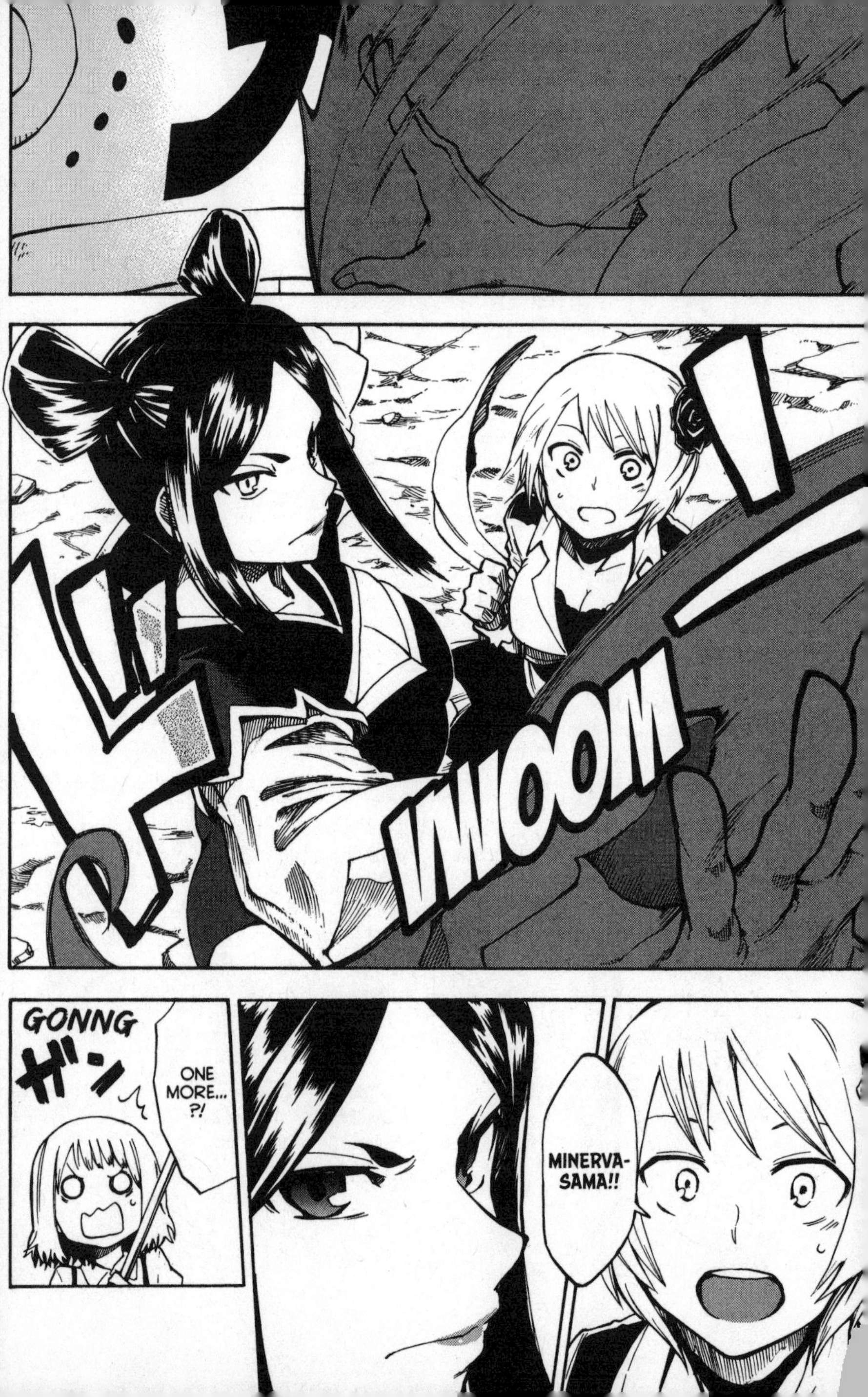
VWOOM
MINERVA-SAMA!!
GONNG
ガーン
ONE MORE...?!

FAIRY TAIL: TWIN DRAGONS OF SABER TOOTH

Chapter 10: The Battle Between the Woman and the Girl

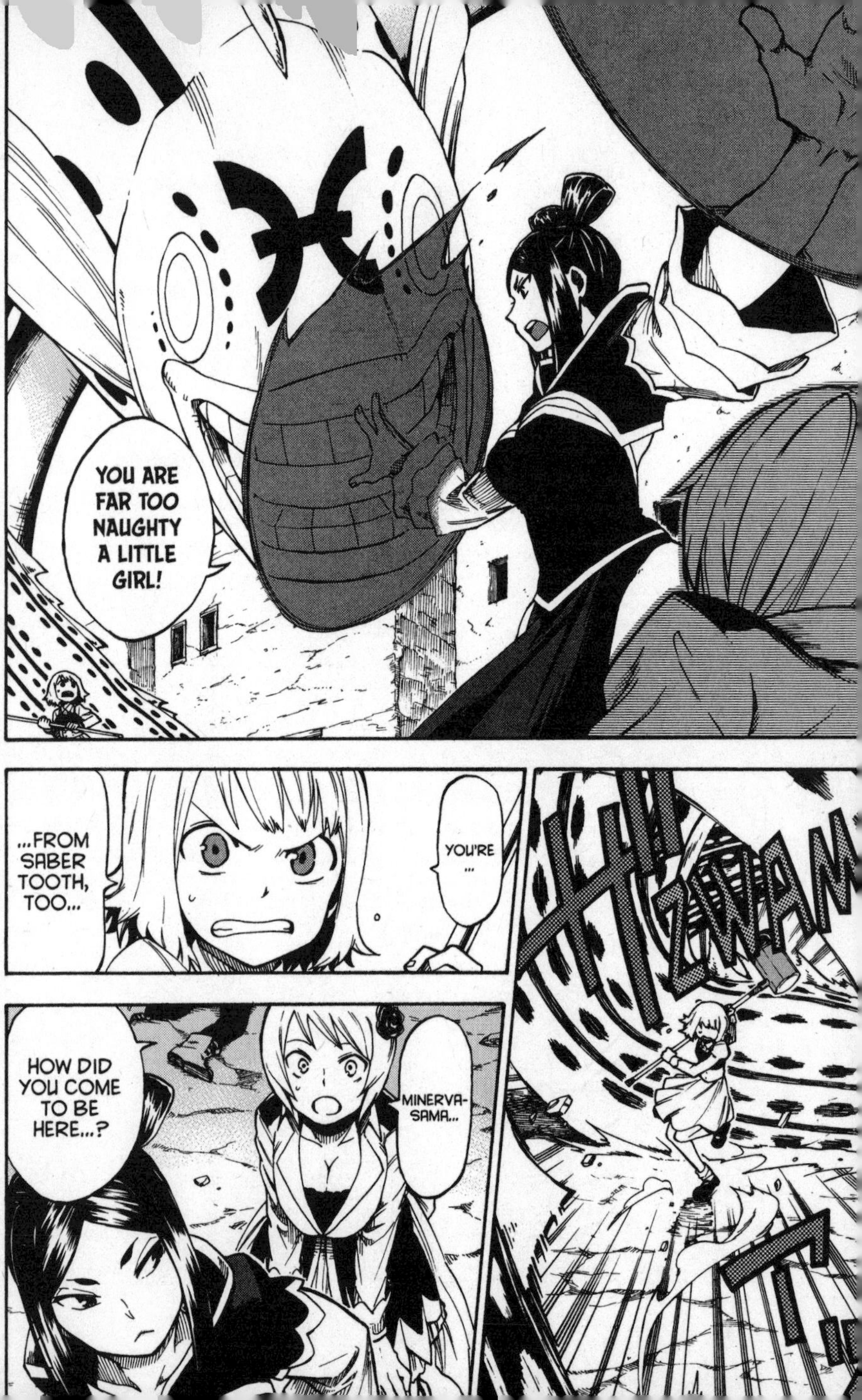
YOU ARE FAR TOO NAUGHTY A LITTLE GIRL!
ZWAM
YOU'RE ...
...FROM SABER TOOTH, TOO...
MINERVA-SAMA...
HOW DID YOU COME TO BE HERE...?

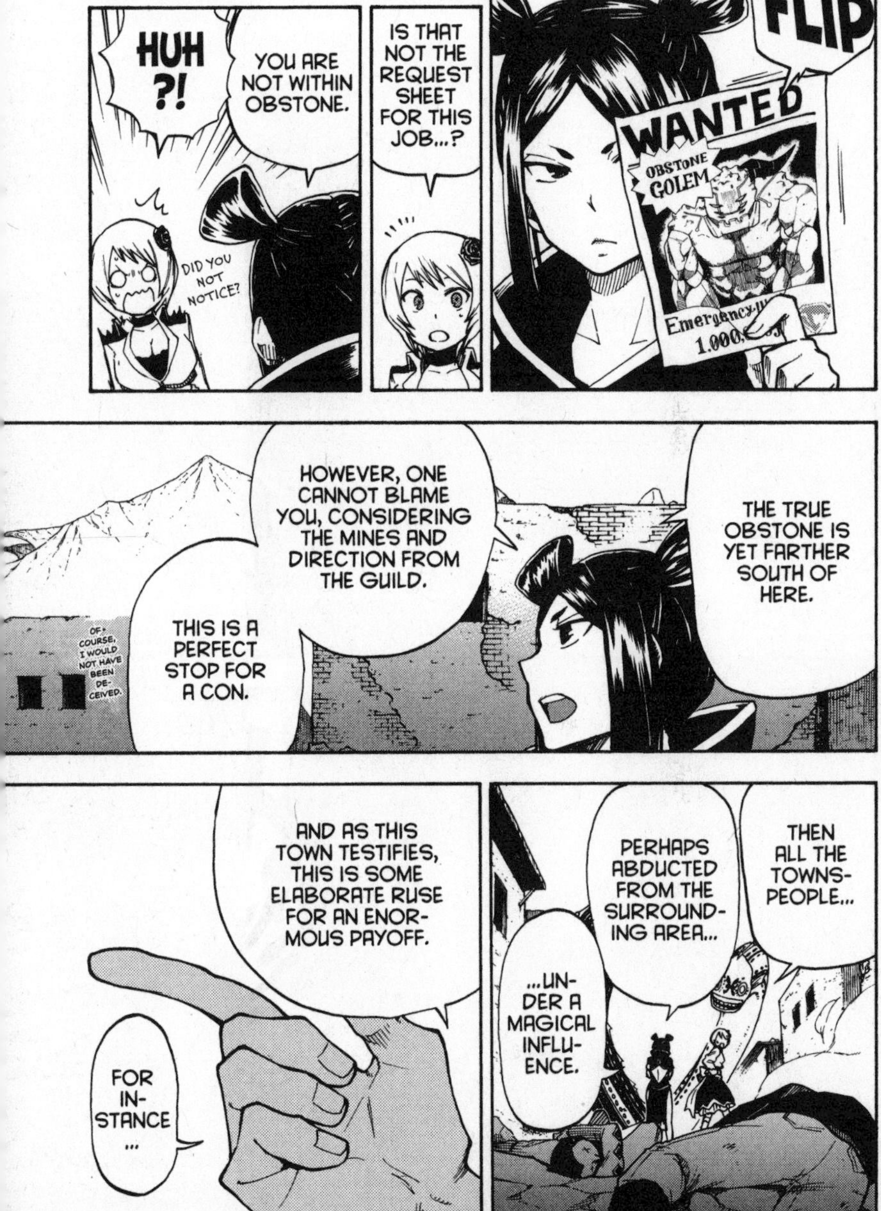
FLIP
WANTED
OBSTONE GOLEM
Emergency!!!
IS THAT NOT THE REQUEST SHEET FOR THIS JOB...?
YOU ARE NOT WITHIN OBSTONE.
HUH ?!
DID YOU NOT NOTICE?
THE TRUE OBSTONE IS YET FARTHER SOUTH OF HERE.
HOWEVER, ONE CANNOT BLAME YOU, CONSIDERING THE MINES AND DIRECTION FROM THE GUILD.
THIS IS A PERFECT STOP FOR A CON.
OF-COURSE, I WOULD NOT HAVE BEEN DE-CEIVED.
THEN ALL THE TOWNS-PEOPLE...
PERHAPS ABDUCTED FROM THE SURROUND-ING AREA...
...UN-DER A MAGICAL INFLU-ENCE.
AND AS THIS TOWN TESTIFIES, THIS IS SOME ELABORATE RUSE FOR AN ENOR-MOUS PAYOFF.
FOR IN-STANCE ...

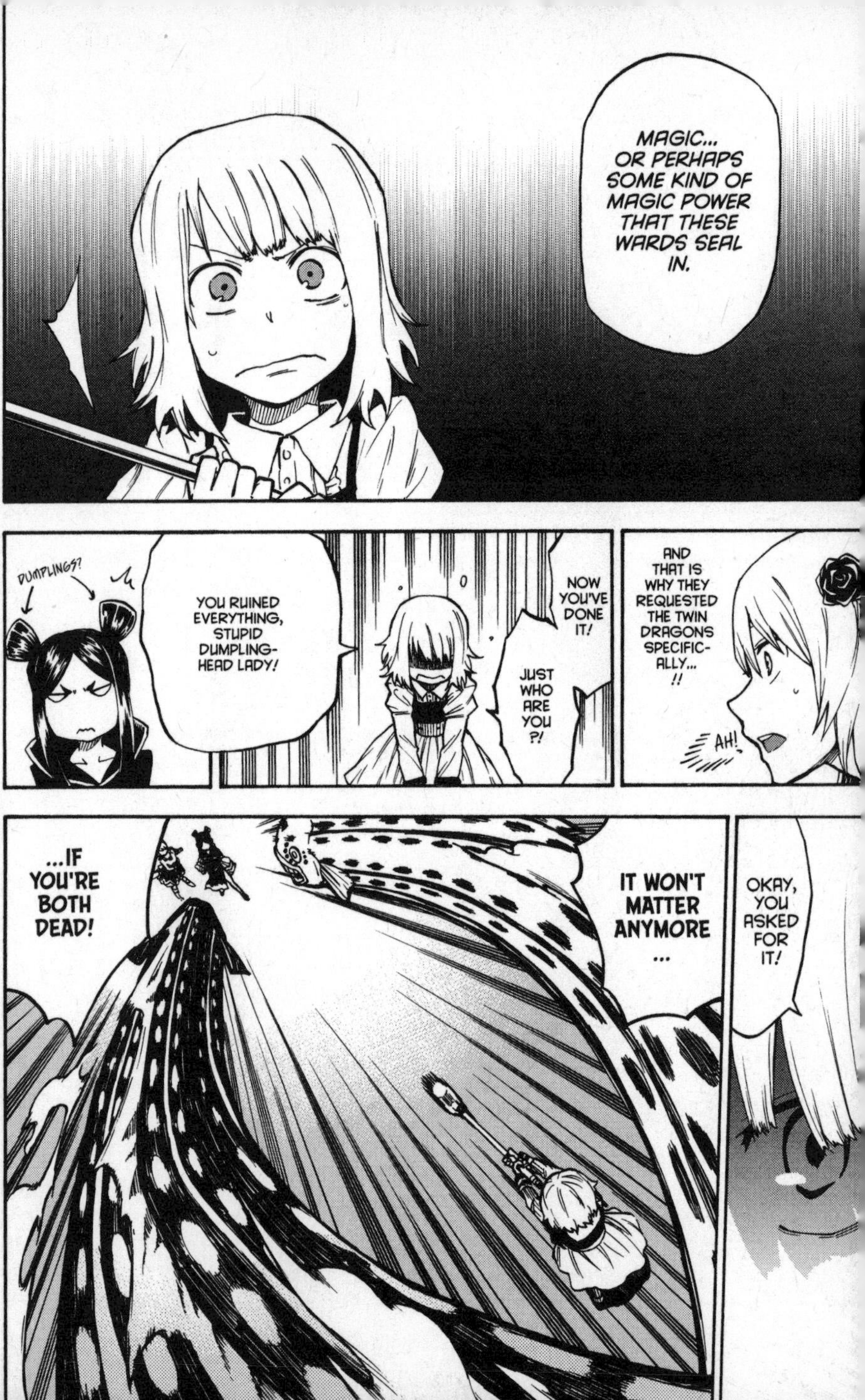
MAGIC... OR PERHAPS SOME KIND OF MAGIC POWER THAT THESE WARDS SEAL IN.
AND THAT IS WHY THEY REQUESTED THE TWIN DRAGONS SPECIFICALLY... !!
AH!
NOW YOU'VE DONE IT!
JUST WHO ARE YOU ?!
YOU RUINED EVERYTHING, STUPID DUMPLING-HEAD LADY!
DUMPLINGS?
OKAY, YOU ASKED FOR IT!
IT WON'T MATTER ANYMORE ...
...IF YOU'RE BOTH DEAD!

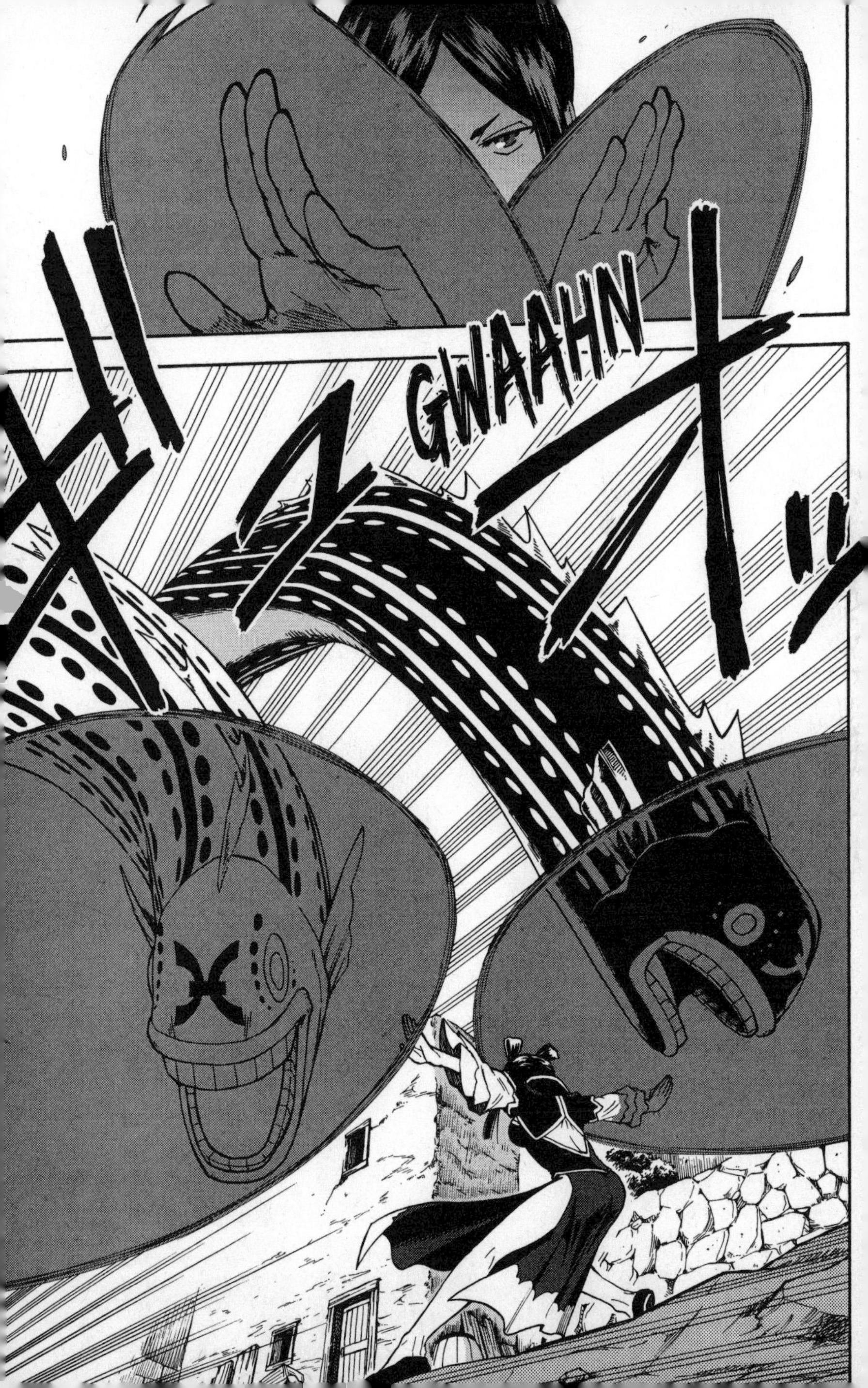
GWAAHN

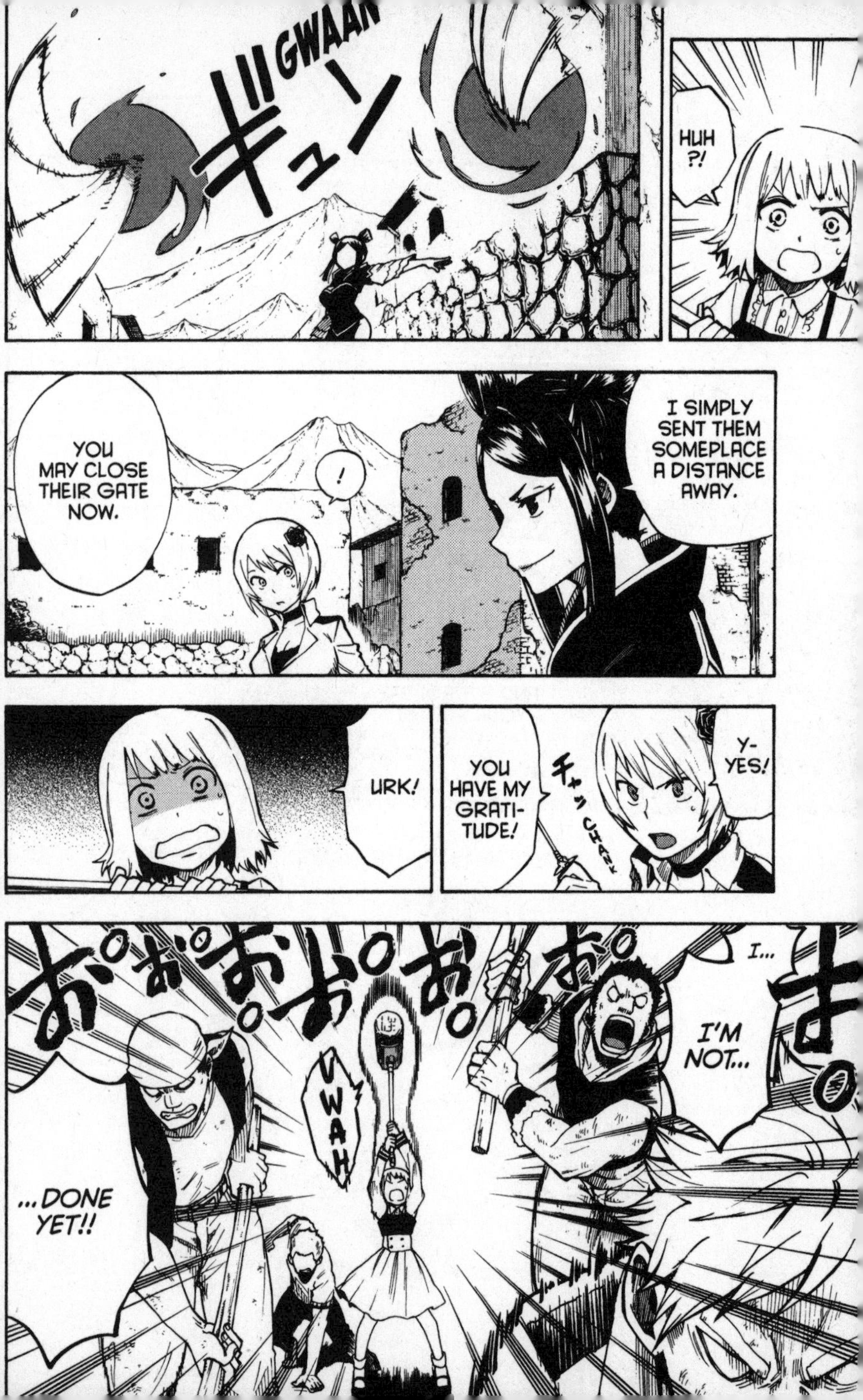
HUH ?!
GWAAN
ギュン
I SIMPLY SENT THEM SOMEPLACE A DISTANCE AWAY.
!
YOU MAY CLOSE THEIR GATE NOW.
Y-YES!
CHANK
YOU HAVE MY GRATITUDE!
URK!
I...
I'M NOT...
UWAH
...DONE YET!!

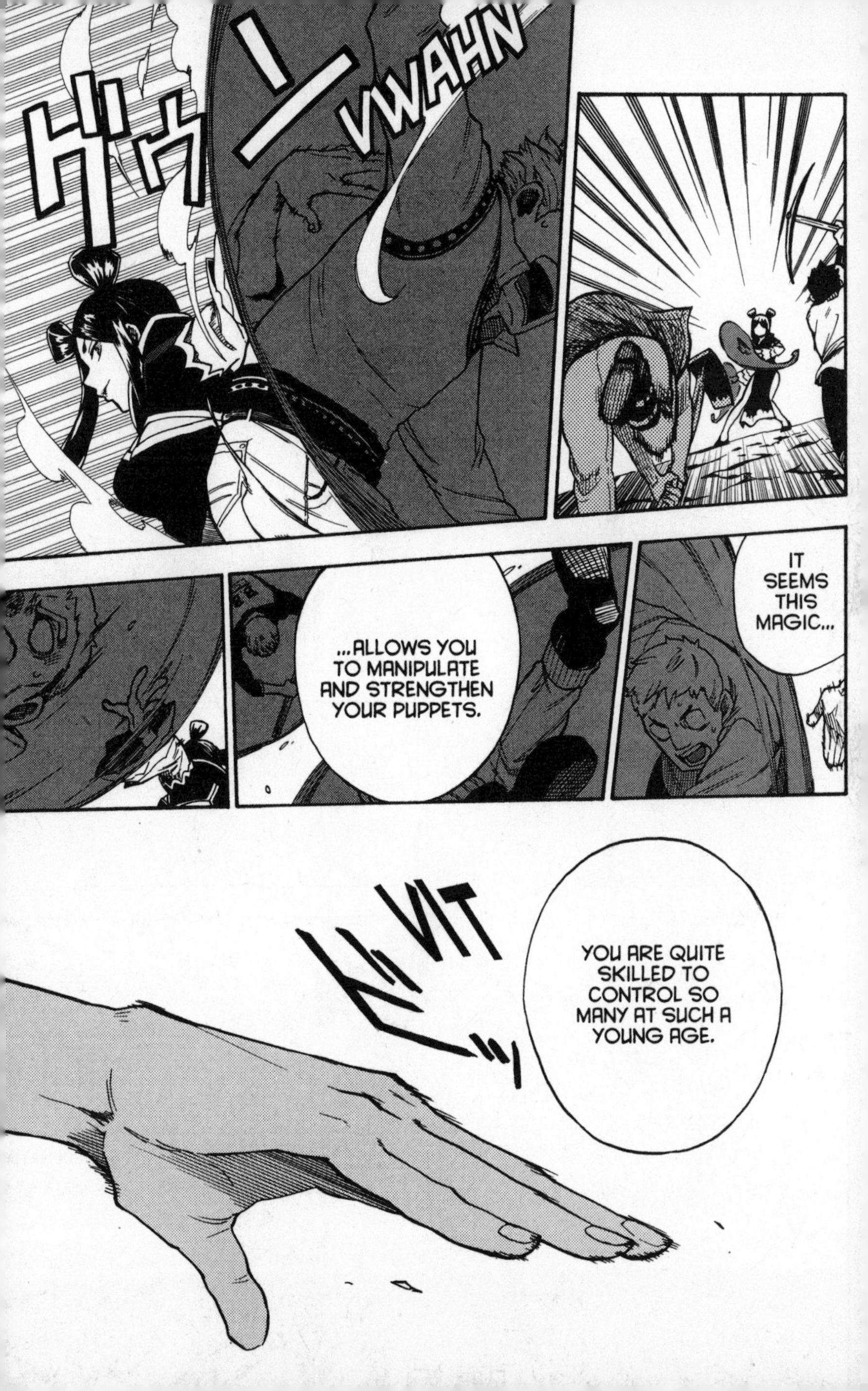
VWAHN
IT SEEMS THIS MAGIC...
...ALLOWS YOU TO MANIPULATE AND STRENGTHEN YOUR PUPPETS.
YOU ARE QUITE SKILLED TO CONTROL SO MANY AT SUCH A YOUNG AGE.

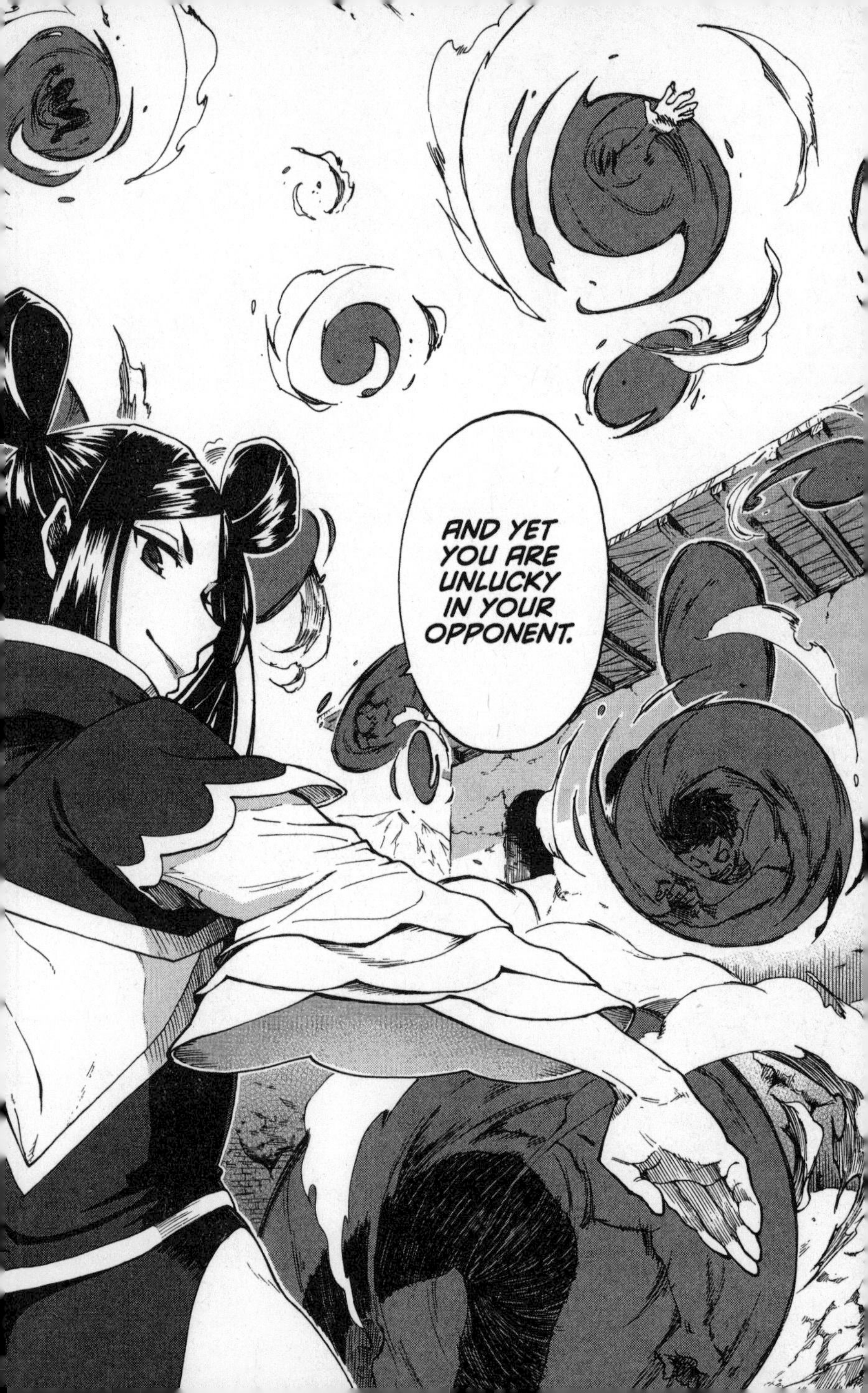
AND YET YOU ARE UNLUCKY IN YOUR OPPONENT.

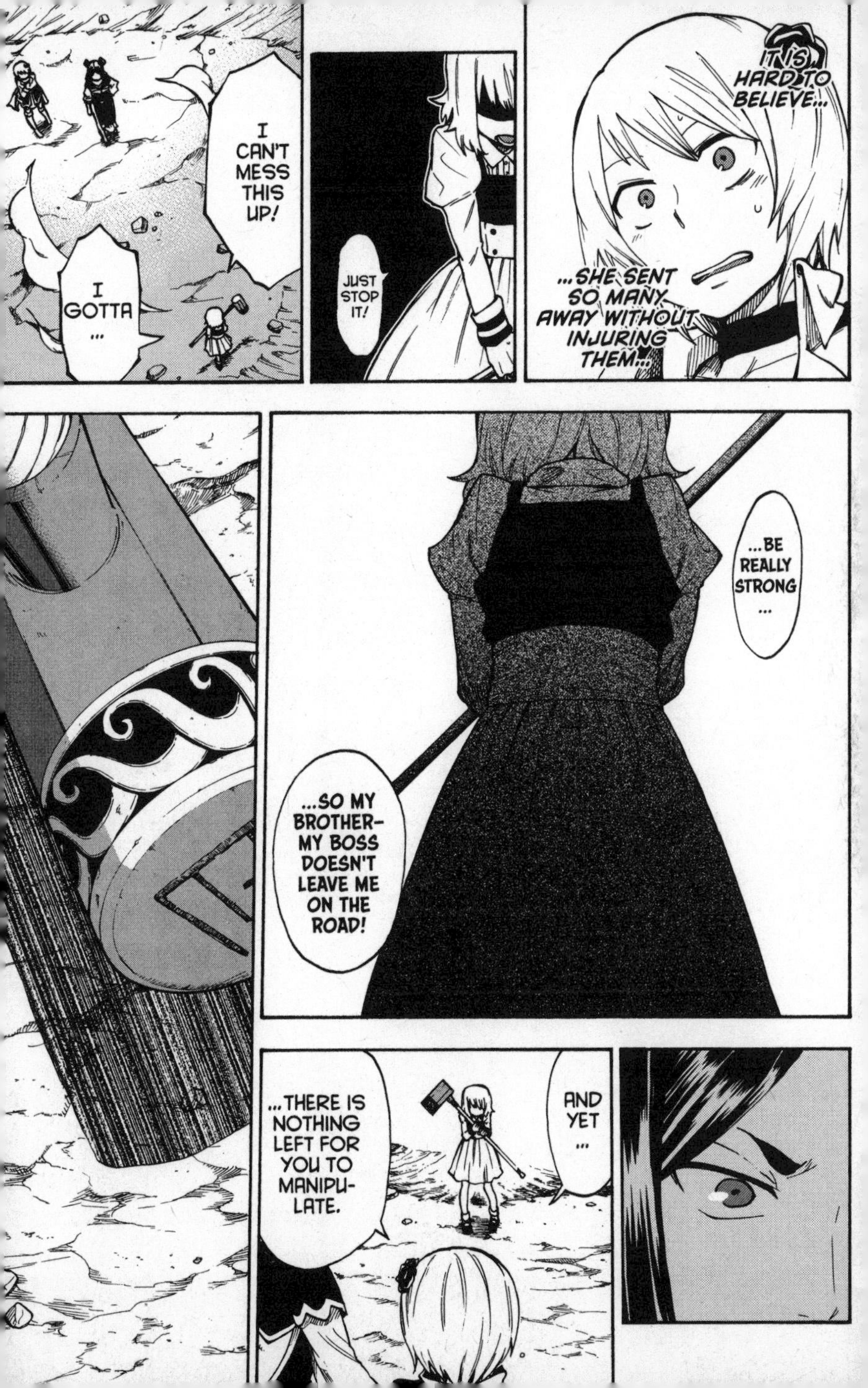
IT IS HARD TO BELIEVE...
...SHE SENT SO MANY AWAY WITHOUT INJURING THEM...
JUST STOP IT!
I CAN'T MESS THIS UP!
I GOTTA ...
...BE REALLY STRONG ...
...SO MY BROTHER- MY BOSS DOESN'T LEAVE ME ON THE ROAD!
AND YET ...
...THERE IS NOTHING LEFT FOR YOU TO MANIPULATE.

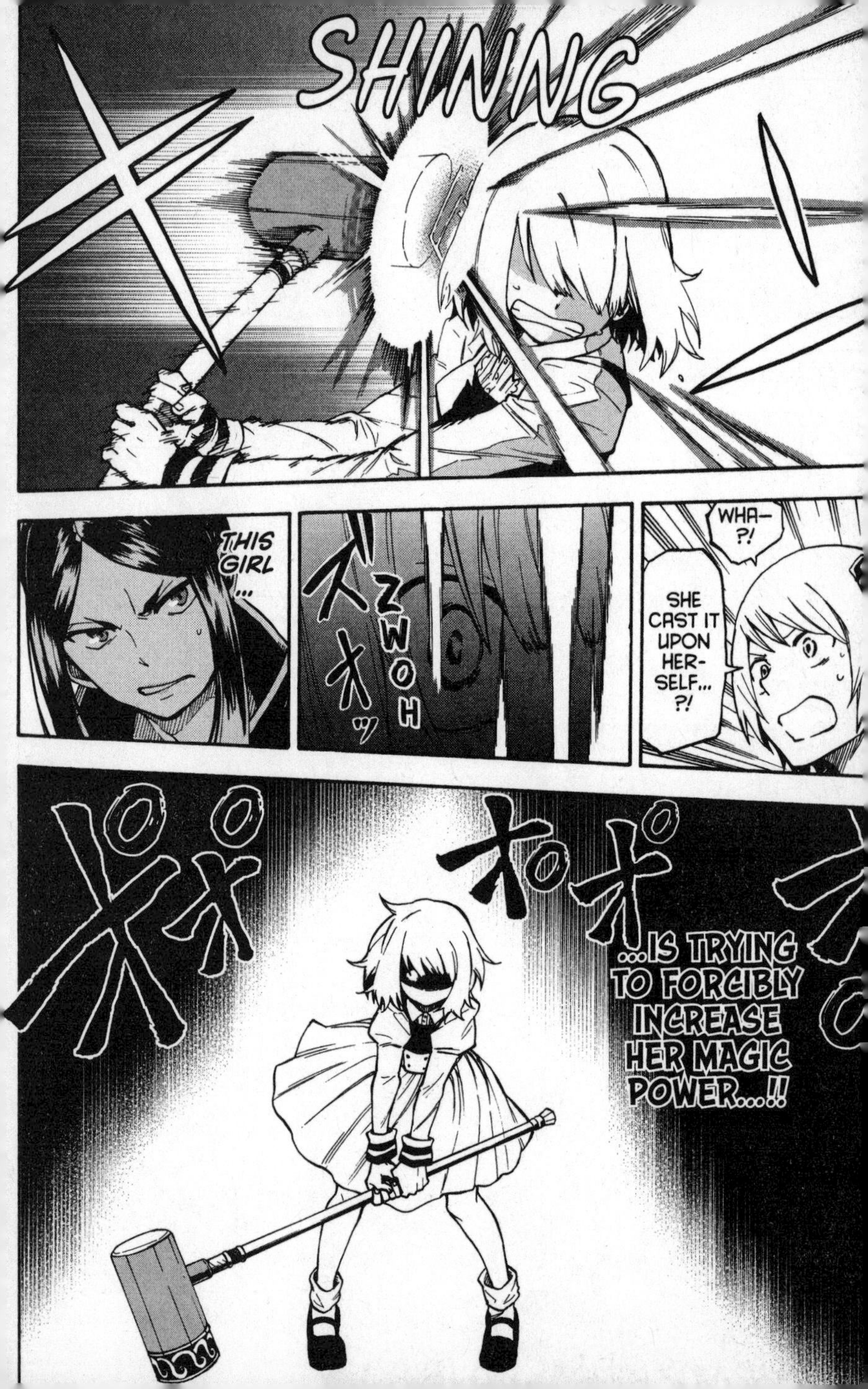
SHINNG
WHA- ?!
SHE CAST IT UPON HER-SELF... ?!
ZWOH
ズォッ
THIS GIRL ...
...IS TRYING TO FORCIBLY INCREASE HER MAGIC POWER...!!

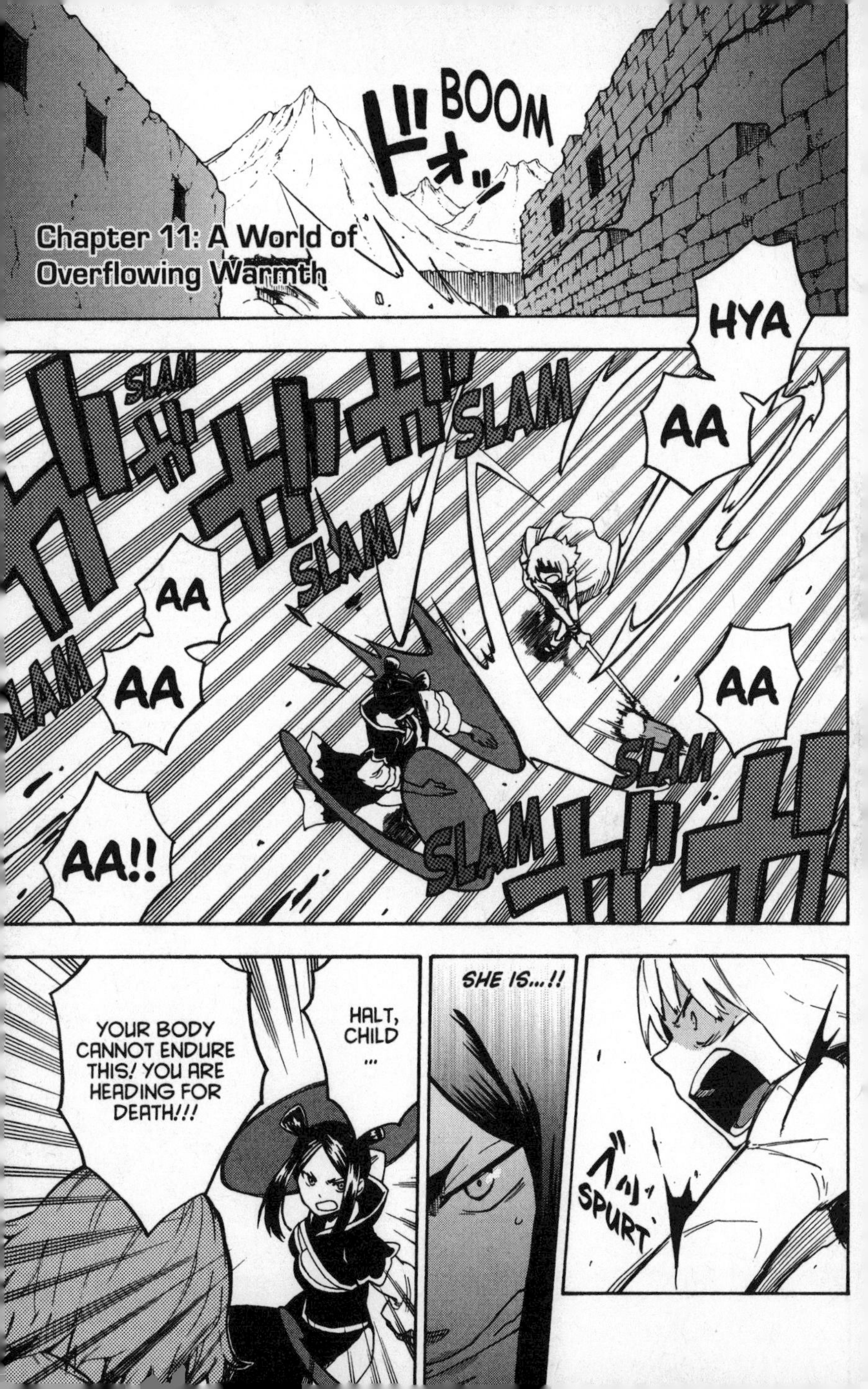
BOOM
Chapter 11: A World of Overflowing Warmth
HYA
AA
SLAM
SLAM
SLAM
SLAM
AA
AA
AA
SLAM
SLAM
SLAM
AA!!
SPURT
SHE IS...!!
HALT, CHILD ...
YOUR BODY CANNOT ENDURE THIS! YOU ARE HEADING FOR DEATH!!!

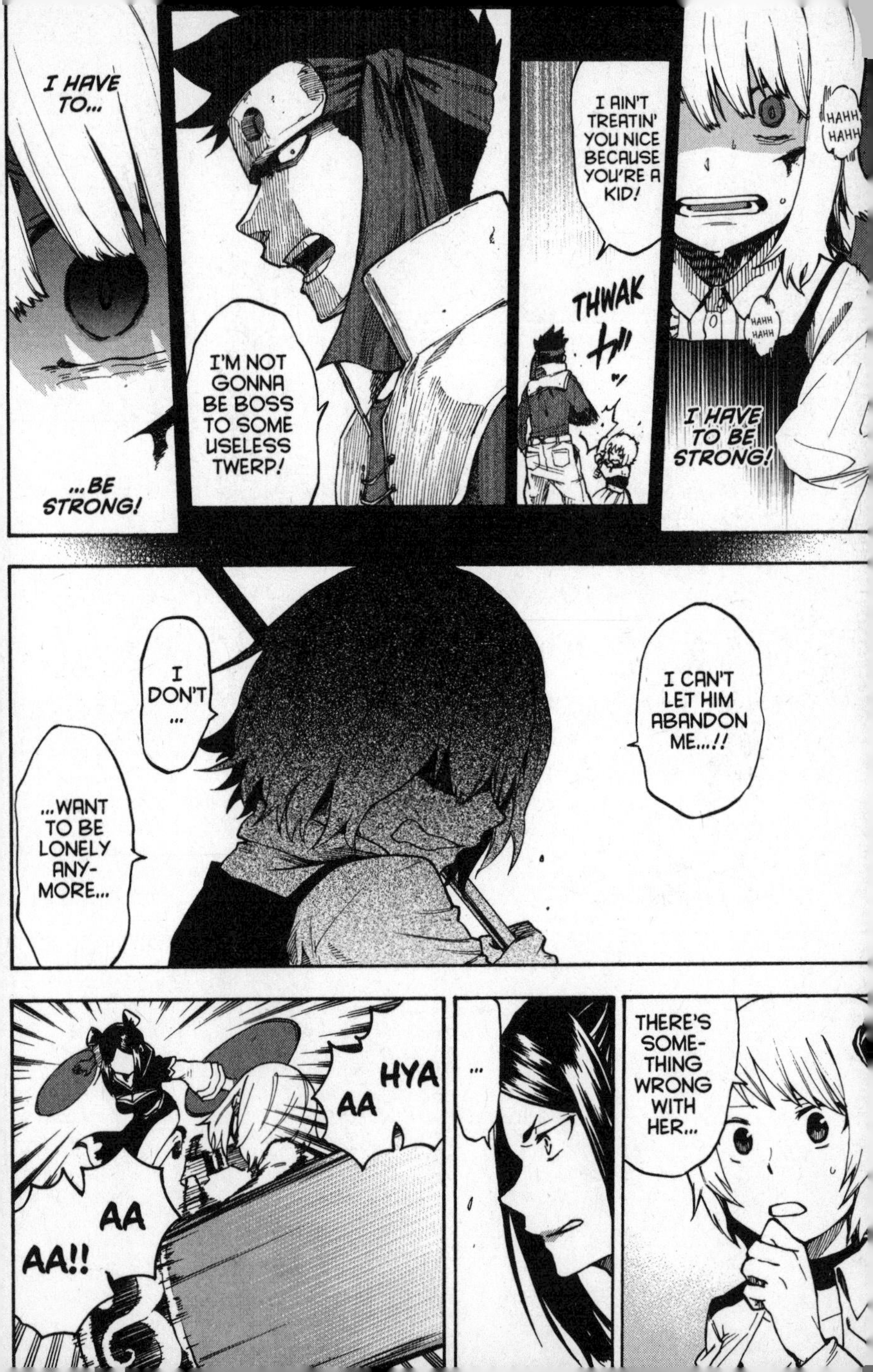
HAHH HAHH
HAHH HAHH
I HAVE TO BE STRONG!
I AIN'T TREATIN' YOU NICE BECAUSE YOU'RE A KID!
THWAK
I'M NOT GONNA BE BOSS TO SOME USELESS TWERP!
I HAVE TO...
...BE STRONG!
I CAN'T LET HIM ABANDON ME...!!
I DON'T ...
...WANT TO BE LONELY ANY-MORE...
THERE'S SOME-THING WRONG WITH HER...
...
HYAAA
AAAA!!

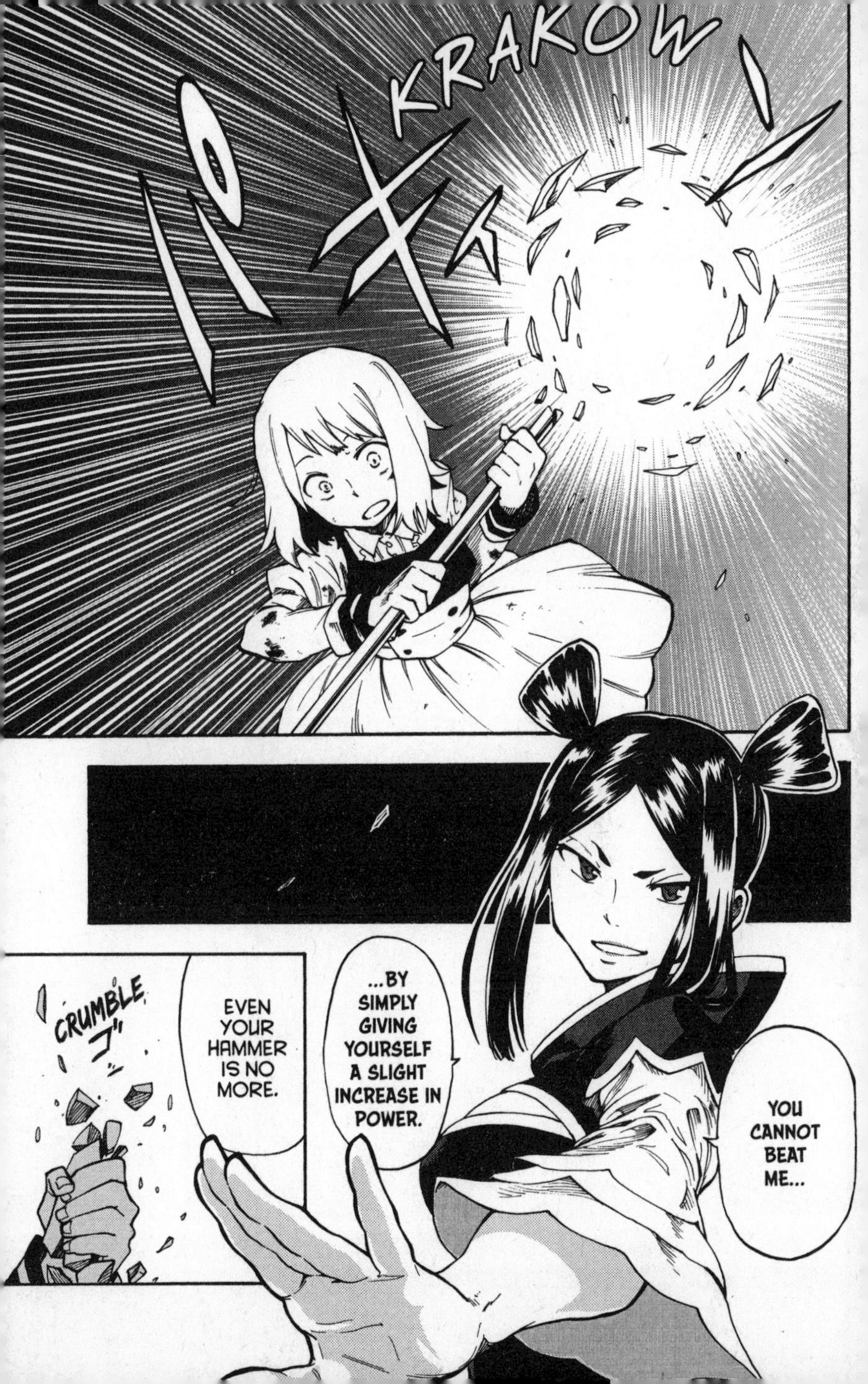
KRAKOW
YOU CANNOT BEAT ME...
...BY SIMPLY GIVING YOURSELF A SLIGHT INCREASE IN POWER.
EVEN YOUR HAMMER IS NO MORE.
CRUMBLE

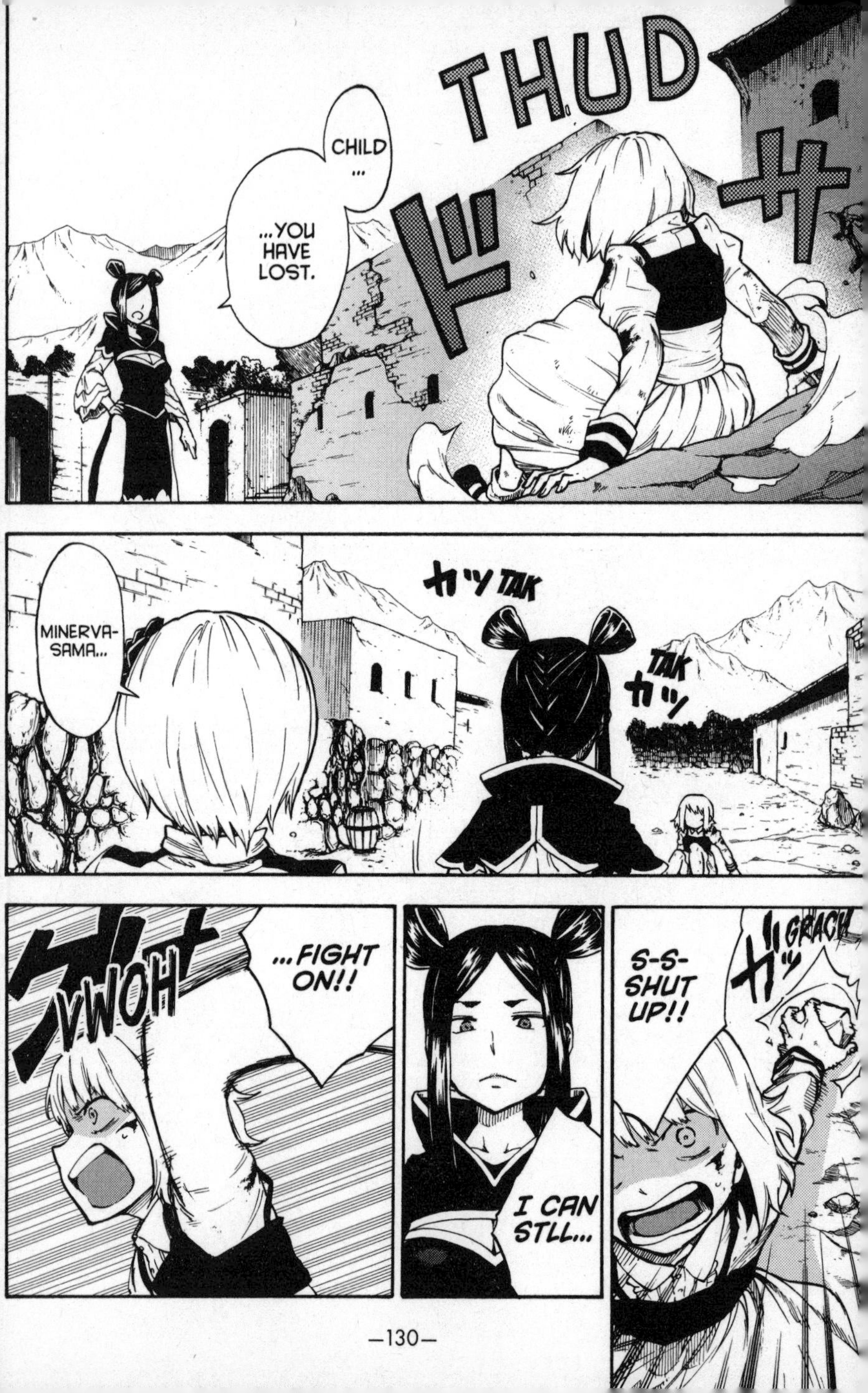
ドサ
THUD
CHILD ...
...YOU HAVE LOST.
TAK
カッ
カッ TAK
MINERVA-SAMA...
ガッ
S-S-SHUT UP!!
I CAN STLL...
...FIGHT ON!!
VWOH

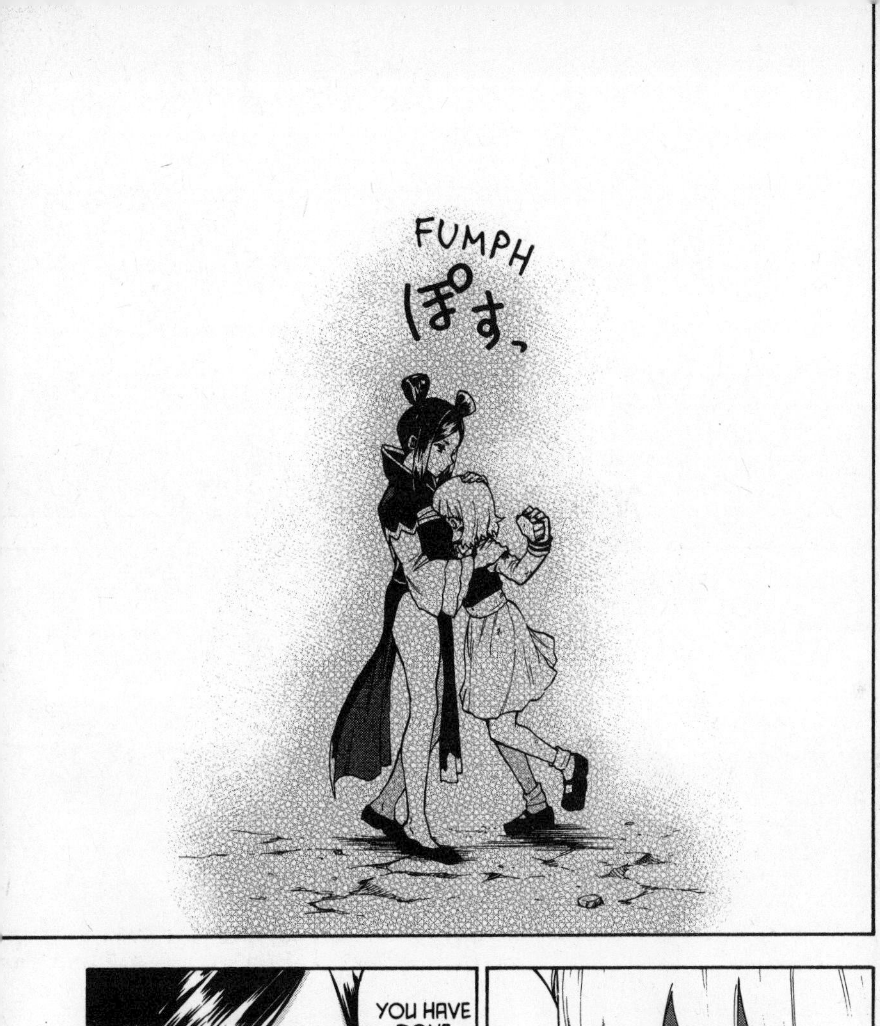
FUMPH
ぽすっ
YOU HAVE DONE PLENTY.

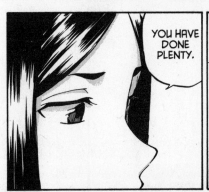

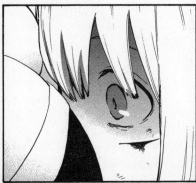

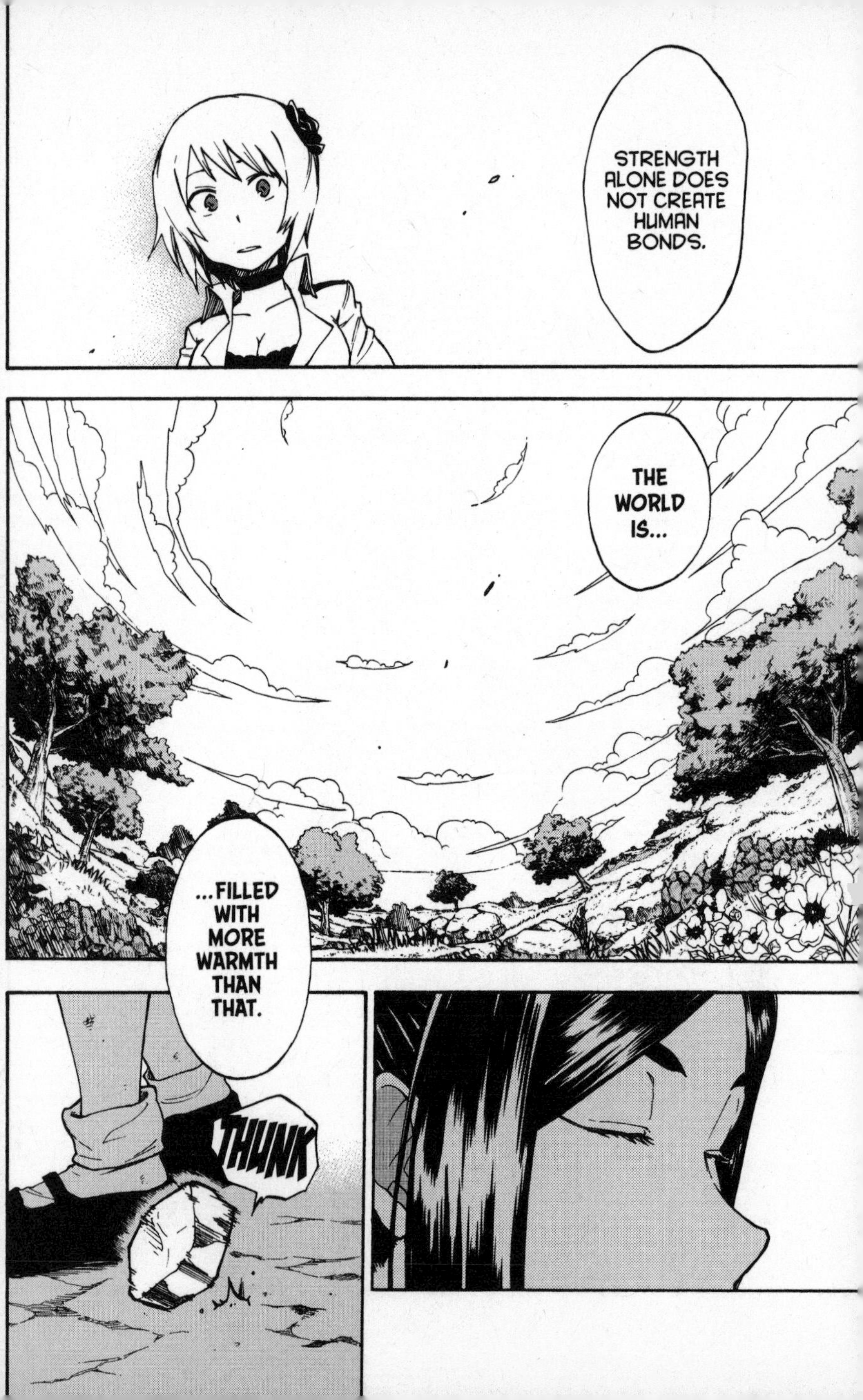
STRENGTH ALONE DOES NOT CREATE HUMAN BONDS.
THE WORLD IS...
...FILLED WITH MORE WARMTH THAN THAT.
THUNK

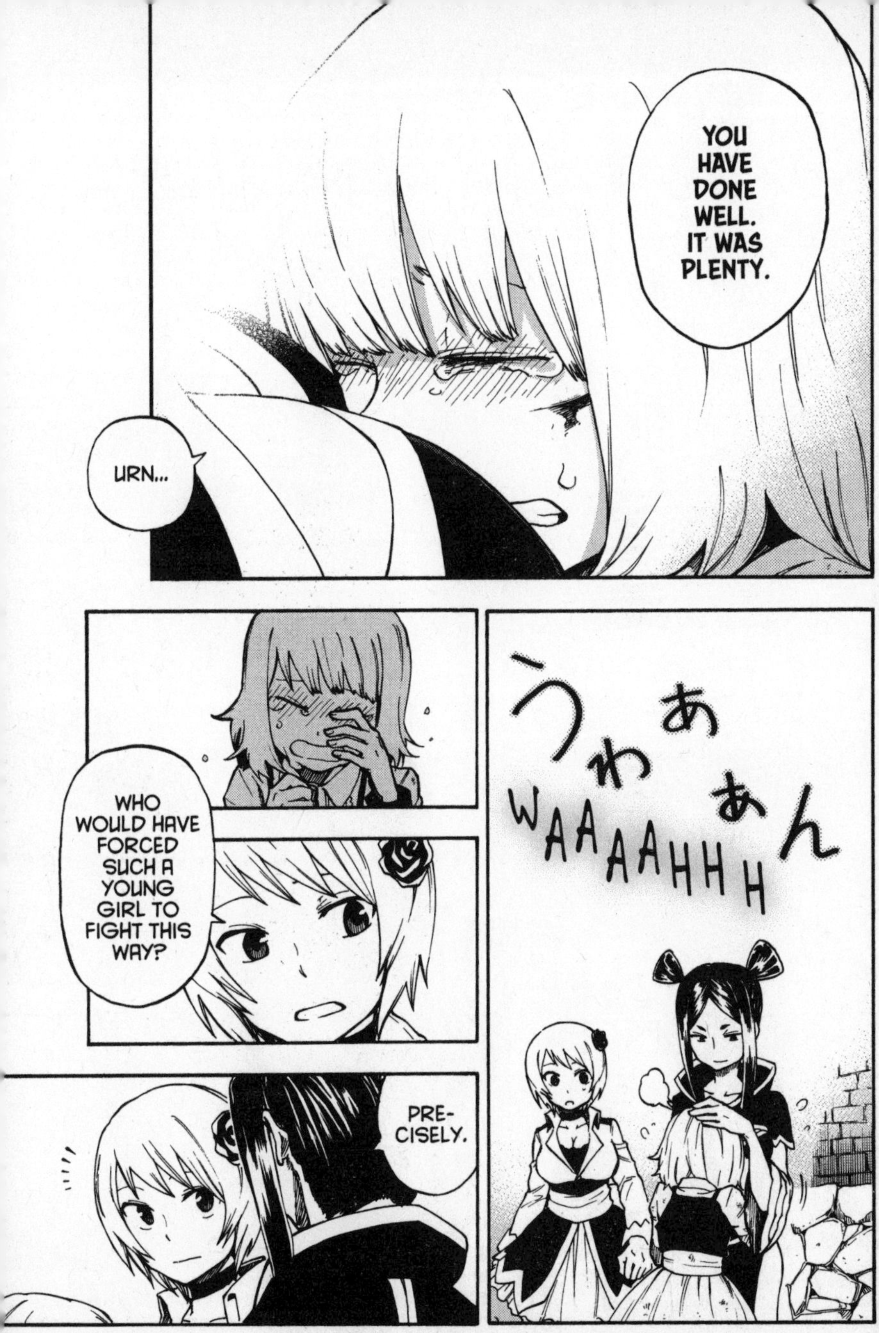
YOU HAVE DONE WELL. IT WAS PLENTY.
URN...
うわああん
WAAAAHHH
WHO WOULD HAVE FORCED SUCH A YOUNG GIRL TO FIGHT THIS WAY?
PRE-CISELY.

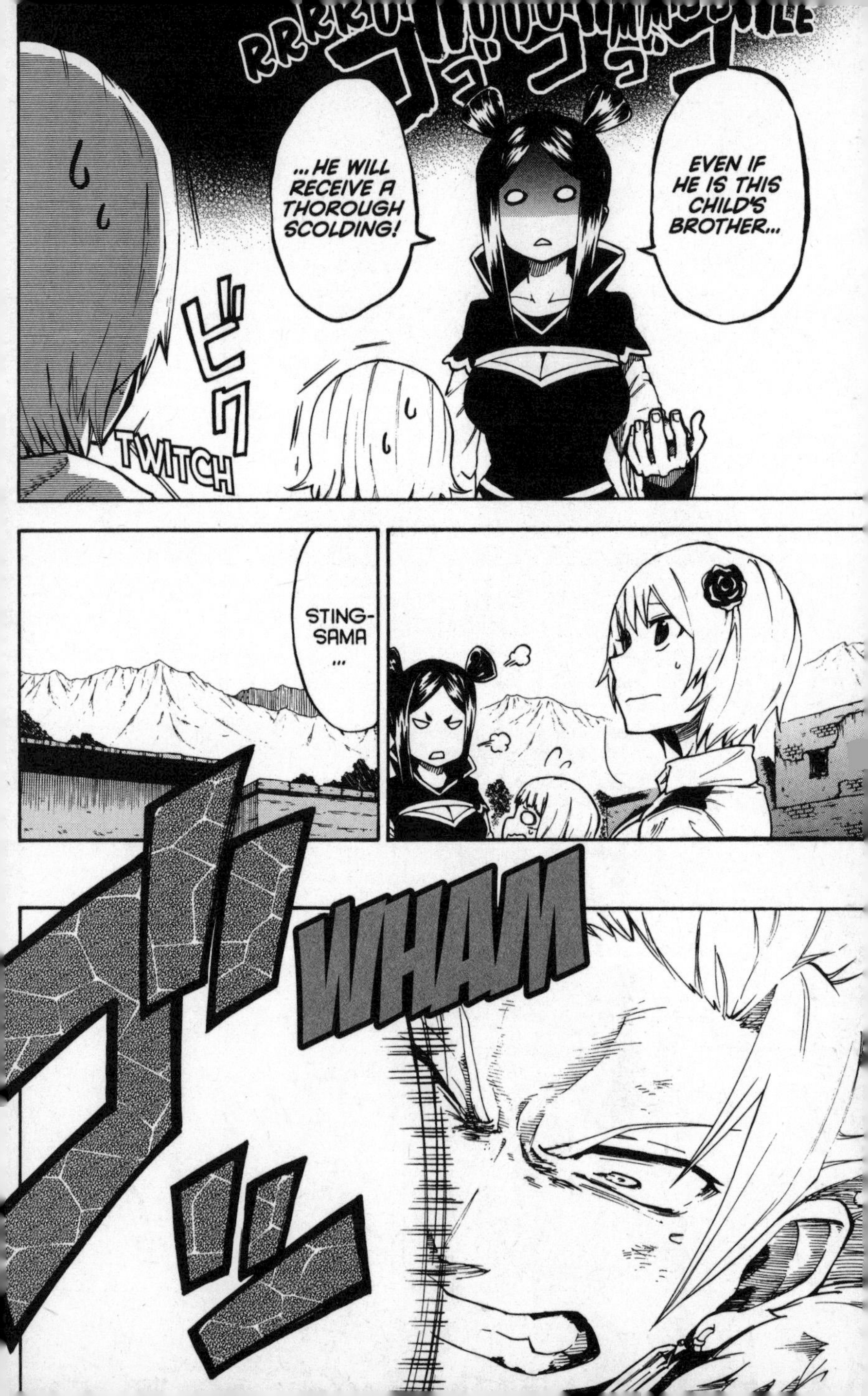
EVEN IF HE IS THIS CHILD'S BROTHER...
...HE WILL RECEIVE A THOROUGH SCOLDING!
TWITCH
STING-SAMA ...
WHAM

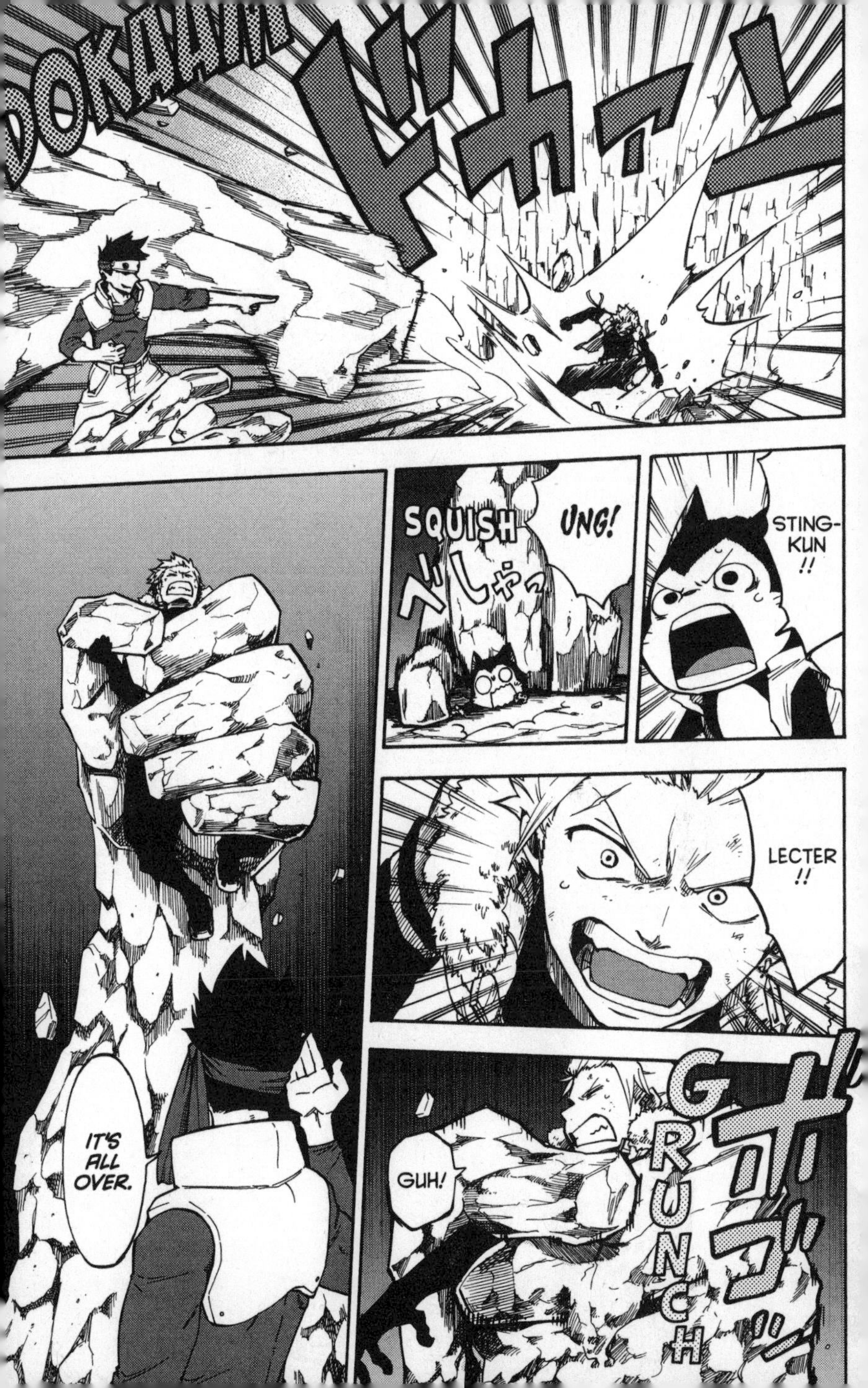
DOKAAAN
STING-KUN!!
SQUISH
UNG!
LECTER!!
GRUNCH
GUH!
IT'S ALL OVER.

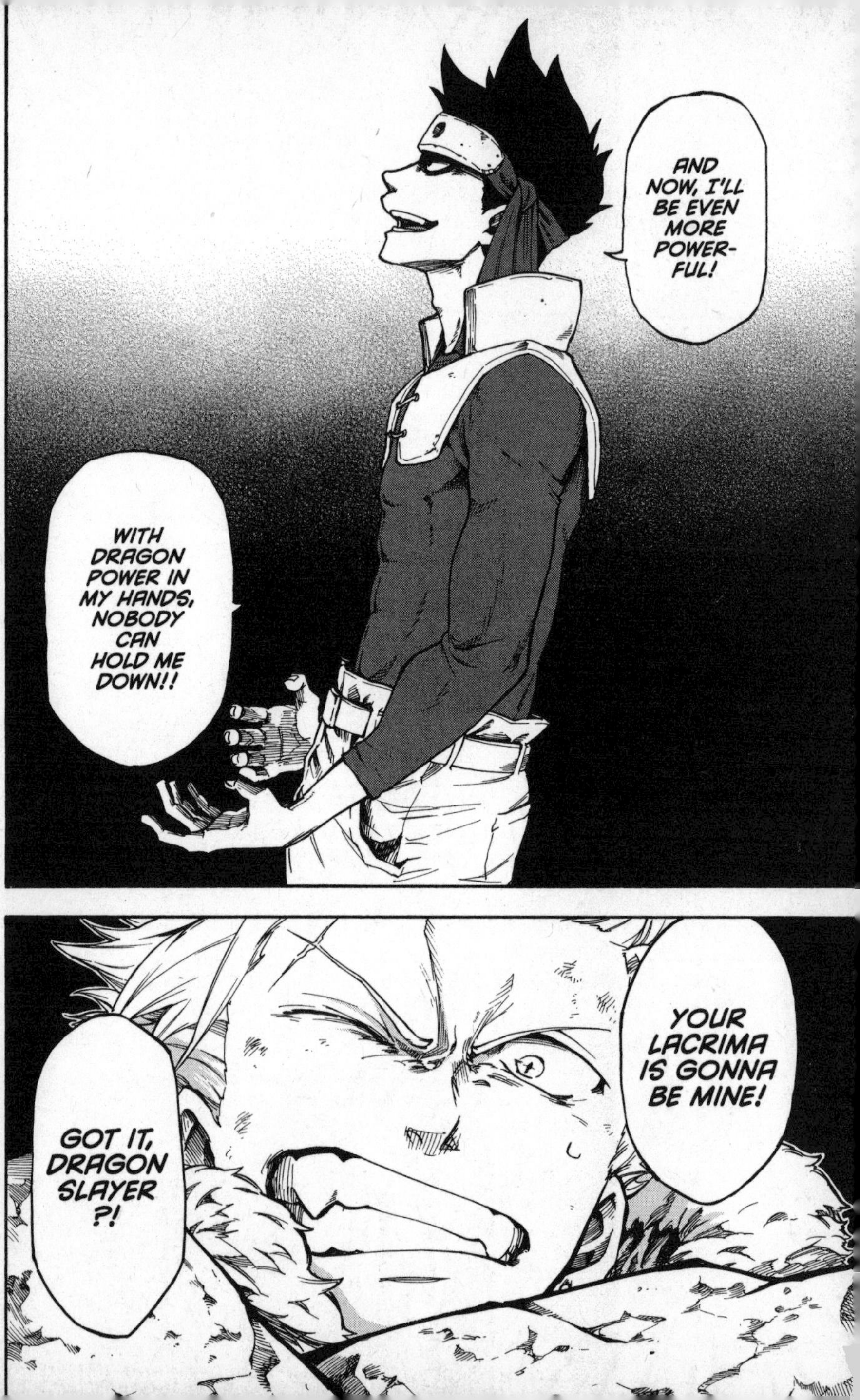
AND NOW, I'LL BE EVEN MORE POWER-FUL!
WITH DRAGON POWER IN MY HANDS, NOBODY CAN HOLD ME DOWN!!
YOUR LACRIMA IS GONNA BE MINE!
GOT IT, DRAGON SLAYER ?!

Chapter 12: It Isn't Going to End Here

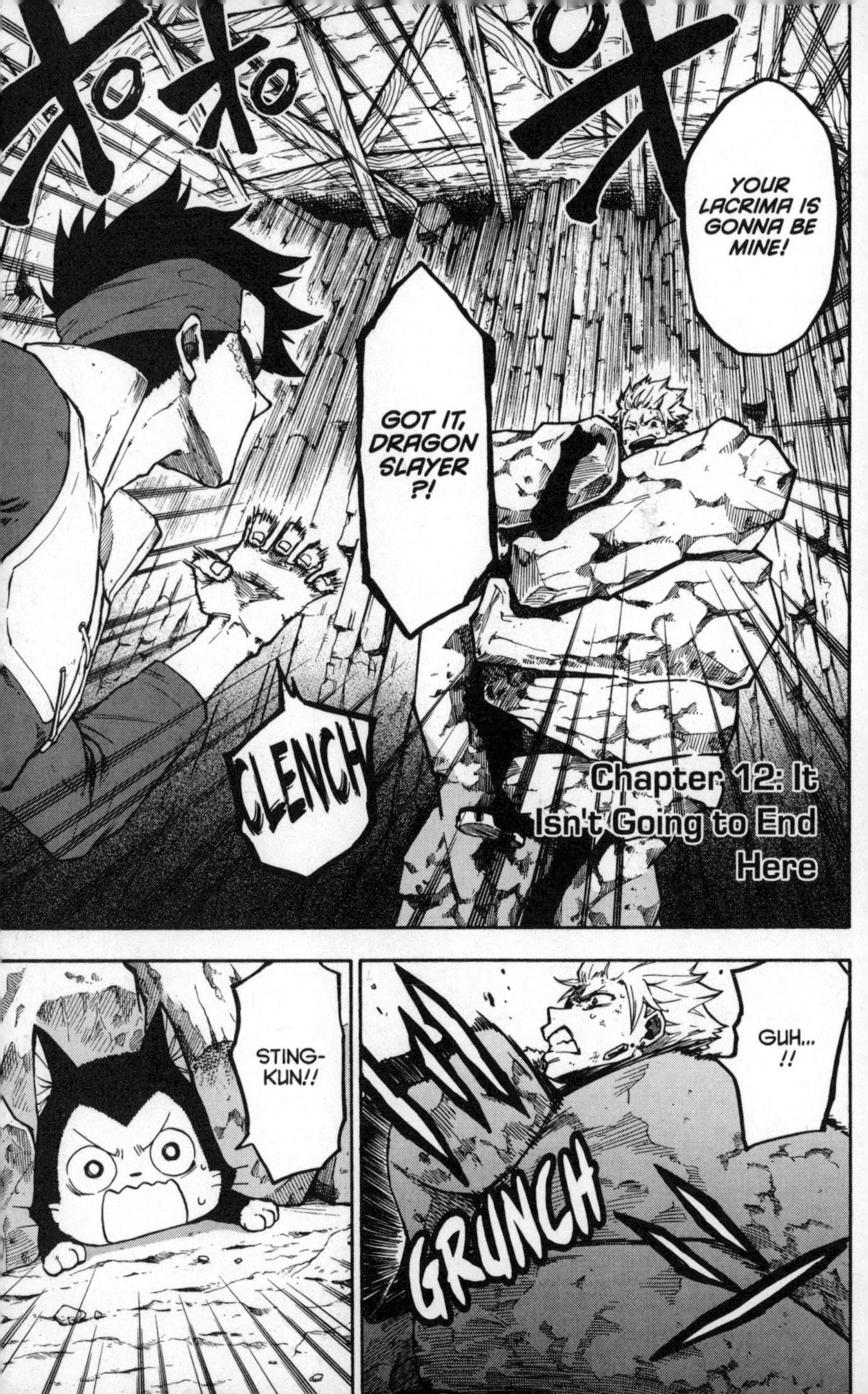

YOUR LACRIMA IS GONNA BE MINE!
GOT IT, DRAGON SLAYER ?!
CLENCH
GUH... !!
GRUNCH
STING-KUN!!

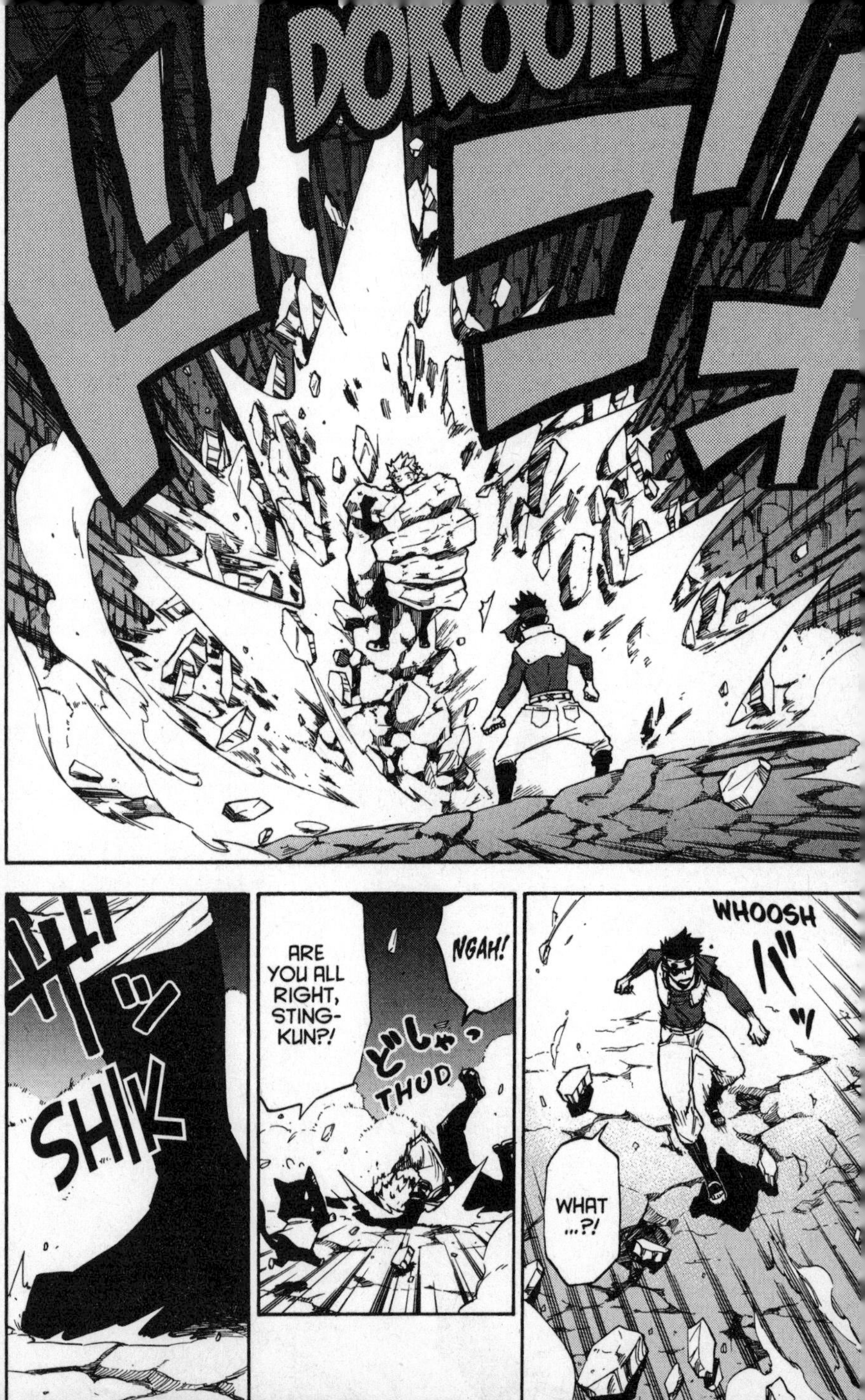
DOKOOM
WHOOSH
WHAT ...?!
NGAH!
ARE YOU ALL RIGHT, STING-KUN?!
どしゃっ
THUD
SHIK

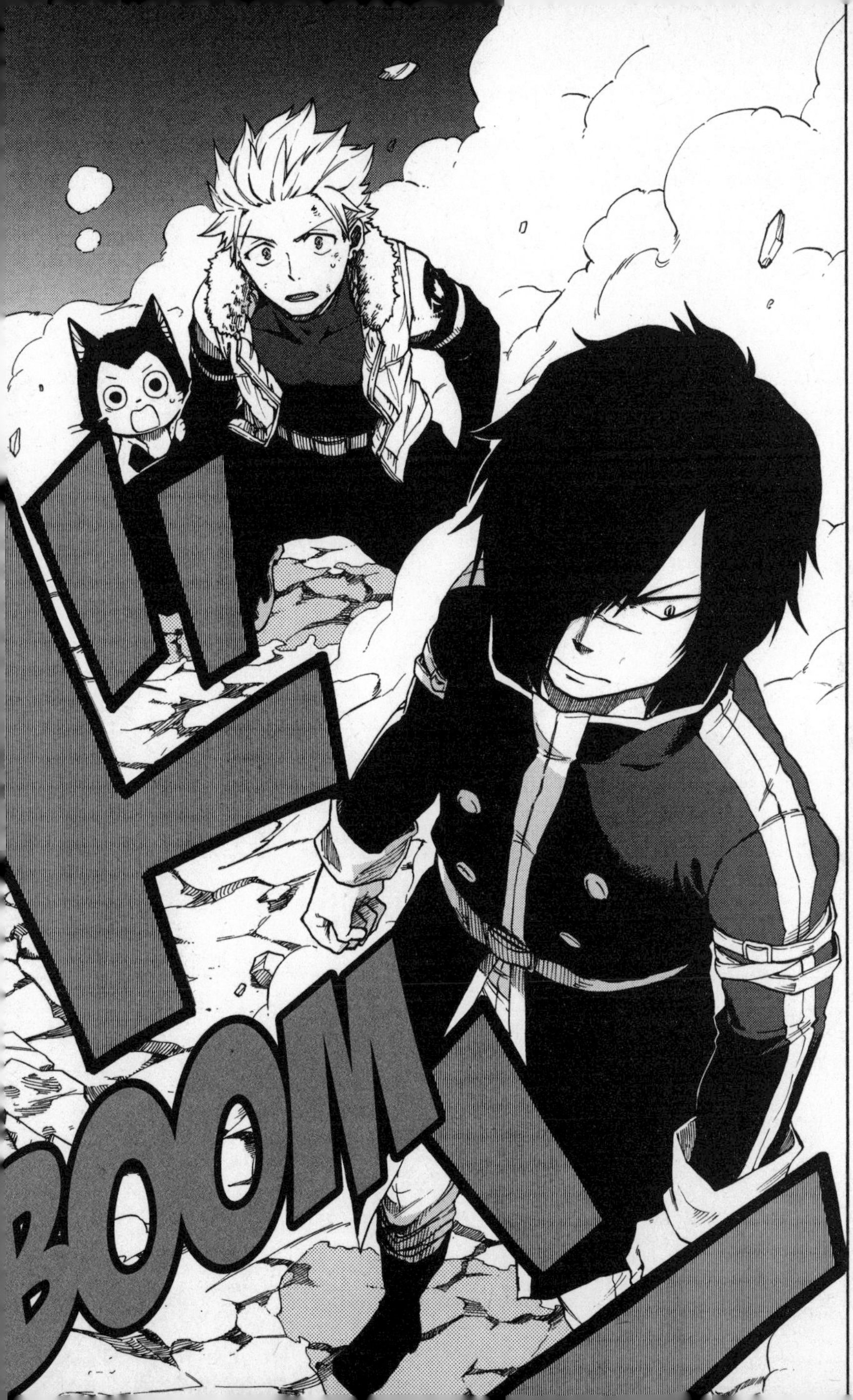
BOOM

EVEN YOU, FROSCH?!

LECTER!

ヒョコ POP

?!

ROGUE?!

ROGUE-KUN!!

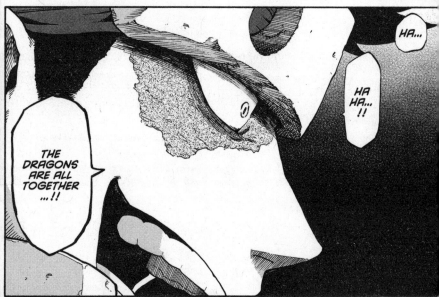

HA...

HA HA...!!

THE DRAGONS ARE ALL TOGETHER...!!

HEH...

HEH HEH HEH...

AND HERE I ALREADY GIVEN UP ON MY ORIGINAL PLAN...

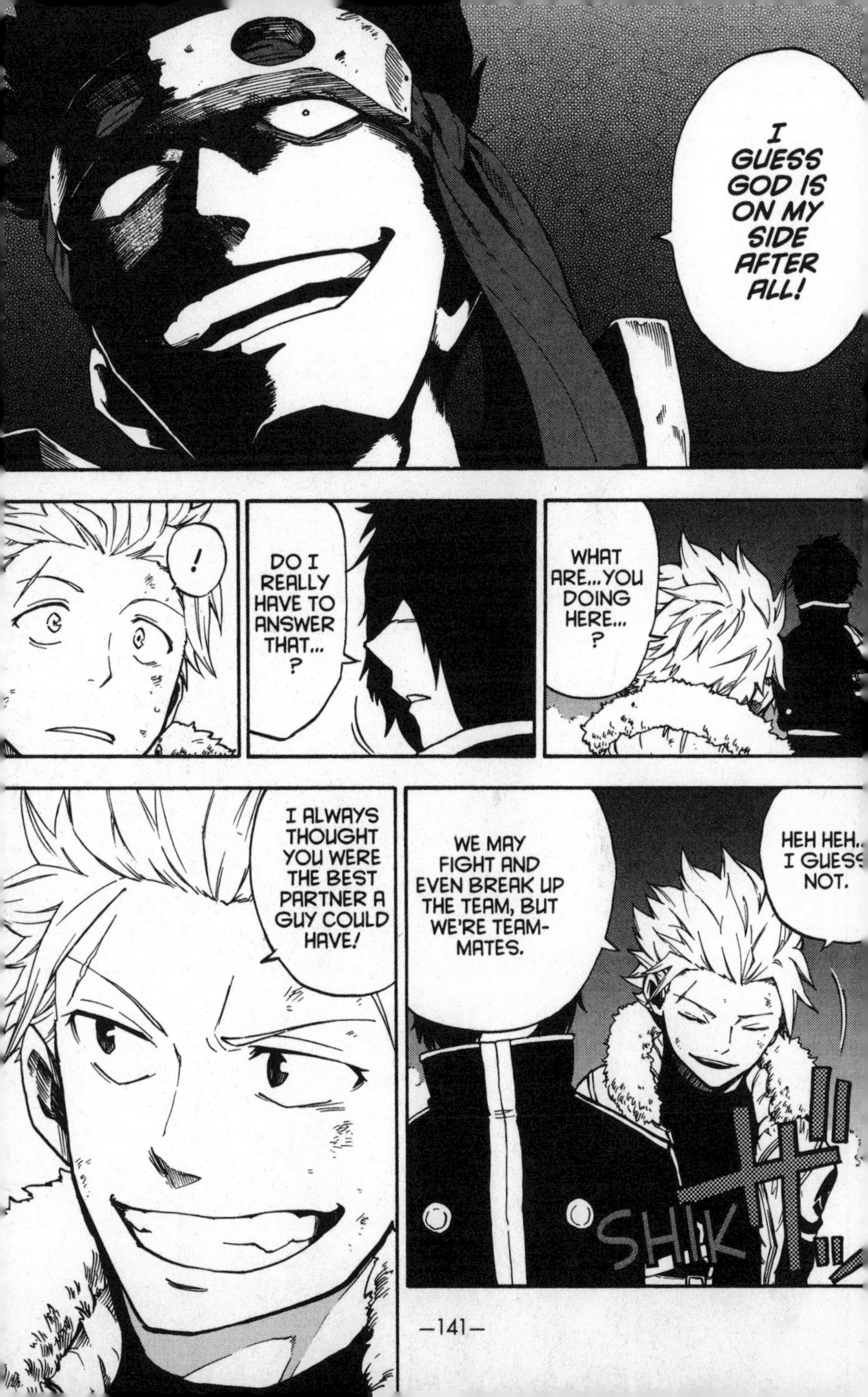
I GUESS GOD IS ON MY SIDE AFTER ALL!
WHAT ARE...YOU DOING HERE...?
DO I REALLY HAVE TO ANSWER THAT...?
!
HEH HEH... I GUESS NOT.
WE MAY FIGHT AND EVEN BREAK UP THE TEAM, BUT WE'RE TEAM-MATES.
I ALWAYS THOUGHT YOU WERE THE BEST PARTNER A GUY COULD HAVE!
SHIK

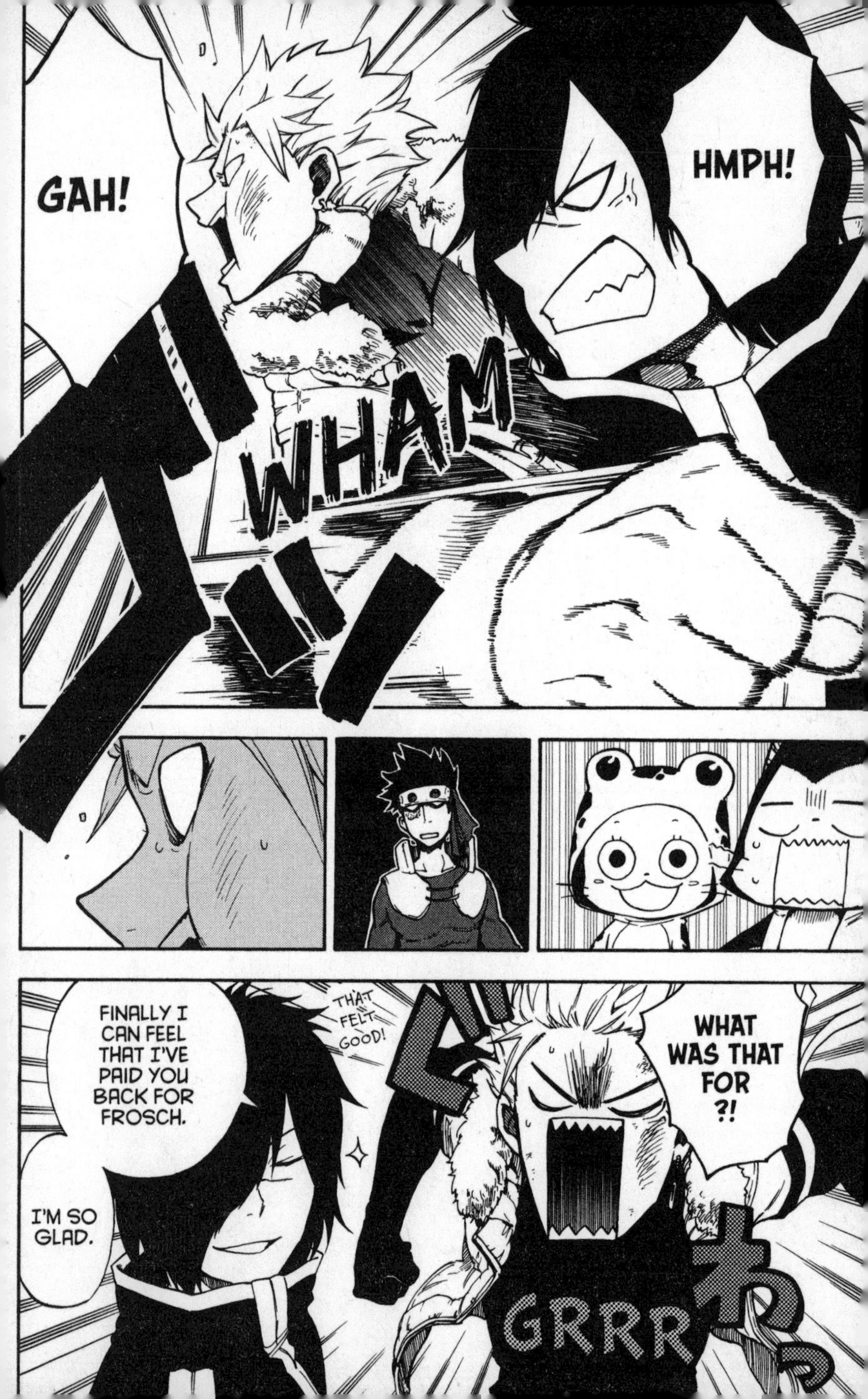
HMPH!
GAH!
WHAM
WHAT WAS THAT FOR ?!
GRRR
THAT FELT GOOD!
FINALLY I CAN FEEL THAT I'VE PAID YOU BACK FOR FROSCH.
I'M SO GLAD.

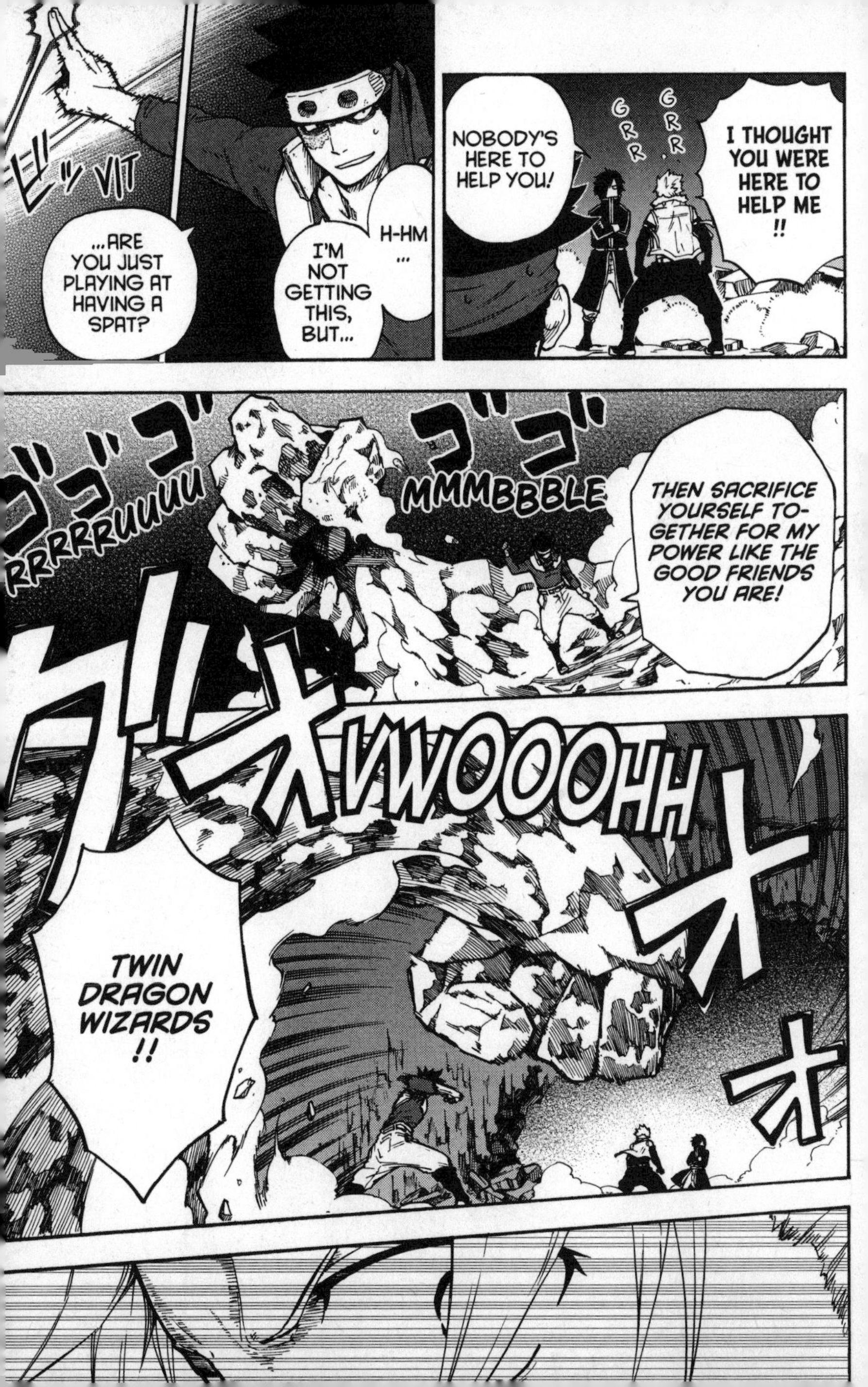
I THOUGHT YOU WERE HERE TO HELP ME !!
GRR
GRR
NOBODY'S HERE TO HELP YOU!
H-HM ...
I'M NOT GETTING THIS, BUT...
...ARE YOU JUST PLAYING AT HAVING A SPAT?
VIT
THEN SACRIFICE YOURSELF TO-GETHER FOR MY POWER LIKE THE GOOD FRIENDS YOU ARE!
MMMBBBLE
RRRRRUUUU
VWOOOHH
TWIN DRAGON WIZARDS !!

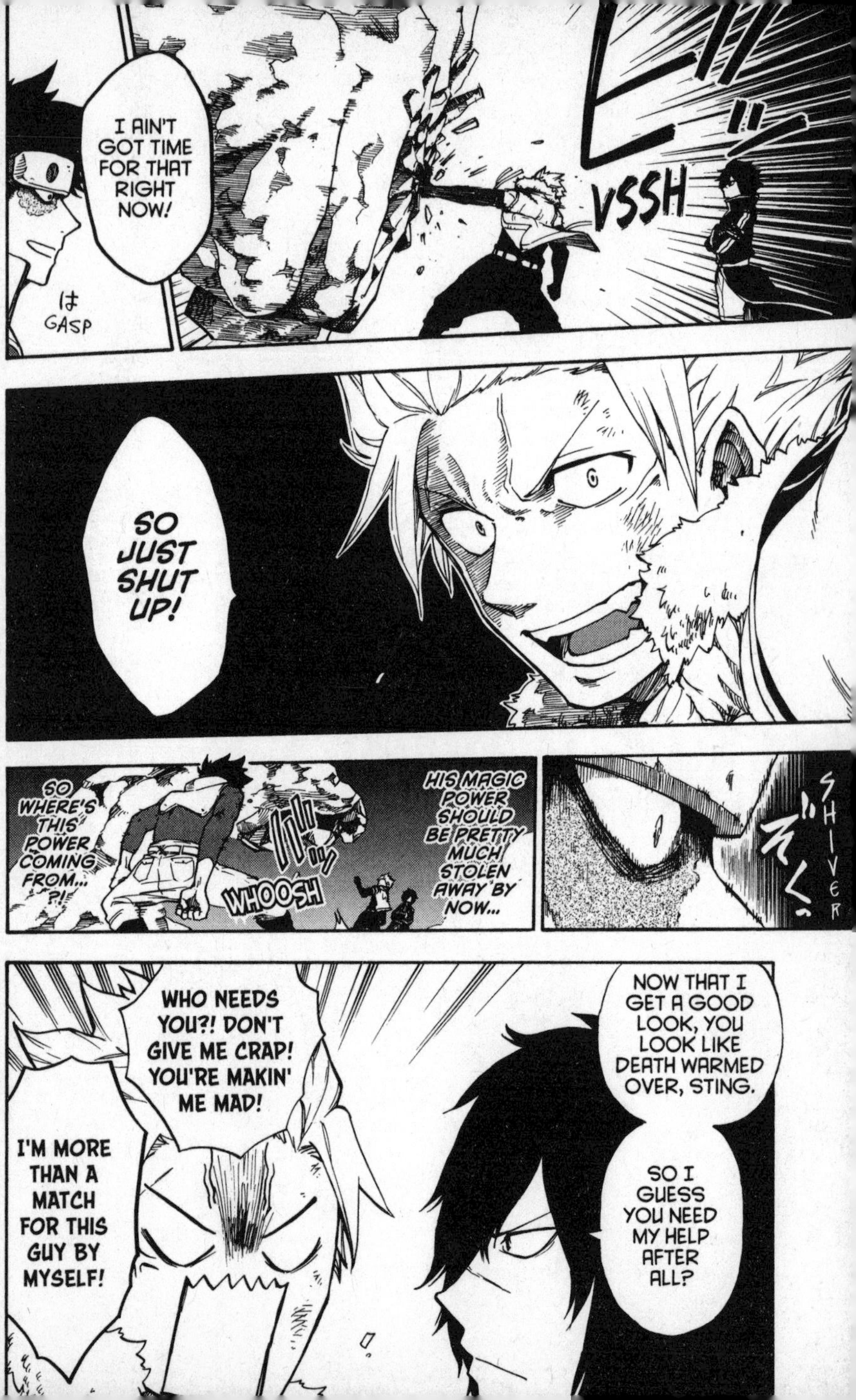
VSSH
I AIN'T GOT TIME FOR THAT RIGHT NOW!
は GASP
SO JUST SHUT UP!
SHIVER
HIS MAGIC POWER SHOULD BE PRETTY MUCH STOLEN AWAY BY NOW...
WHOOSH
SO WHERE'S THIS POWER COMING FROM...?!
NOW THAT I GET A GOOD LOOK, YOU LOOK LIKE DEATH WARMED OVER, STING.
SO I GUESS YOU NEED MY HELP AFTER ALL?
WHO NEEDS YOU?! DON'T GIVE ME CRAP! YOU'RE MAKIN' ME MAD!
I'M MORE THAN A MATCH FOR THIS GUY BY MYSELF!

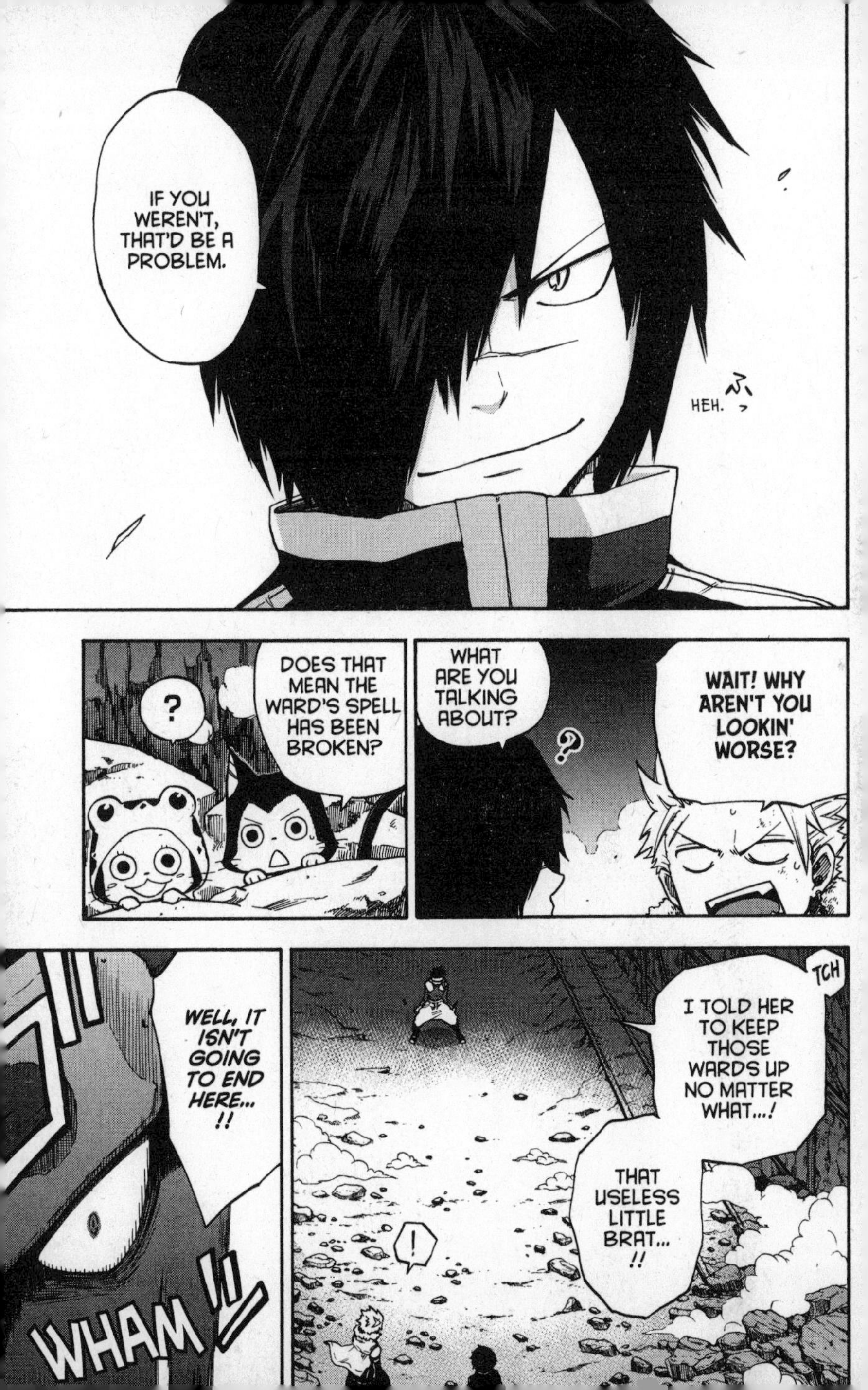
IF YOU WEREN'T, THAT'D BE A PROBLEM.
ふっ
HEH.
WAIT! WHY AREN'T YOU LOOKIN' WORSE?
WHAT ARE YOU TALKING ABOUT?
?
DOES THAT MEAN THE WARD'S SPELL HAS BEEN BROKEN?
?
TCH
I TOLD HER TO KEEP THOSE WARDS UP NO MATTER WHAT...!
THAT USELESS LITTLE BRAT... !!
!
WELL, IT ISN'T GOING TO END HERE... !!
WHAM!!

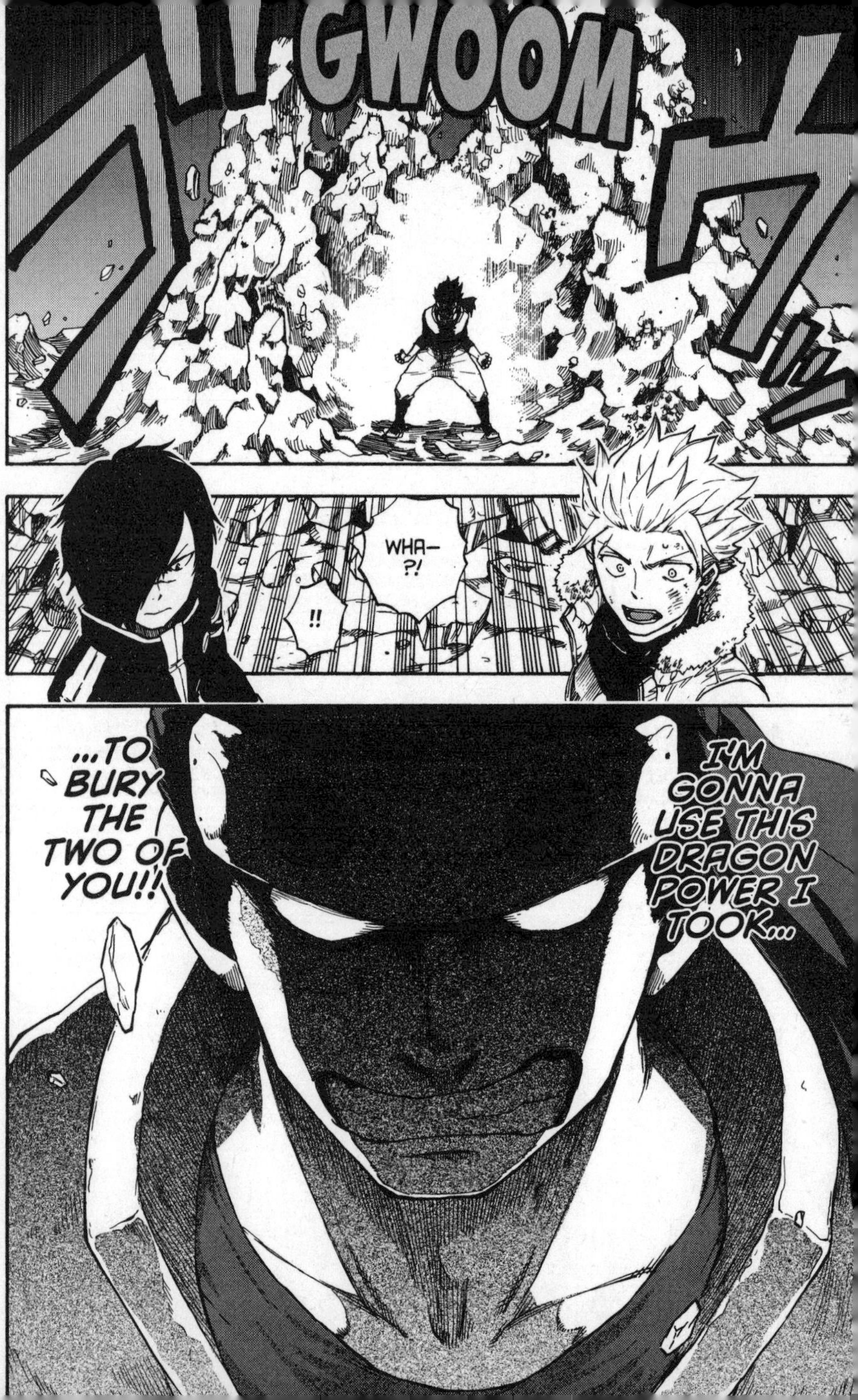
GWOOM
WHA-?!
!!
I'M GONNA USE THIS DRAGON POWER I TOOK...
...TO BURY THE TWO OF YOU!!

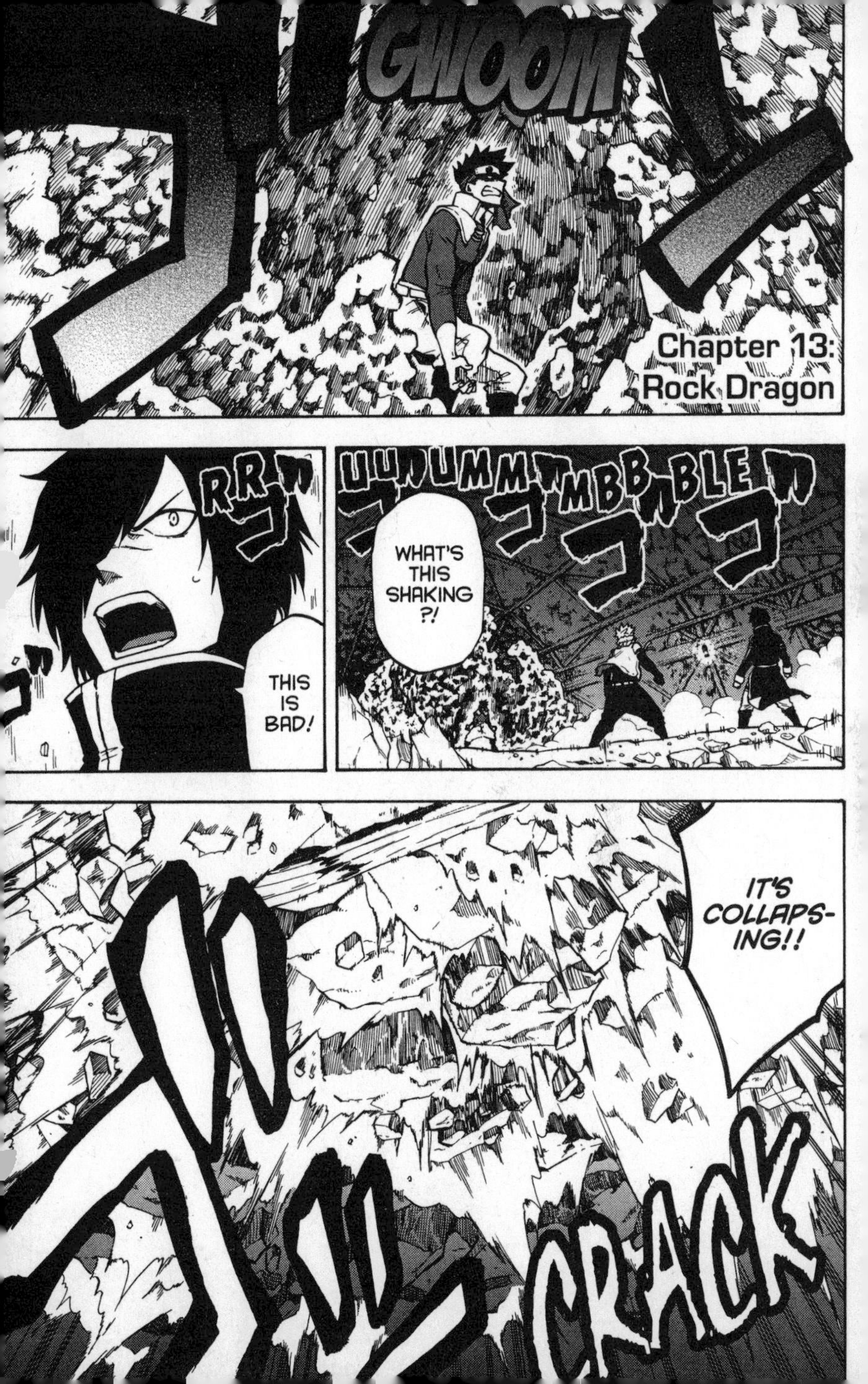
GWOOM
Chapter 13: Rock Dragon
WHAT'S THIS SHAKING?!
THIS IS BAD!
IT'S COLLAPSING!!
CRACK

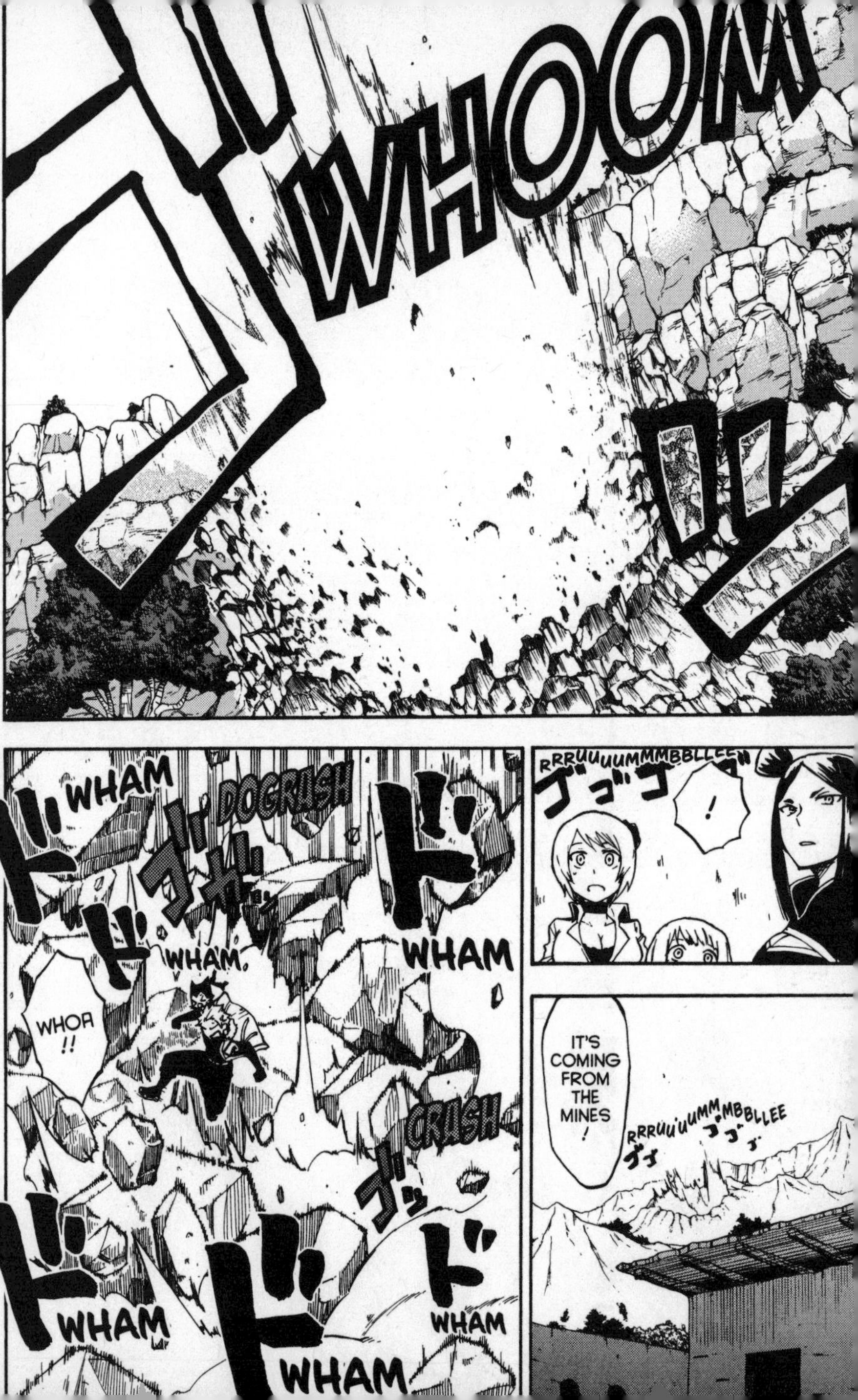
WHOOM
RRRUUUUMMMBBLLEE
!
IT'S COMING FROM THE MINES!
RRRUUUUMMMBBLLEE
WHAM
DOGRUSH
WHAM
WHAM
WHOA!!
CRUSH
WHAM
WHAM
WHAM

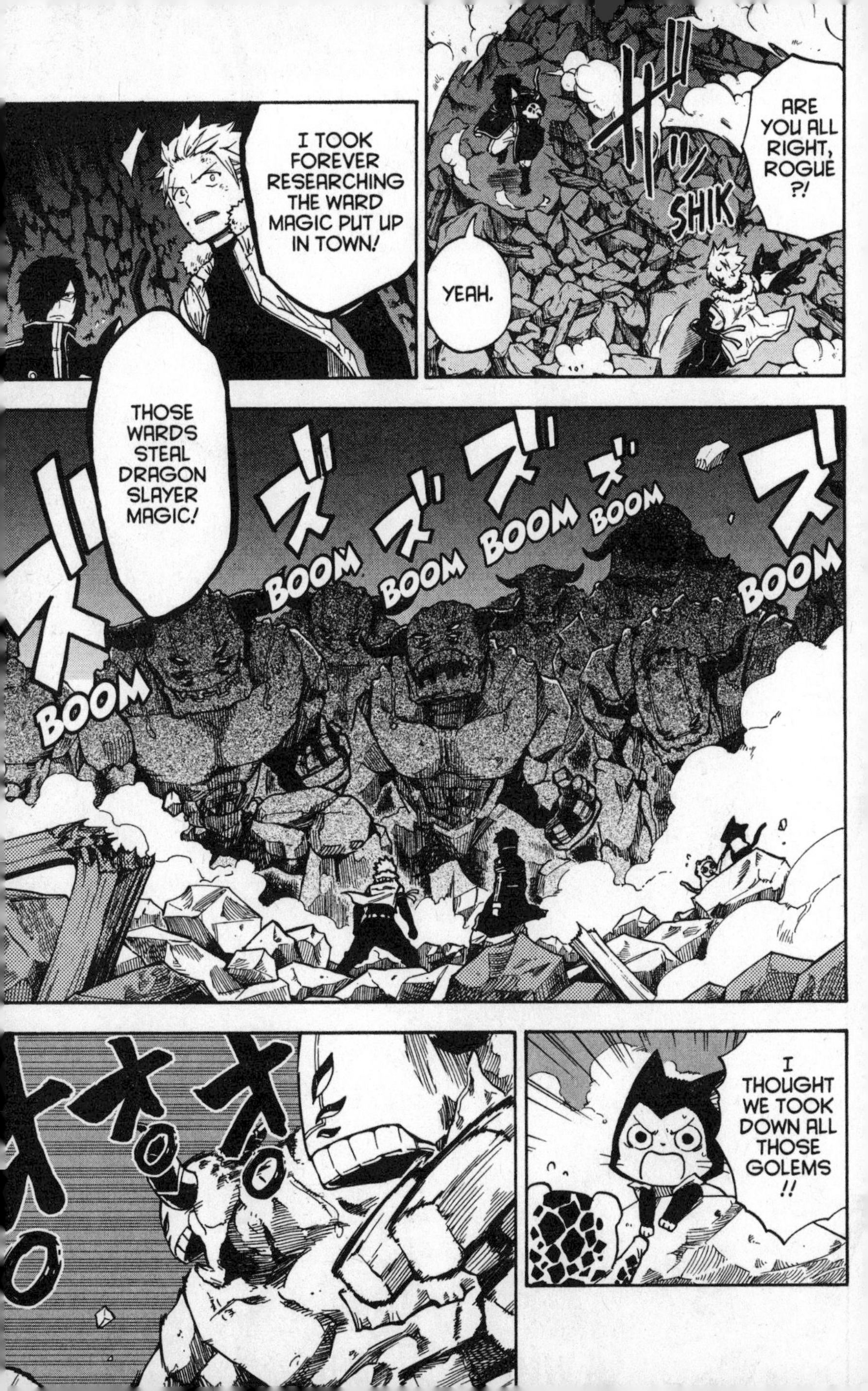
ARE YOU ALL RIGHT, ROGUE?!
SHIK
YEAH.
I TOOK FOREVER RESEARCHING THE WARD MAGIC PUT UP IN TOWN!
THOSE WARDS STEAL DRAGON SLAYER MAGIC!
BOOM
BOOM
BOOM
BOOM
BOOM
BOOM
I THOUGHT WE TOOK DOWN ALL THOSE GOLEMS!!

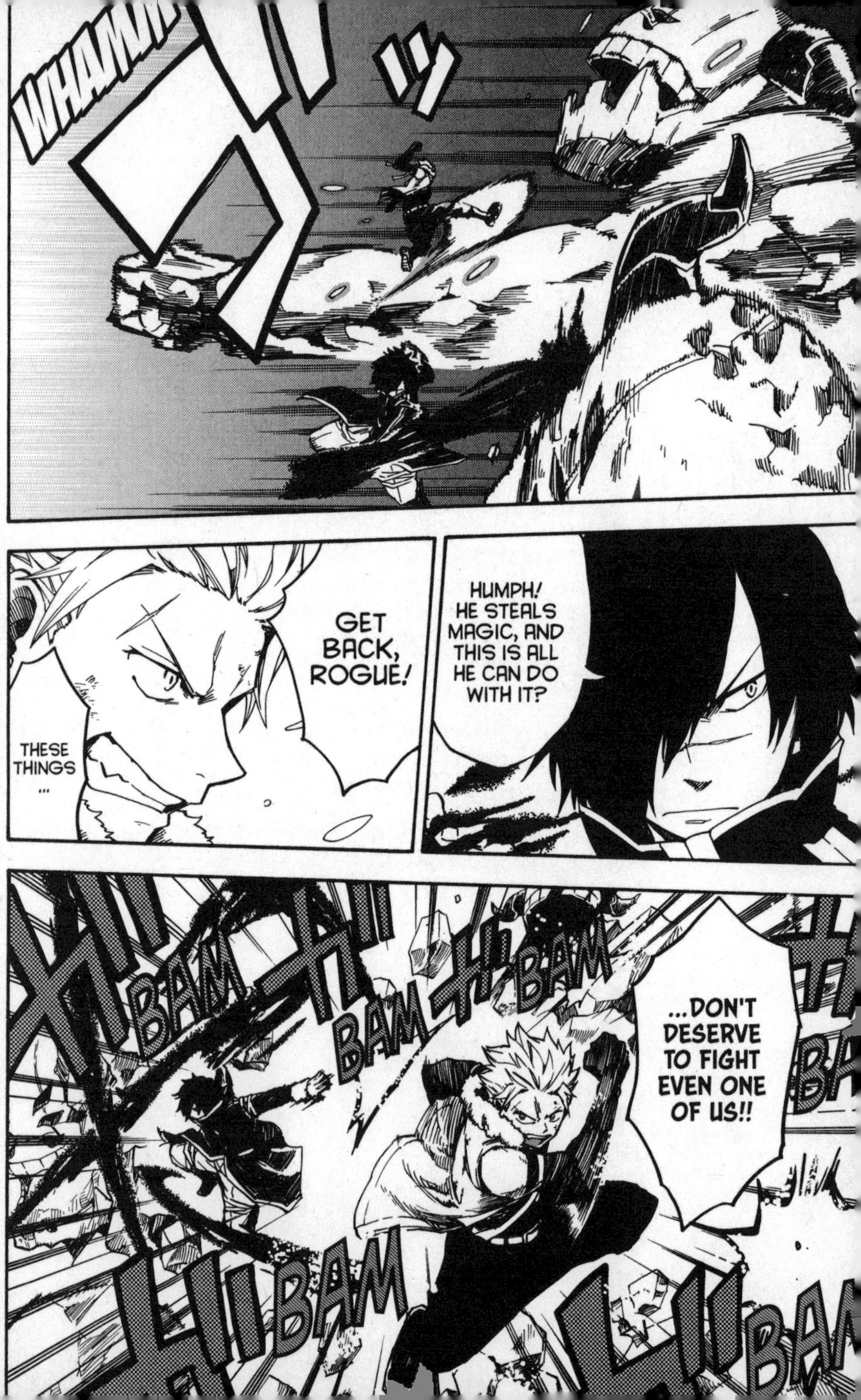
WHAMM
HUMPH! HE STEALS MAGIC, AND THIS IS ALL HE CAN DO WITH IT?
GET BACK, ROGUE!
THESE THINGS ...
BAM
BAM
BAM
BAM
...DON'T DESERVE TO FIGHT EVEN ONE OF US!!
BAM
BAM

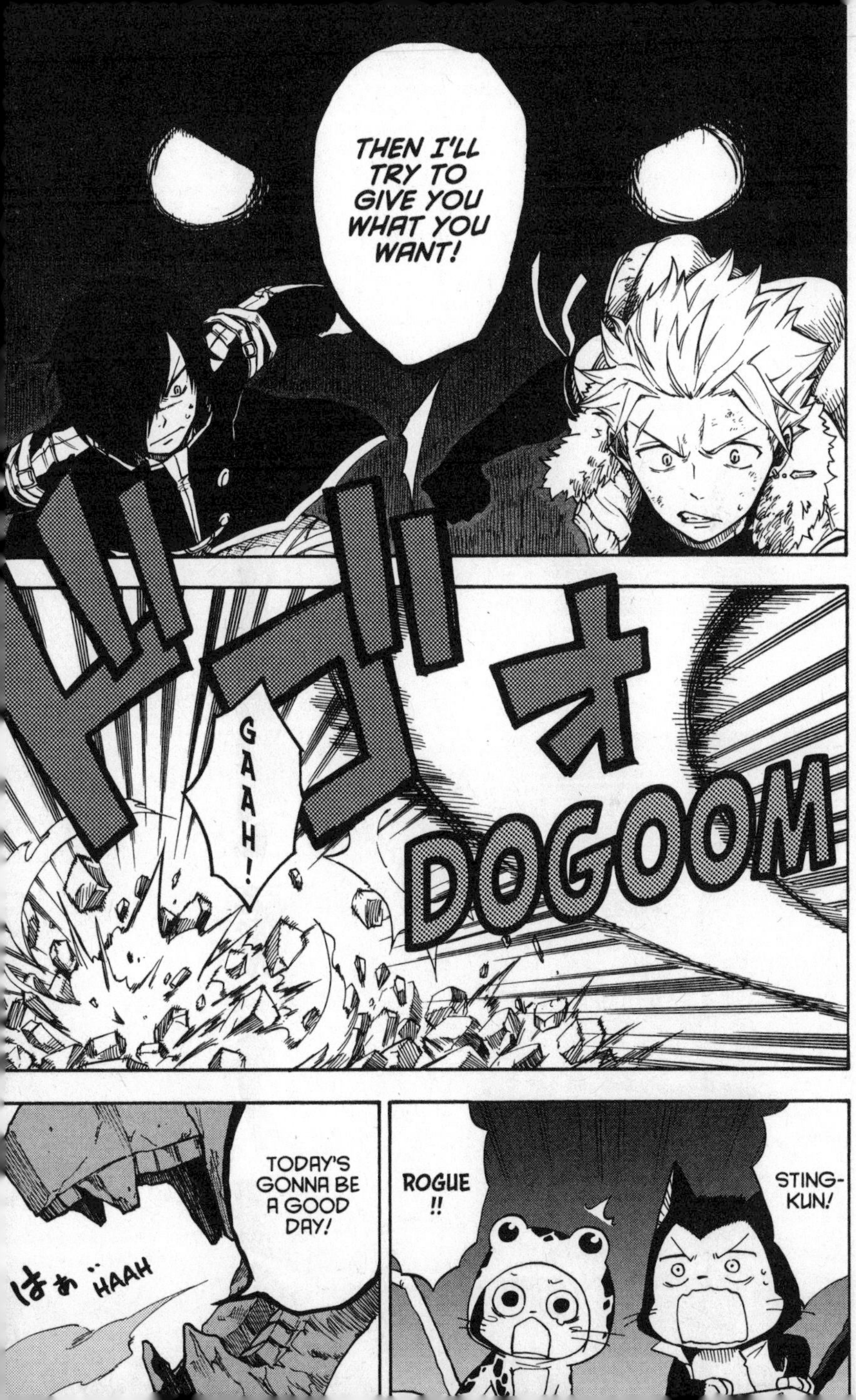
THEN I'LL TRY TO GIVE YOU WHAT YOU WANT!
ドゴオ
DOGOOM
GAAH!
STING-KUN!
ROGUE!!
TODAY'S GONNA BE A GOOD DAY!
はぁ…
HAAH

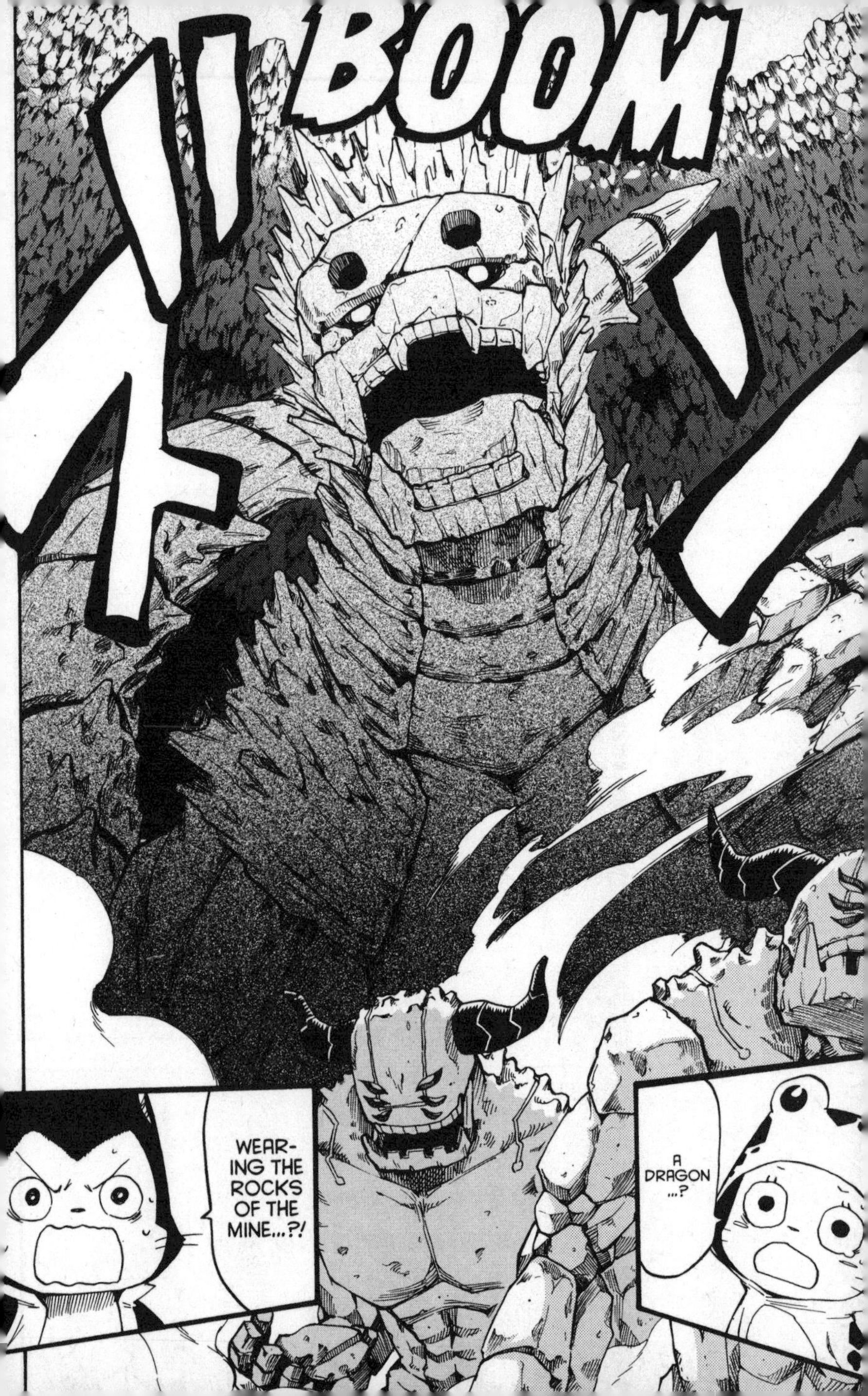

BOOM
A DRAGON ...?
WEAR-ING THE ROCKS OF THE MINE...?!

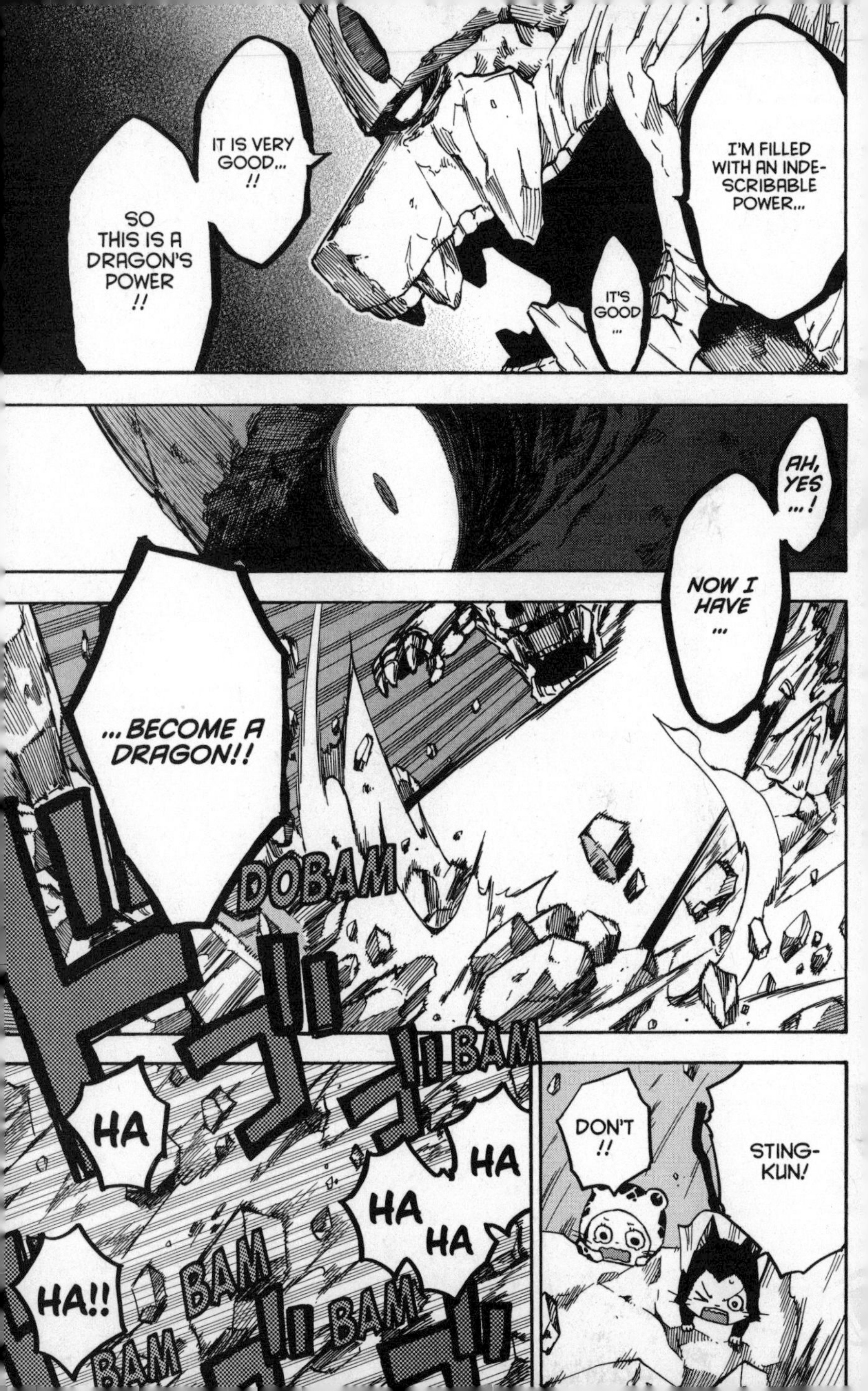
I'M FILLED WITH AN INDE-SCRIBABLE POWER...
IT'S GOOD...
IT IS VERY GOOD...!!
SO THIS IS A DRAGON'S POWER!!
AH, YES...!
NOW I HAVE...
...BECOME A DRAGON!!
DOBAM
STING-KUN!
DON'T!!
BAM
HA
HA
HA
HA
HA!!
BAM
BAM
BAM

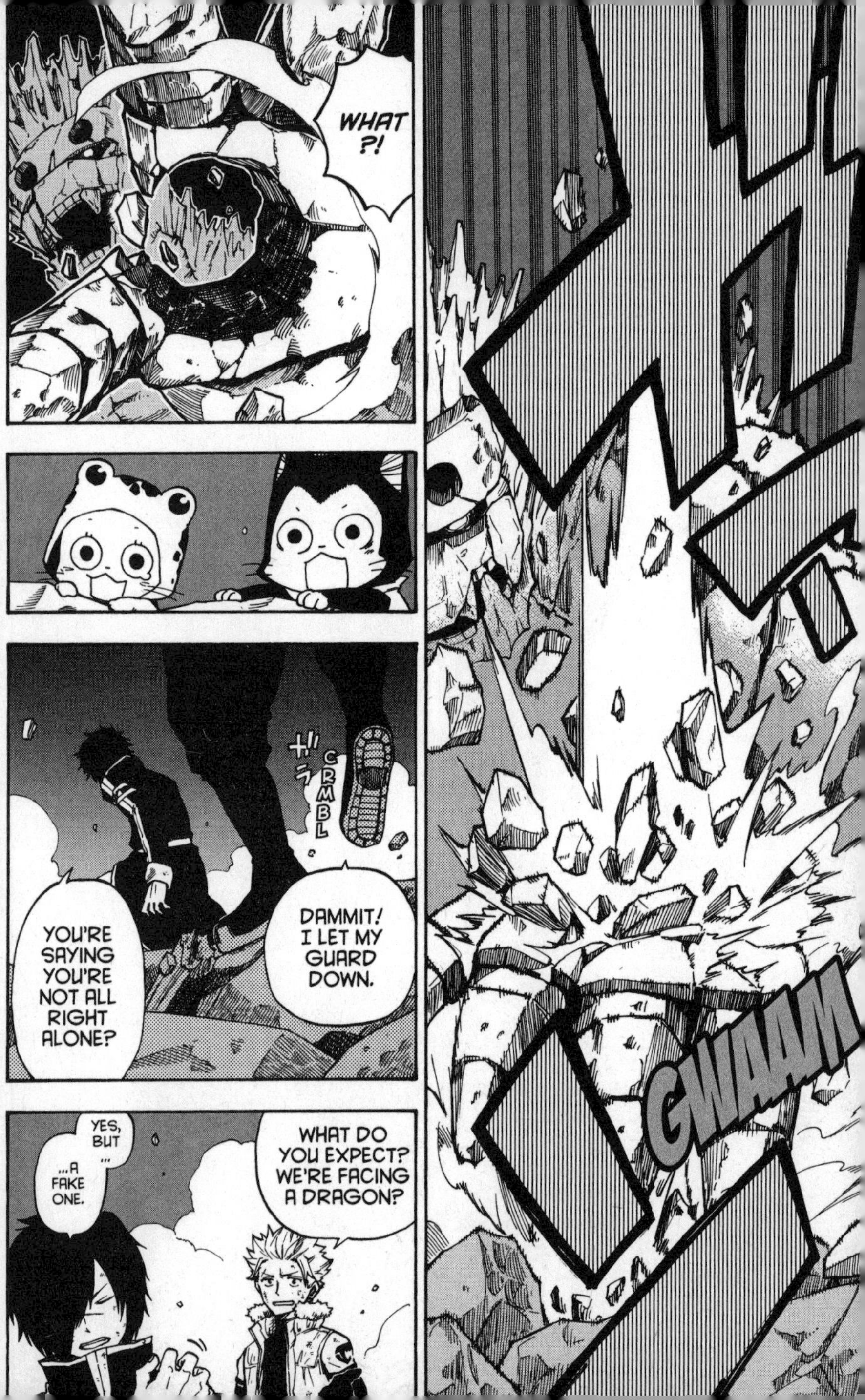
GWAAM
WHAT ?!
CRMBL
DAMMIT! I LET MY GUARD DOWN.
YOU'RE SAYING YOU'RE NOT ALL RIGHT ALONE?
WHAT DO YOU EXPECT? WE'RE FACING A DRAGON?
YES, BUT ...
...A FAKE ONE.

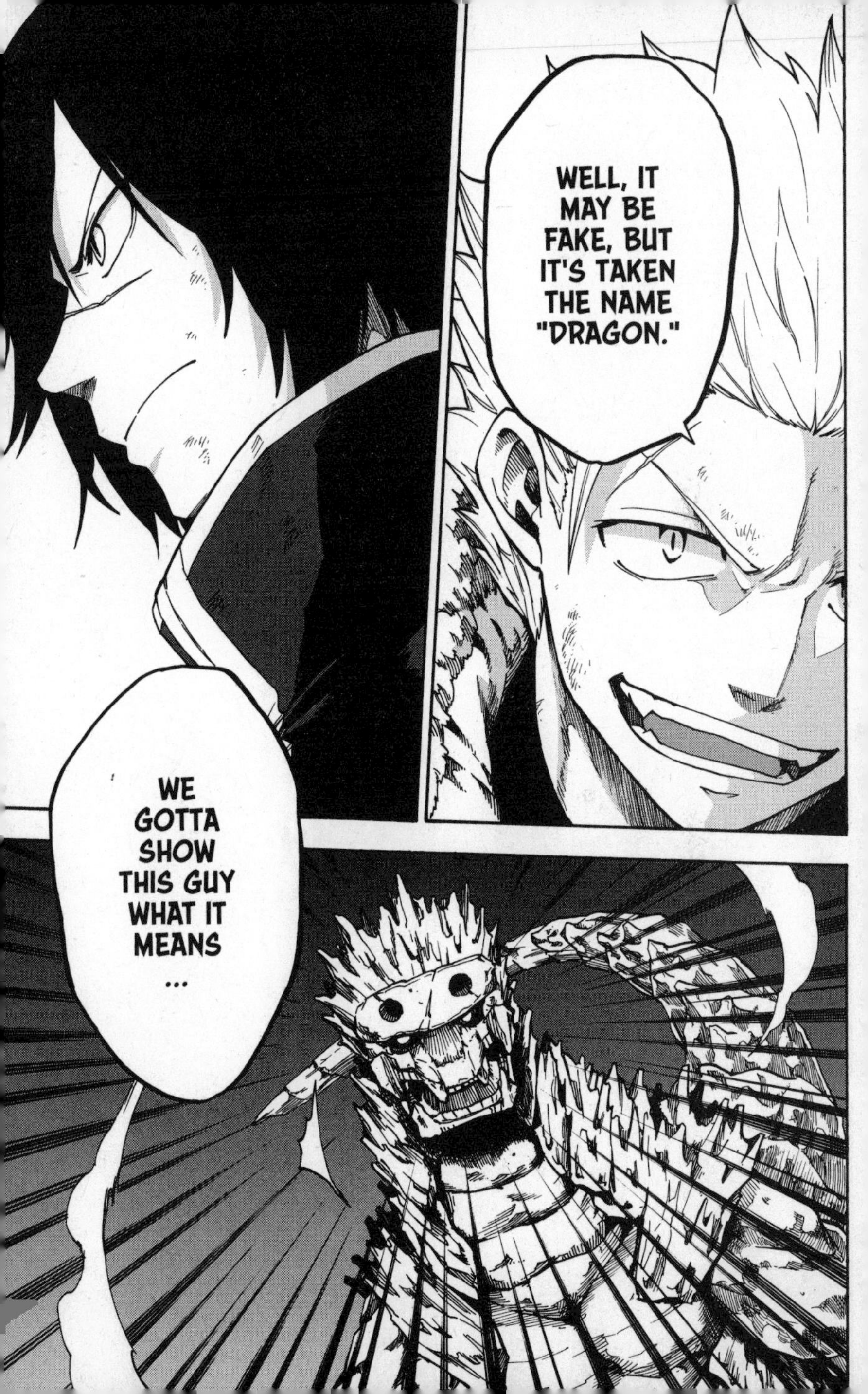
WELL, IT MAY BE FAKE, BUT IT'S TAKEN THE NAME "DRAGON."
WE GOTTA SHOW THIS GUY WHAT IT MEANS ...

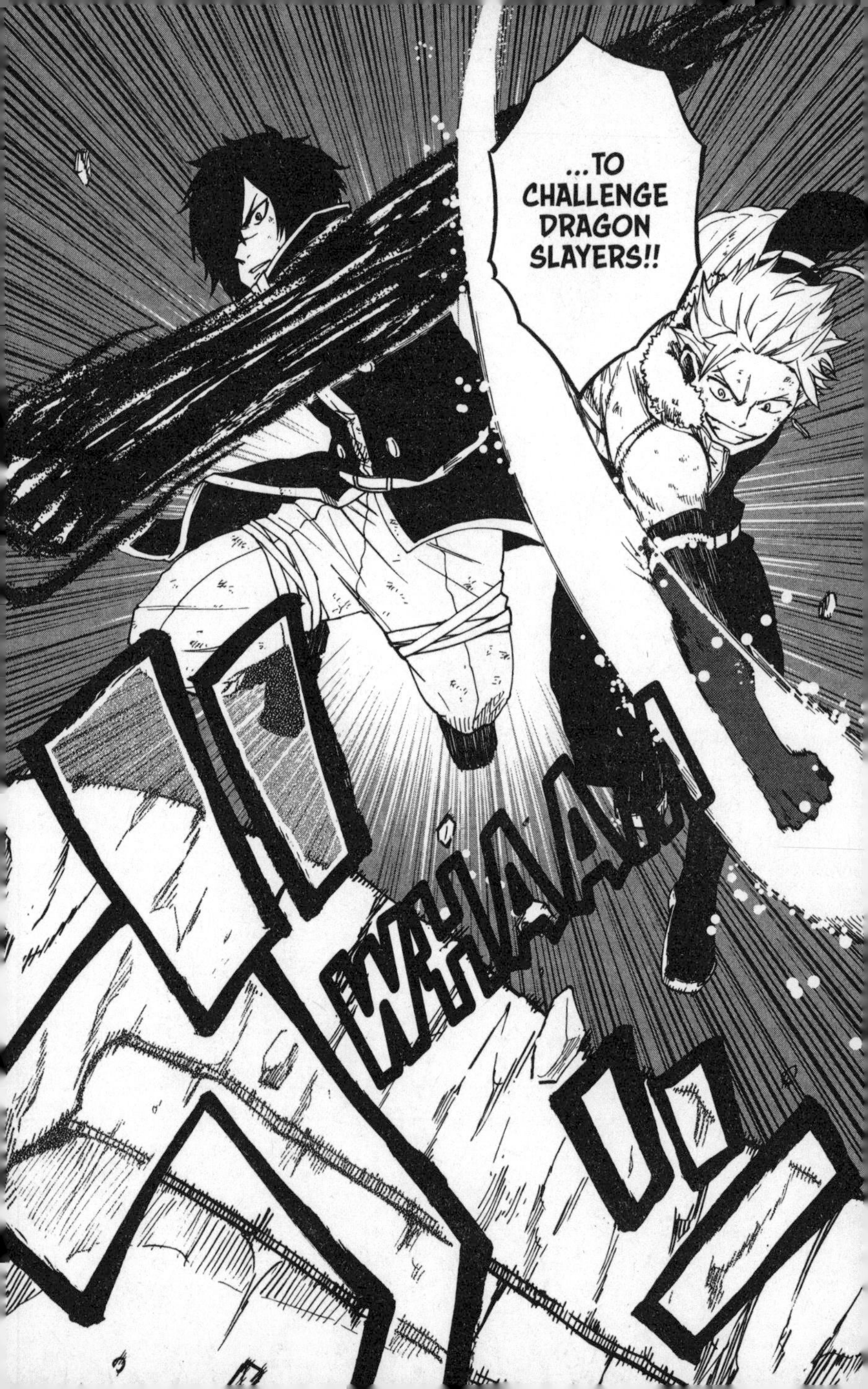
...TO CHALLENGE DRAGON SLAYERS!!
WHAAAM!!

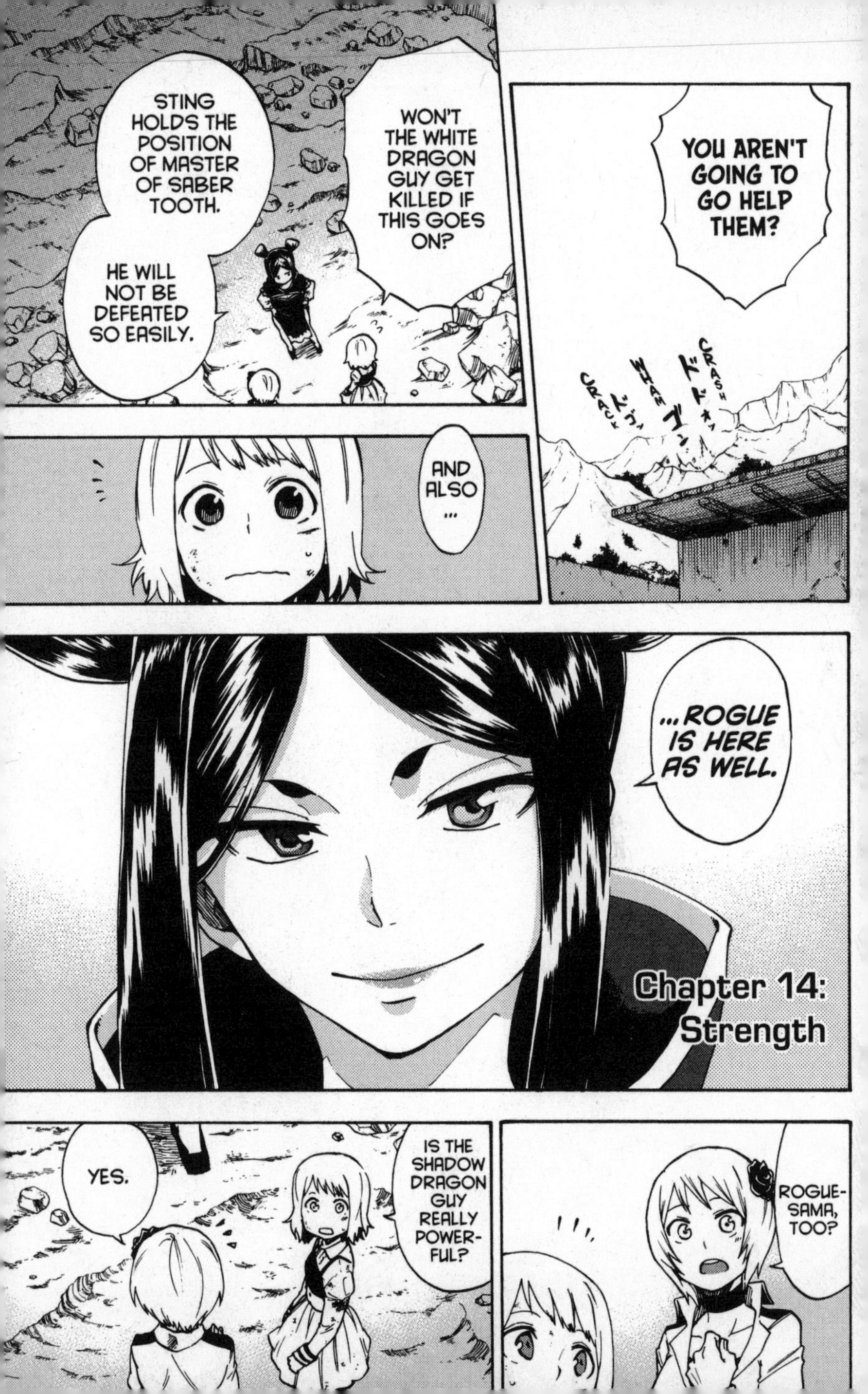
YOU AREN'T GOING TO GO HELP THEM?
CRASH
WHAM
CRACK
WON'T THE WHITE DRAGON GUY GET KILLED IF THIS GOES ON?
STING HOLDS THE POSITION OF MASTER OF SABER TOOTH.
HE WILL NOT BE DEFEATED SO EASILY.
AND ALSO ...
...ROGUE IS HERE AS WELL.
Chapter 14: Strength
ROGUE-SAMA, TOO?
IS THE SHADOW DRAGON GUY REALLY POWERFUL?
YES.

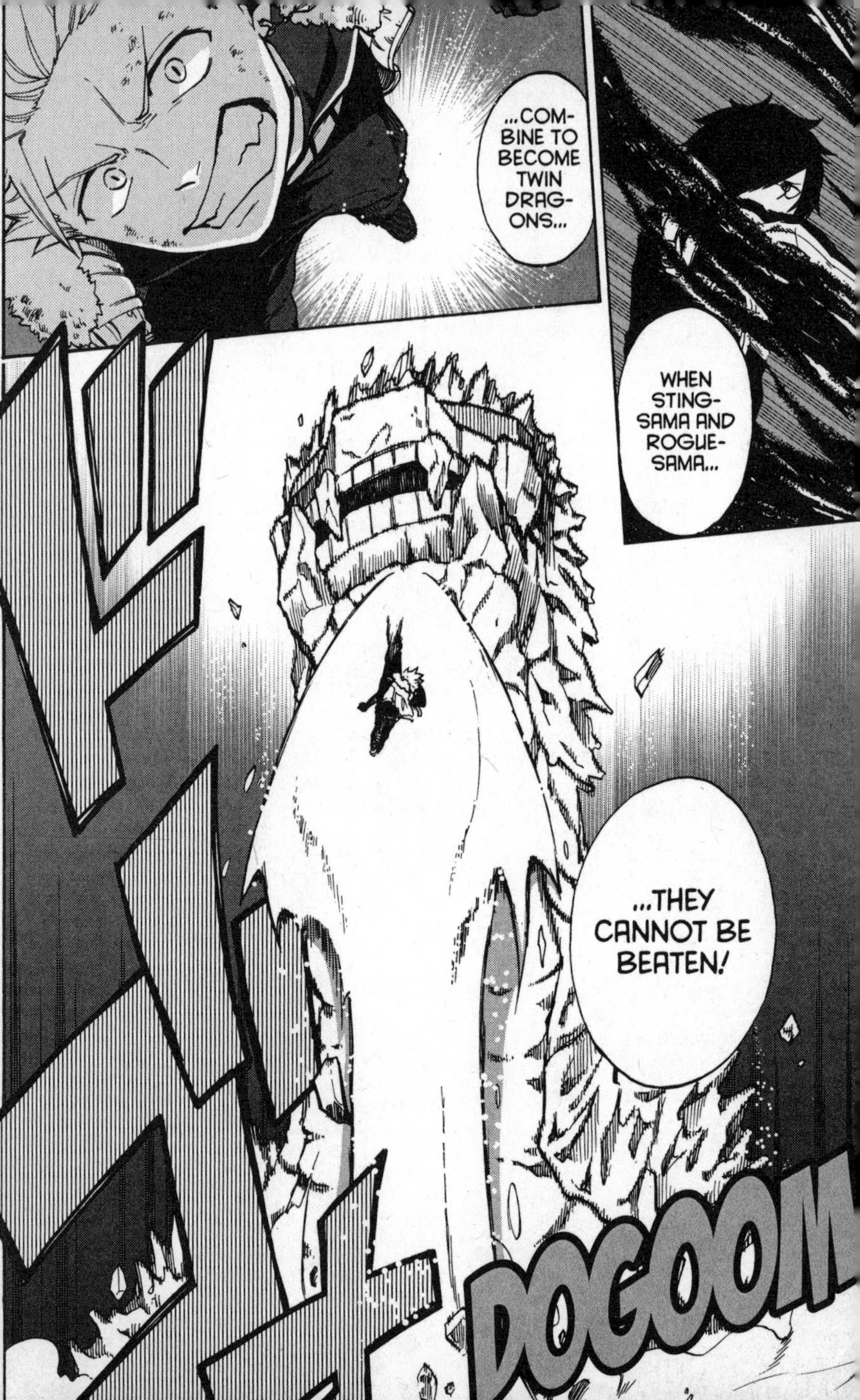
WHEN STING-SAMA AND ROGUE-SAMA...
...COMBINE TO BECOME TWIN DRAGONS...
...THEY CANNOT BE BEATEN!
DOGOOM

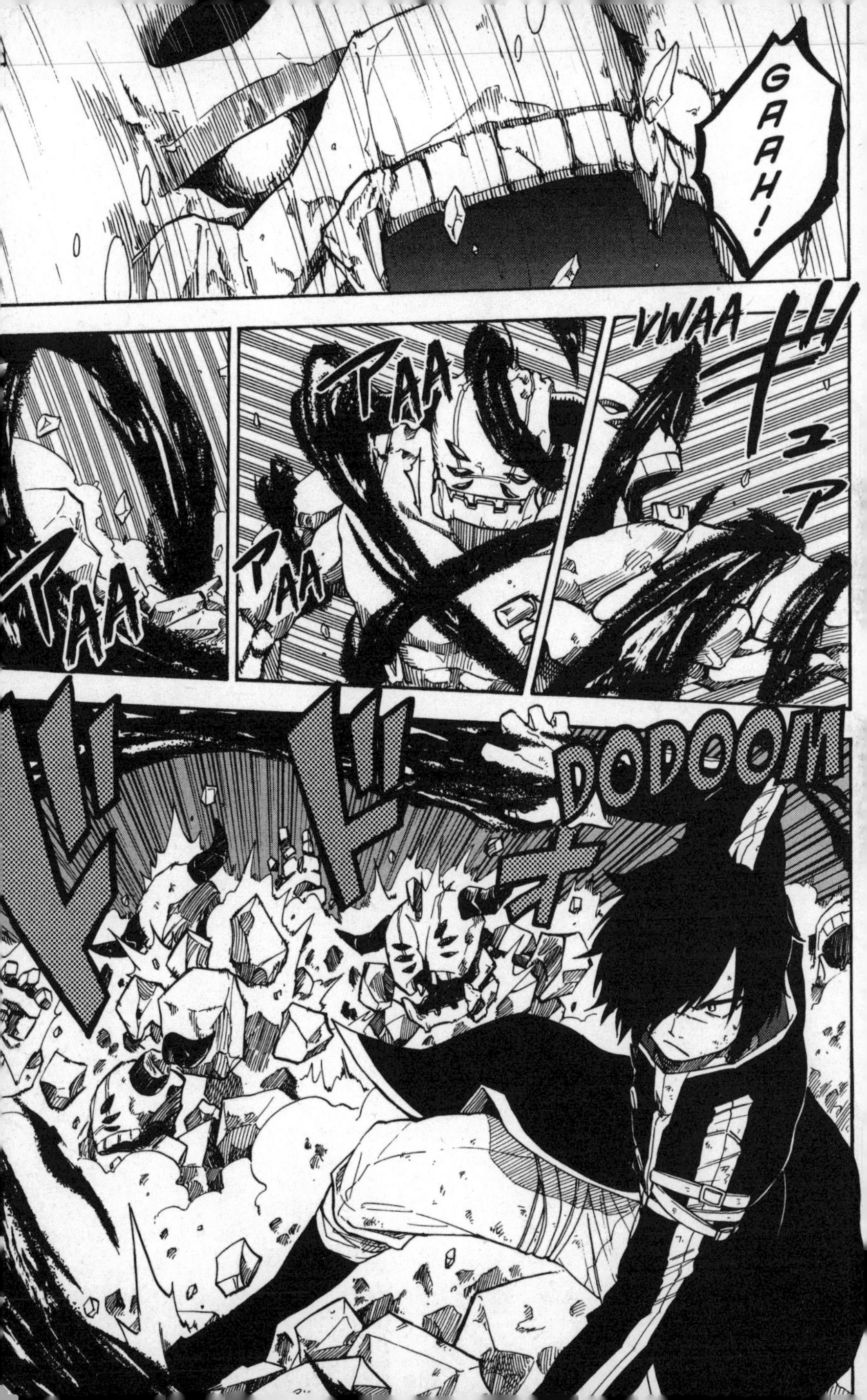
GAAAH!
VWAA
PAA
PAA
PAA
DODOOM

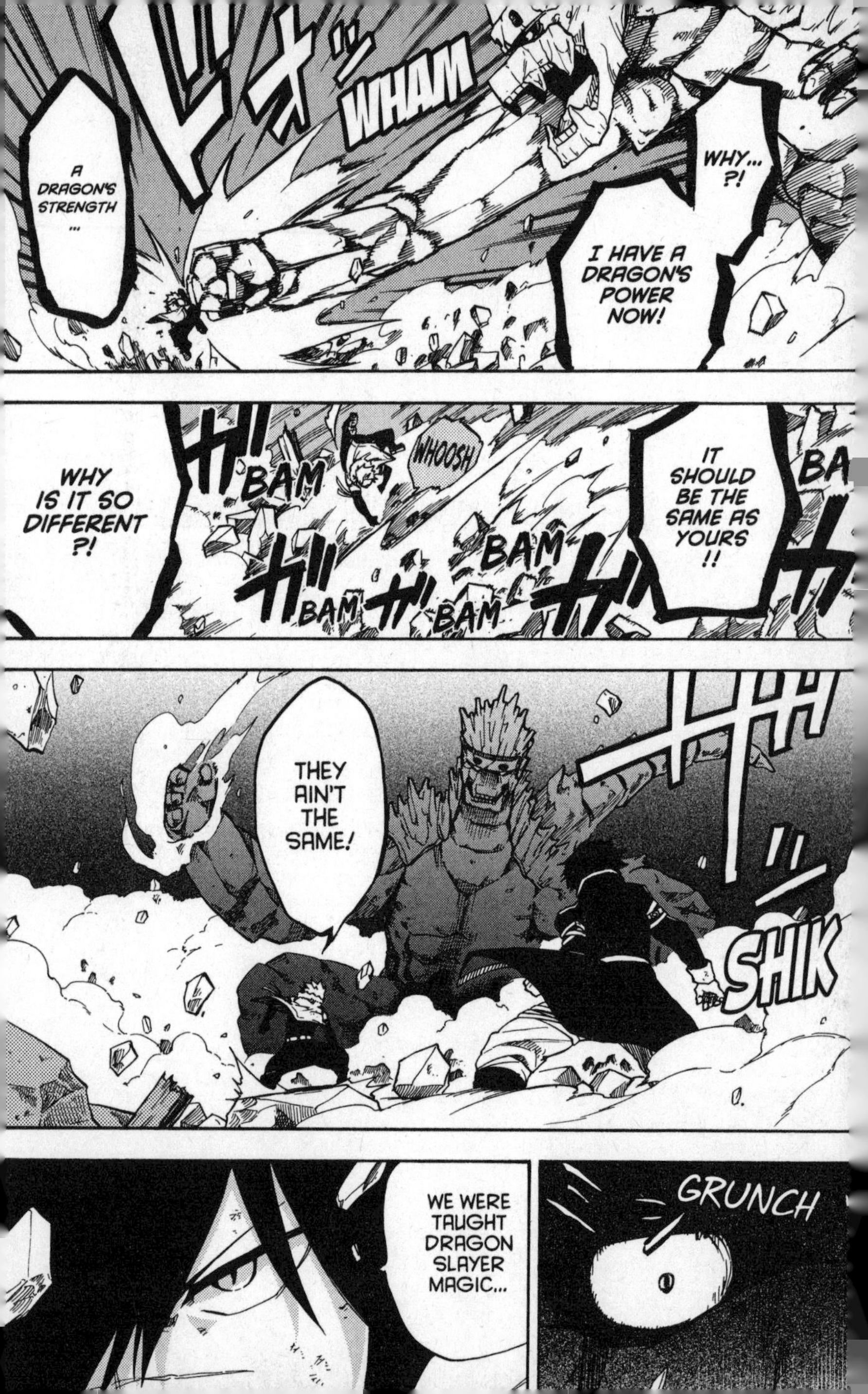
WHY...?!
I HAVE A DRAGON'S POWER NOW!
WHAM
A DRAGON'S STRENGTH ...
IT SHOULD BE THE SAME AS YOURS!!
BA
BAM
WHOOSH
BAM
BAM
BAM
BAM
WHY IS IT SO DIFFERENT?!
SHIK
THEY AIN'T THE SAME!
GRUNCH
WE WERE TAUGHT DRAGON SLAYER MAGIC...

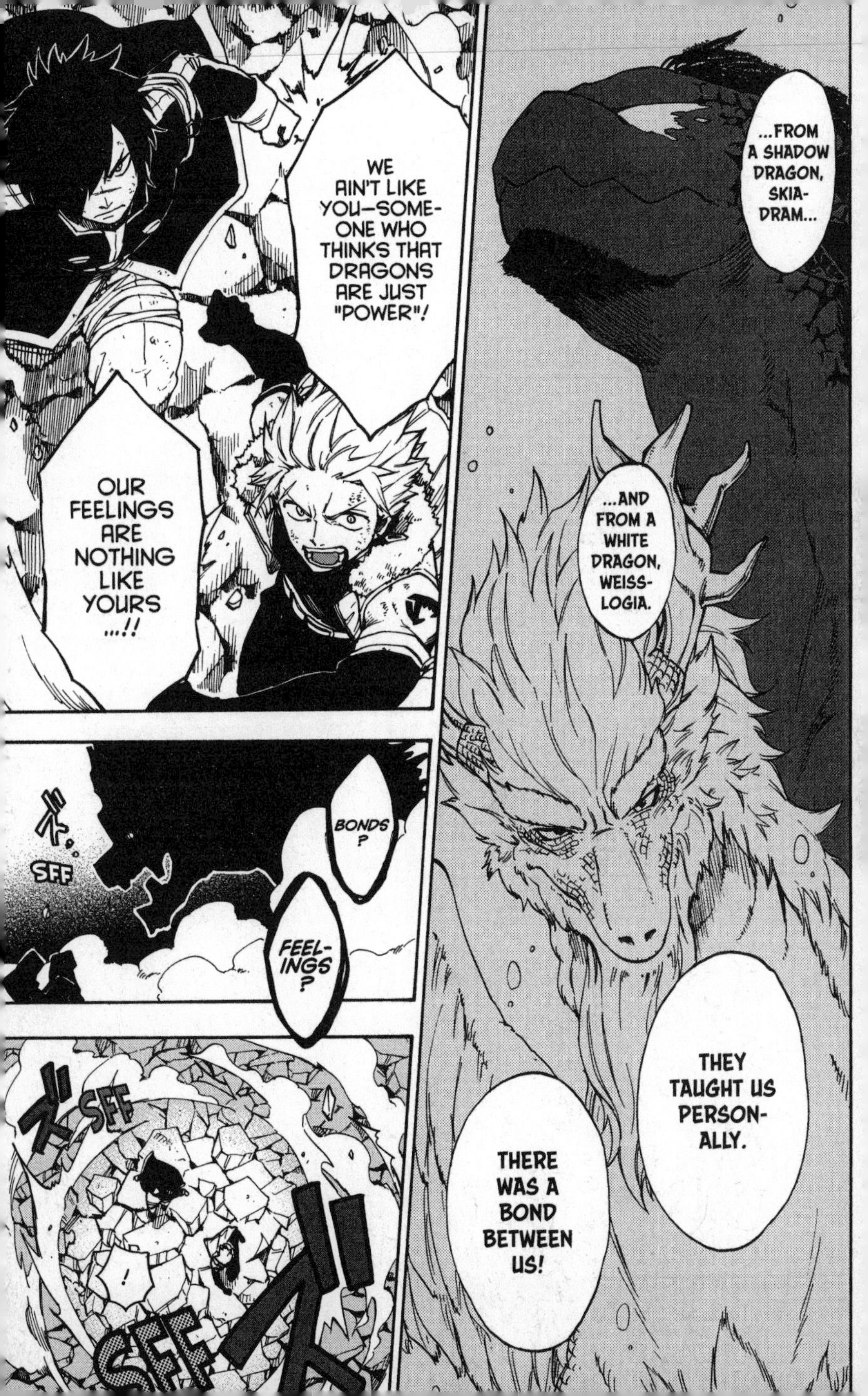
...FROM A SHADOW DRAGON, SKIA-DRAM...
...AND FROM A WHITE DRAGON, WEISS-LOGIA.
THEY TAUGHT US PERSON-ALLY.
THERE WAS A BOND BETWEEN US!
WE AIN'T LIKE YOU—SOME-ONE WHO THINKS THAT DRAGONS ARE JUST "POWER"!
OUR FEELINGS ARE NOTHING LIKE YOURS ...!!
BONDS?
FEEL-INGS?
SFF
SFF
!
SFF

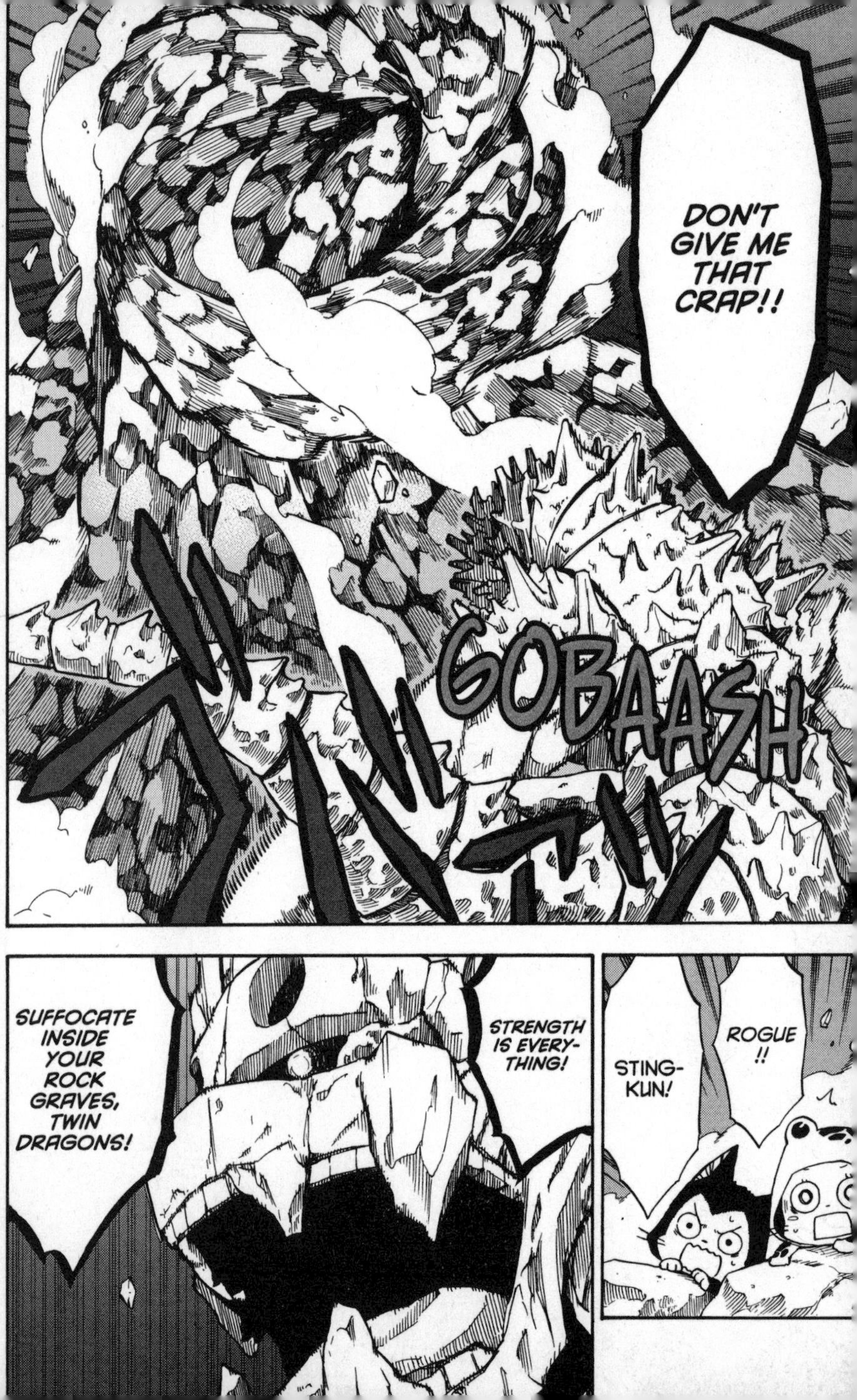
DON'T GIVE ME THAT CRAP!!
GOBAASH
ROGUE !!
STING-KUN!
STRENGTH IS EVERY-THING!
SUFFOCATE INSIDE YOUR ROCK GRAVES, TWIN DRAGONS!

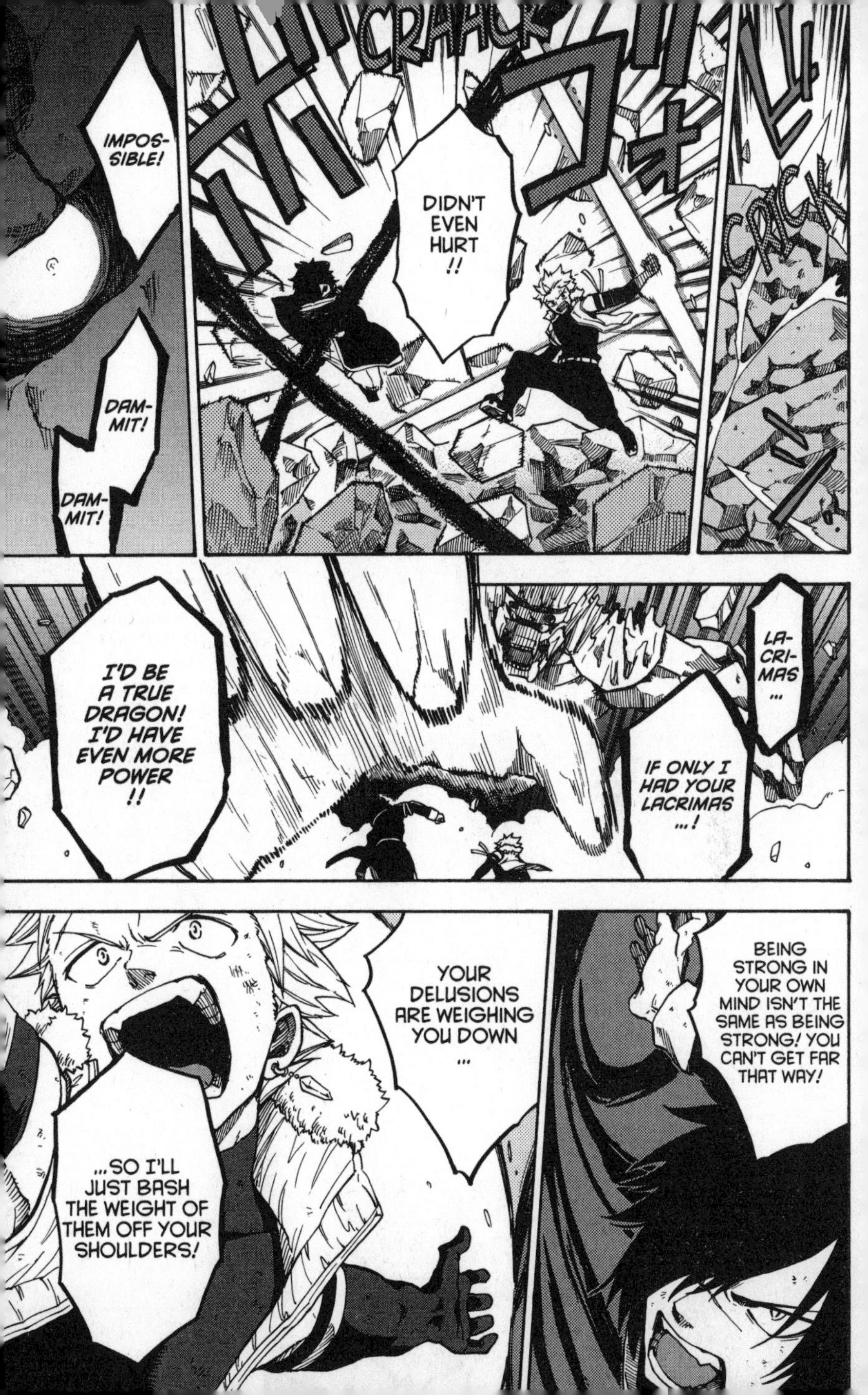
CRICK
CRAAACK
DIDN'T EVEN HURT !!
IMPOS-SIBLE!
DAM-MIT!
DAM-MIT!
LA-CRI-MAS ...
IF ONLY I HAD YOUR LACRIMAS ...!
I'D BE A TRUE DRAGON! I'D HAVE EVEN MORE POWER !!
BEING STRONG IN YOUR OWN MIND ISN'T THE SAME AS BEING STRONG! YOU CAN'T GET FAR THAT WAY!
YOUR DELUSIONS ARE WEIGHING YOU DOWN ...
...SO I'LL JUST BASH THE WEIGHT OF THEM OFF YOUR SHOULDERS!

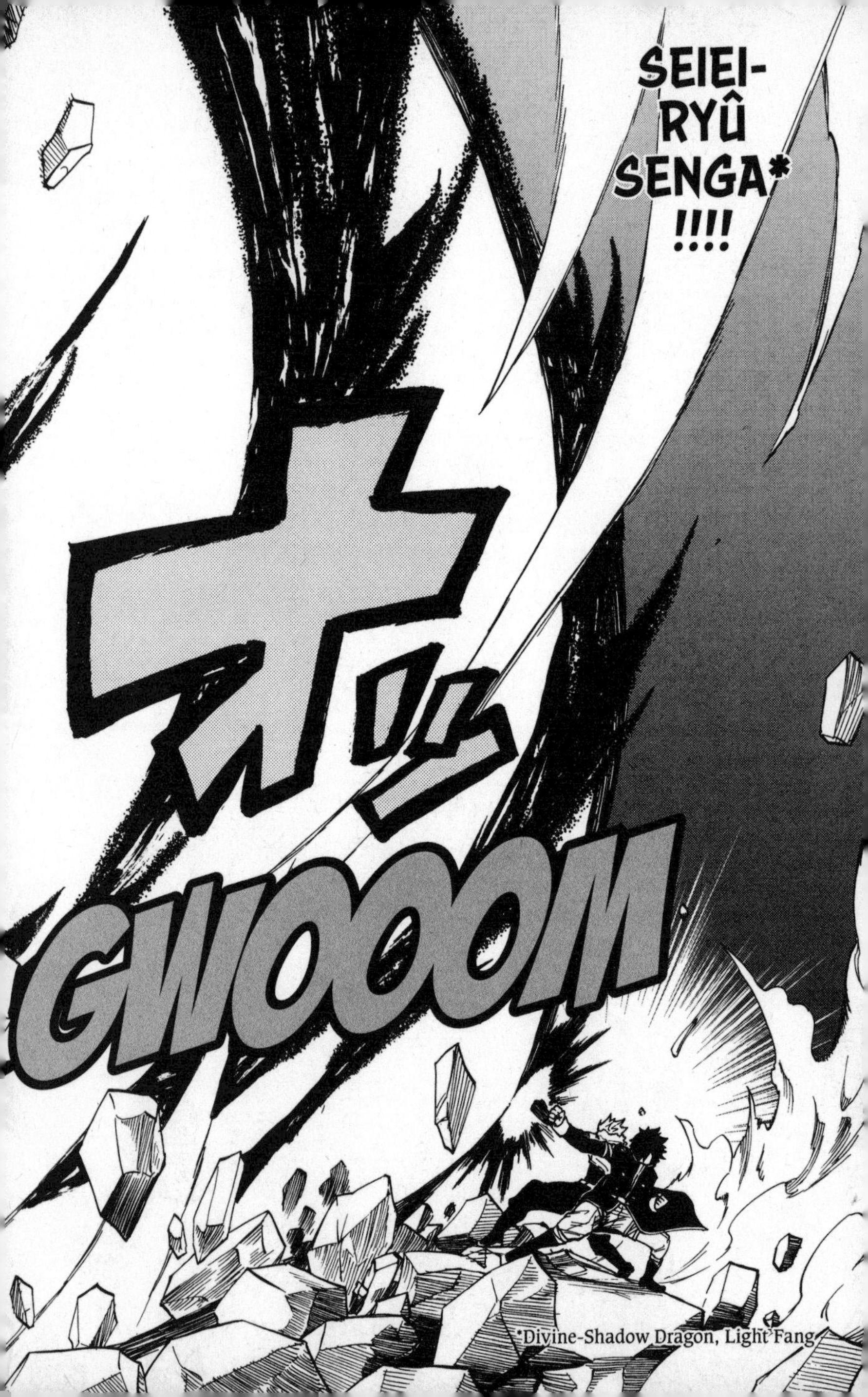
SEIEI-RYÛ SENGA*!!!!
GWOOOM

*Divine-Shadow Dragon, Light Fang

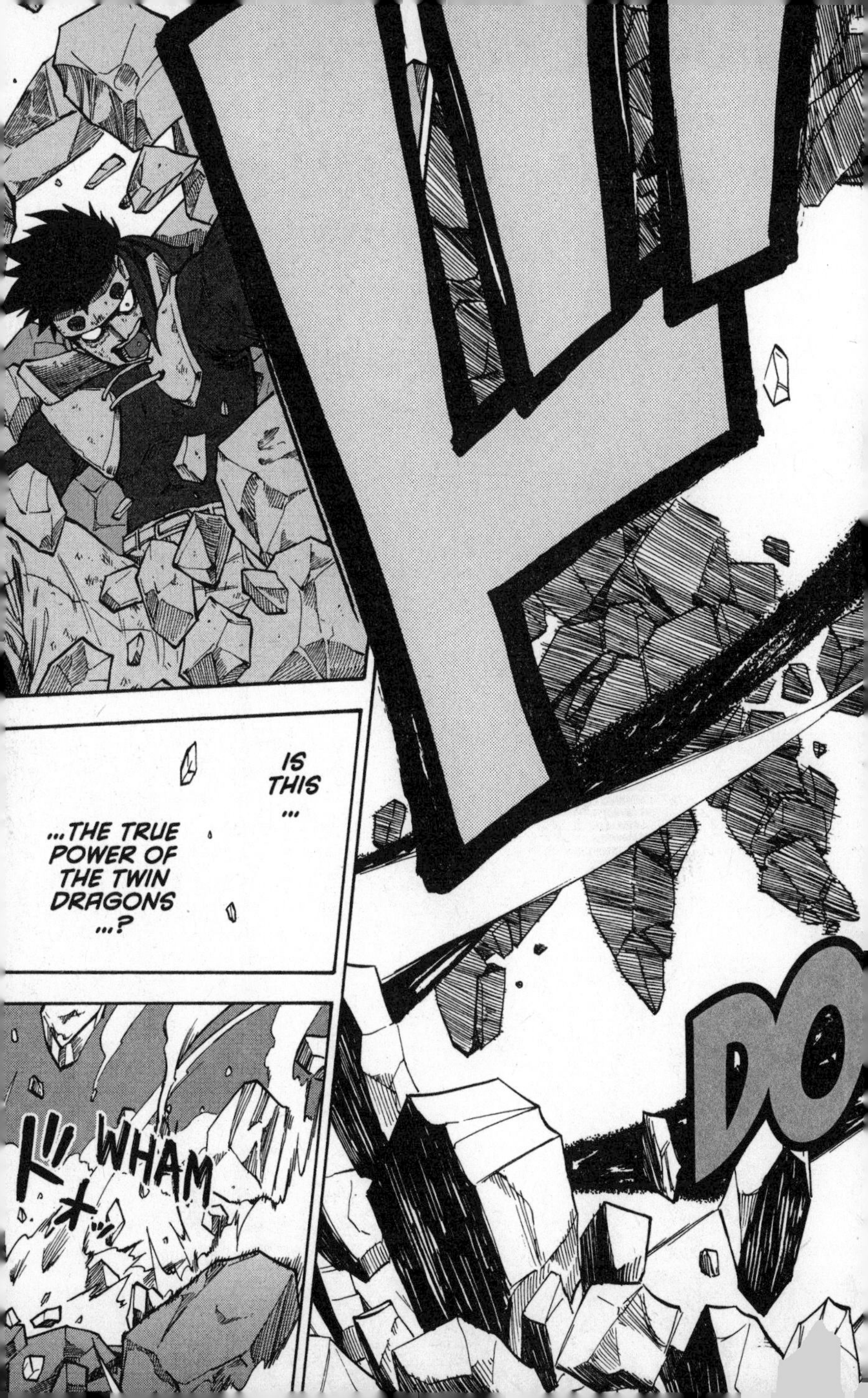
DO
IS THIS ...
...THE TRUE POWER OF THE TWIN DRAGONS ...?
WHAM

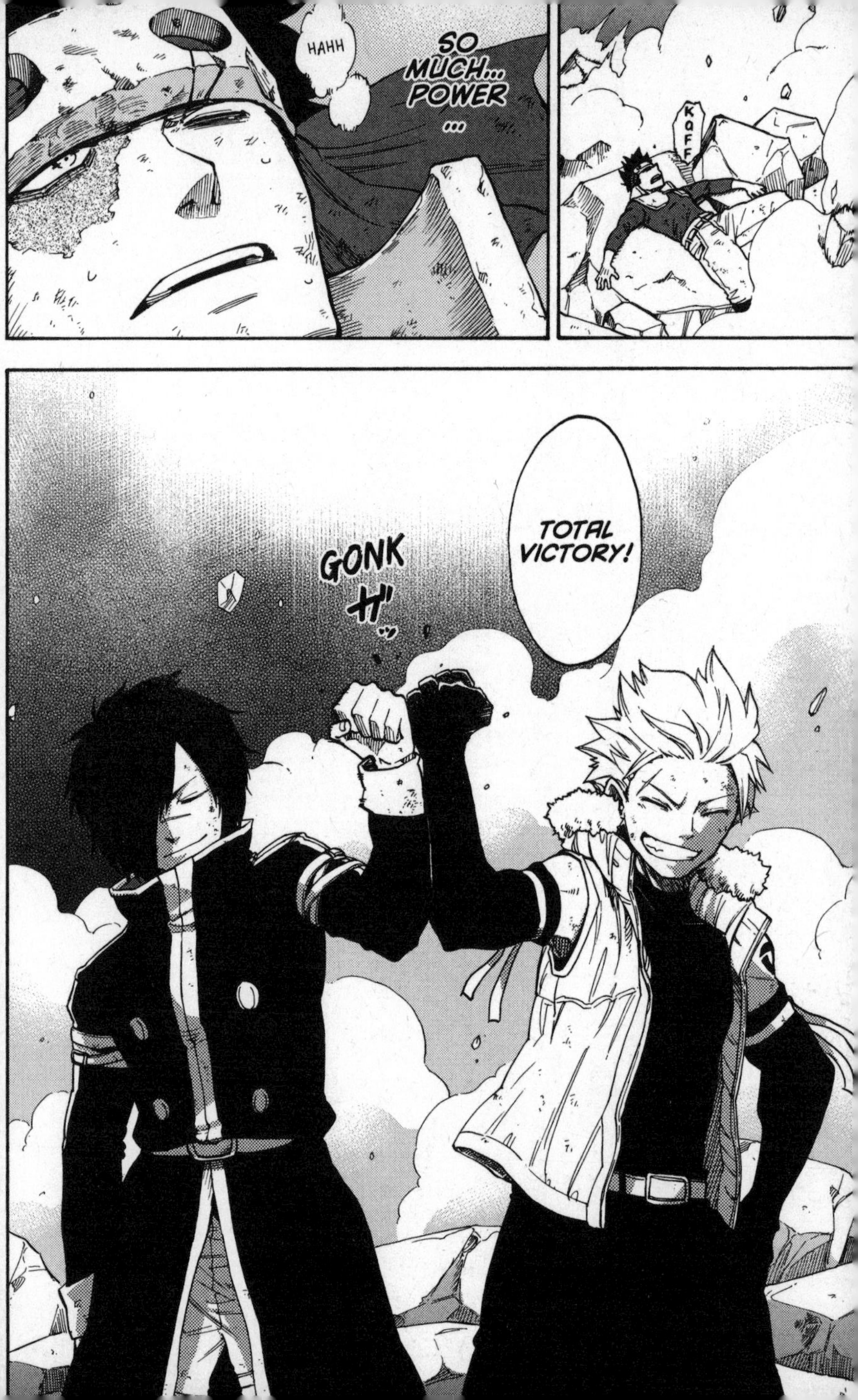
KOFF
HAHH
SO MUCH... POWER ...
TOTAL VICTORY!
GONK

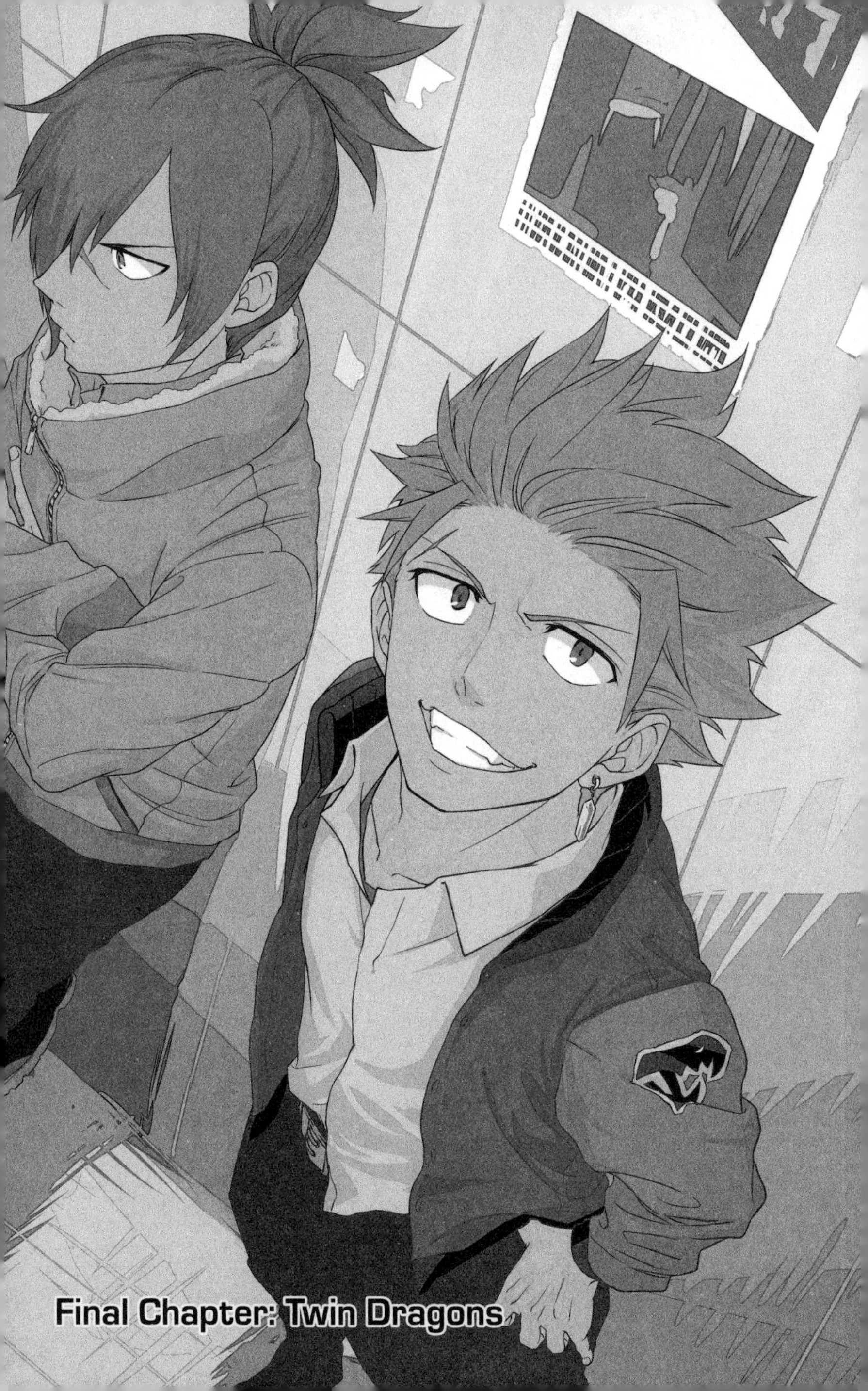

Final Chapter: Twin Dragons

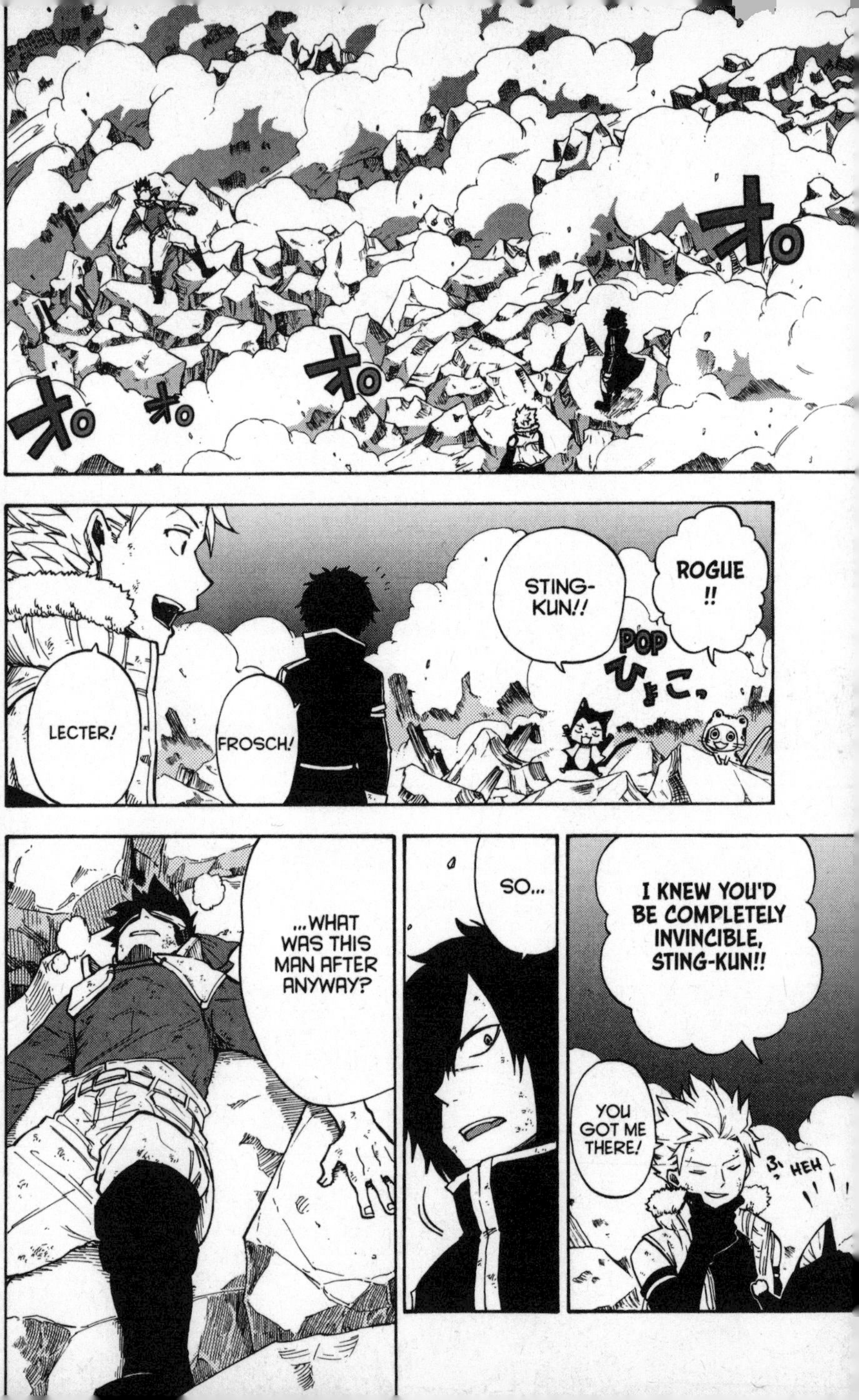
ROGUE!!
STING-KUN!!
POP
ひょこ
FROSCH!
LECTER!
I KNEW YOU'D BE COMPLETELY INVINCIBLE, STING-KUN!!
YOU GOT ME THERE!
HEH
SO...
...WHAT WAS THIS MAN AFTER ANYWAY?

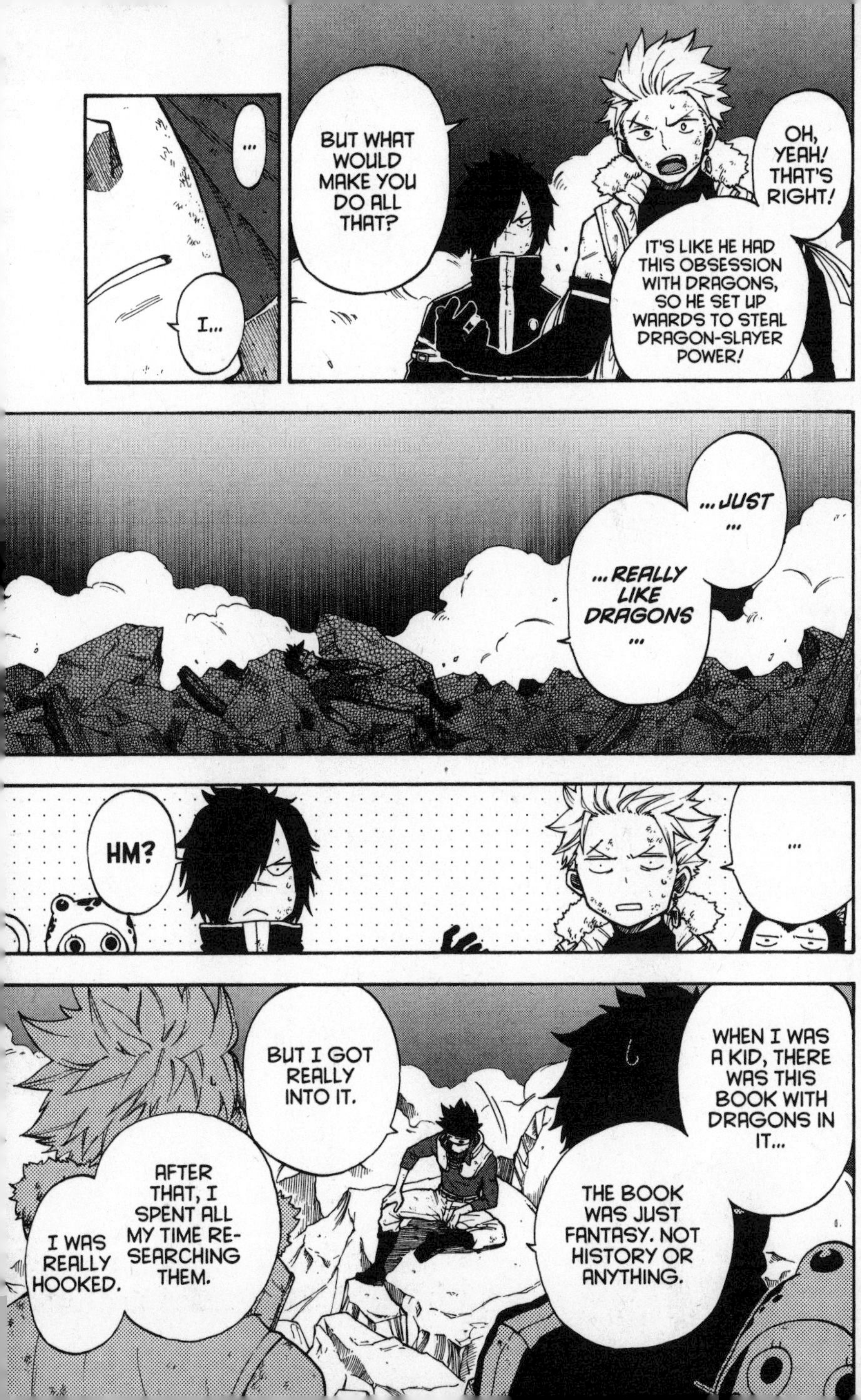
OH, YEAH! THAT'S RIGHT!
IT'S LIKE HE HAD THIS OBSESSION WITH DRAGONS, SO HE SET UP WAARDS TO STEAL DRAGON-SLAYER POWER!
BUT WHAT WOULD MAKE YOU DO ALL THAT?
...
I...
...JUST ...
...REALLY LIKE DRAGONS ...
...
HM?
WHEN I WAS A KID, THERE WAS THIS BOOK WITH DRAGONS IN IT...
THE BOOK WAS JUST FANTASY. NOT HISTORY OR ANYTHING.
BUT I GOT REALLY INTO IT.
AFTER THAT, I SPENT ALL MY TIME RE-SEARCHING THEM.
I WAS REALLY HOOKED.

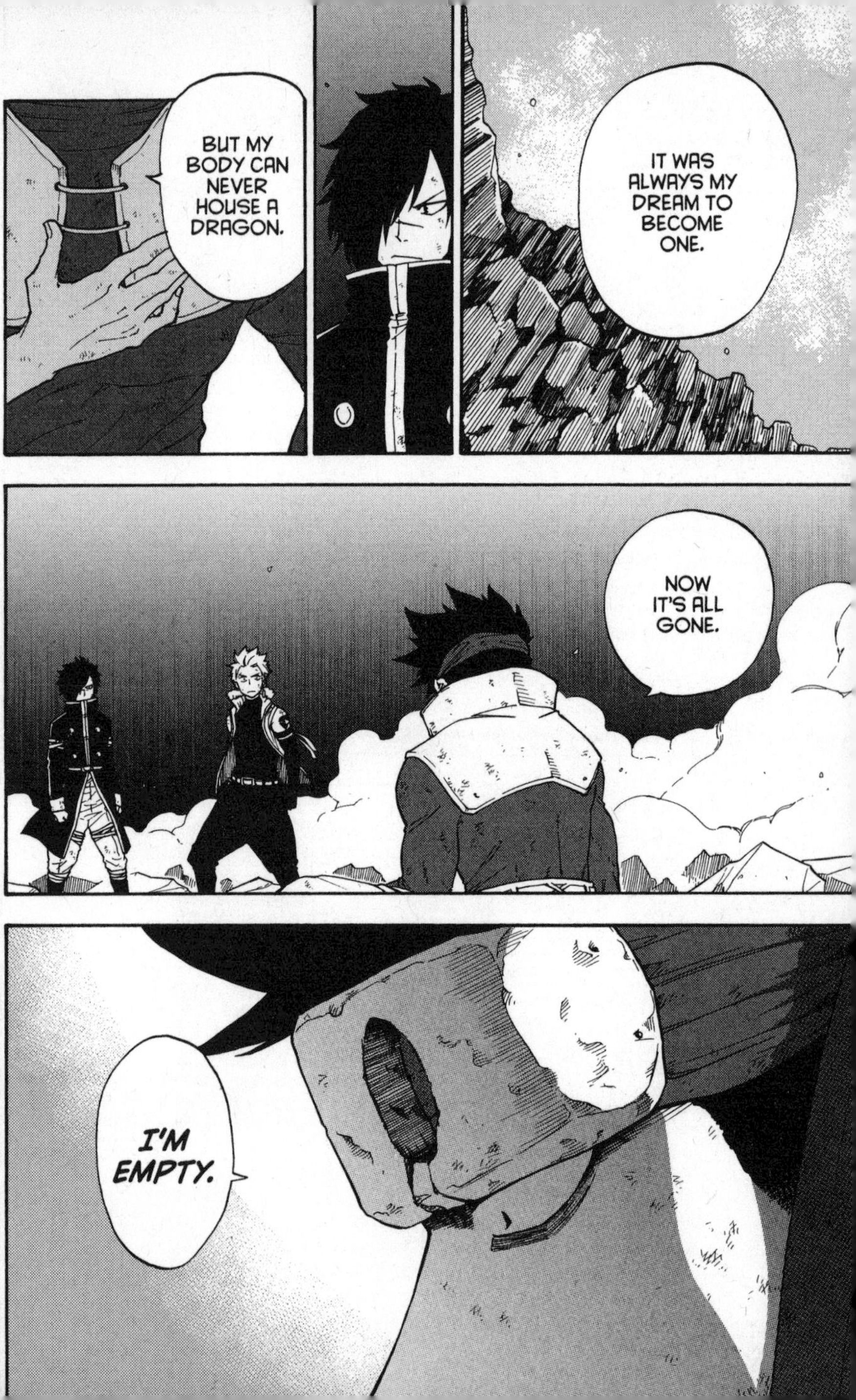
IT WAS ALWAYS MY DREAM TO BECOME ONE.
BUT MY BODY CAN NEVER HOUSE A DRAGON.
NOW IT'S ALL GONE.
I'M EMPTY.

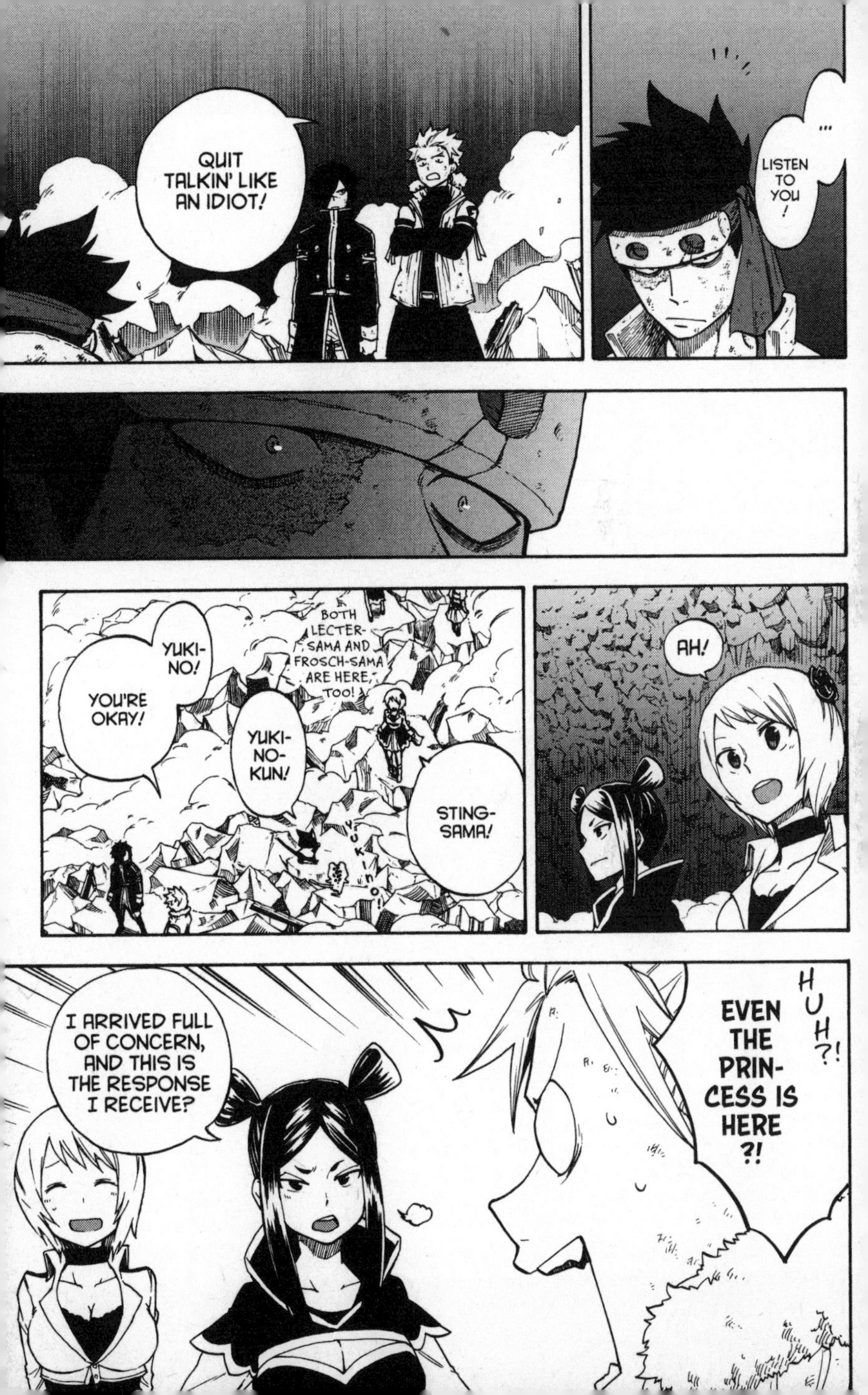
...
LISTEN TO YOU!
QUIT TALKIN' LIKE AN IDIOT!
AH!
BOTH LECTER-SAMA AND FROSCH-SAMA ARE HERE, TOO!
STING-SAMA!
YUKI-NO-KUN!
YUKINO!
YUKI-NO!
YOU'RE OKAY!
HUH?!
EVEN THE PRIN-CESS IS HERE?!
I ARRIVED FULL OF CONCERN, AND THIS IS THE RESPONSE I RECEIVE?

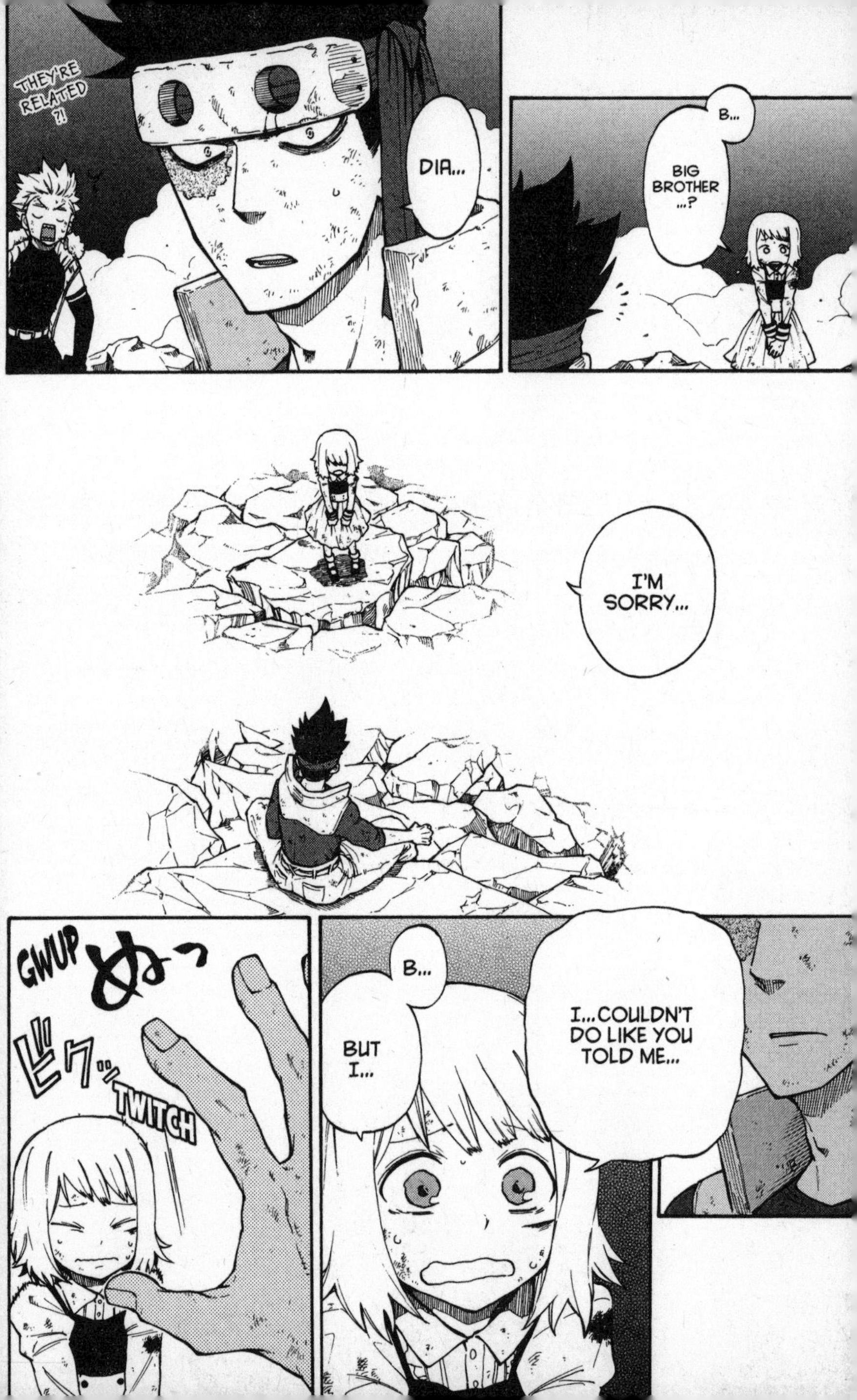
B...
BIG BROTHER ...?
DIA...
THEY'RE RELATED ?!
I'M SORRY...
I...COULDN'T DO LIKE YOU TOLD ME...
B...
BUT I...
GWUP
ぬっ
ビクッ
TWITCH

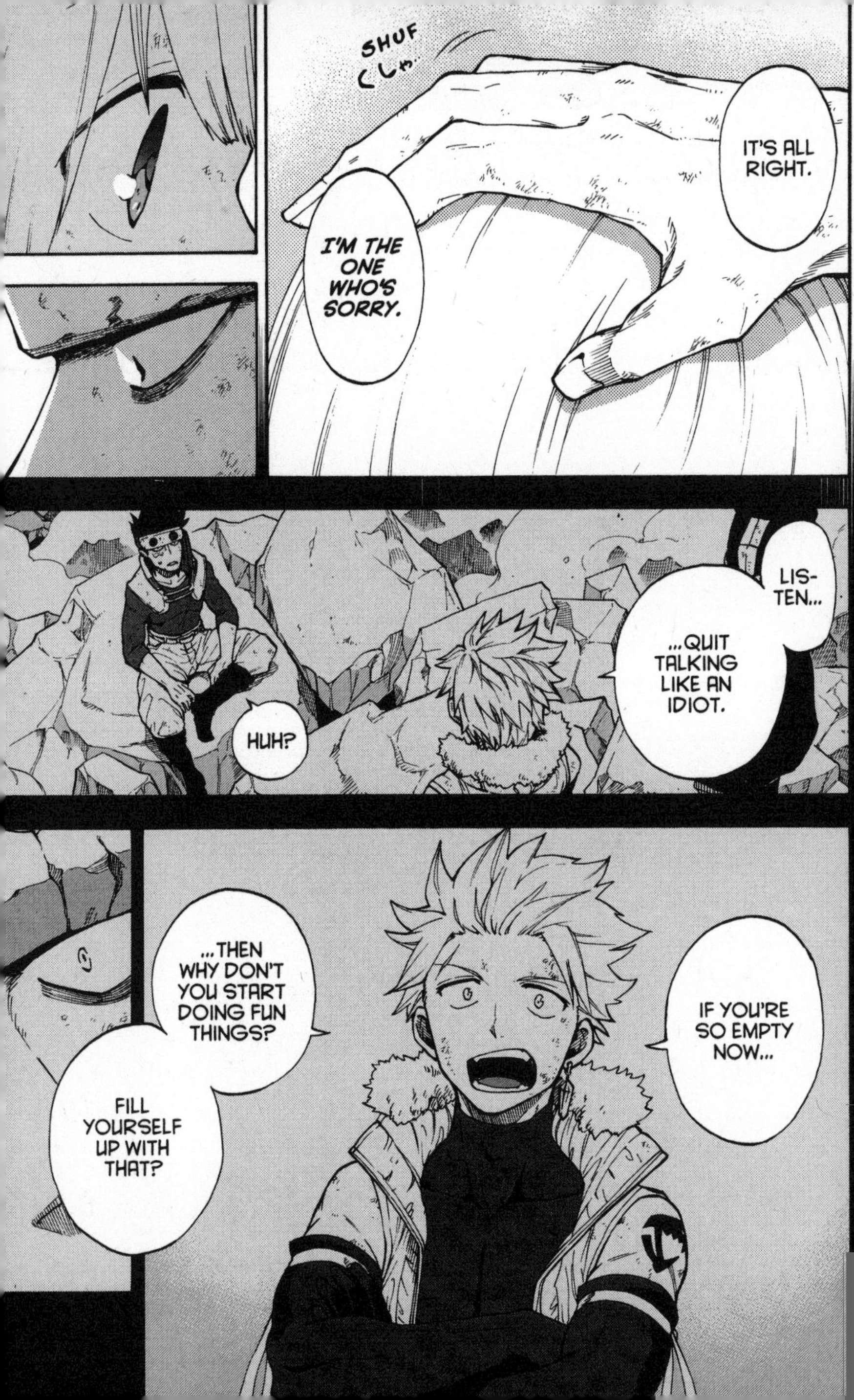
SHUF
くしゃ
IT'S ALL RIGHT.
I'M THE ONE WHO'S SORRY.
LIS- TEN...
...QUIT TALKING LIKE AN IDIOT.
HUH?
IF YOU'RE SO EMPTY NOW...
...THEN WHY DON'T YOU START DOING FUN THINGS?
FILL YOURSELF UP WITH THAT?

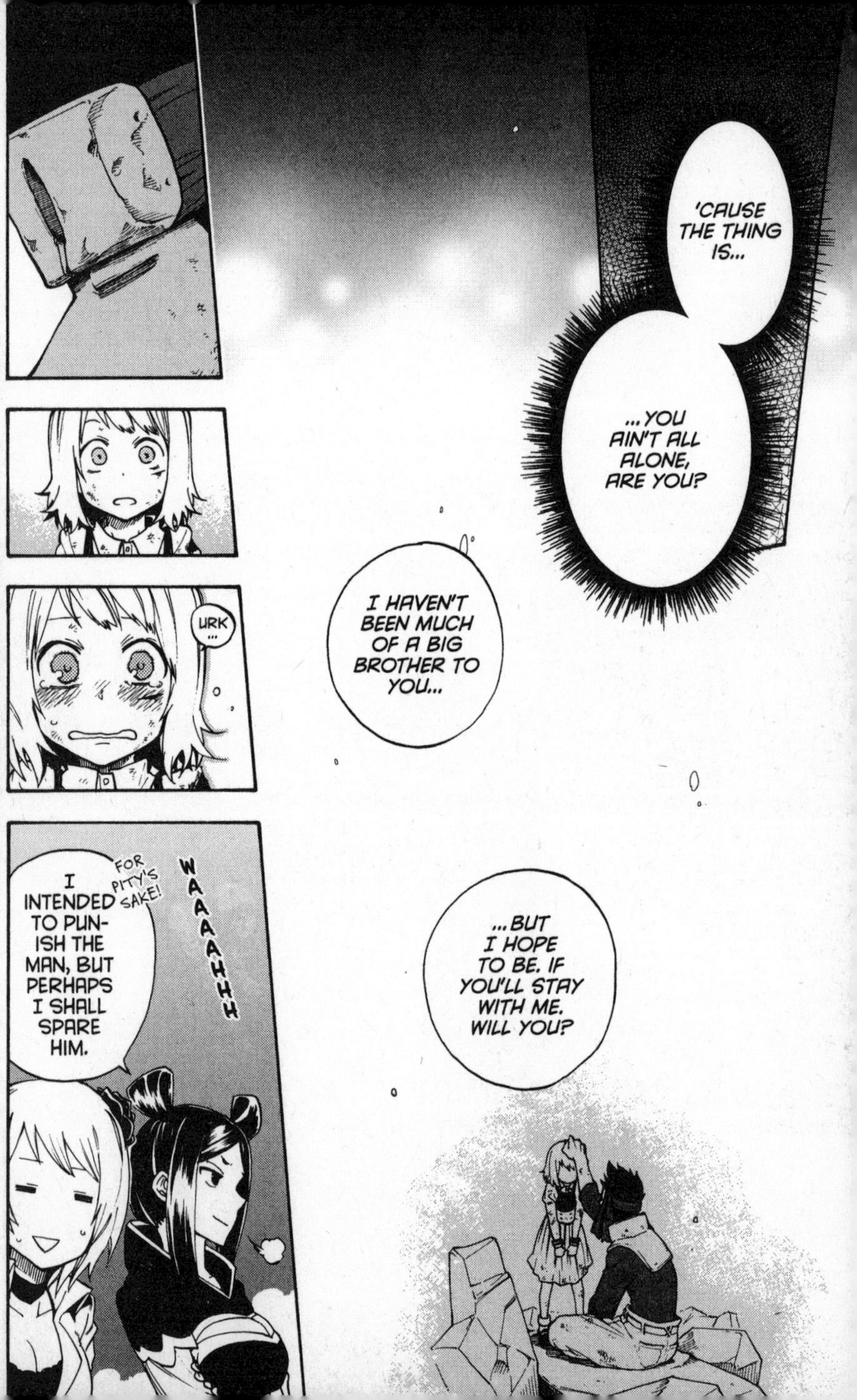
'CAUSE THE THING IS...
...YOU AIN'T ALL ALONE, ARE YOU?
I HAVEN'T BEEN MUCH OF A BIG BROTHER TO YOU...
...BUT I HOPE TO BE. IF YOU'LL STAY WITH ME. WILL YOU?
URK...
WAAAAAHHH
FOR PITY'S SAKE!
I INTENDED TO PUN-ISH THE MAN, BUT PERHAPS I SHALL SPARE HIM.

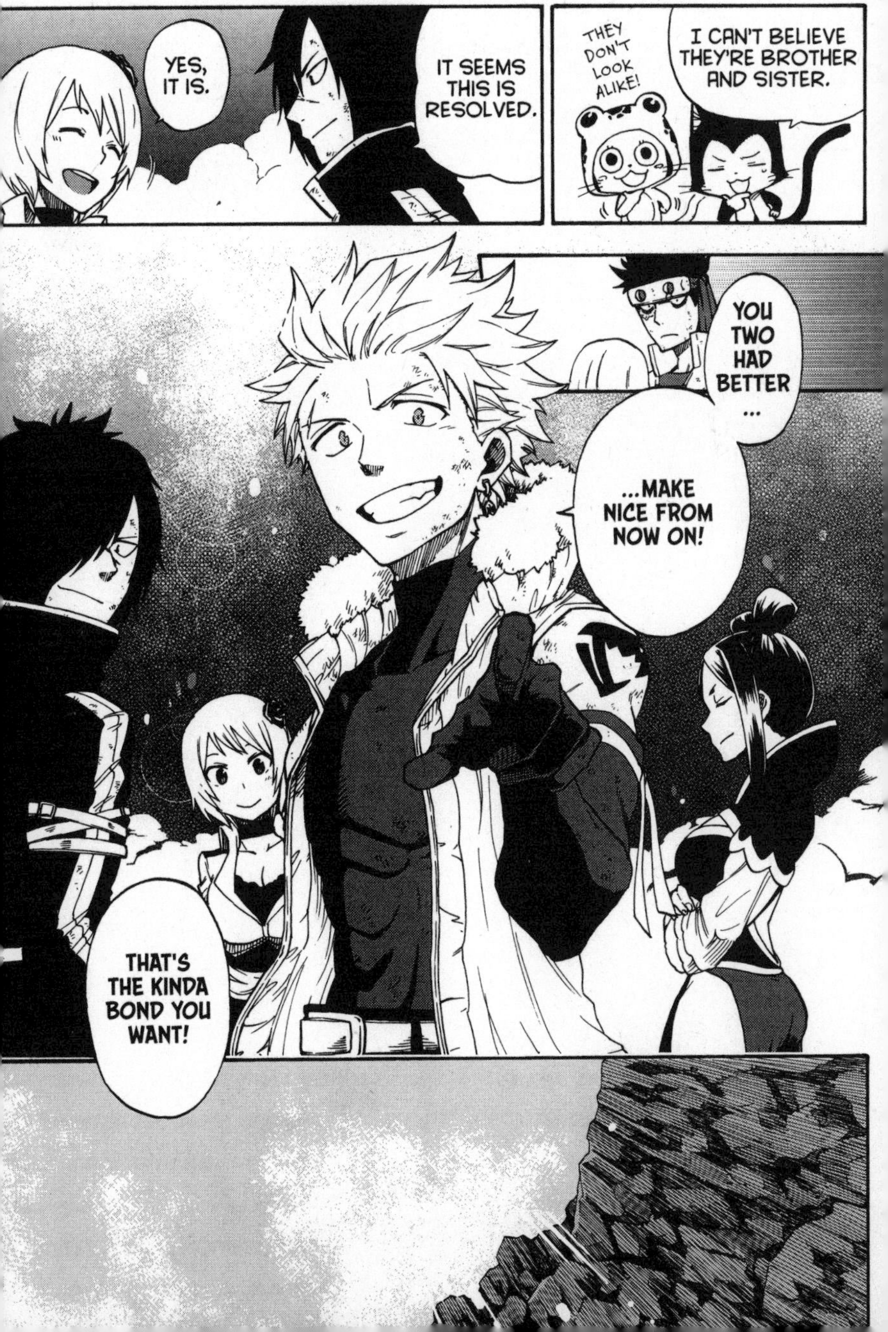
I CAN'T BELIEVE THEY'RE BROTHER AND SISTER.
THEY DON'T LOOK ALIKE!
IT SEEMS THIS IS RESOLVED.
YES, IT IS.
YOU TWO HAD BETTER ...
...MAKE NICE FROM NOW ON!
THAT'S THE KINDA BOND YOU WANT!

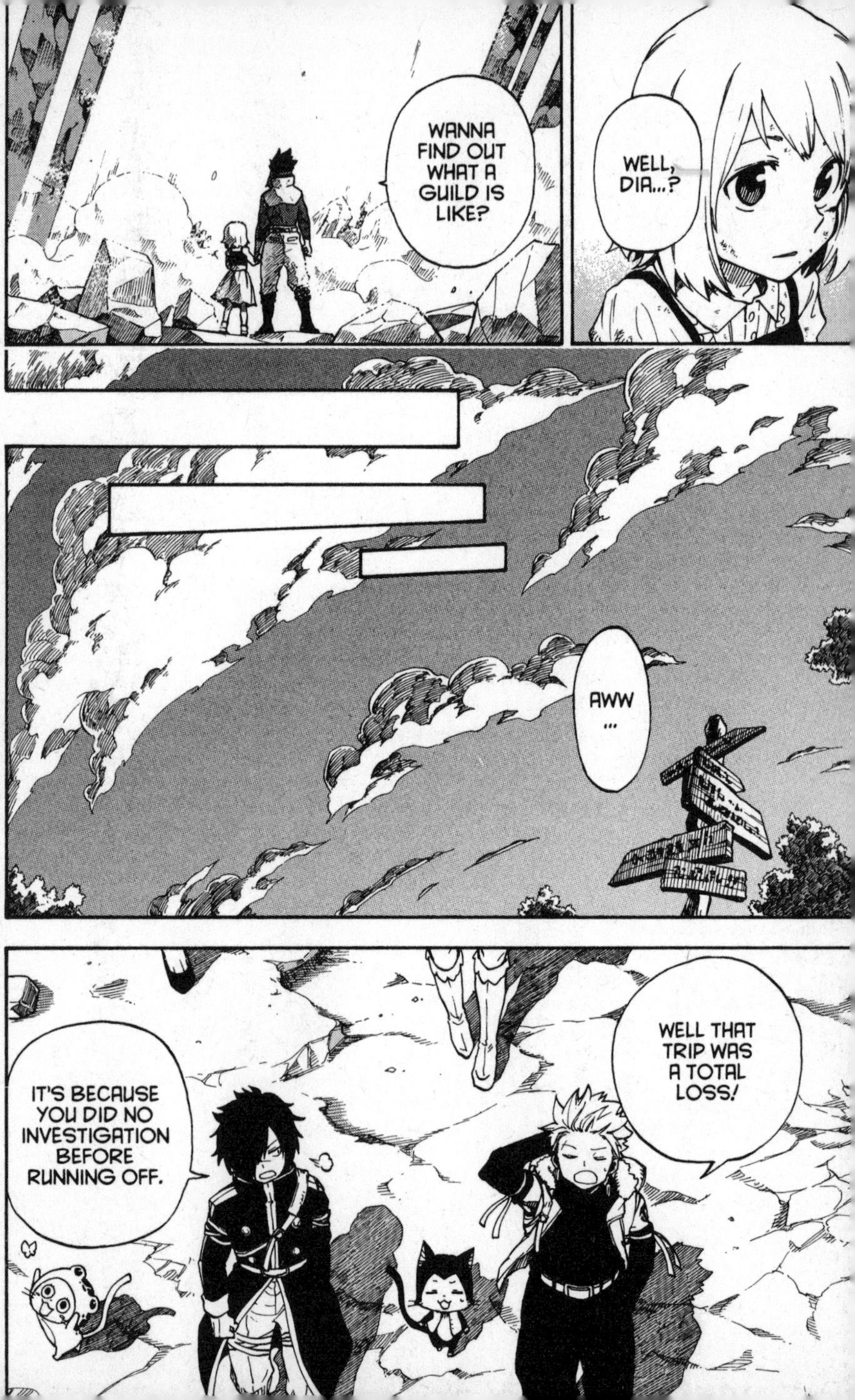
WELL, DIA...?
WANNA FIND OUT WHAT A GUILD IS LIKE?
AWW ...
WELL THAT TRIP WAS A TOTAL LOSS!
IT'S BECAUSE YOU DID NO INVESTIGATION BEFORE RUNNING OFF.

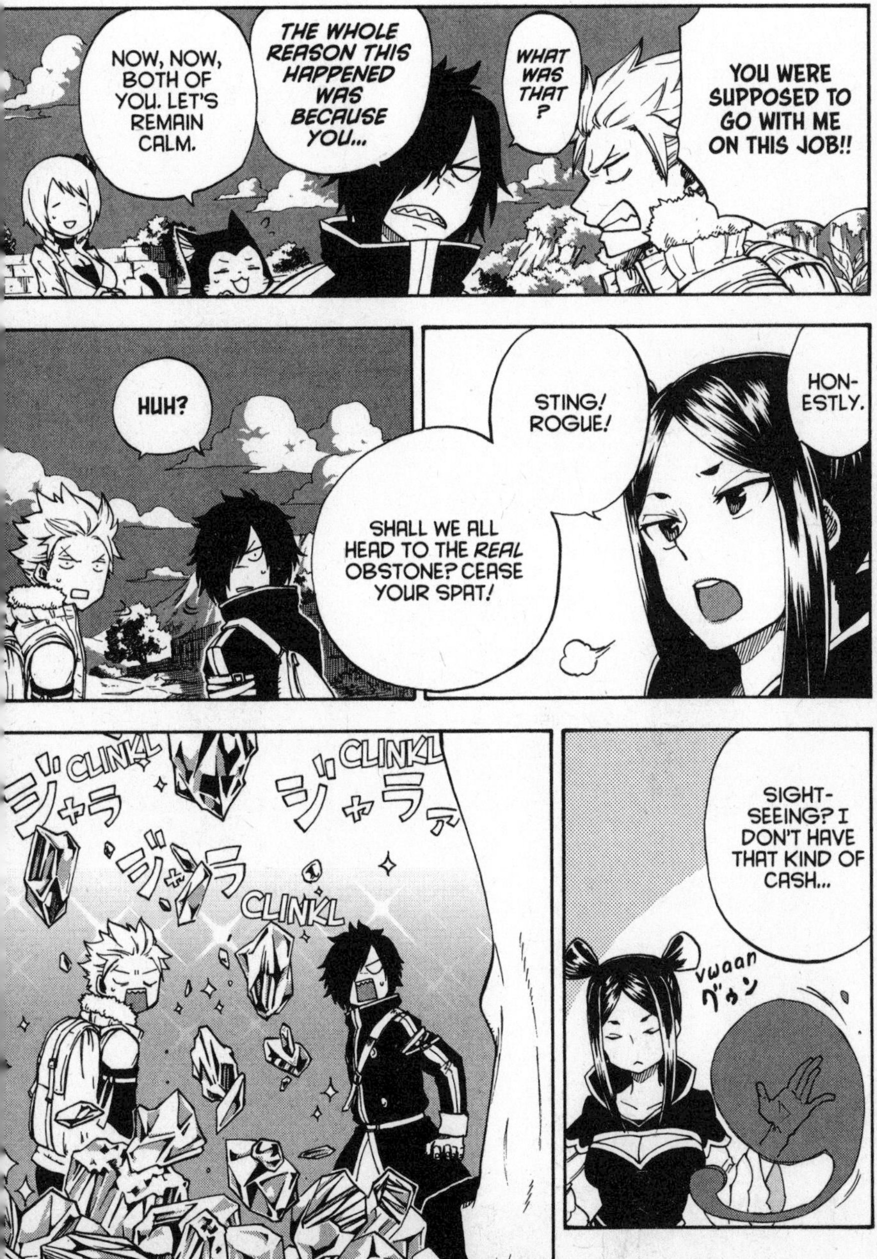
YOU WERE SUPPOSED TO GO WITH ME ON THIS JOB!!
WHAT WAS THAT?
THE WHOLE REASON THIS HAPPENED WAS BECAUSE YOU...
NOW, NOW, BOTH OF YOU. LET'S REMAIN CALM.
HON-ESTLY.
STING! ROGUE!
SHALL WE ALL HEAD TO THE *REAL* OBSTONE? CEASE YOUR SPAT!
HUH?
SIGHT-SEEING? I DON'T HAVE THAT KIND OF CASH...
vwaan
グゥン
ジャラァ
CLINK
ジャラ
CLINK
ジャラ
CLINK

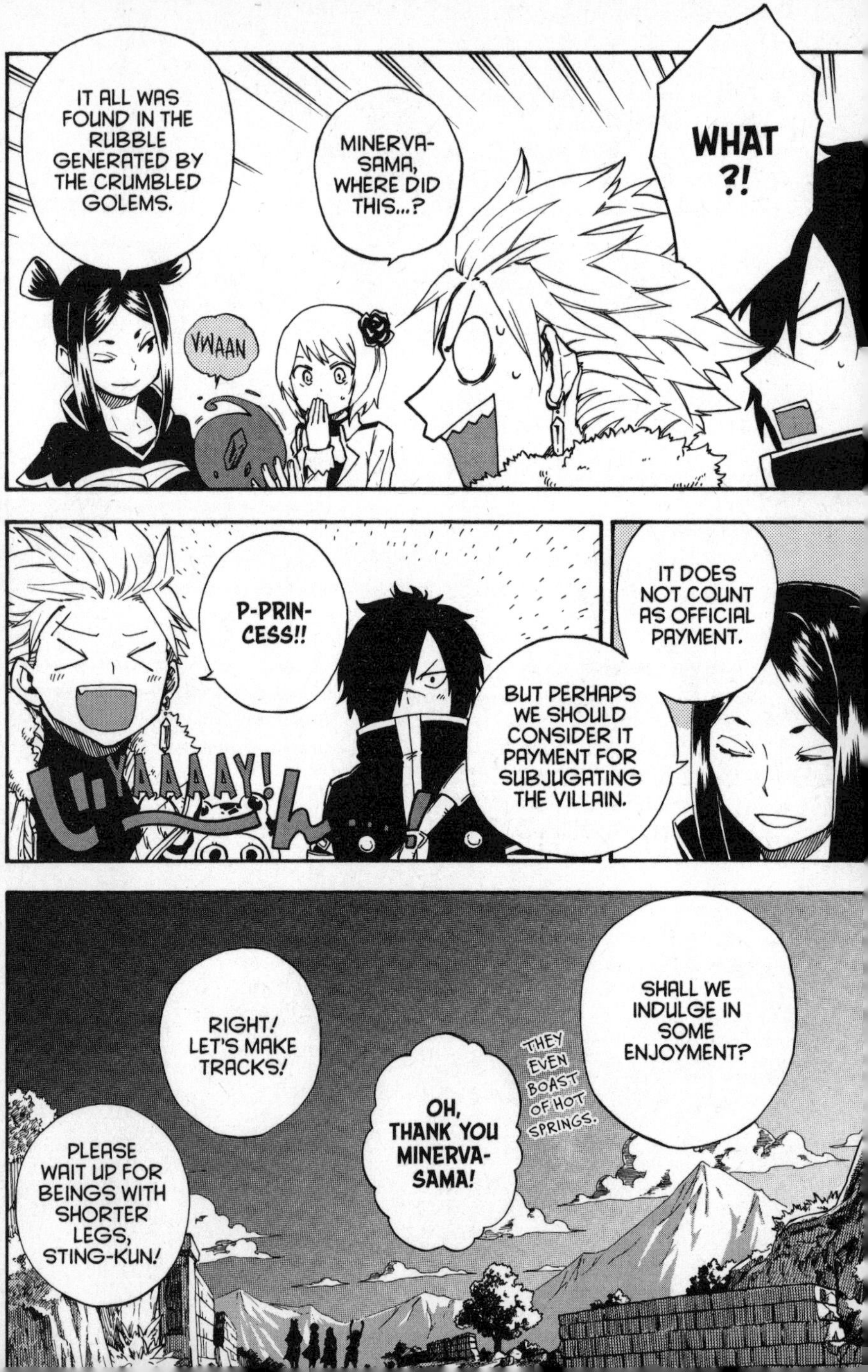
WHAT?!
MINERVA-SAMA, WHERE DID THIS...?
IT ALL WAS FOUND IN THE RUBBLE GENERATED BY THE CRUMBLED GOLEMS.
VWAAN
IT DOES NOT COUNT AS OFFICIAL PAYMENT.
BUT PERHAPS WE SHOULD CONSIDER IT PAYMENT FOR SUBJUGATING THE VILLAIN.
P-PRINCESS!!
YAAAAY!
SHALL WE INDULGE IN SOME ENJOYMENT?
THEY EVEN BOAST OF HOT SPRINGS.
OH, THANK YOU MINERVA-SAMA!
RIGHT! LET'S MAKE TRACKS!
PLEASE WAIT UP FOR BEINGS WITH SHORTER LEGS, STING-KUN!

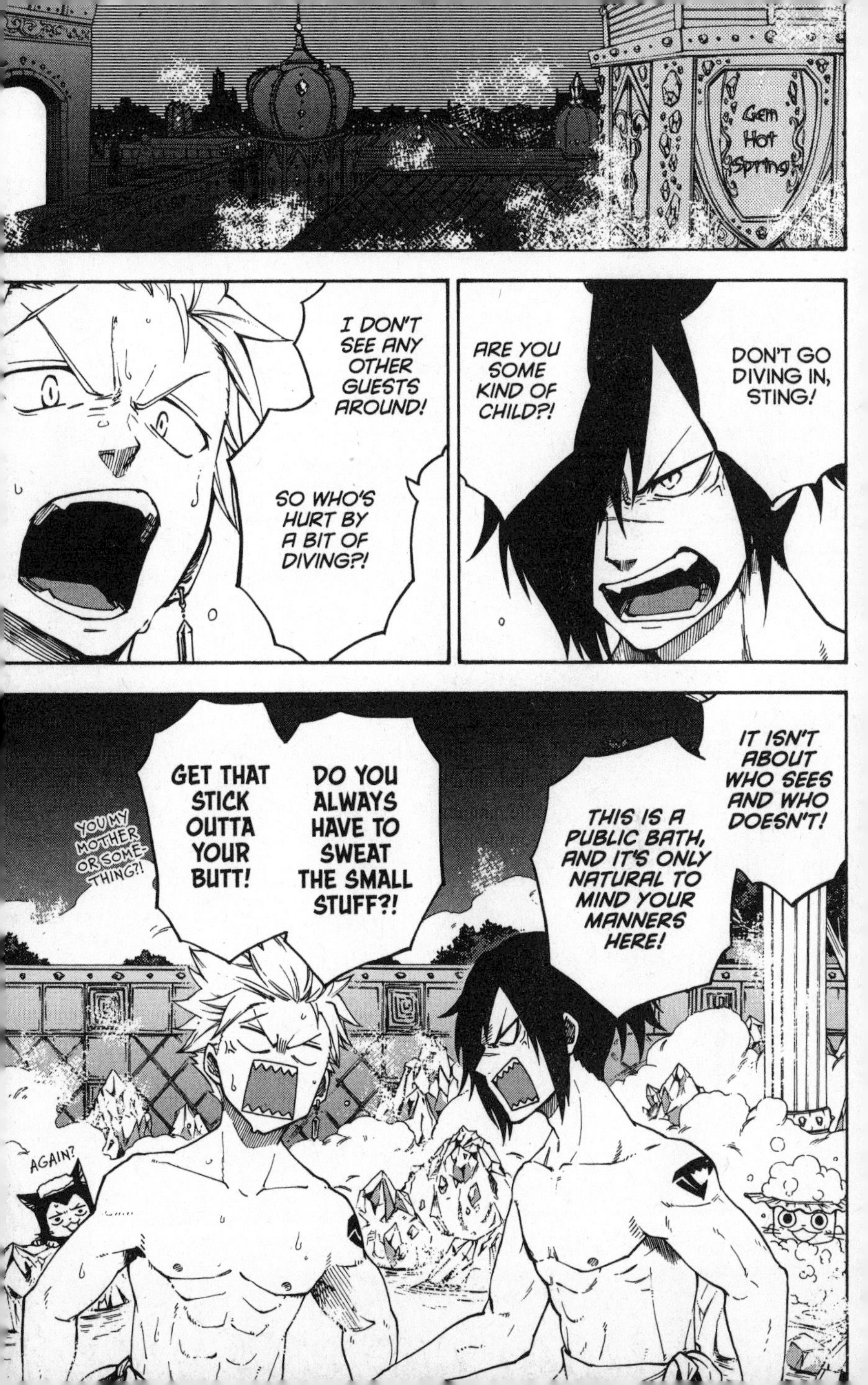
Gem Hot Spring
DON'T GO DIVING IN, STING!
ARE YOU SOME KIND OF CHILD?!
I DON'T SEE ANY OTHER GUESTS AROUND!
SO WHO'S HURT BY A BIT OF DIVING?!
IT ISN'T ABOUT WHO SEES AND WHO DOESN'T!
THIS IS A PUBLIC BATH, AND IT'S ONLY NATURAL TO MIND YOUR MANNERS HERE!
DO YOU ALWAYS HAVE TO SWEAT THE SMALL STUFF?!
GET THAT STICK OUTTA YOUR BUTT!
YOU MY MOTHER OR SOME-THING?!
AGAIN?

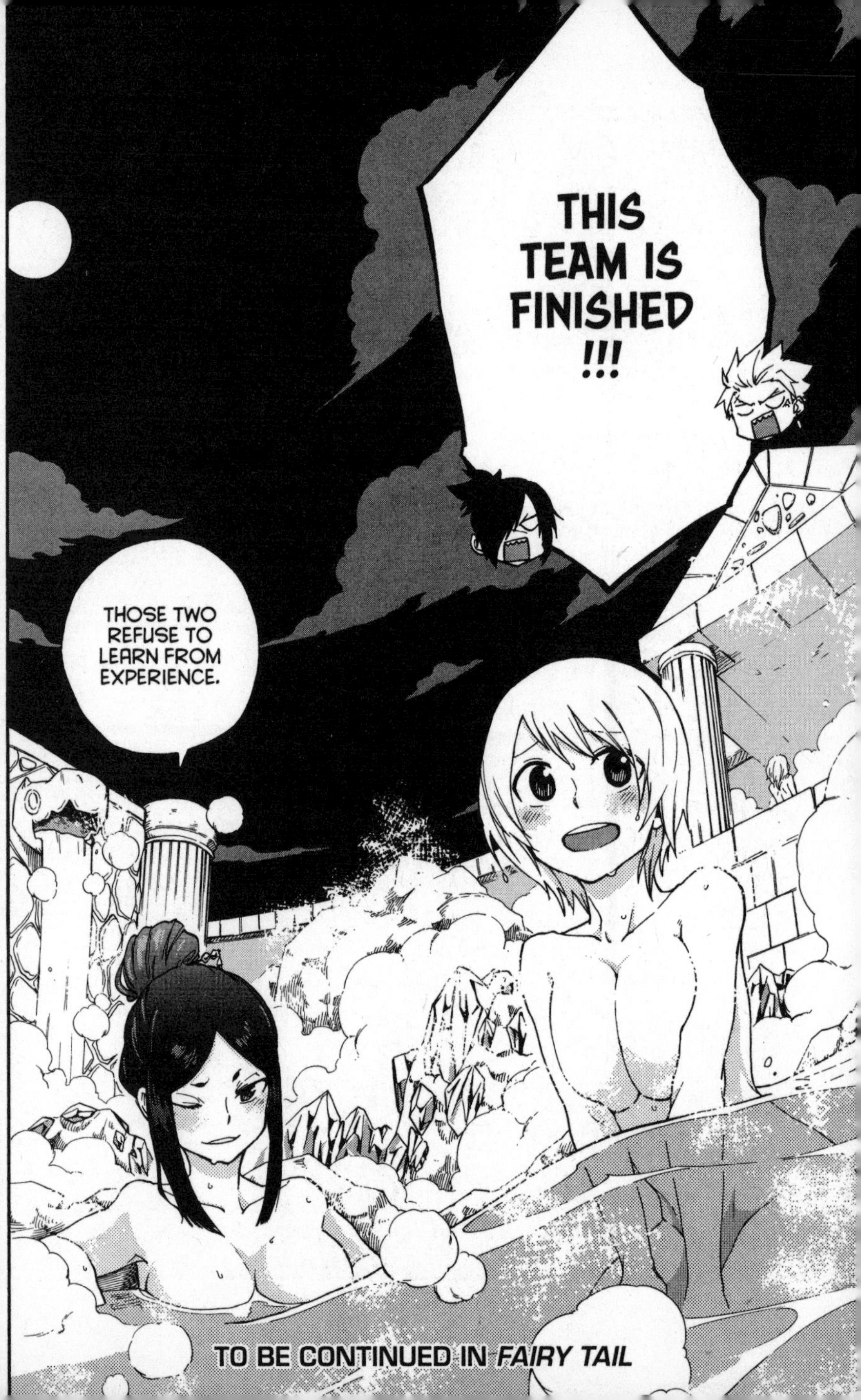

THIS TEAM IS FINISHED !!!
THOSE TWO REFUSE TO LEARN FROM EXPERIENCE.
TO BE CONTINUED IN FAIRY TAIL

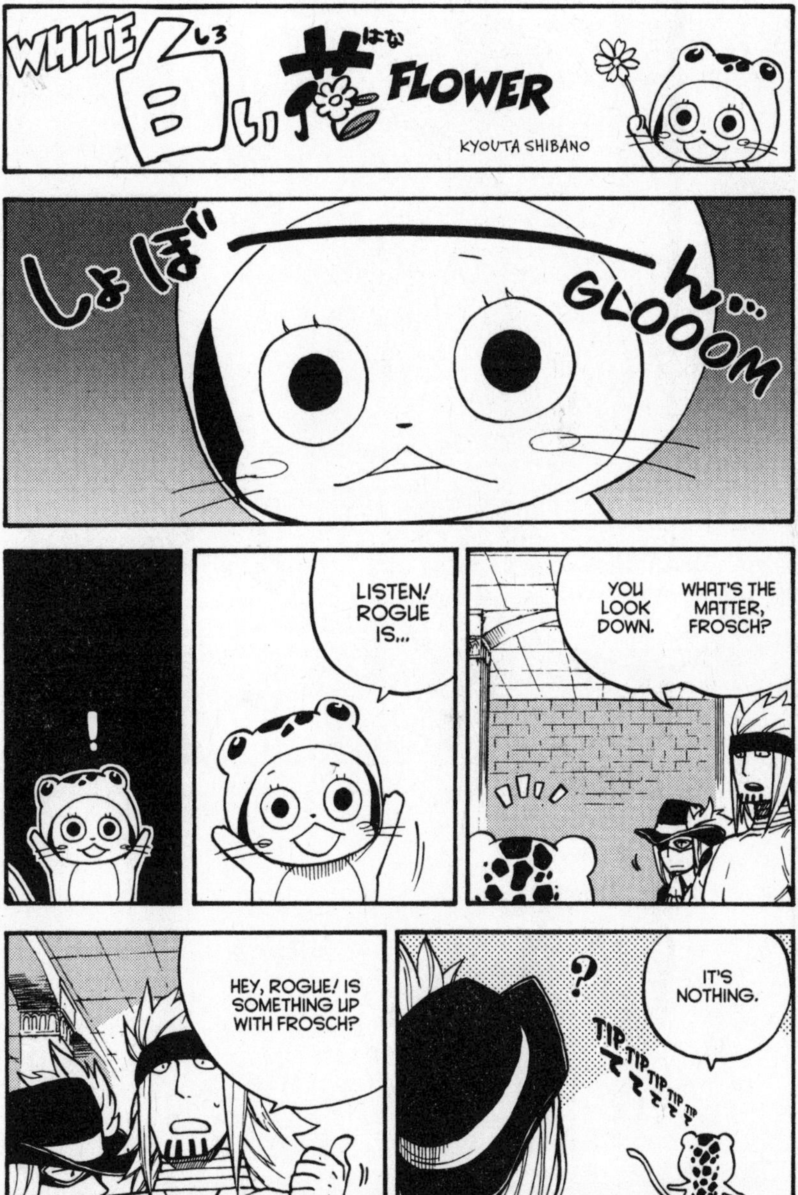
WHITE 白い花 FLOWER
しろ
はな
KYOUTA SHIBANO
しょぼーーーん…
GLOOOOM
WHAT'S THE MATTER, FROSCH?
YOU LOOK DOWN.
LISTEN! ROGUE IS...
!
IT'S NOTHING.
?
TIP TIP TIP TIP TIP
てててて
HEY, ROGUE! IS SOMETHING UP WITH FROSCH?

WHAT, YOU, TOO?!!

GLOOOM

LOOK.

SST

HUH?

WHAT IS THE PROBLEM WITH YOU TWO?

...THE SUIT THAT FROSCH IS ALWAYS WEARING?

ISN'T THAT...

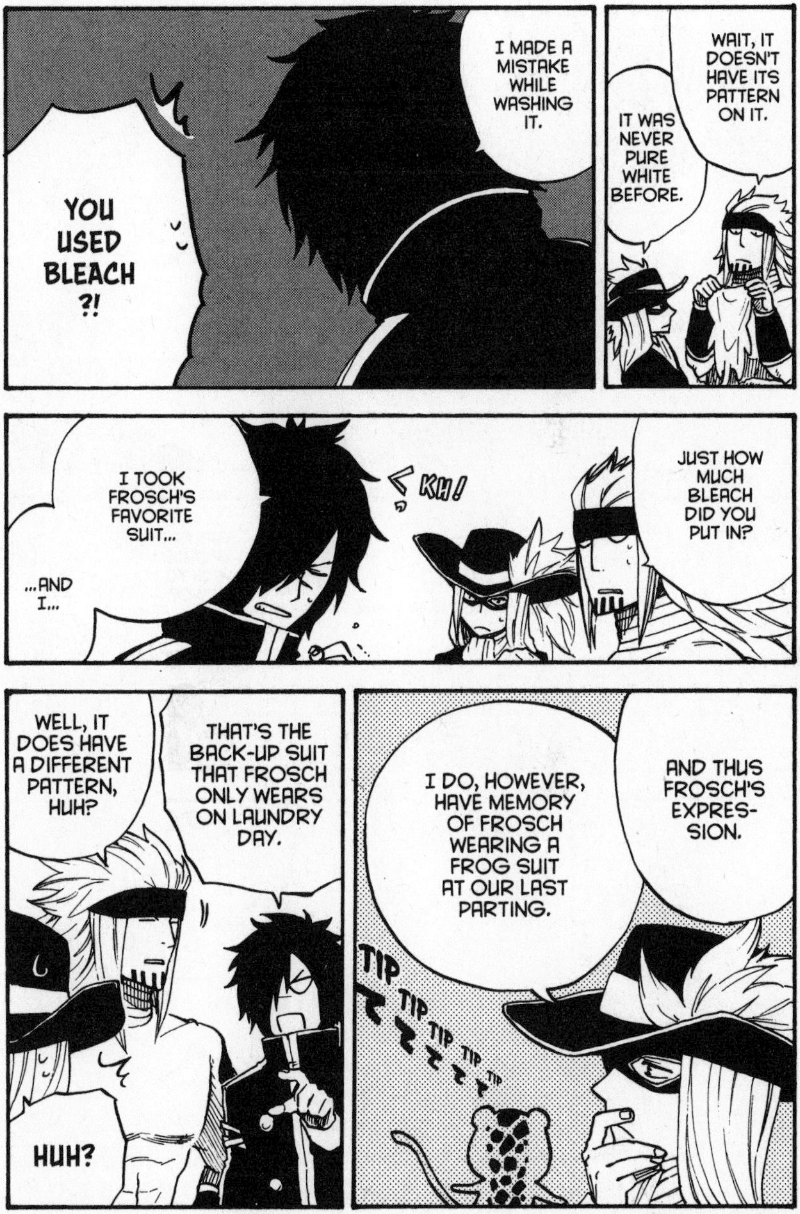
WAIT, IT DOESN'T HAVE ITS PATTERN ON IT.
IT WAS NEVER PURE WHITE BEFORE.
I MADE A MISTAKE WHILE WASHING IT.
YOU USED BLEACH?!
JUST HOW MUCH BLEACH DID YOU PUT IN?
KH!
I TOOK FROSCH'S FAVORITE SUIT...
...AND I...
AND THUS FROSCH'S EXPRES-SION.
I DO, HOWEVER, HAVE MEMORY OF FROSCH WEARING A FROG SUIT AT OUR LAST PARTING.
TIP TIP TIP TIP TIP
THAT'S THE BACK-UP SUIT THAT FROSCH ONLY WEARS ON LAUNDRY DAY.
WELL, IT DOES HAVE A DIFFERENT PATTERN, HUH?
HUH?

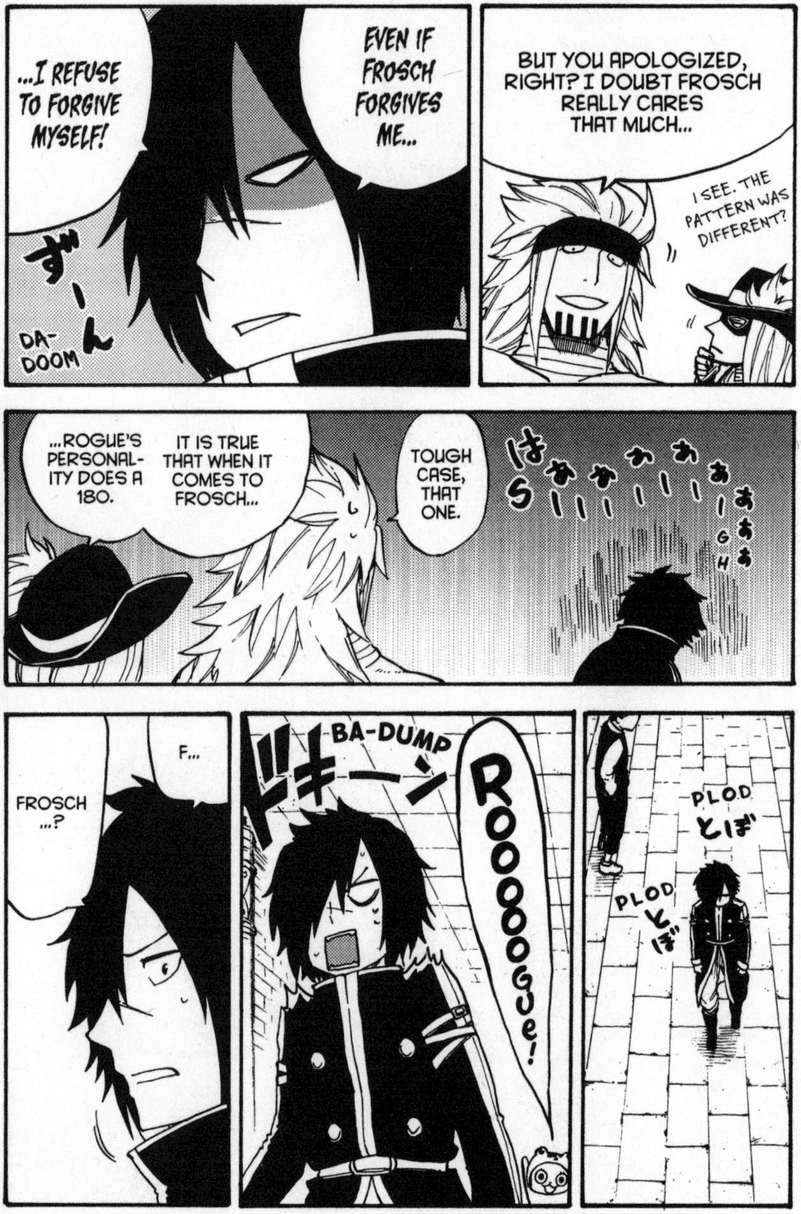
BUT YOU APOLOGIZED, RIGHT? I DOUBT FROSCH REALLY CARES THAT MUCH...
I SEE. THE PATTERN WAS DIFFERENT?
EVEN IF FROSCH FORGIVES ME...
...I REFUSE TO FORGIVE MYSELF!
ずーん
DA-DOOM
TOUGH CASE, THAT ONE.
IT IS TRUE THAT WHEN IT COMES TO FROSCH...
...ROGUE'S PERSONAL-ITY DOES A 180.
PLOD とぼ
PLOD とぼ
ドキーン
BA-DUMP
ROOOOOGUE!
F...
FROSCH ...?

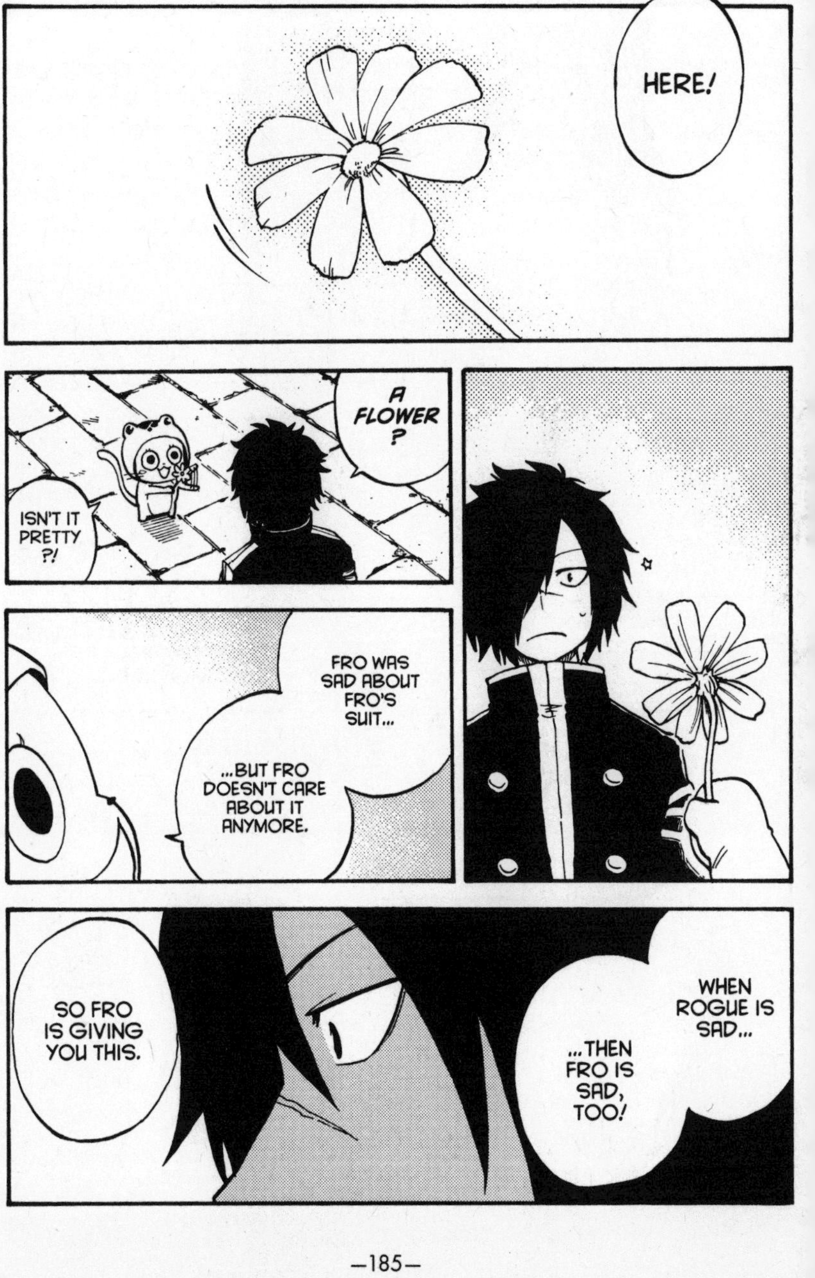
HERE!
A FLOWER?
ISN'T IT PRETTY?!
FRO WAS SAD ABOUT FRO'S SUIT...
...BUT FRO DOESN'T CARE ABOUT IT ANYMORE.
WHEN ROGUE IS SAD...
...THEN FRO IS SAD, TOO!
SO FRO IS GIVING YOU THIS.

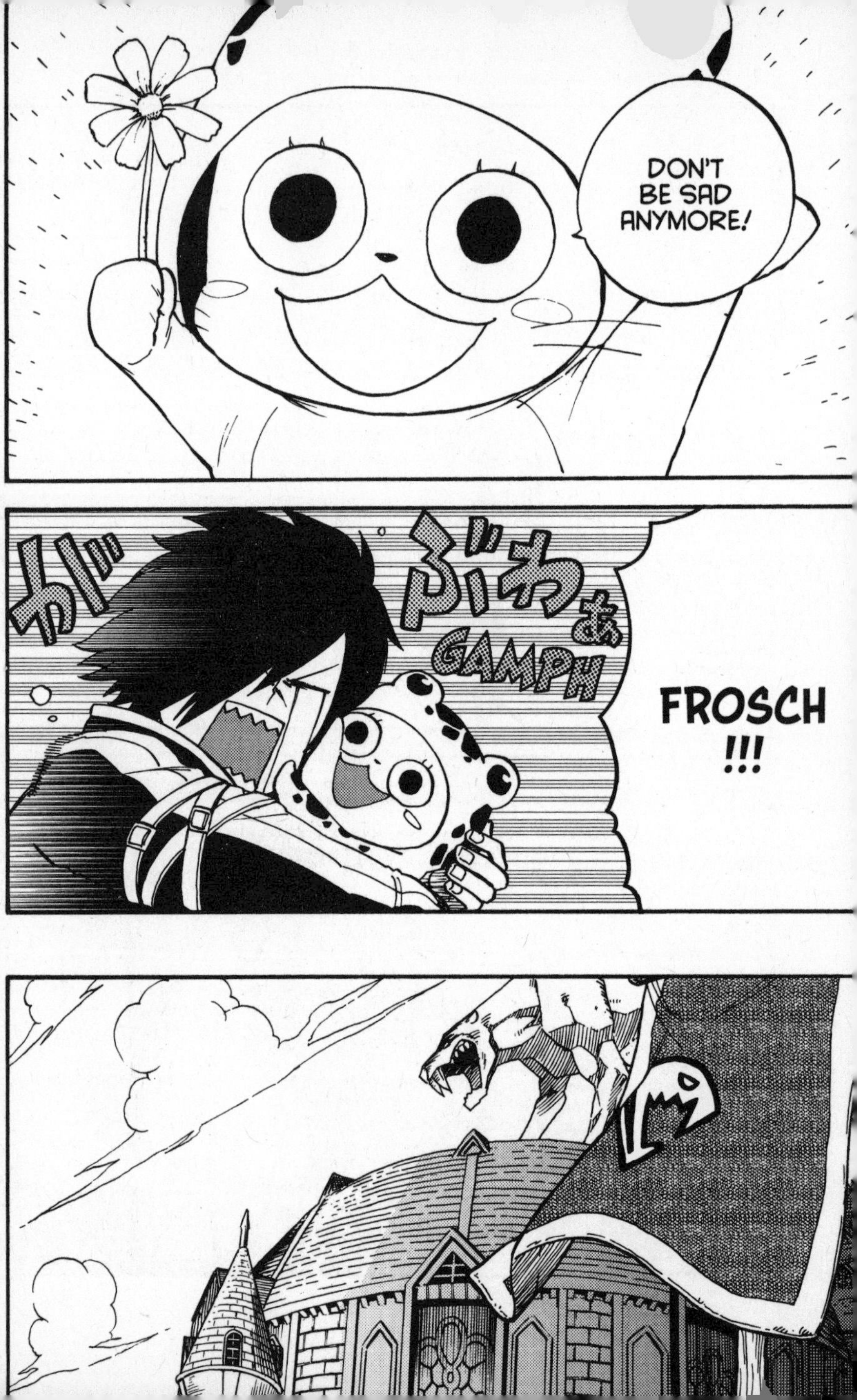
DON'T BE SAD ANYMORE!
FROSCH !!!
ぶわぁ
GAMPH
がば

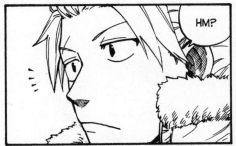

I SLEPT TOO LONG! I'M HUNGRY!
LET'S GO TO THE GUILD BAR AND GET THEM TO FIX US SOME FOOD!!
HM?
YOU SEEM TO BE IN A REALLY GOOD MOOD, ROGUE.
STING.
LECTER, 'MORNING!
HEH HEH HEH. I SUPPOSE I AM.
FEAST YOUR EYES ON THIS!
SST
WHOA! A WHITE FLOWER

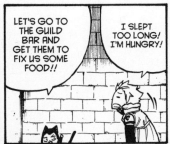

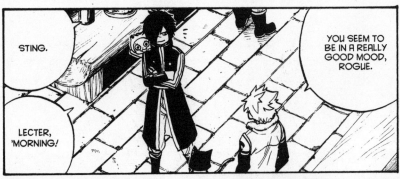

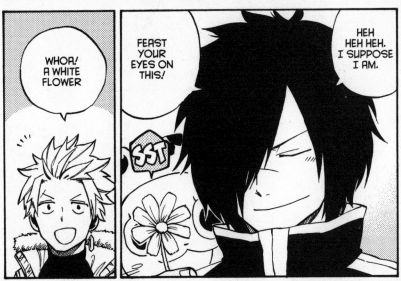

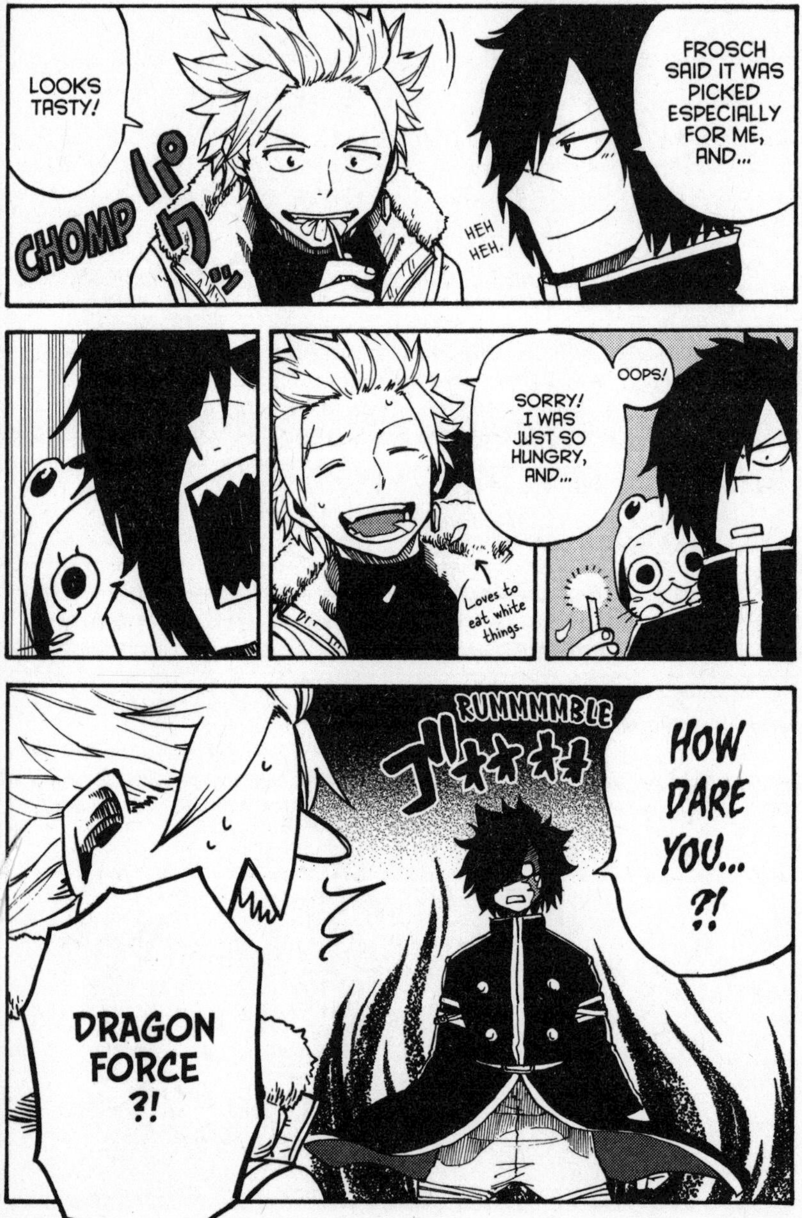
FROSCH SAID IT WAS PICKED ESPECIALLY FOR ME, AND...
HEH HEH.
LOOKS TASTY!
CHOMP
OOPS!
SORRY! I WAS JUST SO HUNGRY, AND...
Loves to eat white things.
RUMMMMBLE
HOW DARE YOU...?!
DRAGON FORCE?!

To be continued in the Obstone chapter.

AFTERWORD

Greetings to all those who are meeting me here for the first time! To everyone else, long time, no see! I'm Shibano.

Did you enjoy *Fairy Tail: Twin Dragons of Saber Tooth*? To tell the truth, I've been a fan of Hiro Mashima-sensei's ever since his earlier work, *Rave Master*. In fact, I was so into it that I remember copying his style at the time, and it influenced my art quite a lot!

I was still a student when *Fairy Tail* first started being published, and I'd be like one of all of you waiting for new volumes of the graphic novel to be published.

And to think that a person like me could now be allowed to draw an official *Fairy Tail* spinoff story is, to be honest...a dream come true.
So I really want to thank the editors who gave me the opportunity to do a spinoff, and to Mashima-sensei who was kind enough to give me the green light!

I'm soooo glad that I started drawing manga!

Fairy Tail: Twin Dragons of Saber Tooth features the people of Saber Tooth as the main characters. And, of course, I wanted to show how cool Sting and Rogue could be, but also, on a personal level, I was so happy when I got the go-ahead to have Minerva and Yukino fighting together, too! I always wanted to read a manga like that! (laughs)

It was also my intention to give the Saber Tooth portion of the *Fairy Tail* fandom at least one book they could really have fun reading.

So now the Saber Tooth chapter is finished, but the extra stories still continue. Please stick with *Fairy Tail* in the future, too! I hope to see you next volume!

KYOUTA SHIBANO

STAFF: MINAMI YASAKA, MERIO YUKINAGA, ATSUO UEDA
YOU REALLY SAVED ME! THANK YOU!

Translation Notes:

Page 6, Jason

With all the odd characters in *Fairy Tail*, it should come as no surprise that some of the more normal ones are (or at least could be) based on actual people. The strange thing is that one of the more outlandish characters is based on an ex-coworker of mine, and a long-time professional in the American manga industry. Jason, the reporter for the *Weekly Sorcerer* is based on Jason Thompson, the author of the *Manga: The Complete Guide*. Jason Thompson is thin, blonde-ish, high energy, and says words like "cool" and "awesome" quite a lot (not as much as his manga counterpart, though). Jason interviewed Mashima-sensei at the 2008 San Diego Comic Con, and Mashima-sensei was so impressed by Jason's character that, within a few months, the reporter for the *Weekly Sorcerer*, Jason, made his debut in the pages of *Fairy Tail*.

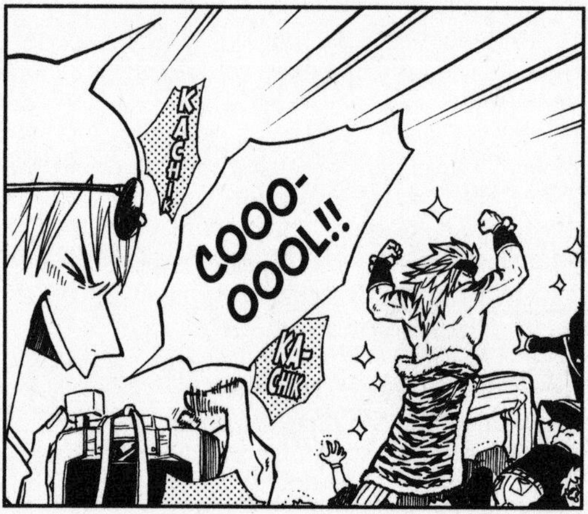
KACHIK
COOO-OOOL!!
KA-CHIK

Page 26, Allocer

Allocer is a demon lord out of middle-ages demonology. According to the German demonologist, Johann Weyer (1515-1588), he comes in the appearance of a soldier on a great horse, with a lion's face and flaming eyes. Apparently he can teach astronomy and other liberal sciences, and he rules thirty-six legions. Similar descriptions of Allocer also appear in *Dictionaire Infernal* (1863) by Collin De Plancy and *Goetia* (1904) by S. L. MacGregor Mathers (it's likely that both of the later versions took their descriptions from Weyer).